Two Cheers for Doctor Arnold

TWO CHEERS FOR DOCTOR ARNOLD

by

Robert Stanier and Leslie Wilson

Edited by Tom Stanier

With illustrations taken from the original edition of Tom Brown's Schooldays

@Tom Stanier 2016
All rights reserved

ISBN-13   978-1530449347
ISBN-10   15330449340

COVAL PRESS

THE AUTHORS

while Prefects at Berkhamsted School in 1925

Bob Stanier and Joe Wilson are seated either side of their Headmaster, Charles Greene (father of Graham Greene). Bob is on Greene's right and Joe is on Greene's left.

PREFACE

Almost every public school has had its history recorded at some time. This book takes a broader look at the great public schools of the Nineteenth Century and offers an overall view of how they approached the different aspects of education . Their approaches were often admirable, often deplorable and often extremely funny. This variety is what appealed to my father, Robert (Bob) Stanier and his great friend, Leslie (Joe) Wilson. They had known each other as schoolboys at Berkhamsted and then as undergraduates at Wadham College, Oxford, before both went into teaching. Bob was for many years the Master of Magdalen College School, and Leslie was Head of English at Bradfield. When they retired, they decided to embark on the joint authorship of this book. It was never published in their lifetime, but my wife suggested that I bring it back into the light of day. It has given me great pleasure to do so.

                              Tom Stanier
                              March 2016

ORIGINAL AUTHORS' INTRODUCTION

The Public Schools have been 'news' for nearly two centuries, and in that time have undergone many changes. It is our belief that many people who are not experts in educational history tend to have in their minds a kind of stereotype of the Public School boy - 'short back and sides', 'stiff upper lip', 'playing up and playing the game' - who proceeds after a rigorous course of fagging and Latin verses to one of the professions, or to a plum job in politics, or to whatever family business might be available to them.

We hope that this brief survey will give the ordinary reader some idea of the waxing and waning of both good and bad qualities in the schools, of their humours and their horrors, of the swing of the pendulum between tyranny and anarchy, of changing attitudes towards such matters as corporal punishment, sexual relationships, and religion, and of the part played by some outstanding Headmasters in bringing about reform. How much reform was needed, our first chapters will show. Disorder, violence, anarchy, and defiance of educational authority are sometimes spoken of as if they constituted a problem peculiar to the present age and to comprehensive schools in particular, but it is unlikely that recent years have seen anything remotely comparable to the outbreaks that occurred in Public Schools in the late 18th and early 19th centuries.

Robert Stanier and Leslie Wilson (1975)

In memory of
Bob Stanier and Joe Wilson

CONTENTS

1.	Some Rebellions	11
2.	The Unreformed Schools	35
3.	Corruption	56
4.	Clarendon's Reforms	69
5.	The Curriculum	77
6.	Discipline	93
7.	The Boy's Life	109
8.	Headmasters and Governors	131
9.	Religion	144
10.	Sport and Recreation	162
11.	Military Training	188
12.	Sex	197
13.	Epidemics	215
Epilogue		226
Bibliography		236
Index		240

CHAPTER 1

SOME REBELLIONS.

"When were you flogged last, eh, eh? Your master is very kind to you all, is not he? Had you had any rebellions lately, eh, eh? Naughty boys, you know, naughty boys!"
(George III, on meeting Etonians in the streets of Windsor)

"When I was a boy at Westminster, the boys fought one another, they fought the masters, the masters fought them, they fought out-siders, in fact we fought anyone."
(Augustus Short, Bishop of Adelaide)

ETON

Eton had several minor rebellions in the 18th century, but the first fully recorded one occurred in 1768. Its origins were rooted in the rather unimpressive appearance and manner of Dr Foster, the Headmaster. He was a good scholar and a strict disciplinarian, but, as the son of a Windsor tradesmen and being of inferior physique, he was at a marked disadvantage in dealing with the more unruly and aristocratic boys in the school. He was also very short-sighted and was reputed to have addressed a large black sow rooting near Long Walk with the words "Come here, you rascally Collegers."

The *casus belli* was an ancient statute of Henry VI which laid it down that scholars were not to leave the College Precincts. Sixth formers were supposed to report boys seen out of bounds, but they could hardly do this without going outside themselves. Hence there arose a tacit agreement between Staff and Sixth formers that the latter should be deemed invisible when met outside College bounds. Dr Foster, however, decided that the Sixth form needed to be taught a lesson, and directed that they should be ordered back to College whenever they were found outside. The Sixth regarded this as an infringement of their rights; and, after some fresh developments, they entered the Headmaster's study in a body and tried without success to prevent him from birching one of their number.

After further altercation, they offered the reasonable suggestion that they should be sent back to college only if they were found in some specifically forbidden place, but this was refused as savoring too much of an ultimatum.

Rebellion was now openly declared, and 160 boys marched off to Marsh's Inn on Maidenhead Bridge, throwing their schoolbooks into the river en route. They then all sat down to a fine dinner, for which the innkeeper gleefully charged them the considerable sum of £55-18s. It all seemed, as to Peter Pan, an awfully big adventure, but reality began to filter through the grey light of the next morning. The rebels now returned to Eton, and, camping on the Playing Fields they sent a deputation to negotiate terms with the Headmaster. A note of uncertainty now appeared, and they soon realised that rebels all hang together, or they are hanged separately. Some negotiators were flogged and expulsions followed swiftly, while those that attempted homeward flight received scant sympathy from their parents. There is a touch of Sheridan comedy in the key-hole exchanges between Lord Harrington and his son, who had locked himself into his room and refused to return to school.

Son: "I return! No, I'll be damned if I do!"
Lord H: "I'll be damned if you don't!"
Son: "Yes, my lord, but you'll be damned whether I return or not."

But wit, like patriotism, is not enough, and the rebels lost the day.

A bizarre episode occurred in 1783 when the boys took the chance to rebel because the staff had gone on strike. Dr Davies, the Headmaster, had, apparently, offended some of his colleagues by his "overbearing manner", and they had appealed against him to Dr Roberts, the Provost, a particularly supine figure, who, by reason of his size and origin, went by the nickname of Double Gloucester. When he refused to mediate between the Headmaster and Staff, they declared a strike and withdrew their labour. This was the signal for the Oppidans (boys outside College) to present the harassed Headmaster with a long list of demands for fresh privileges.

They asserted that if these were not accepted, that they would not be answerable for the consequences, which would be a virtual collapse of the school.

Dr Davies felt that he could not possibly agree to these terms, but he could, at least, escape from his tormentors, and there was soon the unbelievable spectacle of the Headmaster of Eton in full flight from his boys. They chased him like a pack of hounds in full cry out of the Upper School and through his classroom, from which he was able to slip through a backdoor into the Provost's Lodging. Here the rebels paused and drew breath, for they saw that the Headmaster had reached sanctuary. They therefore contented themselves with vengeance by vandalism, and after breaking all the windows of Upper and Lower School and the Headmaster's Chambers, they slashed all his furniture and tore up his papers. The staff at last returned to duty, somewhat alarmed by the scenes of violence, and, after a hurried consultation with Dr Davies, it was decided that the boys should be sent home at once for their Christmas holiday.

In 1818 there took place Eton's last serious rebellion. It was decisively crushed by Dr Keate, who, if not the greatest Headmaster of the age, was certainly the greatest flogger. His record was 80 victims in rapid succession, his aim unaffected by flying missiles thrown at him by the waiting delinquents.
Keate had declared that Eton boys were no longer to be allowed to drive around in tandems and that anyone who did so would be expelled. A harsh penalty, perhaps, for a comparatively venial offence, and when Marriott, one of the school's most famous whips, was caught, and sentenced, a very ugly mood developed.

The first signs were in evidence the following Sunday afternoon when as usual the Upper School assembled for Keate's reading of what he considered a suitable homily. This was traditionally such a noisy affair that passers-by in the street outside used to stop in amazement, but on this occasion there was not only the usual barracking but a volley of shouts of "Where's Marriott?"

Keate, as usual, ignored these interruptions, but when they were accompanied by showers of books and rotten eggs, he slowly withdrew into his library. When the uproar had subsided, he emerged again and resumed his reading of one of Blair's sermons. Once again he was routed and forced to retire. The delighted rebels fell to smashing windows and breaking down part of the long wall. Placards of *Down with Keate* and *Floreat Seditio* appeared in chapel, and five desperate plotters decided on a final gesture that would topple Keate from his throne. While the rest of the school were having breakfast they marched into the Upper School with a sledge-hammer and completely smashed the Headmaster's desk.

Alas, they had reckoned without their host. Keate's trusty servant had seen it all, and the whole school was summoned to meet the Headmaster and the staff. The names of the malefactors were read out, their expulsion pronounced, and the school watched them in silence as they walked out in disgrace. Keate had to face no more rebellions.

= = = = = = = = = = = =

RUGBY

Dr James was a highly successful Headmaster (1778-1794) and a firm disciplinarian, but he could not escape contagion of the times, and there were two rebellions in his reign. Of these we know nothing except that he was able to quell both of them. His successor, Dr Ingles (1794– 1806), was less fortunate. He was an unpopular figure and his nickname, Black Tiger, was a reference to his liking for pouncing ferociously upon offenders.

One evening in November 1797, the doctor was walking down the street when he suddenly heard pistol shots from the yard of Gascoigne's, one of the school boarding houses. He moved swiftly in and found a boy named Astley firing a pistol at the windows of the house next door. His housemaster knew what was going on but seemed to regard it as permissible, so long as the boy did not actually fire at his own house. Dr Ingles demanded from the boy the source of his gunpowder and was told that it was from Rowell, a general purveyor of somewhat dubious reputation. Rowell, when interrogated, professed to have supplied the boy only with a pound of tea, and showed the Headmaster the entry.

Ingles now dealt out justice to Astley for an illicit purchase and beat him soundly. Astley's friends considered that Rowell had behaved badly in not telling more lies than he did, and vented their displeasure by throwing stones through his shop windows. He immediately complained to Dr Ingles, who announced that costs of replacement must be borne by the Vth and VIth forms , who, he suspected, were involved.

Events now moved rapidly.

A round-robin called for rebellion, and a petard exploded outside the Headmaster's house, blowing the door off its hinges. Nothing more occurred that evening, but the next day, on a pre-arranged signal, the whole school swept to the attack. Small boys appeared riding on the shoulders of big boys and they proceeded to smash all the school windows, even those protected by latticework. Next a huge bonfire was lit in the centre of the Close, and all the school desks, benches and even wainscoting were hurled with gusto into the blaze. Dr Ingles tried to get hold of some of his staff but they were all, it turned out, conveniently unavailable.

The situation was eventually saved by the chance presence in the town of a military recruiting squad who had seen the bonfire. The Headmaster wisely posted a soldier with a fixed bayonet outside his study and sat there awaiting developments. The Military were soon reinforced by farmers with horse-whips, only too ready to settle old poaching scores with the boys, and in the face of this alarming show of force, the rebels retired and took up a position in the Island, a building then protected by a sizeable moat. From this vantage-point they hurled insults and well-directed stones and fired guns. Their resistance was spirited, and the Mayor was called on to read the Riot Act. While this was being done, a party of soldiers with drawn swords waded through the moat behind the Island and took the defenders in the rear. They were compelled to surrender and trooped off to the Headmaster's Study to learn their fate. The ring-leaders were expelled, and those that were allowed to remain were flogged so severely that expulsion seemed a lighter punishment.

The Black Tiger hereafter reigned in peace

= = = = = = = = = = = =

SHREWSBURY

Dr Samuel Butler at Shrewsbury, at the height of his success in winning University awards and prizes, seems to have been faced by what his biographer grandson describes as a "period of turbulence." In 1818 three boys ran away leaving notes to say that they were sailing for India. One of them, a Praeposter (Prefect), seemed vague in his letter as to grievances, but finished up by calling Butler "a paltry and despicable pedant". It is possible that the second master with whom Butler waged a feud for 31 years was in sympathy with the rebels, and certainly there were other boys involved. Sentence of expulsion upon the runaways was announced to the school, but the order was ignored and the boys returned.

Butler's reaction to this was purely defensive, and he applied to the Mayor for a constable to protect him. That this was not a theatrical gesture is shown by the fact that previously a 17 year old runaway had drawn a knife on the pursuing Headmaster's servant, and another boy was discovered to be in possession of a loaded pistol, which he was preparing to use if molested by enemies. His parents were told by Dr Butler that he could not allow such a lethal weapon to be brought back the following term. "Further insubordination began" we are told "by the boys eating more than they wanted, and then complaining that they had not had enough; they got up fights in the town; they very nearly killed a farmer's pigs in what they called a boar-hunt and intimidated the farmer himself so greatly that when brought into the school by Dr Butler and asked to identify the offenders, he was too afraid to do so."

Butler himself was threatened with violence, windows were broken and there were other acts of insubordination which made Butler expel three boys and dismiss a fourth.

The only other case of insubordination met by Butler was the so-called "beef row" in 1829. The outbreak occurred on the appearance of a round of beef on the dinner table of the Doctor's hall, whereon the boys one and all - by arrangement preconcerted among themselves before they had seen the beef - left the hall, declaring that the meat was not fit to eat. Dr Butler required an apology from the Praeposter, and as they all refused to apologise, he dismissed them, with the saving clause that on apology being made he would receive them back. The parents of the boys made them apologise, and they all did; and they all did indeed come back. (One of the Praeposters concerned was Robert Scott, collaborator with Liddell in producing the famous Greek lexicon).

Dr Butler, though all accounts agree in stressing the kindness of his nature, was judiciously firm where necessary. In a circular sent with every boy returning home in December 1818 he warns against sending boys "baskets of game and poultry, tempting them to form junketing parties at low houses and exciting to other irregularities" and he added:

"It has come to my knowledge that some of the upper boys, with whose turbulent conduct I have great reason to be dissatisfied, are diligently instilling insubordination into the minds of those younger boys whom they think likely to receive their instructions. I have resolved on removing every such upper boy whom I know of from my school this Christmas; and I earnestly entreat every parent to whom I do not think it necessary to recommend his son's removal to impress him with the great importance of regular and orderly conduct and subordination, and of the impossibility of my showing indulgence to contrary behaviour."

It would be too much to say that boys never react against authority without good cause; but one cannot help wondering whether the food motif which has cropped up above in connection with 'turbulence' may be significant. Any exact knowledge of the feeding at Shrewsbury must now be as far beyond the possibility of human discovery as the song the Sirens sang, but we do know that in 1834 the annual fees at Shrewsbury were: for board 40 guineas, tuition 8 guineas, washing 4 guineas, and 'single bed (if required)' 4 guineas.

We know also that in 1835 there were 160 boarders. Thus, assuming that 160 boarders all had separate beds, they would pay a total of £8,960 p.a. Though fees from boarders amounted to not more than £9,000, Butler says that in spite of heavy family expenses and "keeping a carriage and living in good style", he was able during his last 10 years to put by a full £4,000 a year. "Though my expenses have been enormous" he explained, "I have been able, through Mrs Butler's activity, to keep three houses, each containing fifty boys, in my own hands."

Is it libellous to suggest that if Dr Butler had put by only £3,000 a year, the beef might have been a bit better?

= = = = = = = = = = = =

WINCHESTER.

Winchester, a hotbed of rebellion in the last three decades of the 18th century, seems to have been temporarily out of touch with the motto of its founder, 'Manners Makyth Man'. At any rate, poor Dr Warton, a distinguished man of letters but an ineffective Headmaster, faced a severe series of outbreaks, as shown in this extract from a letter to the Earl of Malmesbury, from his mother. She kept up a constant correspondence with her son, and wrote to him on 23 February 1770:

"This post brought Mr Bowles a letter from his son at Winchester, giving an account of a great riot in that School.
It began on some affront given, I think Monday, by the townsmen to some of the Commoners. Tuesday evening a detachment of Commoners set out, armed with bludgeons, and some with pistols. Dr Warton, on hearing this, locked up what boys remained in the Commoners' Hall, but they forced the door open, and would join their friends. The College was also locked, but they also grew outrageous, and they were let out to join in the fray. About eight they were got home all of them, and put to bed. One townsman was wounded by a shot in his leg.
   On Wednesday night they sallied forth again, armed with weapons of all kinds, and fought in the churchyard. The riot was so great that the magistrates were obliged to interfere, and the Riot Act was read. At length they dispersed, and I do not hear of any further mischief than bruises. Master Bowles was not in it, but by his manner of writing he seems greatly terrified. I am sorry for all this, as the School has got into great repute, and it must give Dr Warton infinite concern, but the spirit of riot is gone forth."

On March 3 she wrote again :
"The riot I mentioned in my last, at Winchester, is all over and no one expelled. It was a formidable thing, for they had several brace of pistols.

"It began, as I hear, by the landlord of the White Hart desiring some of the Commoners, who were drinking at his house, not to drink any more, but to go home. This gave such offence, that the next day some went and broke his windows. The man was obliged to call his neighbours to his assistance, so that brought on the battle between the townsmen and the scholars."

In 1774 another highly disorderly affair centred round 40 of the Commoners and their Tutor, Rev. Huntingford. Some of the boys dressed themselves up in mockery of Dr Warton's hump-backed housekeeper, who was naturally affronted and called upon the Tutor to order them to go to bed before their usual time. This they refused to do, and when Dr Warton entered Hall and tried to exert his superior authority, they loudly hissed him. He angrily retired, and, when he returned, they hissed him again.
"So, gentlemen, " he cried out "are you all metamorphosed into serpents?" In corroboration of the accusation they all hissed him again and indeed refused to let him speak at all.

They also began to show marked hostility towards their Tutor whom they accused of using coarse language and not treating them as gentlemen. Either he or they, it was loudly declared, must leave the school. The Tutor, a future bishop of Hereford, declined their invitation to leave, and so the boys all departed for their homes "The first day," we are told "they suffered much hunger and fatigue and at night going to inns, they, by leaving their watches or other means, got credit to forward them to their several houses."

The long-suffering Dr Warton faced his last rebellion in 1793. The band of the Bucks Militia was playing in the cathedral close and he forbade attendance by the school. The martial strains proved irresistible to a College Prefect, and when he was seen and reported, the whole school in its entirety was punished.

Forty seniors thought this very unfair, and they wrote a polite note of protest to Warden Huntingford in Latin: it said that "while they had implicitly obeyed him, they hoped that he would act differently". The Warden, however, remained obdurate, and the boys withdrew to their quarters, plainly in an ugly mood. Goddard, a popular Usher, was sent to negotiate with them, but he found them armed with clubs and was pelted with marbles. Then they moved over to the offensive, and, seizing the keys, they locked the Warden in his Lodging. He managed to escape, however, and volleys of abuse accompanied his flight through the college gates which were locked behind him. He made his way to the Town Hall where he appealed for help to the Magistrates.

The High Sheriff now tried to intervene, but he observed with alarm that the boys were preparing to hurl paving stones from the Tower in the event of an attack. Swords and bludgeons were much in evidence among the defenders, and the Cap of Liberty had been hoisted. The Headmaster now suggested that the High Sheriff should be accepted as a mediator. The boys agreed; there was a brief amnesty, and the Warden gave his promise that in future all boys should not be punished for the fault of one.

Peace seemed about to be established when one of the masters asked for the restoration of four guns taken from his house. This provoked a fresh spate of argument, but eventually the boys reluctantly agreed. Their mood, however, quickly changed when the Warden began somewhat tactlessly to lecture them on their bad behaviour. When interrupted by hecklers, he was unwise enough to pose a dangerously rhetorical question:

"Eloquar an sileam?" he enquired. (*Shall I speak or be silent?*)
"Sileas" was the reply.
(For the benefit of non-Latinists 'sileas' means 'may you be silent', and if pronounced 'silly ass', it completes a very Wykehamist sort of pun.)

Victory at length came to authority, albeit tardily, because the rebels overplayed their hands and forty seniors presented the Warden with their resignations, expecting them not to be accepted. This was a tactical error, and the Warden at once grasped at his chance of getting rid of all the ringleaders. Soon afterwards Warton retired, solaced for his scholastic anxieties by the possession of two prebends and three fat livings.

Dr Gabell, who had to face the next rebellion in 1818, should have been used to disorderly scenes because he had been present at the storming of the Bastille, and indeed on that auspicious occasion had surrendered his shirt to be torn up for bandages. In this case, the source of the trouble seems to have been an unpopular Tutor who was suspected of abusing the confidence placed in him by the prefects and reporting their out-of-bounds activities to the Headmaster. He promptly put their favourite walk out-of-bounds and added further penalties.

The reaction of the school was immediate and violent. 130 Commoners rushed into college and barricaded it against the Masters. Armed with sticks, they wrested the keys from the Porter and drove out all the servants bar one. The cook was retained by general approval to supply their suppers. In all the school there was only one small boy who rejected all pressures to join the rebellion. His name was William Sewell, and he eventually became Founder and Warden of Radley.

The rebels now settled down for the night and posted sentinels and patrols. They were, however, undisturbed, and their only trial came over breakfast which consisted of an inedible mixture of potatoes, flour and bacon cooked in a very haphazard style. A stately note was now struck by the Warden, who appeared at his window and threw down a paper, reminding the rebels of events in 1793. This, however, merely hardened their resolution, and they immediately drew up a list of their grievances.

One of the Canons now attempted unsuccessfully to mediate, but the boys set about barricading the door of the Warden's House. With a lively sense of the enormity of the crime, the Warden (who was Bishop of Hereford) cried out from the box window above the door that the rioters "would be brought on their knees before the House of Lords for imprisoning a Peer in his own house".

This threat, hardly surprisingly, produced no effect but the rebellion was now defeated by a clever ruse. One of the Tutors appeared at the box-window and announced that the Riot Act had been read and the soldiers sent for, but if the boys would surrender the keys, they could go home for a fortnight. The simple-hearted rebels, overjoyed at this, handed over the keys, threw down their sticks and streamed out, believing that they were on their way home. Almost immediately they ran into the soldiers advancing from two directions and the rebellion was over.

There were some twenty expulsions.

= = = = = = = = = = = =

WESTMINSTER.

Westminster in the late 18th century and early 19th century presented such a picture of anarchy that it is difficult to pick out specific episodes for special treatment. The masters made ineffectual attempts to check visits to the local theatre. Their efforts are here described in the Westminster Annals.

" 'The Westminster Boy', a farce by Captain Topham, was attempted to be acted at Covent Garden for the benefit of Mr Wells. By the most unexampled negligence of the Masters of Westminster School, a number of the gentlemen educated at that seminary were suffered to be at the theatre this evening, and by every species of disturbance put a stop to the performance of the piece. The prologue was written by a Westminster, with whom some of the disturbers may have been at school. To stop these 'schemes' the masters' only method seems to have been to wait in the Palace Yard and the Sanctuary and catch the returning truants. They were seldom successful, for the houses which then stood near St. Margaret's, and whose demolition Southey regretted, were a cover that prevented capture."

Against such a disorderly background it is hardly surprising to read of the internal troubles in the boarding houses. Thus from the diary of a Westminster Usher, quoted in J.Carleton's 'Westminster':

"Opposition and discontent on all sides: such are the pleasures of a Boarding House and an Usher", he writes on 23 February 1792,

And again, on 27 March,
"When I came home to take call over, found the house in everything but open rebellion. Talked to Mrs. Clapham and the boys, and made some miserable temporising shift as to Order."

A month later things were as bad again.

"27 April 1792: Miserably low. At home all the Evening, and in the midst of destruction, noise, tumult and everything but rebellion. Haunted with this damn'd house, in which I think there must inevitably be a riot before the Holydays."

And so the tale goes on. Sometimes the house was 'sullen and silent' or 'in gloomy calm' at dinner, and at other times it was wildly uproarious. On his return from cards one evening he was met by 'a solemn March and Procession' of the boys – a Masquerade of which he 'thought proper to inform Dr Vincent' - and on another evening he returned and 'found the boys and Servants dancing together in the Hall'. There was a riot because the boys did not get enough supper, and another because they did not get enough coal; Mrs Clapham's parlour windows were broken and there was 'sneezing by platoons' in Hall (whatever that might be).

While all this was going on there were, needless to say, innumerable vexatious and time-wasting incidents concerning individual boys. Lawson swallowed a button and Allen kicked down the pantry door in a temper. Dickens got a severe cut from a brickbat thrown from Mrs Grant's yard, and Reynolds was concussed by being tossed in a blanket.

Cory was found drunk in bed at locking-up, Montgomerie 'came home drunk and not 'till 12 o'clock', and Lord Dupplin, on being reprimanded, was 'not deficient in arrogance.'
And, as if all this were not enough, there was endless haggling with Mrs Clapham over House money matters and with his colleagues over fees due to him from several of his private pupils.

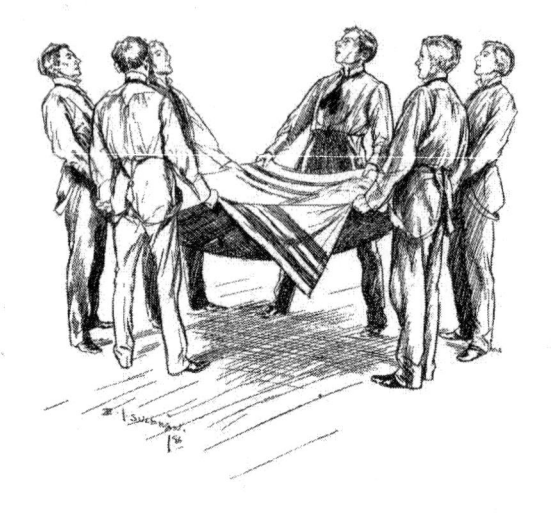

Physical combat seems to have been the breath of life for all at Westminster, and Carey, the Headmaster from 1805-1815, openly encouraged it. "If a boy is a good fellow", he observed to his head boy, "and a good fighter, we must not be too hard on him for his Latin and Greek."

This was evidently a tradition that was faithfully preserved, for Bishop Short of Adelaide records of his school-days in the next generation:
"When I was a boy at Westminster, the boys fought one another, they fought the master, the masters fought them, they fought outsiders, in fact we were ready to fight everybody."

The last extract from the Public Advertiser 26th Nov. 1791 gives a very good idea of the Westminster boys' loyalties and priorities:

"A terrible fracas took place on Wednesday at Westminster School. Two of the boys having had a dispute, agreed to go to the Green, and fight it out. The two heroes were followed by the rest of the boys, and Dr Vincent and the rest of the masters were only left in the School.

Mr Smedley, the Head Usher, was dispatched with orders to summon the Students to their duty. The fight not being over, he returned without completing his mission. Dr Wingfield, the second master, was dispatched, and returned also unsuccessful.

Dr Vincent then went himself, but no obedience could be had till the battle was decided; after which the scholars returned to the schoolhouse, when sentence of flagellation was passed upon Mr Boyley, the head boy, from not having obeyed orders. The sentence was demurred to by the whole school."

= = = = = = = = = = = =

HARROW

Dr Kennedy, later of Latin Grammar fame, was warned in 1835 by Butler, his old Headmaster, that if he became Headmaster of Harrow he would certainly have to face some kind of rebellion. In the event, he prudently chose the Headmastership of Shrewsbury. Harrow indeed had a rare reputation for disorder in an age that was full of violence and brutality of every sort.

Maybe the superior social quality of most Harrovians gave them an arrogance and confidence that naturally led them into angry disputes with the Governors, especially over the appointment of their Headmasters. Indeed, in the late 18th century there were at Harrow at the same time five dukes, two marquesses and thirteen earls in addition to five future Prime Ministers. So when in 1771 on Dr Sumner's death Benjamin Heath was selected to succeed him rather than the school's choice, Dr Parr, the outcry and opposition was immediate, and the following letter was dispatched to the Governors.

"Sirs,
We, the senior scholars, as the voice of the whole school, have heard that you propose, contrary to our desire of each of us, to appoint Mr Heath, or some other person from Eton, as successor to our late Master, Dr Sumner. A school of such reputation, as our late master has rendered this, ought not to be considered an appendix to Eton. Mr Parr cannot but be acquainted with those rules which his predecessor has established, and will consequently act upon the former successful plan. We hope private attachments or personal affections will not bias your minds to the prejudice of the school. A school cannot thrive when every individual is heartily disaffected towards the Master."

It is difficult not to suspect that "those rules" were concerned mainly with preserving the privileges of senior scholars, and the Governors, not surprisingly, disregarded the directive. The school was then torn asunder by furious divisions while the defeated Dr Parr led away forty rebellious boys to Stanmore where a rival school was set up.

It did not, however, last very long. Other sympathisers stoned the carriage of Bucknall, one of the hated Governors, and pushing it down the hill, wrecked it and broke it into pieces. One of the pieces was born off in triumph by 11 year old Richard Wellesley. He was prominent among the rioters and was duly expelled. Later he was transferred to Eton where he was soon followed by his younger brother Arthur. But for this incident, the victor of Waterloo would not perhaps have made his famous reference to the battle won on the Playing Fields of Eton.

A similar challenge to authority greeted the appointment of the youthful Dr George Butler in 1805. The popular choice was the Rev. Mark Drury, the retiring Master's nephew, and the school's fury knew no bounds when their favourite was outvoted. In vain the retiring Dr Drury begged them to restrain themselves. The youthful Byron led the opposition, first by circulating scurrilous verses about Butler, and finally by forming a desperate plot to use gunpowder to blow up a passage that was known to be frequently used by the Headmaster.

He was finally dissuaded from this by those who pointed out how many boards covered with their fathers' initials would be for ever lost to posterity.

An uneasy truce was now observed, and it held till Dr Butler decided to curtail some undesirable features of the monitors' authority. The monitors immediately resigned in a body, and once more the barricades were down and symbols of liberty and rebellion were flaunted defiantly in the Fourth Room. The school keys were taken forcibly from the custodian, the birch cupboard was forced open and pillaged, and the work of the school ground to a halt. All communications with London were cut by carefully posted guards, and authority seemed to be gagged as well as bound. Dr Butler, however, kept his head and, sooner or later, the rebels lost theirs and capitulated.

Nation-wide interest had been taken and George III was among those who sent congratulations to the Headmaster.

= = = = = = = = = = =

MARLBOROUGH.

It is something of an anomaly that a school founded in 1843 to provide education for the sons of the clergy should in 1851 be the scene of the longest and most violent rebellion of them all. On the other hand, on a closer examination of the facts it becomes immediately evident that here was a situation that called for firm and skilful handling. The school had been founded to provide a cut-price boarding school education, and so conditions were primitive even by mid 19th century standards. Most of the school were herded together for all purposes into a huge room which reproduced all the worst features of the Eton Long Chamber. The food was coarse and dirty, and beatings incessant and particularly severe. Prefects had privileges but no responsibilities, and there was no provision for cricket or football at all; poaching, thieving and rat-catching were the chief occupations of the boys, and a staff of a dozen faced an unruly mob of 500, the second largest school in England.

The 1851 rebellion began on Guy Fawkes Day with a particularly savage attack on the small brick house at the school gates, occupied by the boys' most hated enemy, Sergeant Peviar. He was regarded by them as a cowardly informer, and they usually threw stones at his house whenever they could. On this occasion, however, the attack was such a violent one that the Headmaster, Rev. Matthew Wilkinson, confined the whole school to their classrooms as a punishment. Four days of complete anarchy followed. Windows everywhere were smashed and whenever masters attempted to enter the classrooms, they were hissed.

In the face of all this, the Headmaster weakly agreed to rescind the general punishment, but unwisely expelled a ring-leader who was particularly popular.

Next day the whole school followed him cheering wildly to the Railway Station, and on their return journey, they encountered another old enemy, the local Miller, always known as Treacle Bolly. The Miller reciprocated the boys' feelings by reason of their continual thefts of his ducks. There was, therefore, an angry confrontation and he was pushed off his horse and man-handled. His appeal to the Headmaster' resulted in a further explosion, and window-smashing was now followed by the Racquet Courts being set on fire. To crown everything, the school champion sought out the hated gate-sergeant, fought him and thrashed him.

The character of the Headmaster may be gauged by the fact that at this moment he enquired from the rebels what their grievances were. They replied that they wanted their privileges restored. These were largely opportunities to roam even more widely in their poaching and visit public houses. The Headmaster agreed to restore them provided that the boys paid £10 for the damage done to the school property. This seems a modest sum, and they agreed to pay. The rebellion appeared to be over, but there was a final outbreak by a splinter group who carried out a raid on the Master's desks and books and set fire to them all. They refused to own up, and the rest of the school viewed them with slight disapproval.

It comes as no surprise to hear that the Rev. Wilkinson retired next year to a quiet country living.

= = = = = = = = = = = =

CHAPTER 2

THE UNREFORMED SCHOOLS

"I admit that Eton has its faults, my Lords;
why the Ocean has more dirt in it than your little streams."
(J. Hope-Scott to the Clarendon Commissioners)

"We were packed like sardines, without the oleaginous comfort
in which sardines repose."
An Old Salopian (1836)

"I do not know why there is all this fuss about education.
None of the Paget family can read or write,
and they do very well."
(Lord Melbourne, in a letter to Queen Victoria)

The great Public Schools, in spite of their wealthy and aristocratic clientele, provided no exception to the generally intolerable conditions in which so many of the population lived. The average boy was ill-accommodated, under-fed, overworked as a fag, underworked, or at any rate undertaught, in the classroom, and liable to bullying from any one older and bigger than himself. As he himself grew older and bigger, he probably became more capable of securing a bigger share of the food provided, and of bullying rather than being bullied.

But over old and young alike ruled an inadequate number of usually underpaid masters, whose answer to nearly all education problems was the birch. Nowadays nothing is better calculated to bring angry protests from enlightened opinion than the advocacy of any kind of corporal punishment. Yet, it is interesting to reflect that ours is the first age in which the generality of both parents and teachers have ceased to regard beating the young as either a pleasure or a duty or a mixture of both. Scripture tells us plainly that we spare the rod at the expense of the child's character, and the good monks of Canterbury in olden Saxon days used to fall upon their pupils with thongs of bulls' hide in a special ceremony five days before Christmas. This was done deliberately so as to check undue hilarity in the recipients during the festive season. The practice was on one occasion interrupted by the visitation of the sanctified St Dunstan himself, who successfully begged clemency for the victims.

Among members of the church on earth such merciful kindness was rare indeed. Cardinal Wolsey, however, was an exception, and we read with surprise his directions to those who should teach at his new foundation at Ipswich. He was suggesting that pleasure is to be mingled with study, and that boys should find learning an amusement rather than a toil.

He then goes on to say:

"Tender youth is to suffer neither severe thrashings nor sour and threatening looks, nor any kind of tyranny; for by such usage the fire of genius is either extinguished, or in a great measure damped."

If Henry VIII had died suddenly and the Wolsey project had been developed, the whole story of English education might have been different. As it was, Wolsey's school fell with him, and the chance of a new look in Scholastic discipline faded away.

As teaching passed increasingly out of the hands of the church to the laity, the flogging tradition was zealously preserved. Indeed a schoolmaster without his birch was as unthinkable as a soldier without arms. Robert Mulcaster, the great 16th century schoolmaster, was as famous for his flagellations as for his learning, but he sometimes, as the chronicler tells us, infused a touch of sardonic humour into the proceedings. Thus, on one occasion, pausing over a bared bottom, he asked the waiting victims, in a grim parody of marriage service parliaments, if there were any cause or just impediment why the buttocks of the culprit and Madam Birch should not be joined together. A sturdy and intelligent boy spoke up, objecting that the parties were not, and never would be, in agreement. Mulcaster was pleased with his wit and forgave the one's fault and the other's presumption. The boy was spared.

There was, however, no humour in Dr Gill, one of his successors at St Paul's. He not only rained blows unmercifully on his scholars, but even considered a visiting ex-pupil suitable for such attentions. One of them, a future Archdeacon, had an ingenious revenge, as the antiquarian John Aubrey tells us:

"He hired a Pitcher of Oxford who had a sweet and strong bass voice to sing an insulting song beneath the Headmaster's window." It began:

> "In St. Paul's Yard in London,
> There dwells a noble Firker,"

It has several scurrilous verses, each ending with the refrain:

> "Take him up, take him up, sir,
> Untruss with expedition."

This was, apparently, a favourite expression of Gill's before administering corporal punishment. The song relates in each verse how Gill beats a whole succession of mere passers-by. One of Gill's contemporaries was the celebrated Dr Busby of Westminster, whose endless and genial floggings seem to have endeared him to some of the greatest in the land. "The fathers govern the nation", he used to declare gleefully, "the mothers govern the fathers, the boys govern the mothers and I govern the boys".

The later 18th century seems to have seen a slight decline in the cult of beating but Dr Johnson produced a vigorous defence of it, as recorded by Boswell:

"Langton one day asked him, how he had acquired so accurate a knowledge of Latin, (in which, I believe, he was exceeded by no man of his time). He said, 'My master whipped me very well. Without that, Sir, I should have done nothing.' He told Mr Langton, that while Hunter was flogging his boys unmercifully, he used to say, 'All this I do to save you from the gallows.'

Johnson, upon all occasions, expressed his approbation of enforcing instruction by means of the rod.

"I would rather," said he, " have the rod to be the general terror to all, to make them learn, than tell a child if you do thus or thus, you will be more esteemed than your brothers or sisters. The rod produces an effect which terminates in itself. A child is afraid of being whipped, and gets his task, and there's an end on't ; whereas, by exciting emulation and comparisons of superiority, you make brothers and sisters hate each other."

In the early 19th century, however, the pupils, as we have seen, took the offensive in a series of violent revolts in such schools as Eton, Westminster, and Harrow, where the youthful Byron led the way in a daring Gunpowder Plot. The hour called forth the man, and to combat the growing tide of lawlessness there arose in Dr Keate the greatest flogger of them all. He stands to flogging much as W.G. Grace stands to cricket. Faced with bitter unpopularity, savage opposition and misdemeanours of every kind, his unfailing remedy was vigorous and incessant flogging.
"Sir, I'll flog you" was so often on his lips that no one felt surprised or resentful when he flogged a group of Confirmation candidates instead of instructing them.

As we peer through the moral and emotional ambience of today at those early 19th century punitive methods, it is difficult to imagine how Keate's former pupils could tolerate, let alone love, him. But read what Gladstone has to say about the old Etonian dinner in London in 1841, which celebrated the 400th anniversary of the foundation of the College. The gathering was larger than usual, and, no doubt, packed with peers, bishops, and generals, the vast majority of whom, says Gladstone, had endured Keate's floggings in their day':

"In those days at public dinners, cheering was marked by gradations. As the Queen was suspected of sympathy with the Liberal government, the toast of the Sovereign was naturally received with only a moderate amount of acclamation, decently and thriftily doled out. On the other hand, the Queen Dowager was believed to be, Conservative; and her health consequently figured as the toast of the evening, and drew forth, as a matter of course, by far its loudest acclamations.   But upon this occasion, when his (*Keate's*) name had been mentioned, the scene was indescribable. The roar of cheering had a beginning, but never knew end.

Like the huge waves at Biarritz, the floods of cheering continually recommenced; the whole process was such that we seemed all to have lost our self-possession and to be hardly able to keep our seats. When at length it became possible, Keate rose; that is to say, his head was projected slightly over the heads of his two neighbours. He struggled to speak.. I will not say I heard every syllable, for there were no syllables; speak he could not. He tried in vain to mumble a word or two, but wholly failed, recommenced the vain struggle, and sat down. It was certainly one of the most moving spectacles in my whole life that I have ever witnessed.."

Well, well! There are the facts; what is the explanation?

Chatham said that he "scarcely observed a boy who was not cowed for life at Eton", but doubtless the cowed ones did not attend the dinner of 1841. Those who did were clearly under the spell of a powerful emotion comparable to that felt and displayed by a Welsh rugby crowd at Cardiff Arms Park. They were members of a tribe, all of whom had undergone terrifying and painful initiation rites. They had entered as normal small boys; they had been case-hardened; they had emerged as Old Etonians, able to play their part in the world as normal men, but on an occasion like this dinner, irresistibly inspired to identify themselves with the shaman, the totem-pole of the system that had made them what they were - John Keate.

Keate seems to have been put out of countenance only twice in his life. The first occasion was a challenge to a duel from one of his pupils whom he had wrongly accused of not speaking the truth. Expulsion for the boy was the only answer. The second occasion was the presentation to him of 500 guineas from his old pupils. Again he acted appropriately, and raised his hat.

Not all, however, were as amenable to Head Magisterial discipline as Dr Keate's boys. Dr Samuel Butler of Shrewsbury recalls an early incident in his own career (1798):

"An event which, though grossly misrepresented, gave colour to the prevailing gossip, took place about six years ago. Two boys whom I received into my house, apparently on good recommendation, but who, I have since learnt, had been previously expelled from the Charterhouse, went without leave to the races. They did not return till eleven o'clock at night, when they came home drunk. I called for them to punish them the next morning. They refused to submit, instigated the other boys to support them, and ran away. They were followed by my servant and myself; the former first came up with them, when the oldest, about seventeen, drew a knife on him. I had them secured, and punished them with the ordinary school discipline, and, on their contumacy, I expelled them as an example which was become necessary for the preservation of my authority."

Flogging by Headmasters could be said to have reached its zenith with Keate's marathon flagellations, and, after that, this feature of school life entered upon a slow decline, so much so that nowadays it seems likely that it may die out altogether. Physical punishment by senior boys, however, presents some very different aspects. For a long time it seems to have been largely unaffected by adult opinions and controls inside the school and outside, and to have been regulated entirely by the current tastes and inclinations of the senior boys themselves.

The row over 'tunding' (the Winchester name for a beating by a prefect with an ashplant) is fully described by Sir Charles Oman, the historian, who was a small boy at Winchester at the time. His picture of his schooldays is by no means a complete indictment of the system, and there are glimpses of richly comical figures such as the eccentric Fellow who believed that his nose might fall off. He therefore used to strap it on with strips of black sticking plaster 'which gave him the appearance of a venerable tiger'.

Oman arrived at Winchester just when a wave of sadism appears to have invaded the prefectorial body. For a period of several weeks so many tundings were handed out that at least one small boy was reduced to spending all his spare time hiding in a fives court in order to avoid any contact with prefects. The Oman parents, deeply alarmed at the accounts given in his letters, had taken lodgings in Winchester, so as to be near at hand, when suddenly the whole reign of terror was terminated and the Senior Prefect became involved in a controversy which made headlines in the national press.

It transpired that the prefects had decided to stiffen up what they deemed the slackness of the lower school by a rigorous testing of 'notions' - the rather ridiculous slang vocabulary whose use was compulsory at Winchester. One William Macpherson, 'the village Hampden of Winchester', as Oman calls him, claimed that as a 17-year-old he was exempt from such a test, and accepted a tunding of thirty strokes rather than yield the point. (He was indignant not about the beating but about the point of principle.)

His father, when he heard the story, angrily told all to the Times and correspondence followed in other newspapers.

Headmaster Ridding, though he defended the Prefect concerned as being 'in ordinary circumstances a good and gentle boy', was compelled to investigate the whole system of tundings. He was appalled by what he found – 111 beatings for 13 boys over a few weeks. The total figure terrified even the prefects , says Oman. The guilty prefect was made to apologise publicly to his victim; tundings were reserved in future for moral offence or deliberate disobedience; and William, for the rest of his school career, bore the honourable sobriquet of Tunded Macpherson.

We need not suppose that conditions at Winchester were normally like this either before or after the 'reign of terror'. Equally there is no reason to think that Winchester was unique in having passed through such a calamitous period. But, whatever fluctuations in bullying and brutality there might be elsewhere at different schools and at different times, the notorious Long Chamber at Eton provided, till its planned destruction in 1846, a horrifying and unparalleled record of hardship and misery.

If the Long Chamber at Eton had not existed it would have been necessary for Dickens to invent it: for it was a cross between Fagin's Kitchen and Dotheboys Hall. In a room 172ft long, 27ft wide and 15ft 6ins high, 52 boys lived in rat-infested squalor. There was no floor covering of any kind and the wind whistled through broken windows and gaping casements. Except for a privileged few, there was not a table or a chair. There were no washstands or basins and indeed no means of washing at all.

A request for running water to be laid on was in 1838 contemptuously refused by the Fellows with the words: "You rascals, you'll be asking for gas and Turkey carpets next."

Here are the first impressions of a hapless new boy in 1824: "On arriving at my Dame's, I was told that I must go into College at once, and that I should find my sheets and bedding in Long Chamber, and that as 'lag of the School' my bedstead was at the bottom. On entering that renowned dormitory, a scene of indescribable confusion greeted me. It was nearly dark, and there were no lights except a few tallow candles carried about here and there by the boys.

The floor was covered with the bedding, each bundle being wrapped in a coarse horse-rug, far inferior to what would now be used in a gentleman's stable. This was intended to serve as counterpane. The noise and hooting of nearly fifty boys, each trying to identify his scanty stock of bedding combined with the shouts of the elder boys calling their fags, gave me a foretaste of my future lot. There were no servants, to give us assistance.

At 7p.m. after prayers in the Lower School, the doors were closed and we were left prisoners for the night, to settle down as best could. At 7a.m. Dr Keate's servant set us free, and after pacing the Long Chamber twice, armed with a lantern in winter, left us to our morning duties. A person styled a 'bed-maker' came to put the clothes straight, but he did little more, and at nightfall we had to make the beds of our fagmasters as well as our own. A tallow candle was allowed to each boy, and this had to be fetched from a Dame's House."

The condition of a junior Colleger's life at that period was very hard indeed. The practice of fagging had become an organized system of brutality and cruelty.

"I was frequently kept up until one or two o'clock in the morning waiting on my masters at supper, and undergoing every sort of bullying at their hands. I have been beaten on my palms with the back of a brush, or struck on both sides of my face, because I had not closed the shutter near my master's bed tight enough, or because in making his bed I had left the seam uppermost."

"The rioting, masquerading, and drinking that took place in College after the doors were closed at night can scarcely be credited. I do not think that there was even an alarm-bell, although I have seen many a blaze that seemed to threaten destruction to the whole building. In Winter, the Collegers assembled at dusk and then remained in their chambers until after the Latin prayers. had been said. During the intermediate hours, the doors into the School Yard and into Weston's Yard, were open, and a boy stood in the entrance to give timely notice of the Head Master's approach, so that the boys might open their bureaux, light their candles, and put on an appearance of severe study."

Till 1844, these were the quarters considered by the Fellows as suitable for the intellectual cream of Eton. Provost Goodall seriously defended conditions in the Long Chamber by saying that it would be disloyal to Henry VI's wish to provide amenities which might tempt a gentleman to seek admission for his son. It is significant that in 1841 for 35 vacancies in College there were only two candidates. It is significant that in 1841 for 35 vacancies in College there were only 2 candidates.

General conditions were little better for the King's scholars at Westminster, and the Lancet sounded a sombre note of warning about river pollution.
"The waters of the Thames are swollen with the feculence of the myriads of living beings that dwell upon the banks and with the waste of every manufacture that is too foul for utilization."
A Times leader of 1858 describes M.P's staggering out of the portions of their buildings which overlooked the River with handkerchiefs held to their faces. But it was the systematised slavery of fagging that most horrifies the modern reader.

Dacre Adams, a Junior at Westminster in 1829, paints another sad picture:

"In winter I get up at half-past seven, excepting every fourth day, when I get up at six. At eight I carry my master's books into school. I am in school till nine, excepting the times I am sent about messages. From nine to half-past I go into the birch-room, and there I make rods. I cannot do more than half a rod - it is such hard work. From half-past nine to ten I go to breakfast, and at ten I go into school to lesson, and there stand all the time. I do nothing in the way of learning. At eleven I go to my seat, where I sit, unless I am sent about messages. I am obliged, every time I go into school, to bring three pens, three quarterns (*sheets of paper*), and a dip *(ink container)*, and a knife. At twelve I go into the green and play at hockey. I may be sent away from play, if anybody chuses. At one I go to dinner, where I have to mash some potatoes for my master, and to toast his meat.

After I have done that, I may sit down to dinner, if there is time, for I have only half an hour to do everything. I am not allowed to help myself till all are helped, and then I may cut off from what is left. It takes me only four or five minutes to eat my dinner, but sometimes I have not time for it - so sometimes I go without. The seniors have all the potatoes, so we have only bread and meat to eat, and it takes us less time. Every fourth day I have things to do for the Third Election (*Third Year boys*), to clean their candlesticks, to get candles for them, and to put them on their desks. I make their ten beds, which takes a great while, for I must do all my master's things just the same.   I have to brush clothes for ten Fellows, fill eight pitchers, and clean eight basins, wash up their ten sets of tea things when they have tea or coffee, and do sometimes a few jobs for them. But if they call me too often, I say, 'Doing something for my master', for I could not always go when they call. We have no supper."

By a curious irony, it seems to have been the most distinguished schools which imposed the greatest privations on their scholars, and it seems likely that the smaller schools escaped much of the systematised fagging. Living conditions, however, with a few striking exceptions, were pretty bad. At Shrewsbury in 1836 a single bed was a luxury for which an extra charge was made. None of the ten bedrooms in the Headmaster's house had any ventilation, and for 50 boys there was one W.C.

The authorities seem to have taken the same attitude towards the boys' nutritional needs as to their accommodation.   When it was suggested that vegetables should be added to the Eton Collegers' menu, the idea was quickly blocked by one of the Fellows, who asked: "But who will peel the potatoes?"

Mutton indeed appeared with such dismal regularity that when the Long Chamber was finally demolished, two cartloads of mutton bones were discovered under the floor-boards. Generations of Collegers had used them for rat-bait. An astonishing and deplorable tradition at Winchester ensured that while the seniors got plenty of meat at the 6 o'clock dinner, the Juniors got none at all.

This was achieved by means of sending the Juniors running around on errands and throwing their meat into the baskets for the poor when they failed to collect it on time.   Their service was further enlivened by boys called candle-holders who wielded not candles but ash-plants, and hit out at any Junior who was so unfortunate as to come within reach.

As late as 1873 a deputation of boys presented a protest against being served with cold beef crawling with white maggots. And all this was just forty years after Dotheboys Hall !

There were, however, schools like Marlborough, where in early days everybody fared equally badly. The evening meal consisted of hunks of bread smeared with butter, this being thrown onto individual plates from a clothes-basket by the dirty hand of the School Porter. Knives and forks seem to have been a luxury in the 18th century Rugby, and, at Uppingham the practice was to clean the dirty forks by driving them into the tablecloth. High Church leanings produced a curious phase of asceticism at Radley, where at one time the school meals were so slender that the boys were driven to plunder the flower beds for tasty bulbs and shrubs. The 'beef row' at Shrewsbury, however, appears to have been the only occasion on which there was any serious protest about food.

Bullying varied between crude practical jokes and elaborate and cruel torture. The most notorious was probably the Rugby 'Lamb singing' in the pre-Arnold days, when new boys were made to sing solos and had to drink heavily salted hot water if their performance was poor. At Winchester a new boy would sometimes be asked if he had a pair of tin gloves. If he said no, his tormentors would then take a red-hot stick from the fire and trace a line of blisters from the knuckles wrist.

Dormitories provided further opportunities for the bullies. Sleepers were liable to have water poured into their ears and then be hanged out of the window by one leg. Bare-footed runners were made to race over tin-tack covered floors, and (a speciality of Eton and Rugby) pink-coated riders with spurs rode small boys over obstacle courses. Even organised games, elsewhere largely beneficial, were converted at Winchester into instruments of terror and misery for the Juniors. 'Kicking in' at football entailed hours of standing shivering in the cold and wet in readiness to recover a ball kicked out of the 'college canvas'. In the summer any Prefect could make six Juniors stand round him while he hit cricket balls at them, sometimes very hard at short range. For the frail or the short-sighted, it must have been terrifying.

The helplessness of Headmasters at an even later date to stop this puerile brutality is well illustrated by this protest against bullying in a sermon, by Dr Hawtrey (1834-1853):

"The Objects of such a kind of ill-usage are not those over whom there is any lawful or conventional Right: they are the Weak, the Timid, the Eccentric, and the Unsociable; and sometimes those who have none of these Failings, yet who from some Peculiarity of Character are not acceptable to all, who are nevertheless capable of warm Friendship, who are even possessed of no common mental Powers, which might have expanded into great private and Public Usefulness, but which may be also compressed and concentrated in a sensitive Mind, till they lead to Misanthropy, or perhaps to the more fatal Error of doubting the Justice of Providence"

The list of these grim activities is endless and their contemplation is sickening. It is only natural to ask the simple question, why were these things so? To begin with, as with a large proportion of the cruelty and suffering that goes on in the world, lack of imagination was responsible for much. Mansfield, in School Life at Winchester College, describing the duties of 'Junior in College' in about 1840, mentions almost casually that "cleaning his Master's basin" was a task that had to be performed by "rubbing it with earth picked up from between the flints of Quad".

After reporting the small boys' difficulties about getting any dinner, he adds that, when a lucky junior was given some dinner by a kindly Prefect, there were still problems to be overcome.
"We had some difficulty eating it, knives and forks being rare articles, unless the Prefect was good enough also to lend us his instruments. I remember seeing Skith with one end of a carcase of a hare in each hand, burrowing among the ribs with his nose and mouth in search of the tit-bits, which, to judge by the delight depicted on his countenance, were still remaining."

As to more deliberate cruelty, there were probably several reasons. There was a deeply implanted hatred of 'telling tales'. To quote Mansfield again:

"A high code of honour was kept up in the school, truth being scrupulously adhered to between the boys themselves, and by them towards the Masters, except in one particular (which exception, indeed, was caused by an honourable feeling crookedly developed). This was when telling the truth would bring another individual into trouble. On these occasions the most tremendous lies were sometimes considered justifiable:
e.g., The Doctor comes suddenly round a corner, and finds Tibbs mopping the rosy fluid from his nose with a rueful countenance, having just received a sharp back-hander from one of his lords and masters, whose basin he has broken:
Doctor: Pray, what may be the matter with you?
Tibbs: Fell down and hurt my nose, sir,
Doctor: But the ground is muddy, and your clothes clean.
Tibbs: Only touched the ground with my nose, sir."

A fairly light-hearted example; but undoubtedly the rigid code of 'no sneaking' was, and is, responsible for the fact that much bullying escaped detection. Staff surveillance, of course, was either insufficient or non-existent; at Eton in 1833 there were only nine masters to 570 boys. Then again, it has to be admitted that it was a cruel age. Boys naturally delighted in injuring birds and small animals; after the Oxford and Cambridge Boat Race of 1860, the rival crews gathered together in a hired shed to watch dogs being set on cats.

Above all there was a widespread belief in the value of a Spartan upbringing. Mansfield supplies these sentiments:

"I think fagging, on the whole, a laudable institution; and in after-life, in the rough struggles of the world, happy is he who has been through such a training. A boy learns to help himself, not to be disheartened in difficulties and to be prepared for any emergency: and, withal, a keen sense of honour, friendly rivalry and patriotic feeling is continually kept in action"

Nowadays organised games have done much to destroy the power of the bully. Mr Gathorne-Hardy in The Public School Phenomenon, refers to games contemptuously as 'canalised aggression'. It seems a pity that they didn't start digging the canals a bit earlier.

There seems to have been only one serious attempt to break away from the system of flogging by the Headmaster and the despotic rule of the senior boys. It was attempted at Charterhouse by Dr Russell (1811-1832) who substituted fines for flogging and abolished the monitors who were promoted on seniority, in favour of young and intelligent boys who were called Praeposters. Steady opposition to these changes developed over the years, and the school numbers fell from 480 to 137. Russell was succeeded by Dr Saunders who restored the *ancien regime* and the school's numbers rose again satisfactorily.

When Dr Saunders (now Dean of Peterborough) was giving evidence before the Clarendon Commissioners he explained in a very few words how Dr Russell's experiment had failed:

"We thought flogging was very gentlemanly, but fines most ungentlemanly".

He then went on to relate how Dr Russell had one day found the Fifth form in a considerable state of disorder:
"Fifth Form" he demanded angrily, "Where is your Praeposter?"
A figure detached itself from a pile of bodies and dragged out a small and dishevelled boy by his collar.
"Please Sir, " he observed cheerfully. "Here he is."

Rejection of Senior boys' authority by their juniors was something of a rarity. The theological preoccupation of the saintly Charles Gore, subsequently a famous bishop, found little favour in the eyes of the rest of his contemporaries when he was a pupil at Harrow. One day they all threw pats of butter at him as he passed by them. Enraged at this affront to the dignity of the Monitors, the Head of the House summoned them all together. He said that he felt that he could not do justice to them all in one marathon beating, and so he would arrange a sweep-stake: the prize for the six winners would be a beating!

Lessons and life in the schoolroom present a hardly more attractive picture than the chaotic world of bullying and disorder already described.   Fagging, in some schools, took up such an enormous part of the junior boys' time that it is difficult to see how in their first year they were able to prepare any school work at all. This is what Dr Kennedy of Shrewsbury meant when he said that he would never care to teach in a school in which fagging was fully operative.

The foundation stone of classroom activity seems to have been some form of Latin translation.   In accordance with this, individual boys each translated a few sentences into English or sometimes merely parsed particular words. An old Uppinghamian recalls the scene as it must have been in many a small school in the 1840's.

"A little construing or repetition, said very slowly on purpose, and sometimes a bit of Latin prose, or some verses looked over (for we did them in the second form then), and at last the hour for release arrived. This master had a way of collecting our exercises at the end of school, and putting them into his desk, from which, if we did not wish them to be looked over, we abstracted them. When asked 'I haven't seen your exercise, have I?', you just answered 'I showed it up, Sir,' and that was all that was needed. A boy might go for a month without being looked over at all."

Classes were often huge - sometimes over a hundred - and no teaching, as we understand the word, can have been attempted. The choice lay between brilliant lecturing in the University style by men like Dr Butler of Shrewsbury, and perpetual flogging in the manner of Dr Keate of Eton. Here then was an unending syndrome of testing Latin hastily prepared, followed often by immediate beating for inevitable deficiencies.

Thring of Uppingham in the mid-19th Century laid his finger on the weakness of the system when he declared that it did nothing at all for the average or below-average boy, for there was nothing to arouse his interest. It was simply continuous punishment for failure to memorise or even understand the linguistic technicalities of a dead language.

For the tiny percentage of real scholars who needed only time or opportunity to educate themselves, or for those who had the good fortune to meet teachers of genius like Samuel Butler of Shrewsbury, the old system had many advantages. But for the non-academic boys, who formed the vast majority, it must have been tedious, painful and quite meaningless.

Thring, himself a distinguished old Etonian, condemned the system:

"A mob of boys cannot be educated. Not five-and-twenty years ago, with open gates up to eight o'clock at night all the year round, and sentinels set the winter through, as regularly as in the trenches before Sebastopol, to warn us of the coming master, the boys of the finest foundation in the world starved their way up to the university. Whistle or hiss marked the approach of friend or foe. Rough and ready was the life they led. Cruel, at times, the suffering and wrong; wild the profligacy. For after eight o'clock at night no prying eye came near till the following morning; no one lived in the same building; cries of joy or pain were equally unheard; and, excepting a code of laws of their own, there was no help or redress for anyone."

It hardly comes as a surprise to find that during the first quarter of the 19th century there was a steadily increasing erosion of confidence in the Public School system. Not only were opprobrious stones cast by influential pamphleteers, poets, and literary figures, but the colours of Jeremy Bentham's teaching began to tinge the whole spectrum of public opinion.

Bentham was a Radical philosopher whose influence extended far beyond the boundaries of England. He was equally critical of both curriculum and discipline at the conventional boarding schools, and he particularly disapproved of corporal punishment. In 1836 two of his followers founded London University School (afterwards University College School) dedicated to the pursuit of 'useful knowledge' and freed from corporal punishment.

In the face of a growing barrage of criticism, schools that had been the very bastions of the old system began to show a significant drop in numbers:

Eton,   627 in 1833 - 444 in 1835
Harrow,   295 in 1816 - 128 in 1828
Rugby   300 in 1821 - 123 in 1827.

Dr Arnold, offered the Rugby Headmastership in 1828 felt a real hesitation in abandoning his comfortable and happy life in his coaching establishment at Laleham. He knew that the Public Schools were facing a vote of no confidence and, Wykehamist though he was, he could not be sure that he would be in time to save them.

= = = = = = = = = = = =

CHAPTER 3

CORRUPTION

"Deans and Chapters may repose a few years longer in their stalls, unshorn of a single item of dignity and revenue; but by and by Reform will come among them as a strong man armed, and will take from them their armour and divide the spoil."
(Bishop Blomfield of London)

"What will a poor scholar, with his £4 cut down to £1-8-4, think of a Prebendary, with his £40 swollen to £900, or it may be £1025, and reading from the altar 'whatsoever ye would that others should do unto you, that do ye also unto them'?"
(Whiston: Cathedral Trusts and their fulfillment)

St Paul held the love of money to be the root of all evil; and certainly corruption may be seen as the canker at the heart of 18th century England. The dispensation of patronage became an essential element of the art of government; and Dr Johnson was not merely exercising his sense of humour when he defined a pension as 'pay given to a state hireling for treason to his country'. By 1800 he might have added 'or for being the friend of Lord This or the nephew of Lady That'. Fantastic inequalities of wealth were almost universally accepted as the dispensation of Providence. While millions were living on the margin of starvation, the Earl of Durham (1792 - 1840) considered £40,000 a year "a moderate income - such as a man might jog on with". Compassion for the poor existed, but the existence of poverty had not yet begun to move the general conscience.

In the history of education the main cause of corruption - apart from the human heart, which, as Jeremiah said, is deceitful above all things and desperately wicked - was inflation. Inflation, of course, is not a modern phenomenon. The flood of gold and silver into Europe from the New World in the 16th century enormously increased the amount of money available, and the development of banking sent the money flying around much more quickly ; and, as far as money-supply is concerned, one pound that changes hands every day is equivalent to £365 that changes hands only once a year. In a nutshell, £10 a year, which was a respectable salary in 1500, became a derisory one by 1800. Such problems were met in various ways by different Governors and Headmasters in different types of school.

In the 15th, 16th and 17th centuries a large number of schools were founded or re-founded, and the Founders who drew up the statutes usually laid down the salaries for the Headmaster (and Usher, if any) very precisely. The Headmaster received, for instance, £10 at Eton, £20 at Winchester, £10 at Magdalen College School, £20 at King's School, Canterbury, and so on.

Moreover, the Founders - good, pious men who had read their Jeremiah - usually took great pains to ensure that future ages did not monkey with their statutes. At Winchester, Firth tells us,
"Wykeham was so doubtful of mankind that he had long wondered whether it would not be better to distribute his wealth to the poor in his lifetime rather than bestow it to the trust of fools through the course of ages. He tied up his successors in page after page of dry, arid regulations."

Everywhere founders made it very clear that the statutes should be obeyed in their 'plain, exact and literal sense' and that no dispensation of any kind granted by any person of any rank from the king downwards should be asked for, or accepted, or acted upon. Founders also commonly ordained that their school should give free education in grammar to anyone who asked for it. At the great collegiate foundations of Eton and Winchester similar methods evolved. Each had a Warden or Provost and a body of Fellows who appointed the Master and Usher. Each was lavishly endowed with land whose value steadily increased as the years went by.

Each, from these growing revenues, increased the income of the Master and Usher sufficiently to attract men who would keep the school going, while the Governors divided the rest among themselves. The extra pay for Master and Usher was produced either by a slight increase of the statutory stipend, or by evading the ban on exacting payment for tuition, or by allowing them to take in non-foundation boys as paying pupils and boarders, or by letting them take livings (contrary to statute) or by a combination of all four methods.

The technique by which Wardens, Provosts and Fellows reconciled it with their consciences to put most of the growing wealth of their establishments into their own pockets was apparently discovered in the reign of Queen Elizabeth.

The income of the Foundation came from lands, which might be either rented to a tenant for a yearly sum, or leased for a longer period. If leased, the rent would be smaller but a 'fine' would be paid at the time when the lease was renewed or granted to a fresh lessee. Thus, if the rent became nominal, and the fine large, the effect was that the College received the real rent, as it were, for several years in advance and was spared the trouble of collection.

This was a sensible device in many ways; but it proved all too convenient for the Warden and Fellows when they adopted the system, apparently common among Cathedral chapters, of paying the 'rent' scrupulously into college funds, but dividing the 'fines' among themselves. As late as 1860 the warden and Fellows of Winchester divided among themselves nearly half the college revenues, and their total share was eight times the amount spent on salaries of the teaching staff. At Eton, in 1818, the Fellows receive a stipend of £50, plus a share of the fines which in a good year might reach £1000 per Fellow. Most of them also held offices such as Librarian 'with a moderate salary' in addition.

It is no wonder that when Henry (later Lord) Brougham set up his 'Committee on the education of the Lower Orders' in 1818, his beady eye fell on Eton and Winchester (which was certainly not paying much attention to the lower orders), or that in presenting his report he wrote that:

'Our enquiries show that considerable and unauthorised deviations have been made both in Eton and Winchester from the original plans of the founders; that these deviations have been dictated more by a regard to the interests of the Fellows than of the Scholars, who were the main object of the foundations and of the founder's bounty. While, therefore, your Committee readily acquit the Fellows of all blame in this respect, they entertain a confident hope that they will seize the opportunity afforded by the inquiry of doing themselves honour by correcting the abuses that have crept in, as far as the real interests of the establishments may appear to require it.'

This picture of the Fellows of Eton and Winchester eagerly disembarrassing themselves of their questionable emoluments was to prove a mirage. When the Clarendon Commission reported nearly fifty years later they noted that:

"There are but few portions of the Eton statutes which at the present day are, or indeed could be, observed at all. The Provost and Fellows rely in part upon a clause appended to the Founder's statutes, which they interpret as conferring a general power to dispense with any of them - a view of its effect and power in which we find it impossible to concur - in part also upon the general principle of desuetude."

There were also rich pickings in the shape of ecclesiastical preferment. The propriety of the holding of livings by schoolmasters is a subject upon which easy generalizations are not possible. The Church of England, both before and after the Reformation, has always had a close connection with education. Everywhere in the early days one sees schools attached to religious foundations and the endowment of chantry priests who should also teach. In Victorian times an enormous share of the provision of elementary education came from the Church, and 'Church schools' still constitute a considerable proportion of the provision for primary, and to some extent, secondary education. Many an underpaid parson over the centuries has supplemented his meagre stipend by part-time teaching. In all this there need be no element of corruption.

There were other cases, however, which were not so blame-free. At Brentwood and Bristol the holding of livings by the Headmasters of these schools made it financially possible for them entirely to disregard their scholastic duties. The multiple livings enjoyed by Dr Warton, when Headmaster of Winchester, may well have caused eyebrows to be raised - even in the 18th century - and the boundaries of the legitimate were definitely breached by the Fellows of Eton. The Brougham committee discovered that the statutes forbade them to hold any ecclesiastical preferment and required them to take an oath that they would not seek a dispensation from this bar or accept any such dispensation if offered. Nevertheless Queen Elizabeth <u>had</u> given them such a dispensation, and the Visitor had given his approval to this practice.

The Clarendon Commission elicited the details of the Fellows' current procedure. There were a large number of college livings ranging in value from £1200 to £100 per annum. Each living, as it fell vacant, was offered to the Fellows in rotation, and, if no one wanted it, it became 'private patronage', which the Fellows took it in turn to dispense to any one they chose to favour. Both at Eton and at Winchester there were plentiful other perquisites in the shape of board and accommodation free of rent and rates. At Winchester, for instance, the Warden received as a fringe benefit 80 gallons of free beer per week. It is only fair to add that at both schools the Fellows were mainly ex-members of the staff, and the emoluments constituted, as it were, a pension, the hope of which made it possible to attract teachers of good quality.

Magdalen College School was in many ways similar to Eton and Winchester, though the Fellows did have a serious job to do apart from running the school - even if not all of them took it very seriously.

This school had a Master and Usher on salaries fixed by the statutes at £10 and £5, and a President and Fellows, who had been dividing the surplus revenues of the College between themselves for several centuries. As at Eton and Winchester, the salaries of the Master and Usher had been increased just enough to keep the school in being. It had, however, dwindled into a choir school for the sixteen choristers, while the name 'payboys', was given to the three or four other pupils who attended. This showed clearly that the College no longer heeded the Founder's instructions - 'to teach free, gratis and without any exaction of money from anyone coming to the Grammar School.'

Rochester may serve as an example of the many cathedral schools either founded or re-founded by Henry VIII, with its governing body of Dean and Chapter, and Master and Usher on fixed salaries. The statutes also imposed on the Chapter the duty of maintaining four Exhibitioners from the school at the universities with a stipend of £5 per annum, and also maintaining the twenty 'grammar boys' and six 'bedesmen', and paying stipends to them all. In 1841 the income of the Canons had risen from the statutory £20 to an average of £1024, though they were in residence for only two months a year, while the Dean was getting £4300. None of the other payments had been increased at all. The Master subsisted on a living; there was no Usher; there were no 'grammar boys'; there were no bedesmen, and the university exhibitioners would soon be extinct also. All this, of course, represented a considerable saving to the Cathedral funds.

The situation at Rochester can be paralleled at Cathedral and Grammar Schools all over the country. At Pocklington, which the Brougham Committee examined, it transpired that St. John's College, who were the Visitors, had recently made a first-ever visitation in response to complaints.

They found that the Master and Usher constituted a Corporation, with which they were unable to interfere.
The Corporation's income was £800 or £900, from which the Usher received £200, the rest going to the Master, who paid the school's expenses out of it. These cannot have been great as the Visitors found there was only one boy in the school. The reason given for this absence of pupils (though 'no applicant was ever turned away') was that the Master spent all his time in London conducting Chancery suits and the Usher was stone-deaf. One is glad to learn that the College made certain regulations relating to attendance, with the result that by 1818 the school roll had swelled to eight or nine.

At Brentwood, Brougham found that the total income was about £1500, and it was customary for the Patron of the living to appoint the same man as Vicar and Schoolmaster.
When Headmaster Jones died in 1768, his widow claimed the Patron had illegally withheld 'fines' from her husband, and she got a settlement of £1000. Jones's successor reduced the numbers of the school to nil; Headmaster Western raised the numbers to about 20; Headmaster Maybody brought it down to nil again, and by 1818 a new Headmaster had raised it to about 20.

At Bristol in 1811 the Master and Usher were drawing their salaries, but there were no pupils. Pressure by old boys led to the appointment of Mr Goodenough. The new Master was allowed to make his own terms with pupils instead of teaching them for nothing, and to hold livings. He raised the school numbers to about 50, which included a few so-called 'free boys'. These were taught just like the rest - if they paid 16 guineas per annum. By 1829, however, Goodenough had decided that he could live well enough on his stipend and benefices, and the number of pupils was again nil.

Berkhamsted provides one of the best (or worst) examples. Thomas Dupre succeeded his father as Headmaster in 1804 at the age of 22, and by 1812 had emptied the school of boys. He was finally induced to resign in 1841 after some thirty years of vigorous if intermittent wrangling with his critics. During that time he had - to quote the school historian - "enjoyed the use of a comfortable and dignified residence enlarged to meet his personal requirements; he had received in cash upwards of £7,500; a succession of Ushers - his uncle, his closest old friend, and two of his sons in turn - had together received half that sum; and he himself was destined, whilst living at ease in Lincolnshire, to receive from Incent's foundation another £5,000. To earn all this, he had done literally nothing at all."

One of the troubles of the Endowed Grammar Schools on which the Commissioners appointed in 1861 laid their finger was 'the incompetency of many of the Masters and the difficulty in removing them.' Ashbourne Grammar School in Derbyshire is a locus classicus. The Governors, who seemed reasonably conscientious, in 1752 appointed the Rev. William Langley as Master, and spent the next 43 years regretting it.

Mr Langley must have possessed a certain charm, for he earned golden opinions from Dr Johnson's friend, Mrs. Thrall, and from Walter Savage Landor, but during his reign thirteen Ushers were driven to resign by his unbearable conduct. By refusing to admit boys of the town to the school and by 'beating and abusing in an inhumane way' those who had managed to get in, he succeeded in reducing his pupils to one. He defied the Governors when they told him he was dismissed; brought an action in Chancery against them and after seven years won it (involving the Governors in costs of over £1400); and spent the last fourteen years of his life enjoying his triumph, his Headmaster's income and the stipend of a nearby benefice.

When he died the Ashbourne Governors drew up statutes (which they could and should have done 211 years earlier) which made their right to dismiss an incompetent Master legally foolproof. Similar stories could be told of schools all over the country - Master and Usher drawing salaries, but few or no pupils. Sedbergh had 8 day boys and no boarders, Sir Roger Manwood's School 0, Whitgift 0, Coventry 1, Thame 1, Berkhamsted virtually none, Bromsgrove '12 poor boys under a writing master' and so on.

Apart from human laziness and greed, the basic reason for this was that Grammar Schools had been founded to teach 'grammar' (which meant Latin and possibly Greek) to poor boys, and in the country towns all over England poor boys no longer wanted to learn Latin or Greek. Lord Eldon's judgment in 1805 had confirmed that a Grammar School Master could not be forced to teach anything except 'grammar', and the masters and ushers of England, whose salaries were often very small, saw no reason to expand their activities in new-fangled directions.

In most of the country grammar schools that we have discussed, the Governors can be criticised more for apathy than for positive dishonesty. Sometimes, however, self-interest did raise its head. At Bromsgrove the descendants of the founder, Sir Thomas Cookes, became permanent 'patrons' of the charity. There were trustees who were supposed to increase the rent-charge for the school when necessary, but as this increase would have come out of the Patron's pocket and as the trustees were nominees of the patron, it is not surprising that no increase was made.

At King Edward's, Birmingham, the original governors of 1552 were a self-perpetuating body, frequently accused of renting the lands to each other at low rates and neglecting the interests of the Headmaster. In 1696 a new scheme debarred the governors from having any pecuniary interest in the school, but apparently the main result was that they lost interest altogether, and by 1827 the scandal was that the Headmaster was pocketing the 'fines'. Similar accusations had been made against William Broxholme, an 18th century Headmaster of Sedbergh.

Finally a more flagrant example of governors' misbehaviour was furnished by St. Bee's School. The Chairman of the Governors was Lord Lonsdale, and the rest of the Committee were either his employees or holders of livings under his patronage. In 1742 an ancestor of this Lord Lonsdale discovered coal under the school estates, and secured a lease of all the royalties for £4. These were soon worth thousands of pounds.

When Mr Wilson, the Headmaster, started to question this state of affairs, two of these governors forced their way into the school office, and abstracted the lease of 1742. They returned it an hour later with, apparently, the date of its expiry altered to 2609 A.D. The original date had been scratched out and was forever more irrecoverable. The Governors punished Wilson's contumaciousness by reducing his salary from £70 to £50, and sabotaged his attempt to get an ecclesiastical licence from the Bishop of Chester by giving him a bad reference.

The statutes of ancient foundations were a fairly successfully guarded secret and this proved an obstacle to reform. When the Brougham Committee wanted to consult the Winchester statutes, they were told that only the Fellows were allowed to see them, and this resistance was broken down only after a long wrangle. The business of obfuscation was also aided by their being written in Latin. "Pray give us credit, Mr Whiston, for being able to understand Latin," said Dr Lushington, hearing an appeal from the Headmaster of Rochester, when the latter, after giving the Court a lengthy extract from the Latin statutes, was about to repeat the dose in English.

But it was not really altogether easy. Such phrases as 'poor and indigent scholars' or 'freely and without exaction of anything' or 'a perpetual annual payment' proved somehow easier to ignore or evade when left in their original Latin obscurity. *Pauperes et indigentes scholares* was applied by Winchester in such a way that the Fellows were obliged by Brougham to admit that, by their interpretation, 'there was hardly a nobleman's son in the country who would not be eligible under this head'.

Asked about the provision that a Fellow must vacate his Fellowship if he possesses a greater income than £10 per year, the Provost of Eton explained that this was always interpreted to be money derived from land.
"Do you think that the distinction drawn between personal property and landed property is a reasonable distinction and one that should be kept up and acted upon?"
"I cannot say, but it is one that has always been held; it was held at King's as well."

The veto on exaction by the Headmaster of any payment was evaded in various ways. At Eton the Headmaster was given a yearly fee, but he did not 'exact' it. It was put on the bill by the Housemaster and handed on by him to the Headmaster; (and, to be fair, if a parent was unwilling or unable to pay, no pressure was applied). There were also entry fees and 'leaving presents' to the Headmaster. At Winchester the Master and Usher were not permitted to charge fees, but £10, 'if allowed', was frequently put on the bill for 'masters' gratuities'.

Dr Goddard, who was Headmaster from 1793 to 1810, took the money but felt uneasy about it, and ten years before his death gave £25,000 to pay the Head and Second Master.

Dr Hawtrey of Eton (1836-42) did not go to these lengths, but he too felt uneasy about his 'leaving presents', and when a boy came in to say good-bye would remark "I think it's rather warm in here, I'll open a window", thus turning his back while the envelope was laid unobtrusively on the table. When the next boy came in the room would have become 'rather cold', and the window would have to be closed.

This then is a long-drawn-out story of the gradual growth of a totally indefensible system of financial corruption, and it speaks of the myopia which afflicted distinguished and otherwise worthy men when they found themselves involved in it.   It is a story that throws an interesting and sometimes hilarious light not only on the 18th and early 19th centuries but on human nature in general. Without being at all smug about present-day standards, we can say that in this respect, at any rate, things have improved.

CHAPTER 4

CLARENDON'S REFORM

"Devon is weak, Northcote pedantic,
Thompson idle, Twistleton quirky, Vaughan mad."
(Lord Clarendon, commenting on some of his colleagues)

The bad old system may be said to have received its deathblow with the passing of the Public Schools' Act in 1868. This was the direct result of the Clarendon Report, which arose from the appointment of a Royal Commission in 1861, to enquire into the Public Schools, Eton, Winchester, Harrow, Westminster, Rugby, Charterhouse, Shrewsbury, Merchant Taylors, and St Paul's. Lord Clarendon, who was Foreign Secretary for a total of eleven years, was the Chairman, and his colleagues were The Earl of Devon, Lord Lyttelton, Sir Stafford Northcote, Rev. W.H. Thompson, H. Halford Vaughan, and the Hon E.Twistleton.

By 1861, when the Commission was established, the Public Schools had undergone considerable changes, mostly for the better. The Commissioners' report which took some three years to emerge, is a remarkable document, and, thanks to it, one can surely say that there is no subject in the whole of British history about which more is known than the public schools of the mid 19th century. The Commissioners received lengthy evidence, written and oral, from hundreds, if not thousands, of witnesses - Headmasters, assistant masters, provosts, wardens, deans, parents, governors, big boys, small boys, old boys, military and naval officers, university Fellows and tutors, heads of colleges, the Prussian government, and interested members of the public. The final result was a document of some 2,000,000 words
(twice the length of the Bible).

Clarendon himself had a certain flippancy of speech that nearly cost him this job. Queen Victoria was not amused when she learnt that he was accustomed to refer to her as 'the Missus'. He was also less than complimentary about some of his colleagues.

But no one can read the document without being impressed by the care, thoroughness, open-mindedness and sincerity with which the work was done, and the concluding words of the report, even if one detects a trace of Mr Podsnap in them, cannot be lightly disregarded.

"That important progress has been made even in those particulars in which the schools are still deficient, is plain. The course of study has been enlarged; the methods of teaching have been improved; the proportion of Masters to boys has been increased; the quantity of work is greater than it was, though still in many cases less than it ought to be. At the same time the advance in moral and religious training has more than kept pace with that which has been made in intellectual discipline. The petty tyranny and thoughtless cruelty which was formally too common, and which used to be thought inseparable from the life of a public school, have in great measure disappeared. The boys are better launched and cared for, and more attention is paid to their health and comfort.

Among the services which the schools have rendered is undoubtedly to be reckoned the maintenance of classical literature as the staple of English education. This is a service which far outweighs the error of having clung to these studies too exclusively. A second, and a greater still, is the creation of a system of government and discipline for boys, the excellence of which has been universally recognised, and which is admitted to have been most important in its effect on national character and social life. It is not easy to estimate the degree in which the English people are indebted to the schools for the qualities on which they pique themselves - for combining freedom with order, public spirit, vigour and manliness of character, their respect for public opinion, their love of healthy sports and exercise."

"The system, like other systems, has had its imperfections; there have been times when it was at once too lax and too severe - too severe in its punishments, but too lax in superintendence and prevention. It has permitted, if not encouraged, some roughness, tyranny and licence. But these defects have not seriously marred its wholesome operation, and it appears to have gradually purged itself from them in a remarkable degree. Its growth, no doubt, is largely due to those very qualities in our national character which it has itself contributed to form."

Complimentary as the above remarks are, however, the Commissioners naturally did not approve of the financial abuses and corruption which still pervaded the great collegiate schools of Eton, Winchester and Westminster. Their comments were worded with characteristic moderation and tact, but contained a clear rebuke:

"We do not, therefore, think it is just to speak with severity of individuals who, like the Fellows of the Eton and Winchester, have succeeded to a position created legally by statute, but virtually moulded into an altered shape by long and inveterate usage, whose domestic arrangements and whole plan of life have been formed perhaps, with a view to that position, and who when placed in it, have done more than their predecessors did, and more than its customary obligations were previously understood to demand. The evil, however, which is inseparable from moral obligations so loose and ill-defined as such a situation imposes, has been strongly and justly adverted to by an eminent witness, Sir J.Coleridge."

"Nor does this evil stand alone. There is evidently no security that practical changes should be made well and advisedly, which are introduced without a deliberate intention, without responsibility, and without the intervention of any higher authority to protect the permanent interests of the foundation from being undermined by private and personal interests."

The commissioners recommended that all governing bodies should be in the position of trustees and should have no personal interest in the finances of their schools; and by the Public Schools act of 1868, Parliament confirmed the change.
Henceforth the Fellows of Eton and Winchester were either unpaid or worked their money. Corruption and dishonesty in some form will no doubt always exist in every human institution until the millennium arrives; but it can safely be said that the public schools, ever since 1868, have been as free from these evils as any institution and freer than most.

How did this improvement come about? Historians sometimes write as if changes are due to something mysterious like the flowing tide of public opinion. But such tides normally have to be set flowing by some individual, and in the case which we are here considering it is pleasant to be able to allot credit where credit is due. It can hardly be doubted that the Clarendon commissioners, who started work in 1861, had either read Trollope's 'The Warden' or at very least, were aware of the beam that this novel had directed upon the financial abuses prevailing in the fictional, but all too typical, cathedral close of Barchester. And we have Trollope's own word for it that 'The Warden' was sparked off by the real-life battle between the Headmaster and the Governors of Rochester Cathedral School which became known as "The Whiston Matter."

Mr Whiston was the Headmaster who found himself faced with considerable problems when appointed in 1844 to the Rochester school. His predecessor, Dr Warner, had resigned in 1841, but the absence of a Headmaster for three years was less inconvenient than might be supposed, because in 1841 there were no boys left in the school, Warner having 'flogged them all away'.

The Chapter had been vaguely disquieted by this absence of pupils, but it did at any rate enable them to give the Usher's stipend and house to a Minor Canon and avoid paying the statutory stipends to their statutory 20 'Grammar Boys' and to the four exhibitioners they were supposed to maintain at the university. They were sufficiently concerned, however, to accept Whiston's requirement that a new schoolroom should be built (it cost them £800), that his stipend should be £150 a year, that an Undermaster should be appointed at £100 a year and that each Grammar Boy should receive his statutory stipend of £2-13-4 as well as free education. The Chapter were not prepared to give Whiston a large enough house to accommodate the thirty private pupils he was bringing with him, so he leased the small house they did give him to his Undermaster, Mr Allan, and bought a large house of his own.

So far, so good. In four years the full complement of twenty Grammar Boys was achieved. Whiston showed himself a good Headmaster of the old style, popular with parents and boys, an enthusiast for games and cold baths. He was also an enthusiastic researcher into statutes and their abuses. In February 1848, Whiston wrote to the Dean and Chapter, suggesting that 'maintaining' four exhibitioners at the university implied - in modern terms - giving them more than the £5 which the 1545 statutes laid down. After three letters of increasing asperity he received a refusal from the Chapter Clerk, coupled with a hope that this correspondence should now be closed.

What a hope! Whiston's response was to issue a Manifesto, pointing out *inter alia* that it was the Chapter's statutory obligation to 'maintain' not only the four exhibitioners but also the 20 Grammar Boys, and that the stipends of the canons, unlike anyone else's, had been increased - from £20 to £600.

Things were now moving briskly towards a head-on collision. The Dean and Chapter might perhaps have done something sooner or later towards meeting Whiston's demands on behalf of the exhibitioners and Grammar Boys, but when he attempted to lay hands on their own incomes they were ready to fight.

As at most cathedrals, the Chapter scrupulously paid the rents they received into cathedral funds, but the 'fines' they looked on as their own. And as the rents remained the same in spite of the change in the value of money, whereas the 'fines' got bigger and bigger, the increased wealth of the cathedral was, in effect, divided between the Dean and the Canons. The Chapter refused to the last to divulge their accounts to any one, let alone to Whiston, but it did ultimately transpire that from 1844 to 1851 the average yearly income of a Canon had been £1024 and the Dean's £4300.

There followed a protracted battle.

Whiston appealed to the Visitor, the Bishop of Rochester, and published a pamphlet *'Cathedral Trusts and their Fulfilment'* - a detailed, accurate and damning indictment of nationwide cathedral delinquencies - which proved a best seller. He was promptly sacked, on the grounds that his pamphlet was a scurrilous libel, but, when the Chapter appointed a Mr Meeres in his place, Whiston took all the boys except six off to his own schoolhouse; and soon Meeres had only one boy left.

Meanwhile Whiston's appeal against his dismissal had finally ended up on the plate of the Visitor, that Bishop of Rochester who was allegedly one of the victims of the 'scurrilous libel'. The stalling tactics of the Bishop, as well as of the Dean and Chapter might have blunted the purpose of a less determined man than Whiston. It was in June 1849 that he had been dismissed, but it was not until April 1852 that the Bishop got round to hearing the appeal, and the decision did not come until October.

Whiston was restored to his office but 'punished' by not getting his arrears of salary. The Chapter 'voluntarily' increased some of the statutory stipends, but not to the level demanded by Whiston. In other words, it was a typically English compromise, which pleased no one.

Nothing was said about the most important scandal - the sharing out of the fines between the Dean and Canons - but it had at any rate been noised abroad from one end of the country to the other. And Whiston was once more Headmaster, in which position he continued to plague the Chapter for another 24 years. All in all, it was only a half victory for Whiston, but we may acclaim him as the originator of a cleaner world.

In his *'Cathedral Trusts and their Fulfilment'* Whiston quoted Paley: "The man who attacks our flourishing establishment writes with a halter round his neck, and few will be found to attempt alterations but men of more spirit than prudence."

Well done, then, Mr Whiston - man of more spirit than prudence!

CHAPTER 5

THE CURRICULUM

"I assume that the schools commonly called Public Schools are to aim at the highest kind of education; and to give that education, I think the classics are decidedly the best instruments."
(Temple of Rugby)

"Scientific knowledge is so generally valued and confers a power so immediately felt, that I think its diffusion may safely be reckoned on.
(Arnold of Rugby)

"Who wants to learn geography?"
(Sanderson of Oundle)

"I never yet knew a boy who was induced, by fair means or foul, to learn Lilly's Latin Grammar by heart, who did not turn out to be a man, provided he lived long enough."
(Borrows Lavengro)

CLASSICS

In the curriculum of the 19th century the classics played so dominant a role that one cannot make any assessment of the value of what the public schools were doing without considering whether this dominance was in general a good thing - as the Clarendon Commissioners thought - or a bad thing , as perhaps most modern educational writers would maintain. This concentration on the classics had been frequently attacked, mainly on utilitarian grounds, from the beginning of the 19th century. In 1809 Sydney Smith delivered a blistering salvo in the Edinburgh Review.

"We will venture to say that there never was a more complete instance in any country of such extravagant attachment to any branch of knowledge, as that which obtains in this country with regard to classical knowledge. A young Englishman goes to school at six or seven years old; and he remains in a course of education till 23 or 24 years of age.
　　In all that time his sole and exclusive occupation is learning Latin and Greek; he has scarcely a notion that there is any other kind of excellence; and the great system of facts with which he is the most perfectly acquainted are the intrigues of the heathen Gods: with whom Pan slept? - with whom Jupiter? - whom Apollo ravished? These facts the English youth get by heart the moment they quit the nursery. They are most sedulously and industriously instructed in them till the best and most active part of life is passed away."

Sydney Smith would have the schools educate every man in Latin and Greek up to a certain point and, after that, let the classics take their chance in fair competition with equally difficult and more useful subjects ('difficulty' and 'usefulness' are the two criteria by which he values the various possible subjects of study).

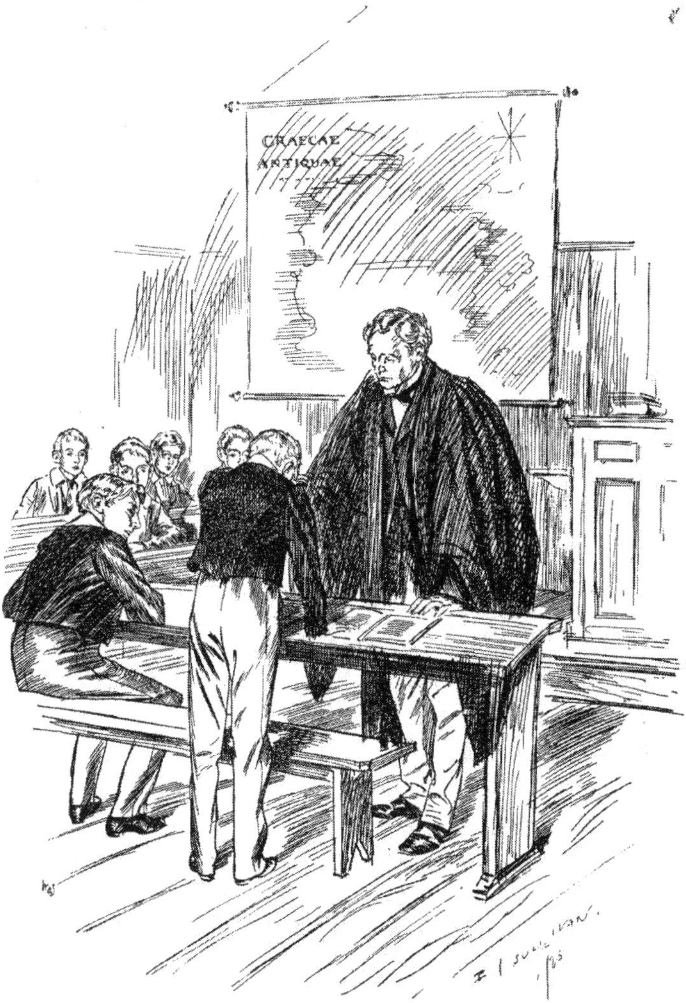
GRAECAE
ANTIQUAE

Smith is only the most eloquent of a large army which has continued the onslaught on Classics with less wit and perhaps less relevance until the present day. Lytton Strachey, for instance, is severe upon Dr Arnold:

"The study of languages,' Dr Arnold said, 'seems to me as if it was given for the very purpose of forming the human mind in youth'. Certainly there was something providential about it - from the point of view of the teacher as well as of the taught. If Greek and Latin had not been 'given' in that convenient manner, DrArnold, who had spent his life in acquiring these languages, might have discovered that he had acquired them in vain. As it was, he could set the noses of his pupils to the grindstone of syntax and prosody with a clear conscience. Latin verses and Greek prepositions divided between them the labours of the week. Under him the Public School remained in essentials a conventual establishment, devoted to the teaching of Greek and Latin grammar."

On the other hand the classics did not, and do not, lack eminently respectable defenders. Goethe, considered by many to be a greater man than Sydney Smith, wrote:
"If our school education always directs us to classical antiquity, which demands a study of the Greek and Latin languages, we can congratulate ourselves that these studies, so necessary to higher culture will never decay."

Gladstone, too, was an enthusiastic supporter of classical education, sufficiently so to volunteer an 1100-word letter on the subject to the Commissioners.

"I by no means require that boys without a capacity for imbibing any of the spirit of classical culture are still to be plied with the instruments of it, after their unfitness in the particular subject-matter has become apparent. I would agree that many boys have to be educated for trades and professions in which the necessities of specific training must more or less limit general culture. Nevertheless for that small proportion of the youth of any country who are to become in the fullest sense educated men, I find that the classical training is paramount.

Is it because we find it established? Because it improves memory, or taste, or gives precision, or develops the faculty of speech? All these are partial and fragmentary statements, so many narrow glimpses of a great and comprehensive truth. That truth I take to be that the modern European civilisation is the compound of two great factors, the Christian religion for the spirit of man, and the Greek discipline for his mind and intellect. St Paul is the apostle of the Gentiles, and is in his own person a symbol of this great wedding. The materials of what we call classical training were prepared, and we have a right to say were advisedly and providentially prepared, in order that it might become, not a mere adjunct, but (in mathematical phrase) the complement of Christianity in its application to the culture of the human being, as a being formed both for this world and for the world to come."

Gladstone's language rings a little old-fashioned today, and is clearly not that of the modern educationist; but there are certain facts which the modern educationist sometimes forgets. The vast majority of men, apart from teachers, do not make the slightest direct use in after-life of anything they have learnt in school beyond the three Rs. Intelligent men go on educating themselves through books and the media; their recreations embrace games, the arts, and various hobbies; they take some interest in politics, and much interest in family life. All this is totally unaffected by whether they studied languages, mathematics, history or science at 'O' or 'A' level.

Temple of Rugby, himself a mathematician, put it well in his written answers to Clarendon:

"When we have to choose between literature, mathematics, and physical science, the plea advanced on behalf of the two latter is <u>utility</u>. Man's chief business, it is said, is to subdue nature to his purposes, and these two studies show him how. Those who use this plea seem to forget that the world in which we live consists quite as much of the men and women on its surface, as of the earth and its constituent materials.
If any man were to analyse his own life, he would find that he had far more to do with his fellow men than with anything else. The study which shall pre-eminently fit a man for life will be that which shall best enable him to enter into the thoughts, the feelings, the motives of his Fellows. That which refines and elevates and does not educate merely the moral nor merely the intellectual faculties, but the whole man.* The highest study is that which most promotes this communion, by giving perfect and pure models of what ordinary experience can for the most part only show in adulterated and imperfect forms."

(* This convenient monosyllable is used, as elsewhere in this book, to cover <u>homo sapiens</u>, male and female, where the context demands.)

With this in mind we may consider where, among the conflicting opinions we have cited, the truth is to be found. Sydney Smith was writing particularly of Eton and Westminster, and in 1809, as far as these two schools were concerned, he probably exaggerated little. Eton, even in 1860, exhibited a conservatism which the most enthusiastic devotee of the classics could hardly commend.

For instance, one of the Clarendon Commissioners asked the Headmaster:

"A hundred or two hundred of the boys in the school are doing the same books?"
"Yes. "
"Do you think that a good arrangement?"
"I think it is."
"I understand that the same boy has to be doing the same authors and the same amount of these authors and the same composition and the same amount of composition in class work for two years running?"
"Yes."
"And in some cases for three years?"
"Yes. "
"Do you think that a good arrangement?"
"Yes, an excellent arrangement."

In fact, all changes in books used had to be approved by the Provost, who was strongly influenced, not only by the natural view that the books he had used when he himself was Headmaster ought to be good enough for his successor, but also by the consideration that any change would diminish some writer's royalties.

But even in Sydney Smith's days not all teaching was dreary. Butler at Shrewsbury (1798-1836) encouraged wide reading and general interests. French, Euclid and algebra were taught. Boys were led to read English history and novels, and they took in papers and reviews. As for Arnold of Rugby, Strachey's would-be satire is so wide of the mark as to be ludicrous. One can only assume that Strachey's dislike of Christianity either blinded him to Arnold's virtues or led him into deliberate mis-representation.

By the end of his first year at Rugby Arnold had arranged the curriculum in such a way that the so-called 'classical' part included not only Latin and Greek, but also Scripture, Modern History and Geography, the 'Mathematical' part included Arithmetic, Algebra and - in the upper forms - Trigonometry, while the 'French' part included the reading of Moliere, Pascal, and Mignet, as well as French composition. Sixteen hours in the week were spent on the various subjects of the 'Classical' part, two on the 'Mathematical' and two on the 'French'.

Moreover, even in his teaching of Latin and Greek, Arnold stimulated his pupils to original thought, led them to read and study the best English authors, and insisted on a high standard of English in translation.

It is sometimes suggested, even by writers sympathetic to Arnold, that his methods, admirable in their effects on the bright boys - the Cloughs and the Stanleys - were nevertheless water off a duck's back as far as the ordinary boys like Thomas Hughes or his alter ego 'Tom Brown' were concerned. Squire Brown's meditations on sending Tom to Rugby are well known:

"Shall I tell him to mind his work and say he's sent to school to make himself a good scholar? Well, but he isn't sent to school for that - at any rate not for that mainly. I don't care a straw for Greek particles, or the digamma, no more does his mother. What is he sent to school for? Well, partly because he wanted to go. If he'll only turn out a brave, helpful, truth-telling Englishman, and a gentleman and a Christian…..That's all I want, thought the Squire."

Tom Brown's father delivers his parting words

What would Arnold have said to such a parent?
Probably he would have argued that what matters is not what they learnt at school, but whether they ended up with acute, well trained, and curious minds, and whether they ended up with a background of general knowledge sufficient to enable them to pursue their further self-education with competence.

FRENCH, MATHEMATICS AND SCIENCE

By the time the Clarendon Commission conducted its investigation, most schools were devoting some time to mathematics and French, though the seriousness of the study seems to have varied and to have depended largely on the views of the Headmaster concerned.

At Winchester, says Firth, from about 1820 one could only learn French as an 'extra' out of school hours, and mathematics from "the writing-master, a despised functionary whose main duty was to clean the slates and mend the pens". By Moberly's time (1853-66) there had been some progress. A quarter of the marks earning 'removes' came from mathematics and an eighth from French. Mathematics was taken seriously at all levels, with the Upper Sixth aspiring to conic sections and trigonometry. But French and German had the worst periods and the worst accommodation allotted to their teaching.

M. Angoville, 'an ideal Frenchman of the old school', was not untypical as a French teacher. He wore a wig that was frequently fished from his head by a rod and line, and he regularly had his classes broken up by cries of 'Waterloo'. M. Angoville assured the Commissioners that his disciplinary problems were far less than they had been ten years previously, but the harsh fact is that the problem of combining knowledge of French with ability to keep order was one that lingered in English schools for a very long time. Arnold pronounced it insoluble and cut this particular Gordian knot in forthright fashion. "I assume" he said, "that boys at a public school will never learn to speak or pronounce French well under any circumstances."
To Arnold , the chief aim of modern language teaching was to enable boys to become acquainted with great men and great books. In other words reading French was more important than speaking it.

All he asked was that the language be taught by the form-masters, that order be preserved, and that the boys ended up tolerably capable of reading French.

Moberly, when he first went to Winchester, "took a leaf ," as he said, "out of Arnold's book, and gave French lessons to one or two classes", but he then gave up the idea because it took up too much of his time, while the other masters did not know enough French. The Commission found the situation equally bad at Eton. Mr Tarver, the only French teacher, had many problems to contend with. French was an optional subject, the lesson times were taken out of the boys' hours of play, attendance was patchy in the extreme, and complaints to Headmaster Balston were ignored. The prize for French, that had been given by the late Prince Consort, for the most part attracted a fair number of competitors, but those who had not attended the classes were apt to do as well as those who had, if not better.

"The opinion of the present Head Master was expressed very distinctly in his examination," said the Report, quoting the following interview with Dr Balston:

"Q. Would it not be considered necessary by the authorities of Eton to render obligatory a thing which they think ought to be part of an English gentleman's education?
A. I should not.
Q. You would not consider it necessary to devote any part of the school time to its acquisition?
A. No, not a day.
Q. You do not think it is a matter which a boy should be required to learn?
A. He ought to learn French before he came to Eton, and we could take measures to keep it up as we keep up English.

Q. What measures would you take to keep up French, and I may also add, what measures do you now take to keep up English at Eton?
A. There are none at present, except through the ancient languages."

Mathematics at Eton also suffered from the low esteem in which it was held. Mr Hawtrey, who came fresh in the 1830's from being 11th Wrangler at Cambridge to teach mathematics, suffered for three years from the incubus of an old and incompetent writing-master, who claimed some kind of a vested interest in teaching arithmetic. Hawtrey was finally allowed to pension this veteran off (out of his own pocket) and to take pupils from any part of the school. He was not given a room to teach in, but was allowed to build a mathematical school (at his own expense) on ground for which he was given a forty-year lease. "Mr Hawtrey states that he has applied for a renewal, but his application has remained unnoticed for four years - an omission due, we presume, to accident or inadvertence. He has also procured by degrees several assistants."

In 1862 Mr Hawtrey's valiant fight was still continuing. In 1851 he had been put on the same level as the classical assistant masters, but his assistants retained an inferior status. Though admittedly equal to the classical masters "in character, education and attainments, as well as birth and social rank", they were not allowed any authority out of school; nor were they invited to the Headmaster's staff-meetings.

Furthermore they were excluded from taking all but the inferior houses; they had only recently been allowed to wear gowns; and - even if in Holy Orders - were not allowed to take prayers or give religious instruction in their own houses . Not surprisingly the Commissioners found that the subject suffered from the inferiority accorded to its teachers, and, though the previous Headmaster (Goodford) had made some effort to lessen their disabilities, "We were," they said, "unable to discover that Mr Balston's influence was likely to be exerted in the same direction."

At Westminster Mathematics and French were studied by all boys, but had no influence on promotions, except for the occasional mathematical high-flyer. Headmaster Scott confessed sadly that, though a few boys, who had learnt French at home, kept it up and improved their knowledge, "the rest neglect the subject and appear blind to the advantages of the subject". It was the old story of the foreigner "finding it a hard task to manage English boys". The fact that the foreigner was paid only £132 a year cannot have improved matters.

In the other Public Schools by 1861 Mathematics and French were being seriously and efficiently taught, and considerable attention was being paid to Ancient and Modern History, Geography and English, while Drawing and Music received a rather surprising amount of encouragement. Altogether it may well be that many of these Victorian classicists received a better all-round education than those 20th century Sixth Formers whose zeal for examination successes has led them to funnel their studies into excessively specialised channels.

By modern standards the great failing was in the teaching of Science. Curiously enough, the poet Shelley was an enthusiast for the subject, and at Eton in 1805 he once arranged a booby-trap, so as to give his tutor an electric shock on opening Shelley's study door. But Shelley, as so often, was exceptional, and the most that Eton provided for the subject was the occasional lecturer on natural science who came down from London. At Rugby a little Science was taken as an optional alternative to Modern Languages; Chemistry was a voluntary subject at Charterhouse, and at Harrow, under H.M. Butler, considerable voluntary work was done in Science. "It was to him," said Farrar, "that we owed the first lectures of Tyndall on sound, of Huxley on the anatomy of the lobster, of Ruskin on minerals."

But in the great Public Schools it is probable that most Headmasters thought like Moberly of Winchester, who was pretty severely heckled by the Commissioners on this subject. The earlier University Commission had recommended that the College should engage a Professor of Physical Science who should, for £500 a year, live in Winchester and lecture not only to the boys but also to the townspeople. The College, on Moberly's advice, had substituted courses of ten lectures during each summer term to be given by visiting experts. These lectures were given on Saturday afternoons and were "shirked" by many of the boys, and Moberly made it clear that he did not greatly mind. He had opposed the idea of a resident professor because, "at £500 a year we should probably get a very inferior person to begin with, and we should have the same lectures over and over again."

Moberly was quite ready to concede that a proper scientific education was a very good thing for boys who were going to be scientists, and that "every man of liberal education is the better for not being ignorant of anything". But scientific facts, he said, do not germinate or bear fruit unless a person is going on to do something practical with them:

"To tell him the fact that such and such is the composition of strychnine, for instance, if he is not going to do anything with strychnine during the whole of his life can lead to nothing. He may remember it for a week as long as his memory is pretty fresh, but let a certain time pass and he will have only the sort of recollection that ladies are apt to have of something they have learned at school; they know there is good deal to be said about it, but they forget what it is."

"Do you not think," asked Mr Vaughan, "the principles of those sciences are, perhaps, more especially applicable to the objects men are pursuing in after life than any other study you could mention - to commerce, professions, arts, even the pursuits of a life of leisure, such as the farming of a country gentleman?"
"I think," said Moberly, "when a country gentleman begins to farm and to farm on principles of agricultural chemistry, he had better not go upon what he learnt at school from scientific lectures."

But by 1862 Darwin's Origin of Species had been out for three years, the tide of science was beginning to flow strongly, and all Dr Moberly's wit could not lure it back again.   New Public Schools like Marlborough, Wellington and Cheltenham were being founded, and others like Uppingham, Sherborne, Oundle and Repton were developing out of what had been local grammar schools. The City of London School, started in 1837, was rivalling the great day schools of St. Paul's and Merchant Taylors; and in the provinces such schools as Manchester Grammar School, King Edward's Birmingham, and Leeds Grammar School were developing into the thriving institutions we know today.   At Clifton, founded in 1862, the first Headmaster, Percival, immediately appointed numerous distinguished science masters, four of whom became Fellows of the Royal Society.

At Leeds the science side, under Henderson, was divided into 'Doctors', with mechanics, physics, chemistry, botany and zoology, and 'Engineers', with mechanism, physics, mineralogy and the theory of the steam engine. Wallis at the King's School, Canterbury (1832-59) was even more wide-ranging: his modern side included surveying, and fortification.

A great leap forward in scientific education took place with the appointment of F.W. Sanderson as Headmaster of Oundle in 1892. His great contribution to education was not so much spending more time on science as in giving it a new dimension and a new vitality. Only the very elect, he said, could benefit from, or be interested in, pure mathematics and abstract science. It was no doubt an advantage that the school which he inherited had been badly run down before his appointment since, for this reason, he was able to lay his hands on some unnecessary dormitories, a common room, and a dining hall, and turn them into Chemistry and Physics laboratories and a Workshop.

Communal activity and creative discovery were the keynotes of his plans, and he was remarkably successful in developing these methods, and, incidentally, in applying them to non-scientific subjects as well. In 1904 new workshops were built, where 'real' engineering could be done; and by the time he died, in 1922, the annual 'conversazione' of the Science Society - a display of experimental work planned and carried out by some 200 boys in their spare time - was comprising 70 or 80 samples, ranging from *'Resistance amplifier of high frequency oscillatory currents'* to *'The significance of bacteria in the farm food cycle'*, and including displays of pigs and poultry which amazed the local farmers.

One wonders how many schools could match this today.

CHAPTER 6

DISCIPLINE

"For this Bowyer flogged me, wisely as I think, soundly as I know. Any whining or sermonising would have gratified my vanity and confirmed me in my absurdity; as it was, I was laughed at and got heartily ashamed of my folly."
(Coleridge, describing how he ran away from school and tried to get apprenticed to a cobbler, on the grounds that he did not wish to become a clergyman as he was an infidel)

The appointment of Arnold to Rugby in 1828 and the retirement of Keate from Eton in 1836 mark something of a turning-point in Public School history; and nowhere is the 'before-after' contrast more marked than in the sphere of discipline. It was not so much that Keate believed in flogging while Arnold, Thring, Vaughan, Butler, Temple and other great Victorian Headmasters did not; the difference was that to Keate flogging was an almost Pavlovian reaction to anything he disapproved of, from fornication to false quantities, whereas Arnold and his contemporaries and followers had really thought out the problems involved. Their solutions to these problems - right or wrong - were rational and defensible.

Arnold, indeed, when first appointed, had hopes of dispensing with flogging altogether, but soon found the alternatives even less desirable. He confined it to the younger boys and to moral offences such as lying and drinking but he had no patience with the idea expressed in a literary journal that it was degrading - even for these offences and even for this age-.group.

Arnold's views were not without support abroad. Baron Pierre de Coubertin, an educationist as well as a future founder of the Olympics, made a comparison between French and English disciplinary methods very much to the advantage of the English.

"For centuries in France education has been an authoritative, an arbitrary, and oppressive process. The object is to give a habit of submission. Nor do students of one country comprehend the results achieved by the other; the French, for example, unreflectingly decry the custom of flogging in English Public Schools, and never realise the fact that in France we flog the spirit, not the flesh."

Arnold was sometimes accused of being too ready to expel boys, particularly when he once expelled six for poaching fish and throwing a gamekeeper into the river. This was the occasion when he said to the indignant school,
"It is not necessary that this should be a school of 300, or 100, or 50 boys; but it is assuredly necessary that it should be a school of Christian gentlemen."

His anger, in this case, was due to his feeling that the school, and even his beloved Sixth Form, had 'ganged up' on him and were sheltering the culprits. Expulsion he used in general not so much to punish particular offences as to get rid of boys who were a bad influence. Stanley quotes Arnold's justification of the practice.

"I can neither theoretically nor practically defend our Public School system, when the boys are left so very much alone to form a distinct society of their own, unless you assume that the upper class shall be capable of receiving and transmitting to the rest, through their example and influence, right principles of conduct. By contrast boys left wholly to form their own standard of right and wrong will often settle for very low standards.
There are some pupils who are not intentionally bad, but whose very low wit and coarseness of character is a great evil and their low and false views are greedily caught up by those below them. In such a case I know not how to proceed, or how to hinder the school from becoming a place of education for evil rather than for good. It follows inevitably that I must get rid of rid of such persons. And then comes the problem for the parents can scarcely be brought to understand why they should remove them; and having, as most people have, only the most vague ideas as to the real nature of a Public School, they cannot understand what harm their sons are receiving or doing to others."

Stanley adds that when Arnold first went to Rugby there was a general feeling that a boy had a kind of right to remain at a school, if he avoided major crimes. Indeed, the parents felt that the more troublesome their sons were, the more suitable was public school education. They felt, in short, that the great end of a public school was to flog their vices out of bad boys, and Arnold saw the whole business of education very differently.

Edward Thring, who was Headmaster of Uppingham from 1853 to 1887, and who was, with the possible exception of Arnold, the greatest of the Victorian reforming Headmasters, strictly limited flogging, but had definite views on the subject, which he made very clear in a letter to a parent who had sent his son to school with instructions not to submit to corporal punishment:

"No man is more alive than myself to the fact that punishment can easily be made by a bad master the substitute for efficiency. The masters here are not inefficient, and take special care with their pupils. I have yet to learn that a society of boys or men gathered from all quarters is to be managed without punishment or ever has been.

The question is reduced to a choice of punishments, and in spite of modern cant, I think flogging is the very best remedy for some breaches of discipline particularly. I demur to the wisdom of perpetual surveillance, and do not mean to allow it here. I demur also to the assumption that if a boy is not known to have bad faults at home, ergo, he learns them at school. Our experience directly contradicts this, and is to the effect that if a boy has a good home we never need be afraid of not succeeding with him here. We have no other fault against your son, excepting that having required great care and forbearance when he came, and received it, he has lately grown very unruly, as might, I think, be expected from the instructions he had received."

" I do feel deeply aggrieved that in utter ignorance of our systems of punishments you should have sent your boy here under direct instructions to mutiny against our authority without giving me any hint of such a thing. How could a government stand if this was often done? It reflects upon us as professional men, it reflects on the school, it sets up our pupils, however young, to be the judges and thwarters of earnest and experienced men. How can good come of it?

But, however that may be, we had a right to expect the choice of refusing to deal with a boy at all under direct instructions to mutiny when sent here. I had a right not to be exposed to the ignorant and impertinent refusal of your little boy to be flogged for a grave disciplinary offence, and the open contempt of my lawful, thoughtful, and experienced authority involved in this. Your boy, too, has much reason to be grateful to M - for his care and consideration during his stay here. Masters do not deserve such a return for their life work. They feel as men. I am prepared in the face of the world to uphold any and every part of our system under a wise criticism and scrutiny, but not to submit it to the caprice of rebellious little boys."

Collapse, one feels, of stout parent!

Almond of Loretto was another Headmaster who had no doubts about the propriety of corporal punishment, according to an admiring former pupil:
"He had no sympathy with the soft humanitarianism which shudders at the thought of inflicting pain, and ridicules the precocious and overstrained idea of honour which renders corporal punishment impossible in France. Yet if, as occasionally happened, a Loretto boy shared the French view, it was characteristic of the spirit of his government that he respected the feeling and substituted some other penalty. In general, however, his pupils had no such ideas, but felt, on the contrary, as the Head

himself observed, an honest pride in not moving a muscle, and going laughing to our seats even after a well laid on six."

This way of taking a licking evidently met with the Head's approval. He was himself in the habit of asking boys whom he had been obliged to thrash whether he had hurt them. If the culprit had the imprudence or bravado to answer 'not much' he laid himself out on the next occasion to correct a failure.
'I cannot make out,' he used to say, 'why people should think it a bad thing for their boys to learn to bear a little pain.'
He regarded it as one of the worst features of his own school-training that it had exempted him from the discipline of the rod. He considered it a happy thing that British common sense had hit upon a penalty which, in an effeminate age, had an educational value of its own. It was the merit of corporal punishment that it was brief."

The ex-pupil rounded off his account as follows:
"There was not a boarding-school in the country where life was so little oppressed by pains and penalties as at Loretto."

H.M. Butler was Headmaster of Harrow from 1859-1885. His account to the Clarendon Commissioners of his system of punishments is worth summarising at some length.
It is so good indeed that it might well be made compulsory reading not only for teachers, but also for those who pontificate upon the subject without having had personal experience of teaching.
Lord Clarendon gives signs of having been one of the latter class.

Q. (Clarendon) "You say there is no absolute uniformity of punishment for similar offences. Is it not the case that uniformity of punishment for similar offences could be very easily arrived at?
A. It is so very difficult to determine what is a similar offence, because there are all sorts of degrees. There is no system of regulations existing on the subject, and I am not aware that there are ever any debates among the masters on the subject; still, as a matter of fact, each master does possess a very fair knowledge of the general amount of punishment given in certain cases. I do not know that I could state the matter more accurately.

Q. I should think there was no subject of more importance to discuss than the amount of punishment that should be awarded for offences that on the whole must be considered so similar?
A. Whatever the general understanding, much must in practice depend on the character of the master."

Lord Clarendon also had strong views on the practice of setting lines, which, he said "appears to me to have no other practical result than that of spoiling the handwriting of the boy."

Q. Is there no other punishment do you think by which some good might be done to the boy?
A. I should observe on that, first of all, that I question the accuracy of that inference as a whole, that it does affect or spoil the handwriting of the boys; and secondly, that it does not by any means apply to the majority of the school, because the great majority of the school are not in the habit of being under punishment. Your Lordship has assumed that the writing is atrociously bad: as a matter of fact it varies very much.

I admit most fully that this punishment is an evil; it is simply a part of the great question of all punishments.
Do what you will, you can never frame a punishment which is not attended simultaneously with some great inconvenience or evil. What we have to do, I conceive, is to hit upon some form of punishment which is at once so unpalatable to the boy as to be a tolerable guarantee that he will not offend again in the same manner, and at the same time, a very important condition, such that the master who sets it shall not be unduly burdened.

If the punishment of learning lines by heart be adopted in the lower part of the school, you have no guarantee that the lines are learnt thoroughly well, because you are most unwilling to turn back a boy if he can just scrape through; and secondly, the amount of time which is consumed in hearing the lines said is something which is very undesirable, I think, to impose on the masters. I see enough of the system to know that in the under-forms it would be quite intolerable for the master to have them learnt by heart.

Q. Is it then true that the system is having in view the convenience of the masters rather than the good of the boys?
A. The convenience of the masters means the time of the masters, and the time of the masters is the advantage of the boys."

Other Commissioners had their suggestions to make:

"Q. (Mr Thompson) I think the cane is not used at Harrow, is not?
A. No, it is not.

Q. Would that be an agreeable substitute for the imposition?
A. It would very often undoubtedly do away with the other. I should not like to introduce it now, but unquestionably if it was introduced, it would do away with many of these troublesome punishments.

Q.   (Sir Stafford Northcote) Would it not be possible to let the masters take in rotation the task of looking at the punishments, so that one master should have the punishments brought to him at a particular time?

A.   A boy, without libelling his nature, will do all he possibly can to avoid a punishment, and the master who sets it will be far more likely to see that it is done.

Q.   (Mr Thompson) Would it also be possible to abridge the labour of the master by setting a boy a piece of uninteresting English prose to get off by heart ?   Perhaps 20 lines of English prose would be more difficult to get by heart than 40 lines of English verse?
A.   No master, I think, would ever wish to hear the repetition through.   And it varies so much with different boys; to one boy it is torture, to another it is nothing.

Q.   I suppose throwing stones would be a floggable offence?
A.   The punishment for that offence would depend upon whether there were any wanton circumstances connected with it .

Q.   (Mr Vaughan) Would the boys understand that you were doing it upon that principle? -
A.   I think so, but I should be exceedingly grieved to have to administer a severe punishment, when the only reason for doing so was the absolute need to put end to a practice which, in itself, was not morally bad.

Flogging, it transpired, took place about twenty times a term.

Q. (Lord Lyttelton) When he is sent up to you, do you always ask him whether he admits the offence?
A. Yes, and while I most scrupulously give him an opportunity of making a defence, it is of the very first necessity to save him from the temptation to tell a falsehood. It is important not to give a boy too much chance of defending himself, thus leading him to evade. If you do, you become responsible, for it is sometimes more than a little boy can stand out against.

Q. You bear that in mind?
A. Yes, generally my short conversation will begin with "How is it that you have done this?"
After a few words, and after taking down the offence in writing in his presence in my book, I then tell him what the punishment must be. In some cases it happens that one has a long conversation with the boy. I may say that if a boy maintains that he has not committed the offence, or if he offers circumstances which if true, seem to me to be seriously palliative, I should not give him any punishment at all, till after communication with the master who sent him up. It would rarely happen that I should punish the boy at all after a conversation with the teacher, if he persisted in denying the offence altogether.

Q. Would you let him off altogether on his own strong denial?
A. To the best of my knowledge, I have never but in two instances punished a boy on a grave charge, when he has persisted in denying the offence. "

The development of these enlightened views on punishment had been accompanied by a great change in the attitude towards boys. There had, of course, been many earlier Head Masters who enjoyed a friendly and civilised relationship with their boys. But by the middle of the 19th century this relationship had become the rule rather than the exception.
True Headmasters - at any rate Headmasters who are any good -

can hardly fail to excite a certain amount of awe in their pupils, even if it is frequently mingled with internal amusement.   As late as the P.G. Wodehouse period , Headmasters rank second only to aunts as inspirers of terror, and certainly few boys would have ventured to treat men like Arnold, Temple, Vaughan and Percival with anything resembling disrespect or casualness.

One of Temple's early sixth-formers was, indeed, beguiled by the Headmaster's informal manner and dress into 'trying it on', but Temple had only to say 'conduct like that will alter the relations between us', and 'conduct like that' was not repeated.   The gravitas of Percival (Rugby 1887-95) was such that when, on one occasion, he slipped on the staircase when coming down to prayers and tobogganed into the hall feet-first, not a titter was heard.

But virtually all accounts of these great Victorian Headmasters agree that they took a deep personal interest in their pupils which had been rare in the 18th century, and that the respect and indeed veneration which they aroused were due to admiration and affection rather than to fear.

Arnold must be given much of the credit for the change, although various attempts have been made to minimise this. The mere fact that in the thirty or forty years after his appointment Headmasters went out from Rugby to Wellington, Haileybury, Clifton, Marlborough, Harrow, Sedbergh and Fettes, must have some significance; but the important thing was Arnold's own educational philosophy.   The Provost of Oriel's prophecy that if Arnold were appointed to Rugby he would change the face of education all through the Public Schools of England, may well have been based on personal knowledge of Arnold's plans in this matter.

People had long been aware of the existence of two widely divergent types of education - the Public School system and what was sometimes called the French or the Jesuitical system. In the one the master taught during school hours, outside which the boys ran their own affairs. In the other, masters supervised every minute of the boys' lives. It was a polarity between freedom and order, between licence and surveillance, each with its own built-in advantages and disadvantages. Arnold, on the one hand, had no very high opinion of Jesuits - certainly not of the methods of invigilation and espionage they were supposed to favour. On the other hand he had had first-hand experience of the evils which uncontrolled boy-rule brought with it. Had not boots been flung at him at Winchester because he knelt to say his prayers in the College dormitory?

Arnold's solution was to break down the barriers between boys and masters. He encouraged all boys to discuss their problems with him, even building a special staircase to give private access to his study and flying a flag to show when he was available. Even more important, he developed a special relationship with the Sixth Form, believing that "those who, having risen to the highest form in the school will probably be at once the oldest and the strongest and the cleverest; and, if the school be well ordered, the most respectable in application and general character."

He imbued the Sixth Form with his own ideals -
"what we must look for here is first religious and moral principles; secondly gentlemanly conduct, thirdly intellectual ability."
And he then gave them the responsibility of running the school. "When I have confidence in the Sixth," he once said, "there is no post in England which I would exchange for this; but if they do not support me, I must go."

There seems little doubt that they usually did.

Among Thring's greatest merits was his concern for the ordinary boy. A member of Parliament acclaimed him as "the most Christian man of his generation, because he was the first man in England to assert openly that in the economy of God's world a dull boy had as much right to have his power, such as it is, fully trained as a boy of talent, and that no school did honest work which did not recognise this as the basis of its working arrangements."

Thring himself wrote that it was a necessary implication of the Public School system that parents sent their sons away in order that they should receive a better training than was possible at home. "This at once brings us to the necessary conditions of a boarding-school as a place of training. It must be better than home. It is an absolute necessity in training, a self-evident truth, that every boy, whatever his abilities may be, should be intelligently cared for and feel that he is so cared for."

Thring, like Arnold, had had personal experience of the evils of boy-rule, having been at Eton before its worst horrors were mitigated. He once expressed the rather cynical but very realistic philosophy that "Good government has no belief whatever in honour and truth. On the other hand good government acts and behaves as if there were no such thing as dishonour and falsehood when it comes to dealing with its human beings."

However that may have been, he certainly achieved a delightfully friendly relationship with his boys, playing fives, cricket and football and skating with them, and helping them with the gardens he encouraged them to keep.

An Old Boy paints a pleasant picture:

"He was the most human of men, delighting in giving pleasure to others. Often at the time when the plums were ripe I have known him call boys into his garden and shake the trees with glee, bringing down large showers of great purple and yellow fruit. He took, I think, even more delight in it than we did, which is saying a good deal. But his love of doing kindnesses was really boundless. In the holidays he was absolutely full of fun and genial good-nature."

Thring's enthusiasm for music was greatly assisted by his German wife, and the art reached such a level at Uppingham that musicians like Joachim, the greatest violinist of the day, used to attend the school concerts. There were also valuable social 'spin-offs', as the same Old Boy describes:.

"About once a month we had what was called a Drawing-room Evening, a term which survived long after the choir had outgrown the capacity of the School-House drawing-room; indeed, for many years the 'drawing-room evening' had to be held in the School-House Hall, where the custom began of ladies taking part in it. The music room then became the tea-room, and when the new schoolroom was built and the concerts transferred to it, the name of 'Drawing-room Evening' was transferred with them and long held its ground. These Drawing-room Evenings were always looked forward to. At 7.30, all went to the drawing-room, and with music and cake and tea and talk spent the rest of the time till ten o'clock. It was one of the ways in which the school was made to feel like home, and the ladies brought into contact with the boys."

It is clear from the glimpses we get in letters, memoirs, and biographies that in the second half of the century something resembling this agreeable state of affairs existed in a large number of schools.

We read of Dr Kennedy's wife at Shrewsbury that "her kind, motherly sympathy was shown to all the boys, whether in the Doctor's house or not".

Dr Vaughan at Harrow used to entertain the Sixth Form to dinner and was "most agreeable", and he feasted the younger boys at breakfast on muffins and sausages.

Pears of Repton, who could reduce the whole school to shamed repentance with a few quiet words, would relax in family gatherings where the boys joined in chamber music and singing.

Dr Blore and his wife used to take the prefects with their family on holidays. Leaving Bromsgrove in 1873, he said, 'I have lived very much among the boys and known them individually. I have never heard a word which has caused me pain.' He came to King's School, Canterbury with a reputation for 'angelic qualities', which his rule there did nothing to diminish.

Elwyn of Charterhouse (1858-63), we are told, knew the origins of all his boys, professional and tradesmen. "This man was living among them in every sense, so much so that when the boys were locked in for the night and anyone needed to be let out for illness or natural purposes, they would call out and he would unlock, wait up for some minutes and turn the key again."

Striking, too, is the attitude to school regulations of Millard of Magdalen College School (1846-64) who did not believe in rigid law enforcement:

"When on the river or engaged in any long excursion, boys will be allowed to take refreshment at inns so long as no abuse of the liberty renders it necessary to withdraw it, but the Headmaster begs that they will not frequent inns more often or longer than is necessary."

And on another occasion:

"As the trees in the Playground, which are not at present a great ornament and advantage to it, have been very much injured and broken of late, the Headmaster wishes boys to abstain from climbing in to them;"

Boys, incidentally, were not the only tree-climbers. Temple, on arriving at Rugby, stole out at night and climbed all the elms in the Close. His alleged reason was to make sure that they were safe, but one suspects he thoroughly enjoyed it. At any rate when Benson, some years later, pointed out a fine beech-tree at Wellington to him, he cried out:
"I can't resist the temptation - look out!" ,
and before Benson could turn round, Temple had made a rush and was scrambling up the bole of the tree. In a few seconds Temple had succeeded in reaching the first stage .where the magnificent limbs diverge in all directions and was grinning with delight at his success.

Headmasters, we may accept, were by no means the austere, even sadistic, figures they are sometimes supposed to have been, but nor does it automatically flow from this that life at a Victorian boarding school was a bed of roses. The douceur de vivre for the ordinary boy doubtless depended a good deal on such factors as food, fagging and the role played by the prefects.

CHAPTER 7

THE BOY'S LIFE

"Thou wyll not beleve how wery I am off fysshe."
(A 15th Century Magdalen Schoolbook)

"All kinds of bulbs were dug up in the park and garden and e agerly devoured. Cowslip roots were a delicacy, nasturtiums, crocuses and hyacinths did not remain long in the gardens. Acorns were collected in great numbers and stored away in holes."
(An Old Radleian)

"The writer of these lines has winter after winter suffered times when neither master nor scholar could write for days together because of frozen ink."
(An Old Berkhamstedian)

DIET AND AMENITIES

As far as diet was concerned, the Clarendon Commissioners found that there had been great improvements since the beginning of the century. There was certainly no shortage of food, as there had been at Christ's Hospital in the days of Lamb and Coleridge.

Lamb describes his school as
"one where each boy can reckon up to a hair what profit the master derives from him, where he views him every day in the light of a caterer, a provider for his family, who is to get so much of him in each of his meals. Boys will see and consider these things, and how much must the sacred character of preceptor suffer in their minds by these degrading associations! The very bill which the pupil carries home with him at Christmas, eked out perhaps with elaborate though necessary minuteness, instructs him that his teachers have other ends than mere love of learning in the lessons which they give him."

Coleridge, more succinctly, writes, "Our appetites were damped, never satisfied, and we had no vegetable."

By 1860 at most schools bread and butter, with tea, coffee or cocoa were provided at breakfast, and dinner consisted of meat, potatoes and sometimes greens, bread and beer; tea was similar to breakfast at some schools, at others supper was the main evening meal, with meat or cheese, bread and butter, and beer, milk or tea. Frequently boys could supplement their breakfast and supper with extras provided by themselves or their parents. Meat was certainly plentiful; a pound per head was normal at dinner; at Eton another half-pound was provided at supper.

Mr Harris, a senior housemaster at Harrow, when asked by Clarendon, said he had never had any complaints about the quality or the cooking of the food, but had had two about the quantity,

"Not the quantity as provided by me, but as consumed by the boys. The boys had got a fancy never to be helped twice to meat. I made a most urgent appeal to them when I got the anonymous letter. I begged and entreated them to save me from the scandal of not allowing them to have second helpings of meat, but it produced no effect. If I had known who the person was, I should have asked him to come to my dining room after dinner is over and see the enormous quantity of food that is left, which we are obliged to give away to poor people. I attribute this fashion rather to the fact of boys eating a great deal elsewhere, and because they do not come with a thorough appetite."

Mr Vaughan: "What induces them to go elsewhere when they have the prospect of a meal before them?"
Mr Harris:, "I am afraid it is the infirmity of boys' natures, a tendency to sweets."

The infirmity of boy natures had led, and doubtless will always lead them, into the field of private enterprise where food is concerned. Jolly feasting in tuckshops is described in Tom Brown's Schooldays and almost every other school story or book of reminiscences ever published.

An Old Westminster (1859-64) provides a succulent sample: "Turning the corner into Barton Street, you came to dear old Mrs. Shotton's, another tuckshop, but more select as to its customers and the food supplied. There was a back-room - where 'the eight' ate their raw beefsteaks when in training - and there was a cosy little box between the fire and the front window where we small

boys ate bread and cheese and pickles, generally onions, for which we dabbed in the plate, turn about, with two-pronged forks."
"The Stilton cheese, fourpence a plate, was always a complete round off the cheese, or red cheese threepence a plate, and pickles twopence, enough for two. The Derby cakes were delicious, round, flat, and crisp, with plums; then there were most excellent jam open tarts, some of them apricot, some strawberry or raspberry; Queen cakes in heart shape, and all manner of good things. She was a dear, roundabout old lady, and made all these things herself."

At Eton there was a certain lack of imagination about the supply of food. For centuries the boys had been restricted to mutton, mainly because sheep were the medium in which much of the College's rental was received; and, though by 1860 there was beef twice a week, and the daily ration in College was one and a half pounds of meat, three pints of beer and two pounds of bread, with butter at breakfast and tea, they had pudding only once a week.

Mr Vaughan: "It is mentioned that pudding is given of a peculiar construction. Is it a good peculiarity or otherwise?"
The Provost : "Good. "

The Oppidans in their houses had a more varied diet with tarts and puddings every day. One housemaster criticised the College dinner because mutton was distributed on the basis of seniority, the seniors getting the haunch, and then, in descending order: legs, loins and necks, while the boys at the bottom are invariably left with the shoulders, the fattest part.

"I never think of putting shoulders before the boys in my own house," he added somewhat self-righteously. "I should never dream of such a thing; they would turn up their noses at it. In my own house I should never think of giving a boy dinner without pudding as well as meat."

The scholars at any rate had good beer. It was brewed in the college brewhouse and the Master in College said he always drank it himself, and it was better than what he got in the tutors' houses. We read occasionally of complaints about the quality of the butter or the beer supplied, but as a boy at Shrewsbury philosophically remarked to the Commissioners, 'Boys always do complain'. Nobody had heard about vitamins in those days, but it is possible that a modern boy living on his 'balanced diet' might sometimes think rather wistfully of the pound of roast mutton and pint of beer at dinner a hundred years ago.

At most of the great Public Schools the accommodation by 1860 was adequate if not luxurious. Arnold, when he arrived at Rugby in 1828, had found boys sleeping sometimes four or even five in a bed unless they paid extra. This he immediately stopped; and he made it a point to recognise the privacy of boys in their studies, never entering one without knocking.

E.H. Bradby wrote home soon after his arrival in August 1839:
"With regard to saying my prayers, I sleep in the rooms with a sixth form fellow who not only does not molest me, but likewise prays himself and is very kind to me.
The Studys (sic) here are comfortable little places and larger than I had expected, having room for a small sofa, a very unnecessary article which I do not intend to get, and have no need of, for the boy with whom I have a study has a good while ago fitted his up with a table, chair, bookshelf and fireplace."

A few weeks later he wrote,
"I have always been able to say my prayers to God, and as in the room where I am now the Fellows do not, I say them in my study."

Later still:

"I have been settled in my own study now for 5 or 6 days, which is a very comfortable one, especially as I am by myself, and I don't think I shall find it very cold in winter. J. Tickell was so kind as to tell me that in winter I might sit by his fire, and this is very kind in a Preposter. My study is next to his."

And again:
"I find that a boy can make the study warm by getting a bit of green baise (sic) and drawing it across the door, which excludes all air and the room soon gets hot, and besides I believe in the winter Anstey's (*his house*) puts those who have no fire with those who have, and each pays half of the coals."

In the severe weather of the following February even these measures did not keep him as warm as he would have liked, but the philosophical little boy wrote,
"As it can't be helped I must bear it with patience."

Thring, like Arnold, realised the value of privacy for boys, and insisted on the provision of individual studies. As to the furnishings, no doubt in schools like Eton and Harrow with separate houses a great deal of variation existed, depending on the housemaster and the ability of the boys to provide luxuries of their own. At Westminster in the middle of the century things were pretty bad for the pupils. The school historian writes that:
"In the dormitory necessary repairs and the calls of sanitation were alike neglected. Broken casements recalled the days of the old granary, and in times of frost it was easy to make a slide of ice upon the dilapidated floor. The holes in it were the delight of innumerable rats. One night a boy would lose his braces, another he was awakened by the thief biting his ear. The rats were as hungry as the juniors, whose frequent fate it was to find in the Hall that, when their elders had fed, there was little or nothing left for themselves."

Dr Phillimore, an Old Westminster, told the Commissioners, "I remember hearing of the present Lord Mansfield's brother being very ill in one of the boarding houses, and his mother, Lady Mansfield, coming to see him. There was only one chair in the room, upon which the poor sick boy was reclining, and a friend who was with him was sitting on the coal scuttle. When Lady Mansfield entered the room the lad who was sitting on the coal scuttle got up and with perfectly natural politeness and good breeding offered it to her ladyship to sit down upon."

At Shrewsbury numbers had declined under Kennedy from about 300 to 140, in spite of the fact that his teaching was perhaps the best in the country; this was probably due to the poor quality of the buildings and amenities.

So at any rate the Commissioners thought. Lord Clarendon, who had not, as a boy, experienced the rigours of a boarding-school education, visited Shrewsbury in person, and subsequently told the Trustees:
"I think there is no father who comes to the school before placing his sons there but would hesitate to send them to a place where they would be so ill accommodated."

The Mayor, who was Chairman of the Trustees and had been a boy at the school in 1836 agreed; but Dr Kennedy pointed out that things had much improved since the Mayor was a boy. In 1836 the Headmaster's house had held 50 boys, living in ten bedrooms with no ventilation and two sitting-rooms; there was only one washing-place, with a brick floor, and only one W.C. Now, he said, the maximum number of boys was 35, there were eleven bedrooms, all ventilated, and three sitting-rooms; they could use the Great Schoolroom in the evenings, there were washing materials in all the bedrooms, and no fewer than two W.Cs.

Nevertheless the Commissioners were probably right. The Second Master's house was far from reaching the Lucullan standard described by Dr Kennedy, and there was clearly need not only for better accommodation but for far more of it if the school was to hold its own with such as Rugby.

Eton accommodation outside College had always been in the hands of Dames, who were not uniformly conscientious in the discharge of their duties. In some houses the floors were sanded and the furniture primitive, while the Clarendon Commission heard from one witness that, as a boy, he had dined exclusively at the Eton cookshop for two years.

In 1838, however, William Evans, the Drawing Master, took over a dilapidated Dame's House and set a new standard by building a handsome Oxbridge-style dining-hall with appropriate trophies and decorations. The boys dined in stately fashion with silver cutlery, and there was wine on Sundays. In the course of the century this trend came to be followed in other Eton houses. In fact, at other schools as well, the Housemaster, able to spend money on the comfort and well-being of his boys, became an increasingly familiar figure in the Public School scene.

= = = = = = = = = = =

FAGGING

"Sir, With the utmost disgust we hear that fagging has been abolished at Eton. As the two most southerly OE's in the world, overwintering in cardboard huts prior to an attempt on the South Pole, we daily empty lavatories, clean and cook. Having spent two to three of our formative years doing menial tasks for others, this comes easily. Many who go to Eton need their self-esteem lowered, and fagging was an excellent way of achieving this."
(Sir Ranulph Twisleton-Wykeham-Fiennes in a letter to the Times of May 2nd, 1980.)

Fagging was one of the features of public school life which Sydney Smith (1810) found most objectionable:

"It is the common law of the place that the young should be implicitly obedient to the elder boys; and this obedience resembles more the submission of a slave to his master, or of the sailor to his captain, than the common and natural deference which would always be shown by one boy to another a few years older than himself.

Now this system we cannot help considering as an evil - because it inflicts on boys for two or three years of their lives many painful hardships and much unpleasant servitude. These sufferings might perhaps be of some use in military schools; but to give a boy the habit of enduring privations to which he will never again be called upon to submit – to inure him to pains which he will never again feel - and to subject him to the deprivation of comforts with which he will always in future abound - is surely not a very useful and valuable severity in education."

Certainly today fagging, like corporal punishment, is a practice which many people tend to react against with automatic horror. Pictures of Flashman roasting fags at the fire rise before the eyes. But it should be noted that the Flashmans of this world were thoroughly stamped out by Arnold. Quite apart, however, from questions of brutality, the notion of a young boy being forced to carry out menial services for his 'master' often arouses instinctive repugnance. But in the 19th century the words 'master' and 'servant' were not so automatically rebarbative.

The word 'service' had a long and honourable history - 'armed services', 'senior service', 'civil service' - and people were perhaps more familiar than they are now with texts like 'whosoever will be great among you, let him be your minister'. In most schools masters, big boys, and little boys were united in their approval of fagging; and when they disapproved, it was the abuses rather than the institution itself that they disapproved of.

The Commissioners thoroughly investigated the matter at Eton. Boys who had been through the system were unanimous that it was a good thing, and that both the fags and the masters would be considerably dismayed if it were abolished.

Lord Boringdon was asked:
"Do you think there is no bad feeling about it
on the part of those who are fagged?"
"Not at all."

"And you do not think there is abuse of power on the part of those who do?"
"Not a bit."

"When you were a fag yourself were you in agreeable relations with your master?"

"Very. I saw him at breakfast and tea, and those were the only times."

The Hon, C.G. Lyttelton, now at Cambridge, was sure 'there was no general feeling against fagging'. It was rarely abused; he personally was still on friendly terms with everyone who had been his fag-master at Eton and fagging 'very rarely' interfered with the work of the fag. Confirmation of the general picture can be drawn from other incidental, references. Julian Sturgis, an Etonian Sixth former, wrote in 1867 to a lady who had asked him to be kind to a new boy whose father she knew.

"My dear Miss P.,
I am sure I need not tell you how flattered I am that you should think me likely to be benevolent to a new boy. I had quite a long talk with him the other evening. I can assure you that you need be in no uneasiness as to his comfort, for bullying is now a thing <u>quite unknown</u> at my Dame's, and though he told me he was rather lonely at first and knew no one, yet by now he must be shaking into the ways of the place and of his schoolFellows. I have told him to come to me if he is in want of the experience of an old boy in the manners and customs of the place. I have also engaged him as my fag."

And A.C. Benson, who went to Eton in 1874, wrote, in *Memories and Friends:*

"We were summoned one evening to the Sixth Form supper-room, where the great men sat at their ease with cold meat, bread, butter and cheese before them. They seemed to me old men, as old as my father almost. We were chosen in turn as fags, and I fell to the lot of a genial boy, J.B. Chevallier, whose bath I filled, made his toast and tea, and did any odd jobs required. But when we came back in January there was a shift of fags, and I was transferred to the charge of Reginald Smith. I did not desire the change, though I felt vaguely flattered at being chosen by a boy who was higher up in the school."

"But from that moment he became a friend. He was endlessly good-natured. He told me I might work in his room, and I trespassed much upon his bonhomie. He would clear a space at his table, ask me what I was doing, help me over a difficult passage. Sometimes two or three Sixth Form boys would come in, when I would listen open-eared to the easy gossip of the gods."

Similar reports came from Winchester, Charterhouse, Rugby, Harrow and Shrewsbury. True, a junior at Winchester did not like 'watching out' (i.e. fielding) at cricket, but said, 'the boys would not mind fagging much if that were abolished'; but another who had recently been through the system, said that
"A boy who watched out well, used to like it because if he made a good catch the prefects used to like him the better for it. A boy who made a good catch, for example, might get off an hour's fagging".

No doubt opinions about cricket will always differ.

A later witness told the Commissioners:
"A sixth former could open his door and call 'fag', and whatever fag heard first had to come."
"Was there a great desire to be the first to hear it under such circumstances?"
"No, not generally."
"Do you recollect what your own feelings were when you were in that capacity? Was it hard work?"
"No, I rather liked it because it gave me the opportunity of talking to the swells of the school."
"Would a master consider himself bound to protect his fag?"
"Yes, your study fag you would always look after and generally have him in to see how he does his lessons."

Fagging in general comprised such jobs as calling other boys in the morning, tidying studies, making toast and tea, sometimes waiting at meals. At Charterhouse, on a rota system, a fag would from time to time be a 'fire-fag' (carrying coal and keeping up fires) or a 'cock's fag' (cleaning washbasins). Semi-compulsory football was looked on as a part of fagging, but was generally enjoyed. Fielding at cricket, as we have seen, aroused mixed feelings. Perhaps nets might have been invented sooner if fags had not existed.

The Commissioners were on the whole satisfied that fagging did not unduly interfere with the little boys' work. In most schools there was a surprising amount of unsupervised prep (at Rugby about five hours school and three hours prep a day) and a fair judgment is probably that if a boy managed his time sensibly, he had ample opportunity to get his work done and to play. Nevertheless, whatever may have been the fagging practices at other schools, the Commissioners got a rude shock when they looked at Westminster. A Mr Meyrick, who had recently removed his son from the College, volunteered information. His allegations and the answers to them in the Report occupy about 80,000 words.

"In consequence," he said, "of the College being wholly in the hands of the boys apart from the masters, there is a system of slavery, for I can really call it nothing else, continued slavery going on from morning to night, slavery of the most irritating and oppressive kind, enforced , as it can only be enforced, at the point of the bayonet.
As an instance of what I assert, it would be supposed that if a boy were taken ill while he was before a master saying his lesson, that fact would be sufficient to prevent him from undergoing a degrading and brutal punishment for a temporary retirement from the room. Still more would it be supposed so if he, previously to retiring, got the special permission of the master to retire.
It does not do so."

"Before he dare leave the room, unless at the risk of a severe licking, he must ask six boys four monitors, his own individual senior and the 'lag', as they call it, of the second election.

I now say not what is matter of opinion. I say what occurred yesterday. He is liable to be had up by one of the seniors. He is made to touch his toes with his hands; the senior sends for a stick or racket, and the boy comes staggering out of the room as white as that paper. I say also, without any figure of speech about it, and without any fear of contradiction, that from the 1st of January to the 31st of December a junior has not a moment during the whole of that time which he can call his own and uninterrupted for any purpose whatever."

Mr Meyrick went on to describe the punishments, 'buckhorsing' (boxing of the ears) 'tanning' (hitting with a stick or racket) and the dreaded 'tanning - in - way', described to the Commissioners by Meyrick junior:

"There is a sink there about the height of this table, and you have to put up one leg, and then the second election runs at you and takes as many kicks as he likes. I know there was one boy who said it nearly did for him altogether."
"Was it quite a common punishment?"
"It was quite a common punishment."

Mr Meyrick went in great detail into all the hard labour and harassment the juniors were subjected, and drew a pitiful picture of the decay suffered by his son. Young Meyrick, he said, had been a townboy for a year and everything had gone swimmingly in work and play. Elected to the College, the first six months had broken him in body and spirit. Previously he had been one of the top cricketers and had won all sorts of prizes at the Sports. Now 'you might as well enter an old carriage horse.'

Young Meyrick confirmed that in his year as a town boy he had got three or four prizes 'for running, jumping, throwing the cricket ball and so on', but in his College year he only won one prize - 'In all the rest I could get nowhere.'

All this naturally led to a close inquisition. Other boys were examined, Headmaster Scott was recalled after he had made his own enquiries, and it became clear that both Meyricks had been guilty of fairly gross exaggeration. 'Tanning- in-way' had been abolished some time before, and young Meyrick had neither experienced it, seen it, nor known anyone else who had seen it; senior boys could remember only one case of a boy being kicked in living memory; the rigmarole about getting leave to go out did not apply to leaving the classroom, but only to getting leave into the town.

Young Meyrick's evidence about his athletic achievements contained a good deal of lying and boasting - his highest cricket score was obtained at the end of his time in College, he had won two prizes for running as a townboy (but none for jumping or throwing the cricket ball), and the only sign of falling off was that in his second year he was beaten by two boys who were in fact not in the school when he won the corresponding event the year before.

The juniors were in bed by 10.15, seldom had to get up earlier than five, and that only once a week; and the Commissioners discovered by a personal visit that there was no room 'more than the width of this table' for the so-called run at the junior to kick him.

Nevertheless it was clear that there was very much wrong with the system. The Meyricks were right in saying that the senior boys were unsatisfactorily controlled by the masters (and indeed Dr Scott's own answers to the Commissioners reveal a rather feeble reluctance to interfere with the traditional claims of the seniors) and that the juniors were being forced to carry out duties, such as early fire-lighting and mounting guard at the entrance to the school, which ought more properly to have been done by College servants.

There were other afflictions. The juniors were obliged to carry round with them pens, ink, paper, indiarubber, and penknives for the convenience of any senior who cared to ask for them, and to learn thirteen or fourteen traditional formulae (not thirty or forty, as young Meyrick said) such as "Will you please to take anything by orders?" Worst of all, perhaps, was the system whereby each 'first election' was under the charge of a 'second election' and was liable to be 'licked' by him if a senior thought he deserved it, while the second election was liable to be licked himself if he did not do his licking properly.

It has been suggested   (J.R. de S. Honey in *Tom Brown's Universe*) that the institution of fagging was connected with one of the reasons which led parents to send their boys away from home - a desire to prevent them from becoming sexually involved with domestic servants. At school, of course, servants existed, but they were largely segregated from the boys and, in any case, were mainly male. The fags at school, as it were, took the place of the maids at home. At this stage we are perhaps in deeper waters than the propounder of the theory intended.

PREFECTORIAL PUNISHMENTS

Clearly when boys are given authority to exercise disciplinary powers and deal out beatings and other punishments, there is a danger that the powers may be misused and unjustifiable suffering may be caused. Those who disapprove of punishment as a system (and a fortiori of corporal punishment) will find this feature of the Victorian Public schools extremely objectionable. Those, however, who, like Thring, "have yet to learn that a society of boys or men gathered from all quarters is to be managed without punishment or ever has been," may like to consider the options more curiously.

In a family or in a small coaching establishment such as Arnold ran before he went to Rugby, it will often be possible to dispense with punishment altogether and to rely on good feeling and admonishment to produce satisfactory behaviour. In a school too big for this to be practicable the choice appears to lie between (A) giving disciplinary powers only to masters, and (B) delegating them to senior boys, with perhaps a via media (C) where prefects check and report misdemeanours but only masters punish. The Victorian Headmasters were unanimously opposed to giving disciplinary powers to (A). Leaving discipline entirely to masters would not only place an intolerable, twenty-four hour a day, burden upon them: it would also turn the relationship between master and pupil into one of spies and spied upon. The third choice would be even more objectionable. The line between 'reporting' and 'sneaking' is difficult to draw, and Headmasters were probably right in thinking that both prefects and offenders would be happier if routine crimes were dealt with without masters being brought into the matter. And so the administration of discipline by prefects became the universal practice. With obvious limitations it was an approach to self-government.

There can be no doubt that at times it went badly wrong.

There were deplorable abuses at Westminster, as we have seen, and at Winchester the reign of terror described by Oman, brief though it apparently was, shows how much harm a few sadistic prefects could do. A sadistic master, however, is equally a possibility, and is perhaps more difficult to discover and control. A far worse danger for the small boy is the unlicensed bully, and not only Headmasters but virtually all the other witnesses who appeared before Clarendon were unanimous that the prefectorial system was the best way to prevent bullying.

"The physical power of irresponsible dolts low down in the school," said Moberly, "is the chief source of bullying, and the instant a prefect comes in sight it stops."

George Cotton was appointed Headmaster of Marlborough in 1851, when it was almost certainly the worst big school in the country. When he left in 1857, it was one of the best in every way. He had come from Rugby and was the original of the 'tall, slight and rather gaunt man with a bushy eyebrow and a dry, humorous smile' who talks so sympathetically to Tom and Arthur in *Tom Brown's Schooldays*. He had clearly absorbed Arnold's theories about the value of prefects. In an opening address to the Marlborough boys he said:

"The Council informed me on my appointment that the school was in a bad state of discipline, and they hoped I would allow no boys to go out unless they were accompanied by a master.
I told them I could not accept office on such terms, that the school I hoped to govern was a public school, not a private one, and I would try to make it govern itself by means of prefects.
The school knows now how matters stand. They must either submit to the prefects or be reduced to the level of a private school and have their freedom ignominiously curtailed. The prefects are and shall be, so long as I am Head, the governors of this school. As soon as I see this impracticable, I will resign."

His reforms were, of course, not confined to the introduction of prefects and giving them major authority, but undoubtedly his success is a proof of what a good prefectorial system could achieve. At most schools a right of appeal existed. At Harrow a boy could appeal, even *in articulo* to the whole body of the monitors, and thereafter to the Headmaster if he thought fit.

Lord Devon: "The monitor has his hand uplifted with a cane in it - what if the little boy says 'I appeal to the whole body of the monitors'?"
Witness: "Yes, he cannot cane him if he chooses to appeal to the monitors. "

Mr Harris, a housemaster, knew of two cases where such an appeal had been made, and he himself had actually expelled a monitor for beating with excessive severity a fag who had committed the unforgiveable sin of breaking his valuable tea-set.

One sees the weakness of the system: the fag would hardly appeal, knowing that he deserved punishment, and by the time it dawned on him that he was being punished excessively it would be too late. It was a pity they did not have the rule which obtained at many schools that if the offence was a personal affront, the punishment must not be given by the prefect affronted. Charterhouse was one such school, where Headmaster Elwyn had made other sensible rules - that caning must be only with an authorised cane, that it must be with the agreement of the other prefects in the boy's house, and that boys can always appeal to the Headmaster.

At Eton there was at this time very little beating. A junior Scholar deposed that he had never seen a boy beaten with a stick, though a careless fag might get his ears boxed. The seven top Collegers had monitorial powers, but seldom beat. The judicious William Cory, an outstanding tutor at Eton, said that good spirit prevented bullying - the ascendancy among Oppidans was due to moral character rather than physical power – and that corporal punishment "was not much liked and was going out."

Alfred Lubbock was at Eton from 1854 to 1863. His autobiography reveals that as a small boy he was a typical 'Just William' type who preferred a 'swishing' - which he occasionally got for slack work - to staying indoors and writing lines. In 1899, when he had four children at the school, he wrote:

"If big boys hadn't a certain amount of disciplinary power over the small ones, what would it lead to? And what would the small boys grow up to be? There is always safety in numbers, and any big boy who used his power or authority indiscreetly, unfairly, or in a cruel, bullying way, would soon find himself in the wrong box, and have the whole nest buzzing about his ears.

One definite proof of the good of the present system to my mind is that the boys themselves approve of it. Either my tutor's house must have been a very well-conducted house, or all the small boys must have been of an exemplary disposition, for during the time that I was there I never heard of a boy being caned (sc. by a prefect). I know it went on in other houses and in college, but never to any severe extent, nor was there anything approaching to bullying."

At Rugby striking evidence of the success of the prefectorial system was given to Clarendon by H.L. Warner, a recent leaver. Warner was impressive for his implicit assumption that certain evils were almost unthinkable. Asked if there was any abuse of the monitorial power, he replied, "I do not think I know of any cases of habitually doing it, because we should at once have an appeal to a Sixth form levy on it."

Q. "Was there any flagrant abuse of monitorial power?" -
A. "The worst would be letting a fellow go by out of bounds or anything of that sort."

Q. "If a sixth-former did commit an offence?"
A. "There would be a sixth form levy called by some fellow in the sixth, and they would probably decide to ask the Headmaster to send him away or to put him down a certain number of places."

Q. "Do you think the body of the lower boys look to the monitorial system as a great protection against bullying?"
A. "I think they do when they think about it; but there is so little bullying that they do not think much about it."

There seems no reason to doubt that this almost idyllic state of affairs did prevail under Temple (1858-69); but the excellent tone of the prefects must have depended considerably not only on their own qualities but also on those of the Headmaster, and on the closeness of the link between them. Thus Rugby saw a sad decline under Hayman (1870-74) and it was not until the time of Percival (1887-95) that the traditionally sound tone of the school was restored.

CHAPTER 8

HEADMASTERS AND GOVERNORS

"A Governing Body without an expert among them - Powerful people attending to a school for two hours twice a year"
(An exasperated memorandum by Benson of Wellington)

"If a master makes an unreasonable request to me, I just say 'My dear chap, the Governors would never hear of it'; and I take care they never do."
(C.M. Cox, Headmaster of Berkhamsted, in an after-dinner speech)

It will be clear already that the relationship of Governors to their schools had varied enormously from school to school, and from time to time; and the prosperity of schools has been greatly dependent upon the success of the partnership between Headmasters and Governors, or Trustees, as they were commonly entitled.

The name is significant. It reminds us that the body concerned was apt to consider that its duty was not so much to make the school as efficient as possible (which is how a modern Governing Body would normally consider the matter) but rather to administer funds at their disposal in accordance with the wishes of the Founder. Even if self-interest did not enter into the question, as it had done at Eton and Winchester, there was frequently room for a reasonable difference of opinion as to how the Founder's wishes should be interpreted in the light of current circumstances.

A constantly recurring problem for the Public Schools was the question of the rights of residents to free education at local schools. There were two conflicting points of view. The Headmasters, conscious of competition from the newly founded schools which had no such charity or commitments, wished to escape from the burden of providing free education for burgesses and residents. The local people, however, of Rugby, Harrow, Shrewsbury, and other towns wished to retain for their sons the prestige of attending a well-known school without being subjected to a largely classical curriculum. At Shrewsbury a conflict between the School and the Town had been temporarily settled by a Chancery decision (1853) which quashed the attempt by the Trustees to set up a new commercial school for the virtually exclusive benefit of the townspeople.

The Clarendon Commissioners made no attempt to disturb this decision, and, rather surprisingly, went further and deprecated Dr Kennedy's very modest non-collegiate class, which offered a classics-free education to a very small number of boys in the school. This the Commissioners considered to be likely to fuel the unworthy demands of the townsfolk that Shrewsbury should renege upon its classical heritage.

The School should rather revert to the terms of its charter and function as a *Schola Grammaticalis*. The Shrewsbury burgesses were also to have their rights to a free education gradually phased out. This was not as high-handed as it might appear to have been; before the Parliamentary Act of 1793, which rescued the school from collapse, the rights of the townsfolk to a free education do not seem to have existed in any meaningful sense.

At Harrow the situation had for a long time been complicated by the increasing number of 'foreigners'. John Lyon, the Founder, had laid it down that the Headmaster be allowed to admit to the School an unspecified number of boys non-resident in the parish. This was soon interpreted by the Governors to mean fee-paying boarders, who, by 1718, outnumbered the Foundationers; this in spite of the fact that the school's official designation was 'the Free Grammar School'. By the end of the 18th century it was described as 'the most patrician school assemblage of which records remain in the entire country'.

This presented a considerable problem for the Foundationers, and in 1853 Dr Vaughan, the Headmaster, made an attempt to appease the local residents with his "English Form", which concentrated on a sound basic education. Unfortunately there was more than a touch of apartheid about this, as Vaughan's Rule 10 leaves no doubt as to the status of the new institution -

'The boys will regard themselves as entirely separate in all respects from those of the Public School at present existing'.

It is only fair to add that this 'Form' was set up against the wishes of the Harrow Governors, at Dr Vaughan's expense and on his own responsibility.

A witness before the Commission, William Winkley, revealed that he had been advised by the School authorities not to exercise his right to send his son to the main school. Lord Lyttelton, one of the Commissioners, appeared incredulous -

"Do you mean to convey the impression that two masters of Harrow, one of them a Headmaster, desire to keep their school exclusively for the benefit of the higher classes?"

Other local witnesses said that they accepted the fact of social differences, and they valued these as the means of obtaining entry to circles that otherwise would be closed to them. The Commissioners, however, were unmoved and their report suggested that these territorial claims to free education should be gradually phased out. To make up for this, the 'English Form' was to be recognised and given an improved status. It was left to the Headmaster, Dr Montagu Butler, to pour oil on the troubled waters. This he did with consummate skill, proposing a new name for the 'English Form', now to be known as the Lower School of John Lyon.

Butler, when explaining his plans to a massed meeting of Harrow parishioners, made a masterly reference to his rejection of the Commissioners' recommendation on this head:

'They offer you a <u>substitute</u> for long-established and long prized privileges. I propose that these privileges should <u>remain</u>, subject to modification.' This was incorporated in the Public Schools Act of 1868, and the John Lyon School, as it is now known, has subsequently had a very successful career.

At Rugby the story was much the same. Dr Temple, the Headmaster, addressed the Commission with great confidence and authority, and wrote a great deal of the Taunton Committee's report himself. He wrote it in his own hand when his secretary flagged. At one point he wrote non-stop for 36 hours, fortified by tea, with the printer's devil standing at his elbow. He said that an exhaustive examination of the documents relating to educational endowments had told him that the aim of the testator had not been to secure exclusive benefits for local, but rather for national education. Thus he favoured the raising of Rugby standards by abolishing free education for the few in favour of open scholarships that were available to anybody.

He also claimed to be catering fully for the needs of the town by founding a Lower School from which it would be possible for a boy of ability to win entry to the Upper School. The Committee found themselves in full agreement with this, much to the indignation of the Rugby residents, who naturally clung to the privilege of free education. This, they believed, had been handed down to them from the days of Queen Elizabeth and her grocer, Laurence Sheriffe.   Temple's plan, however, was determined upon, and the new school, with its semi-classical and commercial curriculum was called the Laurence Sheriffe School after the founder of Rugby. It finally opened in 1878 and has had a flourishing career.

Temple had hoped that the winners of the new Open Scholarships to Rugby would accept a reduction in fees only if they were under financial stress, and that the money saved could be used for the benefit of needier scholars. Thus he wrote to his own son, who was sitting the Scholarship Examination:
"I should be highly gratified were your name to appear among the list of Exhibitioners, but I should like you in that case in some way to give the money back to the school."

Today the welfare state and the apparatus of taxation it involves have produced a different system; the bulk of the scholarship money is subject to a means test, so that the renunciation by the wealthy is compulsory rather than optional. Temple might perhaps regret the necessity for the change, but he would probably be well satisfied with the practical result.

Similar problems occurred, and similar settlements to those of Rugby were made in many of what are now leading Public Schools. At Tonbridge, which had been administered as a small country grammar school by the Skinners Company for centuries, the value of the endowments bequeathed by Judd, the Founder, suddenly leaped up in 1807 owing to a building speculation. The Skinners saw no reason to bestow any of the extra money on the school so long as they continued to perform their statutory duties.
The townspeople, however, thought otherwise.

The Vicar and three citizens successfully brought a lawsuit against the Company, as a result of which a new scheme was introduced. It gave larger salaries to the Headmaster and Usher, and made provision for them to take in 60 and 40 boarders respectively, instead of 12 and 8 as before, while assistant masters and 'housekeepers' could also be licensed by the Governors to take in boarders. They clearly envisaged the large boarding school that Tonbridge has now become. The old rights of the townspeople were preserved by allowing free education, except for extras (i.e. everything except Latin and Greek) to any boys living within ten miles of Tonbridge Church.

Similarly, at Magdalen College School in Oxford a lawsuit was brought to compel the Governors (the College) to do what the local people considered to be their duty.

As we have seen, the Fellows of Magdalen had adopted the common practice of dividing the increased revenues of the college among themselves while paying the Master and Usher just enough to secure (rather inadequate) teaching for their sixteen choristers. A few dayboys attended the school, but paid for the privilege. In 1845 Hester, the Town Clerk, brought an action against the College, claiming that education should be given free to all residents of Oxford, and that the Master and Usher should be put on the same financial footing as the Fellows. All of this was in line with the Founder's statutes, but the Court of Chancery decided that only the Visitor had any authority in the matter. The Visitor, in 1849, finally decided in favour of the College in view of the fact that they had shown themselves clearly aware of their previous neglect and were planning to build a new school for the future. So Hester's case was not entirely fruitless.

Many schools had originally been established in close connection with an almshouse. Charterhouse, thanks to Thackeray's Colonel Newcome, is the best known example, but there were many others. Uppingham, Sherborne, Repton, and Oundle are among those which succeeded in shedding their incubus on equitable terms during the 19th century. Both at Repton and at Oundle the claims of local inhabitants were met, as at Rugby and Harrow, by the establishment of less classical schools.

No Headmaster can have suffered more from his Governors than Benson, the first Headmaster of Wellington. The Governors were extremely distinguished) including the Prince Consort (and later the Prince of Wales), The Earl of Derby, the Prime Minister, and the Duke of Wellington, and they were also singularly anxious to interfere in the running of the school.

Perhaps under-estimating Benson's calibre (they were not to know that they had a future Archbishop of Canterbury on their hands) they treated him very much *de haut en bas*. Governors' meetings were normally held at the House of Lords; Benson was admitted to them only when specially summoned, and was kept waiting, often for hours and on at least one occasion in the dark, with no room to sit in. Even more regrettable, the Governors gave the College Secretary, a Mr Chance, complete power over finance and administration, including the domestic arrangements.

This might have worked if Chance had not (a) lived in London (b) appointed an extremely incompetent Steward, one William Lyne, and (c) been very touchy. Benson's many complaints about Lyne were unavailing, though they were certainly well grounded. We know, for instance that at one Speech Day, when the Prince Consort was present, Lyne failed to provide any lunch for the school and was only with difficulty persuaded to rustle up some bread and cheese; and on another occasion, when Benson had arranged for the Queen herself to inspect the Murray Dormitory, Lyne contrived that, when the Queen entered, the corridor was full of dirty sheets and two charwomen were scrubbing the floor and passing the time of the day with one of the manservants.

The climax came after nine years of this, when Chance stayed the night at the school and two boys poured a jug of water over the bed where he was due to sleep. This was pure mischief - they did not know that it was Chance's bed nor, probably, that Chance and Benson were seriously ill-disposed to one another. Nevertheless Chance persuaded one of the Governors to demand that the two boys should apologise to him in Benson's presence and be made to understand that it was only owing to his (Chance's) kind forgiveness that they were allowed to remain in the school.

Benson was naturally outraged at this encroachment upon his responsibilities and made his final attack on the dual system of control. A Committee was appointed by the Governors, and Benson convinced them that the Headmaster should have the management of the College's affairs, including the control of all servants. Lyne was sacked, and Chance was left with only minor duties. Benson had won, but only by undertaking to produce a healthy financial balance each year . This promise he triumphantly achieved, thanks to his reform of Lyne's abuses, making a profit of £4000 in the first year, two or three times what Lyne had normally managed.

Benson's trouble with his Governors was quite the reverse of general experience. Most Headmasters had to fight their schools' financial battles with little aid from above, and they were frequently called upon to show an enterprise and courage in matters of business which their modern successors are not often asked for.

Samuel Butler reckoned among his greatest achievements at Shrewsbury the successful ending of a lawsuit which had been going on intermittently since the reign of James I. It had been reactivated about 1779, and in 1823 the Governors had paid out over £3000 in legal expenses and were in such difficulties that they decided to reduce the masters' salaries by 50 per cent.
Butler thereupon persuaded them to make him their agent and give him access to all the documents in the case. Then, in addition to all his school work, he carried the suit to a successful conclusion and in 1827 received an impressive tribute from the Master of St. John's: "The School is wholly indebted to your exertions, and few men, if any other, could have surmounted the obstacles which were opposed to an agreement."

The rather casual and empirical development of school finances is well illustrated by the situation in which Montagu Butler found himself at Harrow in 1860. On the one hand his stipend from the Governors, including an allowance for coals, was only £50 a year. Small payments from the 32 foundationers and 22 members of the 'English Form' brought in another £150 or so. On the other hand his profits from boarders and fees from non-foundationers raised his income to about £10,000. One must bear in mind that out of this he had to pay some £3,000 for salaries to assistant staff, and to pay for draining the playing-field, asphalting the school yard, and for the upkeep of all buildings except the Old School.

Thring had to borrow and spend large sums to expand Uppingham, and frequently induced assistant masters to build or buy boarding houses at their own expense as a (well justified) speculation. Pears did the same sort of thing at Repton. Ridding, at Winchester, spent £20,000 on the playing-field and got perhaps £10,000 back. Ralph Lyon, at Sherborne, provided extra dormitories himself, and persuaded the Governors to build more teaching-room at a cost of £1414; but he had to give £414 himself and lend £1000 without interest. This, of course, was not mere quixotry on his part - he would receive fees from all the extra boys that he accommodated.

We may think that the labours of any Headmaster (let alone the Victorian Headmaster with all his heavy teaching load, and lack of secretarial assistance) were arduous enough without these financial responsibilities; but there was a compensation in the authority and independence which they enjoyed. Thring, on securing possession of a piece of land at Uppingham, remarked:
"This puts it out of the power of the townsmen to screw us".

Even more important, the over-all financial arrangements which he built up, put it out of the power of the Governors to screw _him_. When the unsatisfactory sanitary arrangements in the town of Uppingham forced him to take what we should nowadays call industrial action, he neither needed nor received any encouragement or practical assistance from the Governors.

He simply removed the whole school to Borth in North Wales until the drains had been put right. The episode is fully described in Chapter 13. In a less dramatic but equally significant episode, we have seen how Whiston, at Rochester, when sacked by the Governors, took the whole school, except one boy, to premises of his own in the town.

It was really something of a heroic age. These men were not after a safe job and a pension at the end of it. (In any case these commonplaces of today were not then readily available). They hoped, of course, for a decent living, but there was something creative in their approach to the task of Headmastership: they expressed themselves in this work. Arnold and Thring fought for and gained the principle that, once appointed, it was their business to run the school as they thought best. The Governors had hired them, and, if dissatisfied, could fire them: everything else was the Headmaster's responsibility.

We cannot end this section better than with Arnold's letters to Lord Howe, a member of the Governing Body at Rugby who requested to know if Arnold were the author of an article in the Edinburgh Review attacking the Tractarian persecutors of the liberal Theologian, Hamden.

"My Lord,

The answer which your lordship has asked for I have given several times to many of my friends; and I am well known to be very little apt to disavow or conceal my authorship of anything that I may at any time have written. Still, as I conceive your lordship's question to be one which none but a personal friend has the slightest right to put to me or to any man, I feel it due to myself to decline giving any answer to it."

When Lord Howe threatened that he might have to take steps in the matter unless Arnold definitely admitted or denied authorship, Arnold replied:

"My Lord,
I am extremely sorry that you should have considered my letter as uncourteous; it was certainly not intended to be so; but I did not feel that I could answer your lordship's letter at greater length without going into greater details by way of explanation than its own shortness appeared to warrant. Your lordship addressed me in a tone purely formal and official, and at the same time asked a question which the common usage of society regards as one of delicacy - justified, I do not say, only by personal friendship, but at least by some familiarity of acquaintance.

It was because no such ground could exist in the present case, and because I cannot and do not acknowledge your right officially, as a Trustee of Rugby School, to question me on the subject of my real or supposed writings on matters wholly unconnected with the school, that I felt it my duty to decline answering your lordship's question.

It is very painful to be placed in a situation where I must either appear to seek concealment wholly foreign to my wishes, or else must acknowledge a right which I owe, not only to myself but to the master of every endowed school in England, absolutely to deny.

In the present case, I think I can hardly be suspected of seeking concealment. I have spoken on the subject of the article in the Edinburgh Review freely in the hearing of many, with no request for secrecy on their part expressed or implied. Officially, however, I cannot return an answer - not from the slightest feeling of disrespect to your Lordship, but because my answering would allow a principle which I can on no account admit to be just or reasonable."

CHAPTER 9

RELIGION

"Nothing is more fatal to a school than obtrusive religion"
(Thring of Uppingham: Letters)

"My object will be, if possible, to form Christian men, for Christian boys I can scarcely hope to
(Arnold of Rugby: Letters)

Keate managed to hold at bay the forces of disorder at Eton during the weekdays, but on Sunday afternoons he was less successful. In the words of Lytton Strachey, "Every Sunday afternoon he (Keate) attempted to read a sermon to the assembled school: and every Sunday afternoon the assembled school shouted him down". On some Sundays there were even livelier scenes, when he had to retire before a fusillade of books and inkpots, and, on one occasion, a half-brick was included. At this he stood in silent reproof, and then observed: "Boys, I don't think I have deserved this".

Keate's religious attitude, if such it may be called, was an anachronism. To hindsight, it is clear that he was living at the beginning of an age of religious excitement totally unlike anything that had happened since the 17th century. Soul-searching private discussion, public argument in tracts and in the press, all flourished in a way that would have seemed almost insane to 18th century rationalists, and which Christians today may well think partly inspiring and partly tragic - tragic, in that so much of the argument appears to be about matters almost irrelevant to the essence of Christianity.

No simple classification can adequately describe all the varieties and belief that were so enthusiastically supported, but it is reasonable to say that the High Churchmen looked for inspiration to the Oxford Movement led by Pusey, Keble, Hurrell Froude, and (until he went over to Rome) J.H. Newman. They laid great emphasis on the continuity of the present Church of England with the Church before the Reformation.

They claimed to be as 'catholic' as anybody else (a word that sent shudders down the spines of many Englishmen).

They delighted to emphasise their catholicism by the use of ritual, incense, vestments, candles and so on (practices equivalent in many people's eyes to Popery), and they strove vigorously to bring order and decorum back into a Church of England which they considered, with some reason, had become lax, and slovenly.
One hears, for instance, of a clergyman coming out of the vestry before one of his rare celebrations of Holy Communion and asking if anyone in the congregation could lend him a corkscrew.

The Low Churchmen or Evangelicals were largely inspired by Wesley, who had been more or less forced out of the Church of England, but whose burning eloquence and sincerity had not only spread Christian beliefs among the poor, but had touched the consciences of many who remained within the Church of England. Their preaching laid much emphasis on "Redemption by the Blood of the Lamb", and they encouraged a way of life which was highly moral but which easily declined into an excessive puritanism. A third, and very important, element in the Church was the broad churchmanship which survived from the 18th century. The memorial of the Duchess of Buckingham and Chandos who died in 1832, lists among her many soberly balanced virtues, that she was "religious without enthusiasm", a quality which, in spite of Voltaire's gibe about the English having a hundred religions but only one sauce, has probably always been common in this country.

Dr Samuel Butler of Shrewsbury (1788-1836)was probably typical of the Pre-Tractarian Headmasters, very much in the mould of the Duchess of Buckingham; and his religious expectations, says the Shrewsbury historian, were very moderate. "Devotion from a collection of boys in common, may be a very fine thing to talk of, but I must affirm that I never witnessed it and never expect to witness it".

In a letter to the Trustees, he wrote that "the church was a place for private signals and assignations between the girls and my Upper boys" . Indeed Dr Butler himself at Shrewsbury was once reproved by a visiting bishop (a former pupil), who detected him sharpening a pencil during a service, and Dr Kennedy, his successor, found that attendance at communion service was regarded as a duty to be grudgingly performed by the school not more than once a term.

A similar picture emerges at Christ's Hospital. Leigh Hunt, who was at school there shortly after Lamb and Coleridge, criticised the religious practices and the inaudible and indifferent tones of some of the preachers.

"I, Leigh Hunt for one, who had been piously brought up and continued to have religion inculcated in me by my father and mother, began secretly to become as indifferent as I thought the preachers. And, though the morals of the school were in the main excellent and exemplary, we all felt, without knowing it, that it was the orderliness and example of the general system that kept us so, and not the religious part of it, which seldom entered our heads at all and only bored us when it did."

School Confirmation provides an important guide to religious attitudes. Gladstone was from an early age deeply religious, but his diary (Jan. 25 1827) suggests a remarkable vagueness in this matter on the part of the Eton authorities: "Tutor tells me there is to be a Confirmation here next week: notice just received."
On Feb 1st there were more than 200 boys confirmed, and he enters in his diary a 25 line prayer of passionate dedication, and then a mere two lines on the service itself. The final entries for the day are: "Dinner with Wellesley after four. Hallam and Pickering also there. Finished Clarendon, a beautiful history. Finished verses and read some Herodotus."

Looking back on his school days in old age he records as his final opinion: "The actual teaching of Christianity was all but dead, though happily none of the forms had been surrendered."
At Winchester, according to Firth, organised Chapel services, which took place at least twice a day, were a mockery. The three Chaplains, Buggy Swinx, Damme Hopkins and Wise Watkin could 'back themselves for any money against the field to give all challengers a start down to Pontius Pilate in the Creed, and still arrive before them at the Life Everlasting.'

Although the place was stuffed with clergy, sermons in Chapel were rare. One Mr Purnell, then eleven years a Fellow went so far as to mount the pulpit once in 1771, but 'with great tokens of fear and terror'. His rash example was not followed. Warden Huntingford never preached to the boys, nor gave any Confirmation Charge; the matter was considered, but 'some difficulties presenting themselves, the idea was relinquished'. Before Arnold and Moberly set the Victorians going in their torrential spate of eloquence, it was not considered part of a Headmaster's duty to preach.

Such evidence as there is strongly suggests that in religion, as in other matters, the schools mirrored the national attitude, and that any kind of religious enthusiasm was viewed with deep suspicion by the vast majority of English tax-payers as carrying disturbing social and political overtones. Dickens in Pickwick Papers contemptuously derides Methodism in the character of Stiggins, the bibulous hot gospeller. Towards the end of the 18th Century, however, opinion in England was deeply shocked by the spectacle of the French King and his nobles being butchered by the Guillotine, and, soon afterwards, a new kind of refugee began to appear off our shores.

A hundred years before it had been French Protestants fleeing the Catholic persecution, but now it was the Roman Catholic priests and monks who fled from the Revolution. Their pupils had originally come from England where Roman Catholicism was persecuted, but now they were forced to leave a country where, under the Reign of Terror, their religion was accounted high treason. In 1791, however, the passing of the Catholic Relief Act made it once more legal for Roman Catholics to practise their religion in England. And so, between 1795 and 1814, settlements in England were made, which later developed into the great Roman Catholic Schools - Ampleforth, Downside and Stonyhurst.

We have a clear picture of life at St. Gregory's, Douai (the original house of Downside) in the account of a pupil who was there from 1721-1726. There is something very moving in the description of the education of these young exiles whose games and pastimes recall the English scenes that they had left behind, and to which many must very soon have longed to return.
It is shaming too, to read that many years later when a party of these sea-sick schoolboys disembarked at Hull, they were abused by the crowd as "murderers of their King". They then had a weary march on foot to reach the haven of Stonyhurst Hall, given to them by Thomas Weld .

A very different effect of the French Revolution was to strengthen the Evangelical Movement in England which played a great part in the shaping of things to come in the 19th Century.
It was felt by the English Evangelicals that the French Revolution was largely a judgment on the French for their frivolity, and the error of their ways. The only life that was worth living, the Evangelicals thought, lay in total dedication to the service of God.

This meant, among other things, that 18th Century vices were to be regarded no longer as venial offences, but as deadly sins. Drunkeness, gambling, blasphemy and fornication were especially castigated, but there were many other parts of the English way of life, such as Sunday travel and theatre going, on which they cast critical and disapproving eyes. Their leaders were scornfully dubbed by Sydney Smith as belonging to the Clapham sect, and Trollope spotlights their absurdities in the persons of Mrs Proudie and Mr Slope.

But while smiling at their excesses, we are bound to admit that it is to Wilberforce and Shaftesbury that we probably owe more than to anyone else in the 19th Century: the one for his life-long fight against slavery, the other for his dedication to the cause of the poor and needy. Nearly all the Headmasters were conscious of the Evangelical challenge, and, even if they were not fully sympathetic, they felt compelled to take their religious duties far more seriously.

One of Kennedy's Old Salopians records that during his time at Shrewsbury "much attention was paid to the study of the Thirty-nine Articles, which thus became well known and loved by many of his pupils". Few Headmasters, perhaps, aspired to quite such pedagogical triumphs, but many followed Arnold's example, and the Headmaster's Divinity hours with the Sixth Form became one of his most important duties. This, was a tradition that grew steadily throughout the 19th Century and thus we find that Sanderson of Oundle (1892-1922), always regarded as the most scientifically oriented of the Victorian Headmasters, insisted on the paramount importance of Biblical study in the work of the Sixth Form.

"I came that you might have light and that more abundantly." This his old pupils often recalled as his favourite text.

The Clarendon Commissioners found that in all the great boarding schools ample, possibly even excessive, time was devoted to official religion on Sundays. At Rugby, for instance, there were three services every Sunday, as well as Scripture Preparation for Monday, and House Prayers, together with Holy Communion about five times a term. At Shrewsbury every Sunday the boys had prayers and a divinity lesson at 8.05, attended the town church at 11 and the school chapel at 3, did Divinity Preparation from 7 to 9, after which came Scripture Reading and Prayers until 9.20.

"These are the precautions," Kennedy told the Commissioners, "taken to enable boys to use Sunday as a day of religious exercises. I do not see my way to the <u>enforcement</u> of religion by any stricter discipline. Games, of course, there are none on that day, but it is too much to believe that no light literature is ever read. On such points I can only trust to exhortations., and the blessing of God. Espionage I entirely repudiate!"

Most Headmasters would probably have agreed with him. There is nothing in which modern thought and practice differs more from Victorian than in this matter of Sunday observance. It is remarkable, but apparently true, that boys not only willingly accepted this, but also attended the voluntary Communion services in great numbers.

Harrow provides perhaps the only example of a school in which the spiritual influence of an assistant master may well have been even greater than that of the Headmaster. John Smith who taught at Harrow 1854-1880 could best be described as a St. Francis among schoolmasters. His burning faith found expression in his abounding love and charity towards all and sundry.
"I pray for everything, and everyone." he said , "Your father, mother, sisters and brothers; your horses, dogs and rabbits".

It was the measure of his greatness that he was accepted and indeed revered in an age when the schools were still turning slowly from brutality and violence. In his abhorrence of bodily ease and comfort he was positively medieval, but he combined this with a fanatically close observance of personal cleanliness and neatness. This too was expected of his pupils. When he was left temporarily in charge of a Boarding House he addressed the boys at the beginning of prayers in the following words, remarkable for the touch of poetry which often gave impressiveness to his sermons and table-talk:

"As I pass along these wind-swept passages at night, and, going into your rooms, see there your sleeping forms, and beside your beds your clothes unfolded or strewn upon the floor, I think to myself, would the dear Lord be pleased if He came to fetch a boy in his sleep tonight, and found that he had left his things in such disorder? Will you do me the favour in future to fold up your clothes, and leave them ready on your chairs?"

And on Monday came the sequel, overheard in the very words here written:

"I say, what do you think?' - it was a little Lower School boy speaking - 'Last night, of course, I left my clothes about as usual. In came old John. He called my name, but I did not let on that I was awake. So he took up the things, folded them, and put them on the chair himself. Of course he thought I was asleep, but I think it was rather a chouse, as I suppose I shall have to fold up my own after this."

He spoke to boys as easily and naturally about death and Heaven as about events in the next holidays:
"If you reach Heaven before me, dear fellow, keep me a flower. I think I should like a rose best."

Deeply dedicated as he was to his school work, even so, he managed to devote every half-holiday to some charitable work, usually among the very poor. He did all this because he believed so passionately that personal involvement with poverty was the only way to bridge the gulf between 'the two nations', and that therein lay the best hope of achieving a truly united Christendom. The unseen cross which he bore for many years was his fear of the hereditary madness which eventually forced his retirement from Harrow. His last years were spent, at his own insistence, as an ordinary patient in St. Luke's Hospital..
He accepted it gladly as a crowning mercy.

The effectiveness of sermons obviously varied greatly in accordance with the opportunities and abilities of the Headmaster concerned, but there can be no doubt that in many cases it was very great. Regular preaching by the Headmaster was one of Arnold's innovations at Rugby, and it is graphically described by Stanley.

"It is difficult to describe, without seeming to exaggerate, the attention he inspired. Years have passed away, and many of his pupils can look back to hardly any greater interest than that with which, for those twenty minutes, Sunday after Sunday, they sat beneath that pulpit. Their eyes were fixed upon him: their attention strained to the utmost to catch every word that he uttered.
It is true, that, even for the best, there was much that must have passed away from them as soon as they had heard it. But they were struck, as boys naturally would be, by the originality of his thoughts, and the beauty of his language; and in the substance of what he said, there was much that might have seemed useless, because for the most part impracticable to boys, but it was not without its effect in breaking completely through the corrupt atmosphere of school opinion, and exhibiting before them once

every week an image of high principle and feeling, which they felt certain was not put on for the occasion but was constantly living amongst them.

And to all it must have been an advantage, that for once in their lives, they had listened to sermons, which none of them could associate with the thought of weariness, formality or exaggeration. On many there was left an impression to which, though unheeded at the time, they recurred in after life. Even the most careless boys would sometimes, during the course of the week, refer almost involuntarily to the sermon of the past Sunday, as a condemnation of what they were doing. Some, whilst they wonder how it was that so little practical effect was produced upon themselves at the time, yet retain the recollection of his words.

To give the words of one who so describes himself:
'I used to listen to them from first to last with a kind of awe, and over and over again could not join my friends at the chapel door, but would walk home to be alone.'
I myself remember the same effects being produced by them, more or less, on others, whom I should have thought as hard as stones, and on whom I should think Arnold looked as some of the worst boys in the school."

It is surprising to reflect that at the same time that Arnold was preaching at Rugby in this gripping and dramatic style, the sermons at Eton by the Fellows were either inaudible or had as their texts such words as: "Wash" or "This thing was not done in a corner".

At Winchester, by contrast, no one fails to mention the deep impression made by Moberly's sermons. Howe in *Six Great Schoolmasters,* writes as follows:

"His silvery, distinct tones are still in the ears of many who sat 50 years ago in Winchester School. We very greatly preferred Dr Moberly's sermons to those of any other preacher."

The strongest possible testimony to the effect of his sermons is given by a former member of the school who declares that on the Sunday evenings on which Dr Moberly preached 'everybody felt different'. "

Vaughan at Harrow was clearly an equally effective preacher. "Scarcely an assistant master or old pupil who sat in Harrow Chapel in those days fails to record some sermon which, after half a century has passed away, still remains vivid in his recollection."

At Marlborough, when Bradley was Master, Howe records: "A big boy, not by any means a model of excellence once said to his Housemaster: 'I can't understand any fellow going on being bad as he listens to the Master every week in Chapel".

One of the very greatest preachers was Temple, Headmaster of Ruby (1857-1869). We are told that:

" ...his sermons were delivered with such intense earnestness that they could not fail to make some impression even on the most thoughtless of us. He did not urge boys to go to Communion but held a voluntary service late on Saturday when he addressed those boys who cared to go."

It was then that Dr Temple spoke out most freely from his heart, and the boys, knowing this, valued the opportunity accordingly. An eyewitness says:

"Dr Temple always came in alone from his study, his well known Bible in his hand. Nearly every communicant came in any dress - football or cricket, how they pleased - and sat where they liked. Nobody noted who was present. Often the chapel was mainly dark: no lights were lighted. And what a rough and tumble assembly it was! Dirty often from the football scrimmage, they crept silently under the pulpit - and listened."

No wonder that one Rugby boy wrote to his mother, who was apparently worried by Temple's contribution to the controversial 'Essays and Reviews':
"Dear mother, Temple's all right, but if he turns Mahometan, all the school will turn too."

Whatever doubts there may be about the lasting effects of school sermons on the average boy - and none was more conscious of this than Arnold himself - it seems clear that the Victorian Public Schools produced a remarkably large proportion of the Church of England clergy. In Dr Butler's 25 years at Harrow (1860-1885) three hundred of his pupils went on to take Holy Orders. Richard Nettleship, who was Thring's most brilliant pupil at Uppingham, wrote to his old Headmaster from Oxford saying that his education made it impossible for him to consider any calling other than teaching or the Church.

There was another school of thought in matters ecclesiastical, which produced a very striking effect on Education. The Rev. Nathaniel Woodard of Hertford College, Oxford, was strongly influenced by the High Church Movement which called for a return to ceremony and ritual in the Church of England services.

Woodard did not believe that the old foundations could be reformed, and so he embarked upon his ambitious project of starting a number of new schools all over the country in which a respect for elaborate Church Services could be properly inculcated. Hurstierpoint (1853), Lancing (1857) and Ardingly (1870) were the first of his foundations.

His work has certainly prospered, but not quite in the way he envisaged. He had an elaborate design of social stratification, labelling schools as middle class (gentry) and middle class, (lower class). The idea was that the wealthier schools should charge higher fees and make more profit, which would be used for the benefit of the poorer establishments. In practice this proved difficult, and such distinctions between his various schools have now been virtually abandoned.

An equally remarkable religious influence on education was exercised by another figure of the Oxford Movement, the Rev. William Sewell. He shared many of Woodard's ideas, notably that the rich should pay for the education of the poor, and his first plan for a school was that it should number 200 and that 20 of its pupils should receive a free education. Radley Hall was rented (1847) for 21 years, and, after an uncertain first five years, Sewell himself felt compelled to combine the offices of Warden and Headmaster to take over the running of the school himself. His devotion to the Church of England was unqualified.

"I allow no one who has quitted the Church of England for Rome to enter the walls of Radley" he declared, and services were conducted in a chapel which boasted a magnificent Reredos and the finest organ in England.

There was an attempt to create not so much a school as a community in which a new and close relationship was established between pupils and staff, who were at first called Fellows in a style recalling the collegiate life of the more ancient foundations.
In this, Sewell's critics accused him of permitting auricular confession, but he always vehemently denied any such intention. He declared that his aim was to "revive in the 19th Century the graces and virtues of a medieval institution without its corruptions".

There was also a lessening emphasis on the importance of manliness, a prime Victorian quality, and a new appeal for tenderness and gallantry to women. Admiration for noble blood too was unabashed, and on occasions those related to the peerage were proudly grouped together for meals at a special table. With their beautiful furnishings, separate cubicles and baths, and piety in chapel and dormitory, Radley must have been from 1851-1859 the most civilised boarding school in England.

"I have made your schoolroom, your dormitory, your hall, and your gymnasium such as no other school in the kingdom possesses", Sewell proudly declared.

Unfortunately this Golden Age could not last, and Sewell eventually found himself faced with a huge debt which was largely the result of his own reckless expenditure on beautifying the school. He fainted away when he was made to read the balance sheet, and he retired from his post broken-hearted. It was the end of an Anglo-Catholic dream, and the Radley that took its place, like many other schools, gradually shed the distinctive markings of its original foundation.

As the century neared its end it was perhaps inevitable that scientific questioning should produce some shift away from authoritative teaching of religion at Sixth Form level.

There was also less inspiration in the sermons, which were no longer based on the emotional appeals of the Gospels that frequently marked the sermons of the great Victorian Headmasters. Religious fervour indeed now became almost as suspect as it had been in the 18th century. This was a logical development of the modern spirit, but it had a dampening effect on school sermons.

Far more damage, however, was produced by what one might describe as the sanctification of the Public School ethical code. Thus H.M. Butler, preaching at the tercentenary service at Harrow, declared that his aim was 'to bring the dispositions that are lovely in private life into the service and conduct of the commonwealth; so to be patriots as not to forget that we are gentlemen.' "Tell me", he bade his hearers, " if that does not express what you would fairly wish the ideal to be of the Harrow man!"

The limits of such an ideal are obvious, but even less satisfactory to us seem the sporting sermons that soon began to intrude themselves, portraying God as the Great Umpire whose only wish was that we should play the great game of life as fairly as we played cricket. There were, of course, many exceptions to these two styles of preaching. It was probably no accident that this less mystical view of religion was complemented by a more realistic attitude towards the practical side of Christianity.
Many schoolmasters were becoming aware of the contrast between public school life and slum conditions, and were turning their attention towards social service. This was no novelty. Thring had been the first in the field, with school chapel collections for an East End parish; and Percival was a pioneer of such activities both at Clifton (1866) and Rugby (1873).

These examples were followed by Haileybury (1873), Marlborough (1882), Tonbridge (1883) and Shrewsbury (1896).

All such ventures could claim varying degrees of success, but few escaped the general charge that the School Mission was something chiefly connected with a near-compulsory House Subscription. Winchester's Mission in Portsmouth, however, seems to have been something very different. This was run from 1884 to 1895 by Father Dolling, an Irish Anglo-catholic priest of rare originality and charm, who had a positive genius for commending himself to both old and young. Part of the secret of his success was his remarkable capacity for sizing up the many people who sought his help. It was said of him that he always retained a touch of Sherlock Holmes about him to balance the spirit of St. Francis.

He not only subdued and finally captivated an extremely rough Southsea parish, which boasted fifty well patronised public houses in a population of 5,000, but he also formed close personal links with Winchester College, where he preached regularly, gave talks to the school, and made lengthy visits to each house in turn. With staff and boys alike he was a deeply loved and trusted character, though one of the boys commented in a letter home that "once get him on to the subject of vestments etc and he is a ranting maniac."

His visits to Winchester were not the only link. Every Saturday in term time two senior boys from College came for a short weekend to share the life of the Southsea Mission - a shining example of how a School Mission and a slum parish can be drawn together. It is especially remarkable because Dolling's Anglo-Catholicism might have been expected to give offence in the more conventional atmosphere of Winchester. It was perhaps a case of personal charm and integrity transcending the barriers of creeds.

Since the turn of the century the claims of formal religion have become steadily more muted. Sunday observance is everywhere very different from what it was in Kennedy's day; and even in the practical field of social service, the welfare state, with all its shortcomings, has made the helping of the poor a less urgent imperative. This does not mean that religious feeling in its truest sense is dying out. Perhaps the idealism of the young is focussed now more on such matters as 'world peace', 'the third world' and 'community service'.

Any discussion of the 'true sense' of religion raises profound questions that are beyond the scope of this book. We may legitimately hope, however, that the Keatian days of contemptuous irreverence are over, and that never again will a Headmaster of Eton, preaching to his boys, have to dodge a hail of missiles.

= = = = = = = = = = = =

CHAPTER 10

SPORT AND RECREATIONS

"I have no opinion of a boy who keeps a badger."
(Keate of Eton).

"I never knew a boy worth anything who was not fond of cricket."
(Ridding of Winchester)

"The games of cricket and football are so zealously pursued, with such organisation by the whole school, that it is vain to expect extensive reading and sound scholarship."
(Kennedy - speaking of Harrow).

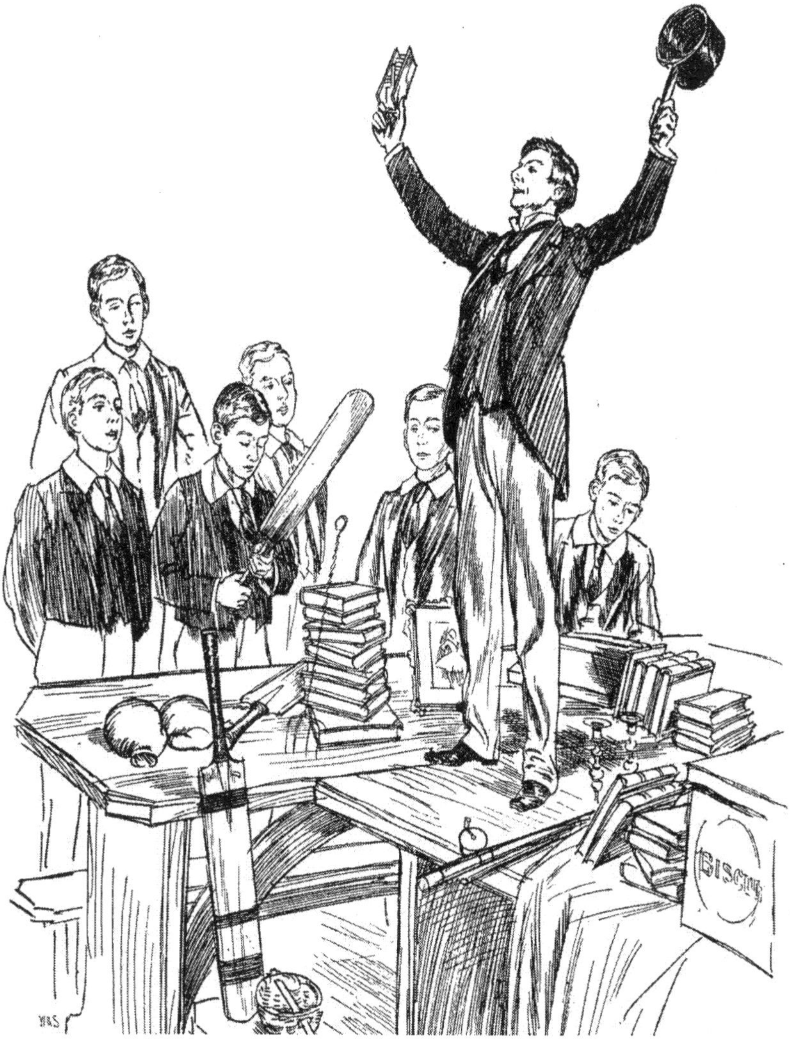

SPORT

Samuel Butler, Headmaster of Shrewsbury, strictly prohibited football and pronounced it a game "fit for butchers", but subsequent Headmasters of other schools took a very different view. Indeed, when in 1829 William Webb Ellis of Rugby "picked up the ball and ran", thus violating the game's principal rule, he took a step that was ultimately to set football beside cricket and rowing as the new figure in the scholastic pantheon. Up to this time, indeed, football had been little more than a running fight, punctuated by kicks at the ball or one's opponents. The rules were so vague that they were very confusedly recalled even by those who had actually taken part in the game. The numbers involved varied between small groups of well-protected, hob-nailed experts, and large crowds of frantic spectators who eventually joined in the fray.

The climax at Rugby was the "maul in goal" when the final attempt to score was made. Here everyone could lay hands on anyone else with the saving clause that "this holding does not include attempts to throttle or strangle which are totally opposed to all the principles of the game".
(Taken from Football Rules: Big side Levee 1849.)
One feels a certain sympathy with the horrified Rugby parent who, standing watching the game with Dr Temple, the Headmaster, enquired anxiously: "Does anything ever cause you to stop this kind of thing?"
"Nothing short of homicide", was the genial reply.
Temple, indeed, took a great interest in football and was directly responsible for the abolition in 1860 of "hacking over",
a particularly brutal and dangerous form of tripping.
This reform carried matters further towards the comparative safety of the code of Rugby Football rules issued in 1871.

The spirit in which the earlier form of the game was played is illustrated by the attitude of the Loretto boys, who with true Scottish fortitude considered it cowardly to pass the ball to another player rather than force a way through by sheer physical effort.   Finer points of the law were hotly disputed. Matches between Magdalen College School and St. Edwards were suspended in 1881 after a serio-comic row when MCS had won a game by 'unsportingly' heeling the ball from the scrummage. St. Edwards claimed that this 'too clever-by-half' stratagem was illegal, and wrote to the Secretary of the Rugby Union who, however, replied that he was 'sorry to say' that it was allowable.

Loretto were trained up by their Headmaster Dr Almond, who was probably the most original educationalist of the century. He was a highly educated Anglo-Scot who started with twelve boys in 1862 and in twenty years produced a school with a unique reputation for physical stamina and hardihood. He was a fanatical believer in the value of physical fitness, which was to be sought by many means: notably fresh air, cold baths, strenuous exercise and sensible clothing. On this last he was most insistent, declaring that the Greeks won the battle of Marathon chiefly because their clothing was less constricting than that of the Persians. In fact, he achieved what was little short of a sartorial revolution, abolishing the wearing of caps, ties, waistcoats and, under certain conditions, jackets also.   Fresh air poured in through open windows at all times, and good fresh food in plenty replaced the usual unappetising fare of the average school.

Almond's ethics owed nothing to existing systems and seemed, in fact, to be a complete reaction against the conventional style. He was a great admirer of Mill and Herbert Spencer, and declared that his aim was   "a community living according to the dictates of reason".

Religion too was harnessed to the need for physical fitness and the Pauline theme was frequently presented to the school of rendering their bodies a living sacrifice to God by striving for strength and purity. Games and athletics were obviously important elements in the plan, but Almond's view of them was strikingly original. Thus he valued them entirely as occasions for physical exercise and displays of hardihood, and he was more interested in the chest expansions of his team than in their match record.

His pupils, however, did not entirely subscribe to this view and they harboured more conventional sporting ambitions when they passed on to the University. In 1882 there were no less than seven Lorettonians in the Oxford Rugby Football XV and between 1884 and 1891 Loretto had four captains of the Oxford XVs. A remarkable record.

Music too, was approached as if it were almost a branch of physical education:
"For boys at least" wrote Almond, "I think that music should be of a broad, robust and diatonic kind. I do not like most modern music and utterly object to anything of a sentimental nature." Exams too, he objected to, on the grounds that anxiety over them impaired physical fitness.

Yet with all his eccentricities and extravagance, Almond's ideal was always to produce in his school "the rational spirit which chooses what is best rather than what is customary".
A photograph of the Oxford team in 1885 shows three wearing shorts and twelve wearing knickerbockers, but in 1886 knickerbockers have entirely disappeared. As in the years 1881 to 1886 a third of the Oxford Blues came from Loretto, it may well be that Almond's ideas of rational dress were responsible for the ultimate triumph of shorts on the football field.

At Uppingham. Thring, the Headmaster, actually played both Football and Fives with his boys. He writes in his diary that "the boys played beautifully", which could hardly be applied to the scenes in the Close at Rugby. A doughty clergyman on his staff, the Rev. Hodgkinson, we are told, played regularly in full clerical attire, choker, black trousers and a tall hat. Yet another style is suggested by a contemporary description of A.G. Butler, Haileybury's Headmaster (1862-1867):

"I remember how Arthur Gray Butler, in November when football was played on the Terrace field, would suddenly appear from the Master's garden, dressed in black cloth, with cap and gown; and, as he watched the struggle approaching the wall, there would be visible a light in his eye and a certain working of the nostrils, like a Warhorse scenting battle, and his voice would be heard calling in thrilling tones: 'In with you Stripes! In with you, Whites! Well played! Well played!'
An impatient movement would ensue, cap and gown would be given to the nearest small boy and a figure presenting to view an immaculate shirt and a pair of red braces would be seen dashing headlong into the fray. Sometimes he would emerge triumphant with the ball held aloft, and sometimes he would be bowled over in the mud like the humblest forward, before eventually retiring from the fight with great detriment to his clothes but none to his dignity."

Eton's version of football was a mixture of the Field and the Wall game. Here, as A.C. Ainger tells us, the most important features were "The privileges of 'the behinds' ".
Any attempt to understand this, A.C. Ainger tells us, is unnecessary because "the rules of the Wall game have always been unintelligible except to a limited number of its professors." However, for those who were not professors, there was a rich variety of compensatory games listed by Sir A. Maxwell Lyte:

Shirking Walls, Bully Cally, Pig in the Ring, Hopscotch, Conquering lobs, Marbles, Puss in the corner, Cut Gallow, Kites, Humming Tops, Hunt the hare, Chuck, Sinks, Hustlecap, Starecaps and Slides in the School.

At Harrow they retained their own brand of Football, and this included one particular tradition: on the first day of the Christmas holidays a marathon Harrow Football match would be played, which lasted for six hours. Players were allowed to drop out for refreshments as often as they liked and for as long as they liked.

Dr Moberly of Winchester adopted a somewhat ambivalent attitude towards the growing popularity of games. Refusing, as he said, to play the part of King Canute, he took what was for Winchester the unprecedented step in 1851 of appointing Lillywhite, a professional, to coach the school Cricket XI. As a result, Winchester promptly beat Eton four times in succession. Moberly then, however, attempted to redress the balance by arranging that the Eton-Winchester match should be transferred from Lord's to the home grounds of the two schools, thus withdrawing the match from the public view. He is also on record as having spoken of "the idle boys, I mean boys who play cricket".

His son-in-law Dr Ridding, who succeeded him (1866-1884) had a very different view. He greatly increased the area of the Playing Fields and declared: "Give me a boy who is a cricketer and I can make something of him".
There were plenty of other cricketing devotees. Robert Barter, the genial Warden, was such an enthusiastic and successful batsman that a particular stroke at the wicket was named after him. At Rossall in 1876, the Headmaster and his deputy put on 200 for the first wicket against the School, and in 1883, the staff at Wellington collected the massive total of 524.

Cricket fever was now reaching its height; Eton's XI spent thirty hours a week on the game and it is significant that in 1878 the average age of the Harrow XI was 18.5 years. It was at this time that the music of J.H. Farmer and the verse of Edward Bowen added a new dimension to organised games by supplying an ethic and a religious sanction that had not elsewhere been observed before. The songs which were now produced bathed the world of Harrow's athletes in a lustrous light that gave a triumphant answer to those who had previously queried the value of games.

> 'Follow up, follow up, follow up, follow up'.
> Till the field ring again and again
> With the tramp of the twenty-two men.

Dr Butler, the Headmaster, was frankly dubious about Forty Years On, and took exception to the line: "God give us bases to guard or beleaguer" on the grounds that it smacked of blasphemy. He soon, however, forgot about it. Future ages were not, therefore, robbed of their favourite end of term song.
Its author, E.E. Bowen, may be regarded as the High Priest of the late Victorian games cult, and it is easy to deride his claims and excesses. But it is also only fair to notice that he was far removed, as a type, from the modern games master.

He was a man of considerable intellectual stature, and, as a young man, he had been a member of the Cambridge Apostles. His interest in classroom education fully matched his enthusiasm for games, and the verdict of his pupils was that not only were his lessons more interesting but he made his pupils work harder than anyone else. His history lectures on such subjects as the Peninsular War never failed to hold his audiences spellbound. He spoke fluent French and German and his interest in questions of the day led him to stand, albeit unsuccessfully, as a Liberal Candidate for Parliament. It is clear that as a games master he was something of an outsize.

There were other poems where the association between games and ethics is plainly made. As in these lines written on the death of Lord Bessborough, a notable cricketer:

> Our fields have lost his presence. Never more,
> In the long splendour of the summer days,
> Game after game, as swells the mounting score,
> His temperate voice shall gladden into praise.
> Others will toil as he did; still shall hold
> The chain that binds us; skill nor love shall cease,
> But he, the first, the purest friend of old,
> rests in the silence of the endless Peace.
>
> Yet, O dear memory of the friend of youth,
> Die not, but stay, and quicken, at his name,
> All that we have of valour and of truth,
> Honour in strife, and simpleness in fame,
> Still keep his teaching fresh, with arm and foot
> Supple, and firm, and scorning sloth alone;
> Keep fieldsmen watchful, batsmen resolute,
> But make our hearts as loyal as his own!

Robert Grimston, another cricketer, is lamented in a similar style:

> Well played. His life was honester than ours;
> We scheme, he worked; we hesitate, he spoke;
> His rough-hewn stem held no concealing flowers,
>   But grain of oak.
>
> No earthly umpire speaks, his grave above;
> And thanks are dumb, and praise is all too late;
> That worth and truth, that manhood and that love
>   Are hid and wait.
>
> Sleep gently, where thou sleepest, dear old friend;
> Think, if thou thinkest, on the bright days past;
> Yet loftier Love, and worthier Truth, attend
>   What more thou hast.

Grimston found the suspense of watching the Eton and Harrow match at Lords so unbearable that he could only be prevailed upon to attend when Harrow seemed sure of an easy win. (Cricket being such an uncertain game, this was difficult to arrange and was only once attempted).

Of course, the simple ethic that it is good for the individual to subordinate his own inclinations for the good of the team had been long established, and this was now enshrined in the Eton Boating song with its insistence on the oarsman's simple creed:

THE ETON BOATING SONG

> Jolly boating weather
> And a hay harvest breeze,
> Blade on the feather,
> Shade off the trees,
> Swing, swing, together,
> With your backs between your knees;
> Swing, swing together,
> With your backs between your knees
>
> Harrow may be more clever,
> Rugby may make more row,
> But we'll row, row for ever,
> Steady from stroke to bow,
> And nothing in life shall sever
> The chain that is round us now,
> And nothing in life shall sever
> The chain that is round us now.

These verses were composed by William Cory, who taught at Eton from 1845 to 1872. He was a brilliant classical scholar and a gifted if eccentric teacher; his translation of Heraclitus has already outlived the fame of its author. He reacted strongly against the old flogging tradition at Eton and his view of Education was highly elitist. Very much the aesthete, he dedicated himself entirely to the development of the talented few who were generally aristocratic and good-looking as well. Cory indeed inaugurated the cult of the Eton Shrine. Thus he wrote in a letter to a pupil entering on his last term:

"The life of the last summer months at Eton is probably as happy as any kind of life. It is pleasure set in a framework of duties: daily obligations are , as it were, the hem that keeps the garment from unravelling."

Cory retired from Eton with mysterious suddenness, and subsequently married a female pupil who was 36 years his junior. Even Fives at Eton, played by four participants between three stone walls, had its lessons for life. It was often played by truants against the chapel buttresses when the sermon palled. The original Fives Court formed by the Chapel buttresses and duplicated later all over the world, can be seen at Eton today.

A SONG OF FIVES

Oft you'll think, in after lives,
What is life? a game of Fives:
Partners to their partners true;
Courteous to their rivals, too -
Here and there alike the aim
In the end to win the game!
Chorus - Here and there, etc.

Oft in life you'll meet with knocks
Gainst harder "pepper-box";
Fingers scraped and fingers bruised;
Ball and player roughly used -
Till "cut down", or slow or fast,
Into "dead man's hole" at last!
Chorus - Till "cut down", etc.

So let Fives its lessons teach;
Hit all balls within your reach;
If you fail for want of pluck,
Don't abuse your rival's luck -
Everyone can win who tries,
For the struggle is the prize.
Chorus - Everyone can win, etc.

School attitudes and enthusiasms often mirror those favoured by the general public, and this is certainly true of sporting tastes. Dr Craddock, Principal of Brasenose Oxford (1853-1886) made it clear that anyone who had been in the cricket XI or the 1st Boat at Eton need not bother about the matriculation (entrance) exam.
C.B. Fry (the great Oxford all-rounder and multi-talented champion), was once escorted all the way back from the Parks to Wadham College by wildly cheering crowds after he had played a fine innings against the Australians.
Baden-Powell's famous defence of Mafeking was conducted amid regular announcements by the garrison about the length of the siege in terms of a cricket score.
Frank Benson's Shakespearean company prided itself on being able to produce not just good theatre but a really good Hockey Team. Conan Doyle scored a century for the M.C.C. at Lords, and it is surely highly significant, too, that Raffles, the famous gentleman crook of fiction, was credited with the same feat for England v. Australia.

The truth is that by the end of the Victorian age the country was games-oriented as never before. To blame this on the schools who did not originate this, but merely shared in it, is highly unfair.
It is unreasonable , too, to look upon the phenomenon, as some have done, with a highly disapproving eye and declare scornfully that the schools originally aimed at nothing but classical scholarship, then concentrated on piety and gentility, and finally settled for gamesworship.

Thus Gathorne-Hardy goes so far as to say that "by 1900-1914 the Public Schools, as far as the majority of their pupils were concerned, had really ceased to be academic institutions".

But if the phrase 'academic institutions' refers to places devoted to books and learning, no one surely could claim this as a description of pre-Reform Public schools like Dr Keate's Eton. Nor is it true that boys lose interest in things of the mind simply because they exchange fighting and poaching for football and cricket. The truth of the matter is that for many years sports of various kinds have been the centrepiece of the English scene. Fox hunting and horse-racing held pride of place throughout the 18th and 19th century, and it is said that in 1815 there was more excitement over the championship fight between Tom Cribb and Jim Belcher than over the Battle of Waterloo

The Public Schools may, in a sense, have led the way in the great spread of organised games between 1860 and 1880, but in this they were certainly preaching to the converted. If the Public Schools had never existed, the modern sports arenas would still be drawing the same huge crowds that they do today. Indeed, the much derided team loyalties of the Public Schools have very little in common with the vast nexus of modern professionalism with its unabashed materialism, its mass hysteria, and the gang-warfare of its supporters.

It is also true that while the ethical and physical benefits of games have been overstated in the past, it would be ridiculous to maintain that such things are entirely imaginary. Most games demand a high standard of physical fitness and a certain amount of self-control. The best players, it is often said, never give up, and never lose their tempers. There are many features of games which make them enjoyable for the spectator as well as the player, but the most important one is the release felt by the individual who can identify with a group, school, university or nation.

This is a psychological fact of great antiquity, and, strange as it may seem, there is a clear connection between the raging of the Greek Bacchants and the more restrained behaviour of modern group-therapists. In both, a person escapes temporarily from the burden of individuality and becomes part of something larger.

Finally, it is worthwhile to examine the astonishing case of what we might well call the Marlborough Revolution (See Chapter 7). Although Cotton, the new Headmaster, had restored a certain amount of law and order, in 1854 he was faced with a financial crisis which threatened the school with immediate closure. He met it in a way that not only dealt with the pressing problem of money, but began the process of solving the serious issue of chronic disorder and indiscipline. He managed to import, as the old staff quickly retired, an enthusiastic group of young masters, largely from Rugby, who were prepared to ease the School's finances by accepting salaries that were well below the normal rates. They were also eager to attempt the conversion of the boys from bullying and poaching to the playing of school games. They were young and athletic themselves, and they knew this change had to be accompanied by total involvement of the staff in every part of the boys' lives.

The school responded to the invitation, but responded very slowly. The last idol to be abandoned was the 'squaler', the traditional Marlborough poacher's weapon which threw a large piece of lead with deadly accuracy. This was used principally on small animals and birds, but could also be used to maim the Savernake Forest deer. Poaching raised its head for the last time when the arrival of a new Headmaster in 1858 was the signal for a general outbreak, involving not only poaching but the selling of game. G.G. Bradley, the Headmaster, acted very swiftly indeed. Within hours the culprits were convicted and severely punished, and the day of the Squaler was over.

The games-cult had obvious extravagances and quite absurd pretensions, and it would be extremely naive to maintain that organised games resulted in a sort of Golden Age in the Schools. But at the same time, desirable things followed in its wake. It is undeniable that it was partly by the new prestige of the Playing Fields that the power of the bully, like that of the poacher, was being steadily eroded. They were cowed by the tramp of the twenty-two men. It is probably not a coincidence that at United Services College, where, largely for reasons of economy, there were virtually no organised games, bullying in 1870 reached unprecedented levels of fiendish cruelty. Lord Birkenhead, Kipling's biographer, writes:

"Boys were held out of windows five storeys high by their heels. They were hanged from the top floor staircase blindfolded, with slack on the rope to give a violent jerk under the arms when they fell into space... their ears were held up against the thin wooden panel of a form-room door, and a violent blow was struck by a hammer on the other side of the panel, producing the sensation of a bomb exploding in the head."

It is not inappropriate to conclude with an extract from the Clarendon Report (1862) on the subject of games:

"Pursued as a recreation and voluntarily; they (*Games*) are pursued with all the eagerness which boyhood throws into its amusements; and they implant the habit, which does not cease with boyhood, of seeking recreation in vigorous exercise. The cricket and football fields, however, are not merely places of exercise and amusement; they also help to form some of the most valuable social qualities and manly virtues and they hold, like the class-room and the boarding-house, a distinct and important place in public-school education."

"Their importance is fully recognized, and they have ample encouragement in general from the authorities of the schools. A Headmaster, who had himself as a boy played in a school 'eleven', is not likely to be indifferent to the game in after life; and those who are most anxious that their pupils should work diligently are desirous also that they should play sport heartily and with spirit.

It is possible to carry this too far, and at some schools we fear that this is now the case. It is carried too far, for instance, if cricket matches are multiplied till they engross almost all the interests, and much of the time, of the boys during an important part of the year; it is certainly carried too far if boys are encouraged to regard play as on the same level with work, or to imagine that they can make amends for neglecting their duty by the most industrious pursuit of pleasure. There is the less excuse for this because it is certain that the two things are by no means incompatible. It happens frequently that boys who are diligent and distinguished in school and at college earn distinction also in the cricket-field or on the river; and as it appears clear that the idlest boys are not the most successful in games, so neither, we believe, are the least hard-working schools.

On the contrary, there is reason to think not only that at such schools the distinction between the player and the worker is more strongly marked than elsewhere, and that intellectual activity is less often united with a healthy interest in games, but that there is more in proportion of that vacant lounging which is sheer waste of time and a prolific source of bad habits."

One should remember, finally, that the Marlborough Revolution was not achieved at the expense of scholars. In 1859 the academic world was astonished by the spectacle of the top two Balliol scholarships being awarded to the *arriviste* Marlborough.

RECREATIONS

Before the triumph of organised games in schools there had always been plenty of play. Even for the big boys at Eton and Westminster, cricket in 1800 took a relatively minor place among such sports as marbles, tip-cat, pitch-farthing and the bowling of hoops, to say nothing of birds-nesting, tree-climbing, poaching, fighting and the stoning of passing bargees on the Thames; and if the Duke of Wellington ever did say that the Battle of Waterloo was won on the playing-fields of Eton, it is anybody's guess which of all these methods of training His Grace had in mind.

There were other entertainments at other schools, Sir Charles Oman describes some at Winchester:
"The common round of term was occasionally broken by some festivities of a more or less compulsory sort. One was College singing - a musical festival held at night in Seventh Chamber, which would hold almost the whole of the population of Chamber Court. Every junior was supposed to have mastered a certain number of songs of official sanction, and might be called upon to warble them. For this purpose it was necessary to possess a 'song book', transcribed in manuscript from one of many originals afloat in College.

I possess my own copy still, written in a very childish hand. It includes not only 'Domum', the Wykehamists' national anthem, but a curious list of songs dating back to various periods of the early nineteenth century. Some are decidedly archaic, such as 'Soldiers Cheer', which relates to Wellesley's capture of Seringapatam, and ' I likes my drop of good beer', which sings the praises of William IV. Others are songs of the Dickens and Thackeray period, celebrating 'Villikins and his Dinah', the misfortunes of Peter Gray, who was scalped by Red Indians, and the grim tale of the 'Workshop Boy".

"Having good lungs I rather enjoyed these festivities. Not so another outbreak of exuberance, called the Buggy Hunt', which consisted of putting the smallest boys in College into boxes on wheels, and running them at full speed round Chamber Court after evening Chapel. Collisions might occur, and sometimes did, but I never saw any which caused serious injuries. But it was a silly game, and hard on the diminutive juniors selected as victims."

Mansfield (1840) gives a vivid account of badger-hunting:

"If one can't follow a fox on horseback, one may do worse than follow a badger on foot - that is, if one's lungs and legs are in as good condition as ours used to be in those days. At some appointed meet, 'Turner', the badger provider, clad in a rusty velveteen shooting jacket, with a cur or two at his heels, and the noble animal in a sack, used to meet us.

On the mouth of the sack being opened, away went badger at a steady enduring pace across the downs. He did not run extremely fast, but then he could go for ever, His strong point was going up a steep hill, when he could beat the fastest runner; going downhill he was not so brilliant. We generally gave him one hundred yards start before we followed, Turner bringing up the rear with the dogs in couples. Sometimes, instead of crossing the downs, he would make for the water meadows, and then the runs were more exciting as he took to the water like an otter; and as there were several pieces of water to pass, our swimming as well as running powers were fully called into play.

When we had had enough, the dogs were let loose and the badger stopped. Turner's excitement at this moment lest his badger or dogs should receive any injuries was intense, and indeed with some reason, as a badger and dog, locked in an embrace, are reluctant to forego their hold.

He used to throw himself on the combatants, and eagerly exhort some of those up to 'lay hould of his tail,' while he himself would chew away at that of the badger or of any dog that would not quit his gripe. The badger being extricated from the dogs, or the dogs from the badger, as the case might be, he was returned to the quiet of his sack again till the next morning Hills."

Lamb Singing at Rugby acquired some notoriety, when at one time new boys were made to sing solos and had to drink heavily salted hot water if their performance was poor. In Dr Arnold's time the new boys were not called upon to perform until they had had half a term to settle down, and the custom does not seem to have been particularly objectionable to the performers.

E.H. Bradby at his first half-term wrote home:
"Last night I had to mount upon the Hall table and sing my song. I sang 'Mrs John Prevot'. It is a nervous thing to have to mount upon a table and sing before about 39 boys; if you don't sing well you are floored, and have to sing two next Saturday. However, I got off, and strange to say sang the best of all! But it was because I determined not to be in a fright, and sing, and not say it."

Apart from amusements of this kind there had been of course, for many years, several traditional schoolboy celebrations. Guy Fawkes' Day, for example, was an occasion which made the most seasoned schoolmaster blench and reach for his cane. Marlborough's hilarious observance of the rite in 1851, already described at some length in Chapter 1, is probably the most famous event in the school's history.

A very different annual ceremony was held at Magdalen College School on the first of May. Nowadays, the picture of silver-voiced choristers greeting the dawn of May Day with song high up on Magdalen Tower, arouses for many people nostalgic yearning for dreaming spires.

The scene, however, as recalled by Millard, the Master 1846-88, was not entirely idyllic.

"The old custom was revived of hurling rotten eggs off the Tower on May Morning. The 'Daily Express', a manuscript paper produced daily by the Choristers for some time, in its issue of May 1st, 1840, informs us that 'nearly a hundred rotten eggs descended on to the multitude of spectators below, bedaubing their garments with the fragrant contents'. This custom apparently arose by way of retaliation against the town boys, who attempted to drown the singing by blowing on trumpets and horns. It was forbidden by the authorities.

The authorities, however, did not at that time, climb the Tower to enforce their orders. But what they failed to accomplish was effected by the sagacious old Porter. Standing at the foot of the narrow staircase at the base of the Tower as the boys ascended it in single file, he would tap with his heavy key the bulging pocket of the leader. The rest, warned by the intolerable stench which followed, wisely retraced their steps and broke their own putrid eggs in the quad below."
(Tuckwell, Old Magdalen Days)

Not surprisingly, the most elaborate junketings took place at Eton, in the shape of the triennial 'Montem' and the annual celebrations of George III's birthday on June 4th, both of which became national occasions comparable to Derby Day. The origins of the Montem are lost in the mists of time, but in essence the object of the exercise had been to collect money from visitors to meet the Captain of the School's expenses at King's College, Cambridge.

There was, however, a great deal more to it than that. Days of extravagant feasting preceded the great occasion, and the whole school put on a sort of military fancy dress of varying splendour in which they confronted the fashionably-dressed visitors, claiming money from them, in exchange for salt or tickets.

Wild and extensive celebrations closed the proceedings. The money collected was considerable, and, although the lucky recipient had to spend about half of it in entertaining his friends and supporters, he was still left the possessor of a sizeable Sum. Thring of Uppingham, one of the last Captains of Montem, received about £300 (equivalent to several thousand pounds in today's money). This, for a worthy clergyman's son, was no bad thing.

But it was the accompanying drunkeness, riotous disorder and vandalism that came to arouse the anger and resentment of an increasing number of people, who were suffering the consequences. Its defence was suitably made by an anonymous Etonian who wrote: "It (the Montem) makes even the wise feel there is something better than wisdom, and the great that there is something nobler than greatness."

An even more remarkable claim for it was made by one of the Fellows, a rigid Tory of boundless Protestant zeal, who maintained that the Montem had taken the place of a pilgrimage to a Shrine of the Virgin, and that it remained a standing protest against Popery.

Parkinson's Life of Edward Thring, records:
"The festivities among the boys began more than a fortnight before Montem day. Bills for large breakfast parties appear as early as May 14th.

For Montem day itself, W. Atkins sends in accounts for: -

160 gentlemen at breakfast at 6s.3d.	£ 50.0.0.
330 do. - dinner at 6s.6d.	£107.5.0
60 polemen at 5s	£ 15.0.0.

These charges only include the solid portions of the two chief banquets of the day.
Botham, landlord of the Windmill Inn sends in a supplementary account. Some of the items must have furnished weighty arguments for the abolition of Montem.
I select a few:

84 bottles port - 5 returned ..	£23.14.0
84 sherry - 16 returned	£20.8.0
72 cider - 30 returned	£4.4.0
48 do - stewards order	£4.10.0
48 porter	..£2.8.0
96 champagne - 14 returned	£35.17.6
2 bottles brandy	£1.0.0
1 barrel ale ..	£1.16.0"

The Reverend G.C. Green, who attended Montem in 1841 and 1844, recalls the scene:
"So we streamed out, over 600 strong, into the Slough Road on the march for Salt Hill. The procession was swelled along its route by the thousands of visitors from all parts of England, on horseback, on foot, in every kind of conveyance, ladies in their gayest dresses, all combining to make such a picture as will be never seen again."

Martial music in abundance was supplied, by the bands of the Life Guards and the 60th Rifles. Even the inventive genius of a Kerry Packer could hardly have improved on this.

Rather sadly, a sombre note is sounded in an account given in the life of Edward Thring:

"When dinner was over it was the custom of the boys to adjourn to the gardens of the Inn and there to use the swords they carried in hacking the currant and gooseberry bushes and decapitating the cabbages and other vegetables. A bill for damages of this kind seems to have been a regular item in the Montem charges; and on this occasion the landlord of the Inn recouped his losses by charging an admission fee to the grounds. This was paid by great numbers of people in order to watch the boys on their work of destruction."

In the Railway Age the extension of the Southern line to Windsor began to bring large numbers of visitors and sightseers who had no connection with the School. These added considerably to the already difficult task of preserving law and order. In 1844 Doctor Hawtrey who had already effected other changes and reforms, abolished the Montem, and from his own pocket, gave £300 to the Captain of the School who had been disappointed in his hopes. It was probably one of the most difficult alterations to a school's traditions that any Headmaster ever undertook, and it required the permission - very reluctantly granted - of Queen Victoria herself.

The celebrations of the Fourth June naturally included a firework display, but the specially Etonian element was the procession of boats, headed by the 'Ten Oar' to Surly Hall, some two miles up stream , and the champagne supper which followed. One of the "Eton Sketches by Quis?", published in the 1840's shows the supper in progress, and useful light is shed by the accompanying note:

"On this occasion each crew obtains some Ole Etonian or other friend to act as 'sitter', whose duty is to sit in the stern of the boat and provide a hamper of champagne. The sitter's health has here just been drunk and he is returning thanks. The tables of the boats are ranged in line, and at the corner of each is fixed the flag of the boat."

It is a curious fact that, although the Captain of Boats was *ex officio*, as Cust says, "the most important and the greatest 'swell' in the school", boating itself was, until 1840, officially prohibited. Consequently river activities were for many years bedevilled by strange anomalies in the attitude of authority. Thus in 1829 when Keate heard that the Eight, in defiance of his orders, planned to row up to Surly Hall before Easter, he arranged an elaborate ambush with some masters concealed behind bushes and others on horseback ready to pursue the delinquents.

When the rowers came in sight, Keate broke cover and rushed towards them shouting , "Foolish boys, I know you all; Lord Alford, Watt, come ashore, or you will all be expelled." The boat drew in to the bank, the rowers stepped out and, removing their masks, gave a lusty huzzah. They were Thames boatmen who had been specially hired for the occasion. Their cheers were soon followed by derisive hoots from the delighted boys who had watched from behind hedges.

A rather different note was sounded by Keate in the following year, when the boys confronted him with a large Newfoundland dog, gay with blue ribbons. He asked them what was the meaning of this, and they replied that it was in celebration of the Eton VIII's victory over Westminster.
"Silly boys," said Keate, and he smiled.
The glories of Henley still slept in the womb of time.

The Fourth of June festivities, which had come to resemble a protracted version of the Montem in the opportunities offered to the general public for disorder of all kinds, were in 1891 finally brought under the control of College. The death of Mrs Hornby, the Provost's wife, on June 3rd led to the cancellation of next day's celebrations, and some weeks later the programme was re-arranged to take place in the comparative privacy of the Weir Stream on the lower river. The Fourth of June now ceased to be a public event.

Acting, like boating, was for many years a forbidden but flourishing institution. We know from Coleridge's memoirs that plays such as The Rivals or Midsummer Night's Dream were rehearsed at dead of night in Long Chamber and produced in hired rooms in Slough or Windsor. Theoretically authority knew nothing of this, but Keate sometimes indulged in sardonic humour by revealing that he knew what boys had taken part in a recent production.

"Lydia Languish, construe!" he would call out, and a blushing youth would stand up and thus own the soft impeachment.

= = = = = = = = = = = =

CHAPTER 11

MILITARY TRAINING.

Except at a few special schools, such as Wellington, military training has tended to be the Cinderella of the English educational system. We do hear, however, of remarkable scenes at Shrewsbury as early as 1581, when Sir Henry Sidney, Lord President of the Marches, visited the area.

"All the scholars, being in number 360, with their masters before them, marched bravely from the Free School in battle with their generals, captains, drums, trumpets and ensigns before them through the town. They met Sir Henry, and the general with the other captains made their orations how valiantly they would fight and defend their country."

It is probable that in other schools at this time the threat of a Spanish invasion aroused similar patriotic fervour, but this seems to be the only one of which there is any record.

The next threat was a much more serious one; Napoleon's sword pointed at England's heart, and once more, Shrewsbury led the way. Two companies were formed (1803) of "dismounted cavalry" and infantry, and though they never had to fire a shot in anger, their spirit is well illustrated by the speech of Sergeant T.S. Hughes, on the occasion of his leaving the Corps to go to Cambridge.

"My brave companions", he begins, "it was the discipline of the Roman Legions that enabled a brave people from a band of robbers, murderers and outlaws, to rise into a mighty nation, to defeat with a handful of men myriads of barbarians, and to become masters of the world? And it was the same spirit that rendered the Grecian phalanx irresistible?"

"I go", he continued, warming to his task, "to range myself under a different standard, and to enrol myself among the brave protectors of our ancient seats of learning, the glory of our country and the envy of all others".

He ends heroically "There among the tombs of our ancient forefathers, those ornaments of their country, will we fight; with them we will stand or fall; amidst them we will conquer or die!"

Rugby too, responded to the call, and formed a company of Volunteers (1804) clad in blue coats collared with scarlet. Their armament was limited to wooden broadswords, but with these, no doubt, they made great play. Nelson's Trafalgar soon removed all serious threat of invasion, and the companies of schoolboy infantry and "dismounted cavalry" alike were soon disbanded.

Almost forty years of peace followed the Battle of Waterloo, and the Crimean War seemed to most people to be a mere echo of old unhappy far-off things, when suddenly the spectre of Bonaparte began to walk again in the person of his nephew Louis Napoleon. Once more there was war-fever and talk of a French invasion.

Volunteer Rifle Corps sprang up in large numbers, and Eton (1859) led the way. Doctor Goodford, the Headmaster, was 'carried away' by the school's passionate concern for suitable uniforms. There was a particular demand for the maximum amount of silver lacing for the officers, and the whole project was entrusted to the capable hands of a London clothing contractor. So magnificent were the resultant uniforms that when Sergeant-Major Gubbins attended Chapel, Provost Hawtrey gravely, but mistakenly, ushered him into the pew reserved for the Vice-Provost. The position of the Corps was still further strengthened when Major Warre, the Commanding Officer, became Headmaster. The watchword now became "No compulsion but you must join." In 1891 they had the unique distinction of an Inspection by Kaiser Wilhelm II!

Harrow's response seems to have been, by contrast, rather muted, and, though a company was formed under the aegis of the Middlesex R.V.C., there was a curious amount of opposition to the idea. E.E. Bowen, the most notable figure on the staff and a keen military historian, never concealed his dislike of the school Rifle Corps.

Rugby, however, recollecting their martial attitudes of 1804, went at it with a will. Four companies were formed 'dressed in sober grey uniforms' and, armed with muskets and bayonets, they did regular drill every day.

Rossall too, were originally dressed like Rugby in grey, but on joining the 65th Lancashire Rifle Volunteers, they acquired a brass band, and exchanged their grey for scarlet. A contemporary account of a Military Review attended by the school contingent gives a good idea of the hilarious atmosphere that sometimes prevailed:

"We were now in rear of the hostile battery, and our friend the Inspector rode up and ordered us to take the guns. This just suited our idea of fun and what a sham fight should be, and we wheeled. I never heard an order to fix bayonets, but we all did. We were as excited as our empty stomachs permitted, and helter-skelter we went for the guns, and meant having them too. It was with much difficulty that we were stopped just in their rear. I don't think that officer will send schoolboys to charge again!
After that exploit we were marched to the rear, and formed behind an artillery battalion, which was and had been in square; the said battalion had refreshed in the town previously to the review, and not wisely.
The face fronting the enemy was ordered to fire, but the gentlemen on the other faces, in spite of the expostulations of their officers, began firing too, right in our faces, as we were some sixty yards in their rear. Presently a hurling sound over our heads announced the flight of a ramrod and then another one came. This was too hot, so our captain did not wait for orders to march us away."

Shrewsbury's military renaissance was this time (1860) striking but brief; and seventy boys out of one hundred and twenty volunteered. They did plenty of arms drill, went for long marches fortified by a drum and fife band, and rather oddly, elected their own officers. Lacking proper support, they were disbanded in 1863, and there was no corps for many years.

Then, in 1900 the Headmaster, Dr Moss, became convinced that there would be war with Germany before long, and he determined that his school should make its contribution. When, therefore he selected the Reverend F. Sergeant to start a new House , he made it a condition of appointment that he should revive and command the Corps.

Another clerical C.O., the Reverend T.G. Vivyan, had appeared at Charterhouse in 1873. The school had recently moved from the city of London, and it seemed natural that they should take advantage of their new, more spacious, surroundings. Their beginnings, however, were humble and "the only shooting was at glass bottles in a backyard in the Pepperharrow Road". Even this seems to have been of little avail because in 1874, on their first appearance at Wimbledon for the Ashburton Shield, out of the 140 shots fired by the Charterhouse team, only 63 hit the target.

This was soon put to rights, however, and in 1882 and 1883 they came first in the competition. This was the more surprising, as numbers had fallen so catastrophically that on one parade in 1880 six officers and only four men had put in an appearance. A new C.O. injected fresh life into the Corps, and by 1892 Charterhouse had won the Ashburton Shield for the fourth year in succession and were treated to a grand civic reception.

Winchester's Volunteers (1860) adopted a uniform of grey with black facings and braid, completed by knickerbockers, which, if slightly unmilitary, at least possessed sovereign qualities of durability. Elsewhere, shooting was generally regarded as a useful carrot for keeping up the numbers of the Corps, but a fiery correspondent in the Wykehamist (1867) drew attention to the dangers of the situation:

"Owing to the extremely undisciplined state of the Corps and the foolish and expensive practice of continuing the shooting throughout the year, it is a fact that some of the most untidy and round-shouldered members of the School are in the Rifle Corps".

He then made a plea for more drill, and the claims that he makes for drill would arouse much amazement in any age:
"A good day's drill over good country is certainly as enjoyable as a day's shooting; there is always an endless variety about drill, always something new to be learnt which makes it exceedingly enjoyable."
Such words from the lips of a Drill-Sergeant today, might cast doubts on his sobriety.

It is interesting that the future Field Marshal Wavell was extremely reluctant to join the Winchester Cadet Corps. He argued, with commendable logic, that he would get quite enough drill when he became a professional soldier.

In 1860 a Rifle Corps was started at Repton, and a contemporary account (H.V. Pears 1872) suggests a rather light-hearted approach to the business.
"In my time the officers wore 'Caps of Honour' (velvet) and the rest of the Corps wore Hallite football caps, dark blue with white star; non-Hallites used to borrow caps from small Hallites. Officers wore white flannel shirts and the rest red football shirts. We used to fire percussion caps and blow out candles with them in the studies. The rifles were kept in racks (in the front hall at the Hall) and in the other houses. The three officers were, I think, the three head boys in the school, and the non-commissioned were elected by the Corps. We only soldiered in the autumn term (from 2 to 3 on Tuesdays and Thursdays) and there was a march-out and a Review every year with a real Volunteer band for the occasion"

The Corps at Repton ceased to function in 1875 and was not revived till 1900 when the Boer War disasters began to throw considerable doubts upon British military skills.

Marlborough in 1859 formed the M.C.R.V.C. and adopted a suitably functional uniform, which could be transformed into a plain grey flannel suit on the removal of the decorative braid. A slightly antique flavour characterised the fire power which was represented by old Police Carbines, and one of the officers who had last seen action at Waterloo. The Corps ran into some tough times till in 1890 the Command was assumed by the Reverend W.H. Chappel. A signalling squad and a cycling section were now added, lectures were given by distinguished soldiers, and a drill competition instituted on an inter-house basis.

In 1875 a Rifle Corps was started at Clifton under the command of Colonel E.C. Plant, the Art Master. It was officially attached to the British Engineer Corps, and masters who joined were given the rank of Sappers. This was the moment of the school's particular preoccupation with cricket, and there was widespread indignation when some musketry practice took place during the match against Cheltenham. By 1895, however, Clifton had a drum and fife band, and had won the Ashburton Shield.

At Haileybury a rather dreary note is struck in a Notice which reads: "From 2.30 till CallOn Tuesday, Thursday, and Saturday Sergeant Bryant, with one or two Masters in occasional attendance, instructs fifty or sixty stalwarts on the Terrace."

St. Peter's, York, were more zealous. Here, in 1860, a Volunteer Corps was formed as the result of the unbounded enthusiasm of a master, F.M. Scargill, the son of a General. Big boys, it is recorded, had rifles; small boys carried short swords which proved very useful as toasting-forks.

At Magdalen College School a Rifle Corps was formed in 1871. "A gallant band", writes a former member, "of some fifty boys, mostly small, who were ready to go anywhere and do anything. We wore a uniform of very dark blue, a busby of imitation astrakhan, with a blue and black plume, carbines, and the long sword-bayonets in black belts, and frogs. We fancied ourselves in this uniform quite a lot, though looking back on things, it was a ridiculous dress and particularly ugly."

Some friendly advice in the school magazine throws a little light on the problems that beset the unit:

"We must ask all members of the Corps to observe absolute silence in the ranks, as, otherwise, they cannot give their whole attention, which is a *sine qua non* in learning drill. They must also listen for the word of command, and when they have received it, act upon it without delay, as by so doing they will render it much easier for the Officers in command to rectify any mistakes they may have committed; and we must also ask those of the School who do not belong to the Corps, but who are led by their patriotic feelings to accompany it in its parades, to preserve a respectful distance, and on no account to attract the attention of those in the ranks."
The Corps appears to have lapsed about 1880.

Bradfield in 1883 was concerned not for national defence, but for school discipline: The Headmaster, Doctor Gray, thought that a quasi-military organization might cure the boys of "slouching". They soon smartened up in their uniforms of scarlet with green facings, and the school's successes in the Ashburton Shield, which they won outright in 1897, provided a further incentive to recruitment.

In general, any kind of military activity was something of a frail and delicate plant in the life of a school. To the average boy, it generally seemed to be neither work nor play, but simply an unwelcome invasion of his leisure. The excitement of a national emergency or the burning enthusiasm of an outstanding commander, evoked a lively enough response, and the large majority of the army officers came from the Public Schools.

A typical list from Sandhurst in 1885 shows that of 304 cadets, 27 came from the universities and 211 from the Public schools. Of these, 189 had been assisted by a crammer, whose services were almost invariably required to bridge the gap between school and Sandhurst or Woolwich.

= = = = = = = = = = =

CHAPTER 12

SEX

"It was half past nine at night and the lower school had gone to bed, but there was Wildney quietly sitting on Eric's knee by the study fire."

(Dean Farrar: Eric or Little by Little)

"I should say that the majority of women (happily for them) are not very much troubled by sexual feelings of any kind."
(William Acton (1813-75), medical expert)

When in 1760 Lord Hinchinbroke was served with a paternity order by a woman of Windsor, the Headmaster, Dr Barnard, gave him a severe flogging. Such an offence, in his eyes, amounted simply to a serious breach of school rules, in much the same category as drunkenness or breaking bounds. In the next century a much stricter moral climate came to prevail, and there was a sharp reaction against the sexual permissiveness of the 18th Century. Headmasters, fired by the fervour of Dr Arnold of Rugby, began to take their spiritual duties much more seriously, and to be concerned, as never before, with such issues as moral purity. Indeed, as the century wore on, one could almost say that this, and not discipline, was likely to be a Headmaster's chief anxiety.

At first, as for Arnold and those who followed his lead, purity was simply part of the armour of a Christian gentleman who was brought up to abhor vices such as lying, blasphemy, drunkenness and gambling. But gradually the word came to have a specifically sexual connotation, much as 'immorality' does with us today. It was in their campaign for sexual purity that the Victorian Headmasters laid themselves most open to modern criticism. But before we join in the general chorus of disapproval it should be remembered that most modern critics occupy a much more untenable position when they suggest that schoolboy sexuality was a largely Victorian development greatly accelerated by organised games. The schoolboys of earlier ages must surely have been just as sexually oriented as their descendants.

Confirmation, if needed, can be found in the stories about Charterhouse in the 1820s referred to by Ann Konsarrat in a recent biography of Thackeray:

"Years later, when Leech had grown into a tall, distinguished and eminently successful cartoonist, they - Leech and Thackeray - mulled over the corruption rife in their shared academy for the edification of colleagues at Punch's weekly dinners, recalling the pornographic literature which had found its way into their hallowed cloisters, and the fresh innocent voices of their contemporaries singing bawdy songs, which few of them understood:"

Sydney Smith's observation that the only way public schools prevented boys being corrupted by the world was by corrupting them before they got out into it, was borne out by another story Thackeray told at Punch. One of the first orders he had received from a senior boy at Charterhouse, he said, 'Come and frig me.' What changed, of course, was not the boys themselves but the Headmasters, who now made a high moral issue of what had previously been accepted or ignored.

Thus Thring of Uppingham enters in his Diary (1871): "Yesterday I was in a fearful dread that I had got into a nest of indecency." By 1885 deep anxiety about these matters had become for every Headmaster an overriding concern.

Thring writes again:
"At nine I had all the Communicants in the Upper School to speak to on the subject of lust. I consider the half-ignorance so deadly that once a year I speak openly to the whole school, divided into three sets. The consequence is that the whole school have virtually pledged themselves to put down all indecency as a school offence."

Unfortunately, Thring did not speak as openly to his diary as he claims to have done to the school, with the result that we are left a little uncertain as to exactly what he meant by 'indecency'. His expression 'a nest of indecency' perhaps suggests that he had in mind any kind of communal sexual activity.

Two of Benson's toughest fights at Wellington were over matters of immorality. Benson was not empowered to expel boys without the Governors' permission, but he was entitled to induce parents to withdraw their sons privately. This procedure was applied in 1861 to a boy who had "struck another boy in an indecent manner", and in 1872 to three boys who had committed offences with a serving-maid during the holidays, "as a result of which the eldest contracted a shameful disease, and younger two, being immature, escaped physical consequences".

In both of these cases the Governors attempted to overrule Benson, but in vain. It is interesting to note that Benson was able to call for support from the Headmasters of Eton, Harrow, Winchester, Rugby, and Marlborough, the Bishops of Durham and Manchester, and Charles Kingsley, while the Governors considered that Benson was being inordinately fussy. The Duke of Wellington described the first offence as "merely an indecent lark in public", and C.W.Penny (a great admirer of Benson), complained a propos of the 1872 affair that the Governors: "had acted like a pack of cynical, hoary old sinners, who looked on youthful immorality as a sort of complaint, like measles."

By this time references to sex began to appear in the school rules, and at Haileybury (1894) impersonation of females in school plays was expressly forbidden, as were also bare legs on the football field. Dr Percival of Rugby was the object of some criticism for the rule he made in the early 90's that boys playing football must wear shorts that covered the knee. It has been suggested that he feared the sight of bare knees might excite the lust of other boys, or even of himself.

The full force of the purity campaign fell heaviest on the new boys on their first day at school, just when they were least fitted to receive it or even to understand it. Dr Warre of Eton (1884) used to harangue his youthful flock like an Old Testament prophet,

denouncing sinners before all the Tribe:
"Beware the evil thing, that which defiles, and let us shun the abomination in our midst. Have none of it: don't touch it: stamp it out."

Reading this today, we can guess that the speaker's reference was probably to self-abuse, but most of his trembling new boys on their first day at School were unlikely to know what he was talking about.

It is only too evident that in this matter, which they regarded as being of tremendous importance, such Headmasters shared the conventional Victorian view of sex as being a painful compound of evil and mystery. Marriage, if it came, provided an apocalyptic revelation, but before that, ignorance was innocence and that was all they knew on earth and all they needed to know. Yet to us it seems something of an anomaly that an age so full-blooded and virile as the Victorian should in this one matter be so tongue-tied and inhibited. At a time when London had more prostitutes than any city in the world, when countless wives died young, worn out by childbearing, sex remained for many men either a deadly secret or a dirty joke.

Gladstone himself provided the most striking illustration of this conspiracy of silence on sexual matters. His nocturnal perambulations over many years among the London prostitutes, however worthy his intentions may have been, provided his enemies with enough evidence to destroy any prime minister of England. But the lips of his would-be accusers were as firmly sealed as those of his closest friends.

Thring himself considered that a single letter from his father had established his own position in this matter for his lifetime, and a similar practice among fathers seems to have been fairly general. Lord Lyttelton wrote identically the same letter to each of his six sons, being careful to conclude each with the firm statement that he would never again make any further reference to this matter.

On the female side, ignorance and prudery were carried to even more preposterous lengths. Not only did well-brought up Victorian maidens enter upon marriage in a state of total ignorance of the facts of life, but the married women themselves seem to have spread the myth that ladies do not enjoy sex: they merely endure it, reluctantly, in obedience to their husbands. This attitude was reported upon good medical authority, which can only have been based on evidence given to doctors by the women themselves.

The task of Headmasters, then, seemed to be not to transmit information or give advice but, simply to utter dire warnings. This they did very faithfully in chapel sermons, school hall harangues and study indictments in the case of actual offenders. In this context, scholarly men who had a high regard for the truth, delivered themselves of passionate tirades which had, in reality, no basis of truth at all. Masturbation was represented as being inevitably followed by venereal disease in its most terrifying forms, and moral leprosy was a term freely applied to the trembling offenders.

The question may well be asked: why should these Headmasters have behaved so monstrously in this matter? The answer may be that they over-reacted deliberately with the mistaken idea that they would be likelier to achieve their aim if they exaggerated the effects of their warnings. Over-reaction after all, is common enough with schoolmasters who have to punish disobedience to rules and regulations. It is a normal part of authority's defence mechanism.

Another explanation is offered with some hesitation. We know that a few Headmasters were personally conscious of the power of the sins and temptations which they denounced. Thus there may have been an element of self-loathing in those judgments which they called down on the heads of the young sinners. This may seem a fanciful explanation, but it is a fact that the rigid monastic regime of the 19th Century boarding schools produced, as was inevitable, a certain number of casualties, and that in a few cases Headmasters were numbered among them.

Dr Percival of Clifton was for many years tormented by nightmares. Doctor Benson, later Headmaster of Wellington, solemnly pledged his troth to a ten year-old girl when he himself was twenty-seven. The eventual marriage was, to say the least of it, a highly unusual one, and it probably imposed a heavy strain upon him. Often he found himself deprived of his wife at a time when he needed her most.

What we do know is that there was a strong if misguided body of medical opinion to which Victorian sex attitudes were related. An eminent figure was William Acton (1813- 1875) a London specialist, whose books on sexual matters were highly praised in the Lancet, translated into French, and went into a number of editions in America. His views on the effects of self-abuse in the young would be almost incredible if we did not have them in cold print. This is his description of a boy who habitually masturbated:

"The frame is stunted and weak, the muscles undeveloped, the eye is sunken and heavy, the complexion is sallow, pasty, or covered with spots of acne, the hands are damp and cold, and the skin moist. The boy shuns the society of others, creeps about alone, joins with repugnance in the amusements of his school Fellows. He cannot look anyone in the face, and becomes careless in dress and uncleanly in person. His intellect has become sluggish and enfeebled, and if his evil habits are persisted in, he may end in becoming a drivelling idiot or a peevish valetudinarian. Such boys are to be seen in all stages of degeneration, but what we have described is but the result towards which *they all* are tending."

Not content with this awesome warning, Acton paints a further description of the ultimate effect of adult insanity:

"Apathy, loss of memory, abeyance of concentrative power and manifestation of mind generally, combined with loss of self-reliance, and indisposition for, or impulsiveness of, action, irritability of temper, and incoherence of language, are the most characteristic mental phenomena of chronic dementia resulting from masturbation in young men."

It is possible to see an explanation in this of what would otherwise be a farrago of nonsense. Acton had enough of the Victorian puritan in him to believe firmly that sex was sin. He was also even further than we are from being able to diagnose the cause of insanity, and the temptation to brand insanity as the penalty of sin proved irresistible to him once again.

When the House-system was fully established, the Housemaster now associated himself with sex-instruction and some degree of improvement resulted. Talks were no longer entirely confined to Head magisterial threats in Assemblies, but could be given in the more relaxed atmosphere of the Housemaster's study. But the limiting factor here was often the Housemaster himself who almost certainly embarked on these talks with considerable reluctance and embarrassment. His utterances, through agitated clouds of tobacco smoke, were often couched in accents of such Delphic ambiguity that they left the youthful auditors no wiser than before.

Such closing advice as never to talk of anything that they would not care to discuss in front of their mother or sister can have given boys little help or comfort.

There was one area of the problem, male friendships, in which there was a marked change between mid and late Victorian attitudes. Tennyson's love for his friend Hallam was accepted on all sides as an ideal relationship, properly consecrated after Hallam's death by a lifetime of mourning and dedicated grief. Charles Kingsley writes of his Cambridge friend C.B. Mansfield, "He was my first love: the first human being, save my mother, I ever met who knew what I meant"

Dickens's most famous novel puts David Copperfield and the handsome Steerforth on a nobly tragic plane, for the generous protector of the youthful Copperfield stoops finally to folly and is destroyed.

Disraeli in Coningsby (1847) apostrophises such relationships in a lyrical passage:

"At school, friendship is a passion. It entrances the being; it tears the soul. All loves of after life can never bring its rapture, or its wretchedness, no bliss so absorbing, no pangs of jealousy or despair so crushing and so keen! What tenderness and what devotion; what illimitable confidence; infinite revelations of inmost thoughts, are confined in that simple phrase - a schoolboy's friendship! 'Tis some indefinite recollection of these mystic passages of their young emotion, that makes grey-haired men mourn over the memory of their schoolboy days. It is a spell that can soften the acerbity of political warfare, and with its witchery can call forth a sigh even amid the callous bustle of fashionable saloon."

Two rather different views of this relationship appear in school stories written in the mid 19th Century, *Eric or Little by Little* and *Tom Brown's Schooldays*. *Eric*, by Dean Farrar, has been very properly derided for its linguistic absurdities, but the following extract is worth attention for the light it throws on relationships between young and older boys. Eric has risen to the dignity of a study and Wildney is a younger boy whom he has "taken up".

"Eric soon learned to like Wildney, who was a very bright, engaging, spirited boy, with a dash of pleasant impudence about him which took Eric's fancy. He had been one of the most mischievous of the Lower Fellows, but, although clever, he did little or nothing in school, and was in the worst repute with the masters. Until he was "taken up" by Eric, he had been a regular little hero among his compeers, because he was game for any kind of mischief and, in the new tone of popular morality, his fearless disregard of rules made him the object of general admiration. From this time, however, he was much in the studies, and unhappily carried with him to those upper regions the temptation to a deeper and more injurious class of transgressions than had penetrated there.

It was an ill day for General Wildney when he sent his idolized little son to Roslyn; it was an ill day for Eric when Duncan first asked the child to frequent their study. It was past nine at night, and the lower school had gone to bed, but there was Wildney quietly sitting on Eric's knee by the study fire, while Duncan was doing some of Arnold's verses for him to be shown up next day."

The spectacle of a junior boy sitting on a senior's boy's knee would cause some raised eyebrows in the later 19th Century, and it is also notable that the small boy is seen as the offender. He is the one to lead his elders astray. In the Tom Brown extract, Tom Brown and his friend East lay hands roughly on a Wildney-type boy.

" 'Hullo, tho', that's past a joke,' broke out East, springing at the young gentleman who addressed them and catching him by the collar. 'Here, Tommy, catch hold of him t'other side before he can holla.'
The youth was seized, and dragged struggling out of the quadrangle into the School-house Hall. He was one of the miserable little pretty white-handed curly-headed boys, petted and pampered by some of the big Fellows, who wrote their verses for them, taught them to drink and use bad language, and did all they could to spoil them for everything in this world and the next."

But the footnote comes to the rescue of the 'small friend system', as the author remembers that the main theme of the book is to be the redemption of Tom by Arthur, the saintly new boy, who weans him away from swearing and cribbing. But in neither book is there any hint of the sexual corruption in this kind of relationship that the later Headmasters sniffed on every breeze.

The battle to keep sex out of the schools was scarcely assisted by the Greek and Latin literature which formed such a large part of the schools' curriculum. The following extract from a session of the Public Schools' Commission is a fair sample of the arguments stirred up by this question. Dr Hessey of Merchant Taylors is here being interrogated by Mr Vaughan on the problems of reading Catullus with his boys.

Q. With an author of that stamp how do you manage the extreme difficulty with regard to his obscenity?
A. All the particular odes that I have selected are comparatively free from that blemish.

Q. Do you put your hand on a particular ode and say 'do not read this, read that'?
A. Some of his odes are no doubt very bad, but we take for instance his first or second ode one day and then possibly the next day we take the 11th ode.

Q. Do you give any reason for passing over the others?
A. I give no reason whatever, but of course the boys understand why they are passed over.

Q. Do you think the boys do not read them?
A. I think the gross odes of Catullus are so gross and the Latin so hard that even if they had the bad taste they would hardly take the trouble.

Q. You think they do not read the objectionable odes?
A. I do not think they do.

It is hard for us to imagine young schoolboys averting their gaze in distaste from an ode that has been indicated to them as unsuitable for their reading. A much less confident note on this subject is sounded by William Acton. He first explains his rather surprising view that the young remain for a long time in a state of complete innocence:

"Thus it happens that with most healthy and well brought up children, no sexual note or feeling has ever entered their heads, even in the way of speculation. I believe that such children's curiosity is seldom excited on these subjects except where they have been purposely suggested."

Having such great faith in primal innocence of mind, Acton then goes on to give a warning on the subject of pollution by means of unsuitable books:

"He *(the boy)* reads in terms of the pleasures, nothing of the penalties of sexual indulgences. He is not intuitively aware that if the sexual desires are excited, it will require greater power of will to master them than falls to the lot of most lads; that if indulged in, the man will and must pay the penalty for the errors of the boy; that for one that escapes, ten will suffer."

It would be true to say that somewhere between 1860 and 1885 the climate of opinion about male relationships underwent a further change, for which the Public Schools were partly responsible. Hitherto, the general attitude in these matters had been what one might describe as Shakespearean in its frankness and absence of inhibition. Tears both of grief and joy were shed by men without embarrassment, physical contacts were eagerly and naturally sought, and emotions were deeply felt and freely displayed.

At a Military Court Martial in 1833 when the accused Captain Wathen made reference to having fought at Waterloo, "many veterans in the court were observed to shed tears". It is hard to imagine such a reaction fifty years later. It had become the age of the stiff upper lip; and tears, even of the manly variety, were not permitted. It is reasonable to see in this the influence of Public School values. Discipline, law and order had been successfully imposed on these schools, and emotional self-control had been established as a cardinal virtue.

The change indeed went deeper still, and a chill wind started to blow where hitherto the atmosphere had been relatively genial and unrestrained. In the claustrophobic conditions of the boarding schools not only did friendships between boys of different ages, which had hitherto been regarded as beneficial, become suspect, but certain teacher-pupil relationships began to exhibit disquieting features.

At Eton William Cory, generally regarded as the College's most successful Tutor, gloried in platonic love between males and wrote pederastic poetry lamenting the deaths of beautiful young men; and Oscar Browning, a Housemaster, was dismissed in 1877 because of his relationship with the boys.

Arthur Sidgwick at Rugby and Henry Dakyns at Clifton were close friends of John Addington Symonds and in early days may have appeared to share his tastes. What they were can be best explained by a brief examination of the Symonds story, because of the allegations he makes against both his school (Harrow) and Dr Vaughan, the Headmaster. The account which follows, is based largely on Miss Phyllis Grosskurth's recent biography of John Addington Symonds.

Symonds was the son of a well-known Bristol doctor and was at Harrow from 1854 to 1858 before proceeding to Balliol College, Oxford. He was a very clever, highly sensitive boy and he found his school-Fellows extremely uncongenial. Looking back at the school in 1866, he says of it in a letter:
"The seeds of vice, sown long ago in this fruitful soil, continue to propagate themselves like mushrooms on a dunghill".
But much more serious than Symonds's aspersions on his Fellows is the actual fact that he was instrumental in forcing the resignation of Dr Vaughan.

During his last year at school he received a note from a friend named Pretor, saying that he was having an affair with Dr Vaughan, and that he had a number of passionate letters from him. A year later, when Symonds was at Oxford, he mentioned this to a don with whom he had become friendly. The don urged him to refer the matter to his father.
Dr Symonds was deeply shocked, and wrote to Dr Vaughan saying he had Pretor's letter and asking for the Headmaster's resignation.

If he agreed to this, Dr Symonds undertook not
to make the matter public, but he warned Vaughan that he would
expose him if he accepted a bishopric.

Vaughan travelled down to Bristol, and agreed to the doctor's
terms. He subsequently resigned on the plea of ill-health, and, was
offered a bishopric two years later. He accepted but then
withdrew, obviously once more under the pressure of Dr
Symonds. (He was, however, allowed to become Dean of
Llandaff.)

It is a strange and tragic story, and also highly relevant.
If it is true, it is a serious reflection upon one of England's great
schools - vicious boys and a corrupt Headmaster. But while
the outline of the story is indisputable, it is unfortunate that we
have only Symonds as a witness, who, after leaving Harrow
became, on his own confession, a practising homosexual. His
judgments on his Fellows are obviously somewhat suspect, and
although Vaughan condemned himself by his resignation,
the full extent of his offence remains a matter for speculation.
His letters to Pretor are mentioned, but their contents remain
in doubt. In fact, no written evidence beyond the one letter of
Pretor's seems to have been produced. Dr Vaughan put a
final seal on further enquiry by directing in his will that all his
papers were to be burnt and no biography written.

There is no doubt, however, that the deep soil of Victorian
sexual repressions and fears was starting to produce some strange
and evil-scented flowers. London had for long been notorious for
its vast number of prostitutes; and now, in addition, there
appeared brothels where male patrons paid large sums to be beaten
by comely females. Male vices and perversions were now carried
on a flowing tide of pornographic literature, aided and abetted by
influences from across the channel. The implications were now
very different from those that had disturbed England at the end of

the previous century. No strident voices cried out for the overthrow of tyranny, but the siren songs of Baudelaire and the French decadents made their subtle challenge to Victorian values in life and literature.

In 1885 an extra clause was added to the Criminal Law Amendment Act. Homosexual acts now became criminal, even if committed in private, and there was further publicity in this matter as a result of the Oscar Wilde trial, and a markedly hostile attitude to homosexuality was maintained until the Wolfenden Report (1957).

So would it be true to say that a problem hardly known to exist in the 18th century reached the proportions of a national scandal in the next century? How wide-spread and how serious was this problem in the schools? Generalising is extremely dangerous in such matters, but it is difficult to believe that sexual tortures and the rape of young boys occurred at more than a very few schools. As to the much publicised cult of romantic friendships, this was obviously much more widely spread, though its intensity varied greatly from school to school. The wildest assertions about it in this generation have been made by modern writers, who have vied with one another in portraying the agonies and the ecstasies of their classroom passions.

E.F. Benson, educated at Marlborough in Late Victorian days, gives his testimony:

"For 12 or 13 weeks three times a year they live exclusively among boys and that at a time when their vigour is at its strongest. Naturally there is a danger about it (for what emotion worth having is not encompassed by perils?) and a strong threat of affection may easily explode into fragments of mere sensuality, be dissipated in mere 'smut', and from being a banner in the clean wind be trampled into mud. But promiscuous immorality was, as far as I am aware, quite foreign to the school, though we flamed into a hundred hot bonfires of these friendships."

The whole subject seems to call for some final general statements. It is difficult to see how far the changing public view of sex is subjective and how far objective. Has sexual behaviour changed or have our attitudes to it changed? Public opinion has certainly changed, and as children are part of the public just as much as adults are, their opinions have changed too. To the average boy of the day which Dean Farrar describes, the picture of Wildney sitting on Eric's knee in his study would doubtless have been unsurprising; to many of his successors, forty, fifty or sixty years ago the picture would have been good for a salacious giggle; most boys today would probably find it funny in a quaint, archaic way or - if sufficiently sophisticated - would be tickled by Farrar's unawareness of the implications.

As for sexual behaviour, we may take it for granted that human urges have not greatly altered, nor has the proportion of boys whose instincts are homosexual rather than heteroexual. What has altered from time to time are the reactions of society to the manifestations of these urges.

The ancient Greeks often awarded the highest honours to male lovers, whether tyrannicides or patriots, but the Christian Church, following the Judaic philosophy, in its determination to improve the status of women, from the very first categorically denounced such practices. It is hardly surprising, therefore, that in Victorian and Edwardian days quasi-monastic iron curtains and moral artillery of a very heavy calibre went into play. This probably had the effect of stimulating homosexual activity even among those to whom it did not come naturally.

In today's permissive atmosphere, it is probably just to say that though plenty of people may disapprove, the restraints applied to the sexual behaviour of the young are, in general, only those which they themselves recognise as reasonable and proper.

As to adult homosexuality, in spite of classical precedents and the shifting standards of our age, a bedrock of disapproval and distrust still remains. The modern view seems to be that homosexuality is frequently a psycho-physical phase through which some pass without being conscious of it, but a few people of both sexes are born with a bias which makes homosexual behaviour as natural to them as heterosexual is to the majority.

In view of the relatively high incidence today of homosexuality in the worlds of affluence and public entertainment, it is hard to avoid the conclusion that education in itself plays a very small part in this problem .

CHAPTER 13

EPIDEMICS

"Those poor continentals: why, there is scarcely a sanely-living man among the lot, so far as I can learn from those who have been abroad."
(Almond of Loretto, in a letter on healthy living)

"It seems as if gentlemen send their sons to school as much to have scarlet fever as to learn Latin - and with much more certainty of catching the fever than the Latin.!"
(Florence Nightingale)

We often smile unbelievingly at the death-bed scene of the Victorian novel in which a blameless child expires, surrounded by his weeping family. Yet it is true that death at an early age was a common occurrence of Victorian middle-class life.

The reasons for this were many, and not least in importance was the primitive state of the drainage system. Britain had not yet faced the full implications of the Industrial Revolution with its crowded factories, slums and concentrations of population. The boarding schools throughout the nineteenth century lay in the shadow of infection or pollution. Dr Keate himself caught typhus in 1825, and cholera dispersed Rugby in 1832.

In June 1841 Doctor Arnold wrote to his sister:
" Very anxious about their (*boys*) health. One boy died from pressure on the brain, another within the last week of a fever, and a third, who went home, is also dead. Four more boys were, at different times, at the point of death"
In the event, one master and seven boys died from what was probably typhoid. The School was closed, and Arnold, together with several of the sixth form escaped to his house in the Lake District.

Florence Nightingale, in her Crimean War days, was a noble and heroic figure; but in the years that followed, she exhibited a distressing narrowness of outlook. Because overcrowding and lack of ventilation in the Crimean hospitals were the major causes of disease and death, she came to believe that these factors were the only two aspects of illness worthy of attention. She scorned the discoveries of Pasteur and Lister as "germ fetish", and regarded infection as little more than an unproved theory.
Her message was a simple one: "Don't overcrowd, and keep your windows open."

When appealed to for advice on the building of a Sanatorium at Bradfield, she wrote:
"If we were asked to provide an Infirmary for 25 beds upon a population of 150, we should begin by asking: what horrible sanitary wrong is there at home to be put right that you must accommodate so many sick people?

If they really ever have such an amount of Scarlet Fever or any sick as 25 to 150 there should be a most serious enquiry into the sanitary state of the school."

After a scornful reference to the deplorable state of the Rugby Sanatorium, she added a sarcastic postscript:
"It seems that gentlemen send their sons to school as much to have Scarlet Fever as to learn Latin; and with far more certainty of catching the Fever than the Latin."

Scarlet fever, a mild disease at the beginning of the century, steadily developed into a killer, and the home itself was sometimes no refuge. In 1856 scarlet fever claimed the lives of five daughters of Dr Tait, former Headmaster of Rugby, in the Deanery at Carlisle. They all died under the age of eleven and they all died within five weeks of each other. Two sons of Dr Moberly died of it in Winchester in 1858 and 1871, and Kilvert's Diary speaks of the deaths of three Marlborough boys in 1870. There then seems to have been a lull, followed by outbreaks in 1886; and two years later it was authoritatively reported that eleven southern schools had broken up as a result of scarlet fever and diphtheria.

Dr Fry, ultimately a famous Dean of Lincoln, had the distressing experience as Headmaster of Oundle, of moving from one infected area to another. Twelve months after his appointment as Headmaster of Oundle (1884), he complained that he and his wife were continually ill as a result of living in such unhealthy surroundings. The water, he said, was undrinkable, and there were frequent outbreaks of chicken pox, measles and, scarlet fever. He therefore resigned and was soon appointed Headmaster of Berkhamsted.

Hardly had he settled in there before the school-town drainage syndrome started again, and Fry began writing to the authorities complaining that :

"the pipes conveying the sewage into the river caused the stream to be at all times dangerous, producing horrible smells, causing illness in the School, and occasioning me deep anxiety."

Furious scenes followed at the Public Inquiry in the Town Hall, and the affronted townsmen at one moment threatened the Headmaster with a ducking in the horse-trough. It seems likely that some of the local residents had a partial immunity to water infection, having been exposed to it for so long, and they refused to believe the Headmaster's comments. Indeed, local witnesses appeared before the Clarendon Commission who were ready to testify that they could not imagine healthier surroundings than those provided at Westminster when the Thames was at its most pestilential and polluted.

So we see that many factors contributed to the sorry tale of schoolboy deaths from preventable causes, but a more detailed study of the experiences at two schools will help us to understand many aspects of the situation as it may have existed in others.

When scarlet fever struck Uppingham in October 1875, Thring's initial reaction was highly characteristic. Parents should only be allowed to take their sons away under very special circumstances, and boys in general should not be allowed to 'run away' from sickness. Those who did so were branded as 'deserters'. His over-riding idea seems to have been not to save the lives of individual boys but to resist at all costs the closure of the school, which would mean to him the destruction of his life's work.

In his diary he writes:
"But it is not a right condition of things, this weakness of schools, which makes even a strong school a prey to the apothecary and his following."

Even his prayers show his priorities:
"Give me not over for a prey unto their teeth (*Apothecaries*) and spare my boys, O Lord. "

Desperate defiance is sounded in the Order to the School: "No boy will be permitted to go home on the bare receipt of a telegram.."

There was, however, a sudden change of mind on the receipt of an official report from the Health Authority in London that the Uppingham water was definitely contaminated. Thring now laid it down at the next Masters' Meeting that if the School Doctor pronounced that a boy was seriously ill, the parents were to be informed. One cannot help feeling amazed that this was not already the rule. Thring next vented the full fury of his wrath upon the local Sanitary Authorities who had allowed this to happen. "The most insulting thing I ever knew; altogether this is a time of humiliation and sackcloth".

When Thring was eventually compelled to disband the school, he attacked the Local Government Board in a lengthy petition, in which he stressed the pecuniary loss to himself and his masters as ratepayers in the loss of fees resultant upon the untimely withdrawal of the school. Strangely enough, he seems to have felt no regret, still less a sense of guilt, that he had not sent the boys home earlier and possibly saved a life thereby. In a statement to the Press he declared:
"Therefore it is not my intention under any conceivable circumstances of illness to break up the school by a public act."

He notes in his diary that some of the parents think his pronouncements are dictatorial. They certainly seem to have been ill-judged, for when a further report from London declared that a sample from Uppingham had indicated polluted water, Thring was compelled to eat his words and break up the school.

Worse was to come. After the school had reassembled for the Easter Term a case of typhoid was diagnosed on February 20th. Thring now acted quickly and decisively. All parents were circularised, and the remaining boys in the house concerned sent home. On March 2nd there was another case of typhoid, and the same procedure was followed.

Thring was now near to despair: "Unless steps are taken in London", he wrote in his diary, "the school is done for."
At a Masters' meeting, however, somebody mentioned the word 'migration', and Thring quickly clutched at the idea as the only lifeline left to him. Another case of typhoid forced him to disband the school again, but he immediately followed this up with a circular to the parents saying that the school would reassemble in three weeks' time at a place as yet unknown which would, at least, be healthy.

The place eventually selected was Borth, a small seaside resort near Aberystwith. A hotel capable of housing two hundred was taken over, and the remaining hundred boys billeted in surrounding houses. It was a remarkable feat of organisation, and yet little enthusiasm for the project was shown by the School Trustees, who sanctioned it with reluctance. The school adjusted well to the new environment, but fate was to deal Thring another heavy blow. After a few months had passed, three boys went down with the dreaded scarlet fever.

A lesser man might have taken this as a sign that he had lost the battle, but not so Thring. He continued to struggle undeterred until in due course the epidemic was brought under control and all the patients recovered. His altercation with the Trustees soon took a new turn when they started urging him to bring the school back to Uppingham, and he kept refusing to do so on the grounds that insufficient improvements had been made to the Town drains.

Dramatic emphasis was laid on this fact by the death from typhoid early in the New Year, of the Chairman of the local Sanitary Board. This seems to have worried the Board more than the death of a schoolboy, and they were now shocked into making some real improvement in the sewage arrangements; and finally Thring agreed to take the School back for the Summer Term of 1877.

This long and bitter struggle had well illustrated some of the most important features of Victorianism: the ignorance of hygiene that led to the pollution and infection; the reluctance of local bodies to spend money on what seemed to them to be trivial and unimportant; the strong conviction that boys should prove their manhood by facing sickness and not running away from it. Above all, Thring showed himself to be a typical Victorian in his belligerence, his energy, his powers of organisation and his all-pervading sense of God's purpose. When a boy died for whom he had prayed the previous day, he entered in his diary:

"God had taken little Cecil Mullins. I misinterpreted His will somewhat, but not the gracious answer to my prayer in the Spirit He gave me."

Wellington provides the most extraordinary and most tragic story of them all. Doctor Benson, the first Master, was a close friend of Frederick Temple, Headmaster of Rugby. In the course of letters exchanged between them in 1869, Temple, noting Benson's good fortune over the past ten years in such matters as school epidemics, jokingly advised him to follow the example of King Polycrates in the old Greek story and throw his ring into the lake for fear that the Gods might become jealous of his unbroken good fortune.

But soon afterwards the first blow fell on Benson.

Early in the Easter term of 1870 there was a scarlatina scare at Wellington. This disease was not only a potential killer but was also liable to leave a sufferer who recovered with some permanent disability. The first casualty by a strange stroke of irony was the School Doctor, Barford, who retired immediately to the Sanatorium for fear of infecting his pregnant wife. His medical duties were taken on by a retired practitioner from Wokingham, and a student called Robotham, who had been assistant to Barford, and was as yet unqualified.

This hardly seems a suitable team to cope with an emergency, and an emergency soon developed. Surprisingly enough, none of the three hundred and twenty boys caught scarlatina, but a boy named Alban died suddenly from a disease that could not be identified. He was the first Wellington boy to die at school, and the effect on the masters and boys was profound. Nine days later Benson preached a deeply moving sermon at the Memorial Service for Alban, and when the school filed out of Chapel they learned that another blow had fallen. A boy named Blacket-Orde was found dead with a window cord round his neck. He had been heard to complain of a blinding headache before the Memorial service, and though the cause of death was obscure, a verdict of accidental death was returned by the Coroner.

There was yet another tragedy to come. Several cases of blood-poisoning occurred in November of the same year, and one of these, William Marriott, died after four days' illness. His death was not only distressing in itself, but was indicative of a growing danger from infection and pollution.

The calamities of 1870 were temporarily forgotten in the succeeding stream of change and development at Wellington. In 1872 Benson resigned, to be succeeded by Doctor Wickham. For ten years Wickham concentrated on educational matters, but in 1882 he turned his attention to medical matters.

The Sanatorium was enlarged to take fifty beds, and a partially successful effort was made to restructure the medical staff. Doctor Barford, however, remained in charge; and when in March 1883 there was a severe outbreak of septic throats, he wrote an angry letter to the Lancet drawing attention to the unsuitability of the Wellington terrain for the maintenance of a boarding-school. The Governors were stung into activity by these words, and a leading sanitary engineer was entrusted with the task of overhauling and repairing the school drainage system. This was carried out at the heavy cost of £13,500. and pronounced to be perfectly safe. Some years now passed, and Doctor Barford eventually retired in favour of Doctor Armstrong, who was to give the school many years of sterling and indefatigable service.

First of all, however, he had to endure in 1891, a baptism of fire. In November, an epidemic of septic throats and tonsils broke out, and with thirty seven boys in the Sanatorium, eighteen became diptheria suspects. Doctor Armstrong acted very quickly, and Sir Andrew Clark, the Throat specialist, with Doctor Bristowe, Senior Physician at St. Thomas' Hospital, were summoned for consultation. Their verdict came as no surprise: the school was on the verge of a diptheria epidemic.

The Headmaster immediately gave orders for the school to disperse (December 2nd.) and arrangements were made to move to Malvern next term. Eventually, the diptheria claimed twenty three victims, of whom two died. A new examination of the drains was made, which, after the passage of only eight years, were found to be dangerously defective.

Hindsight is almost impossible to resist and it is difficult not to feel that much of all this mischief and misfortune was caused by ignorance, prejudice and a parsimony, which in some cases, was the direct result of an acute money shortage.

As a witness before the Public Schools' Commission, the Reverend F. Poynder of Charterhouse, admitted that his dormitories had no chimney ventilation, and when asked if he did not think that this would seriously reduce the amount of fresh air, he replied complacently that the servants had made no complaints about the atmosphere when they tidied the dormitories on the following morning.

In the same context, the Reverend A.P. Saunders revealed revealed that arrangements for an Isolation Sanatorium had broken down for minor administrative reasons and the Reverend C.C. James said that before the installation of an Isolation Sanatorium at Eton, masters had to run round Windsor in search of a house that would take in a fever patient. He then went on to complain bitterly about the finances of such a medical situation. £12,000 had been lent by the parents for this purpose, and the Headmaster had told the staff that after ten years £3,000 of this sum was still owing. The staff were then invited to contribute towards the liquidation of the debt, but they, quite rightly, refused because the Headmaster was unwilling to present any sort of balance sheet.

Money-shortage, or at least, unwillingness to pay, presumably accounted for the low standard of medical service available in most schools during this period. Some schools, giving hostages to fortune, had an irregular medical service, and some, like Sedbergh in 1874, possessed neither a Sanatorium nor a School Doctor. The town drains were said to be a hundred years out of date, and the water-supply, in spite of heavy rainfall, was exiguous.

Not for nothing was the School motto "Dura virum nutrix".

For a long time, indeed, it would seem that the attitude of Victorians in this matter was determined by two not dissimilar sentiments. There was what might be called the Fresh air-and-no-nonsense-about-germs school of thought, who looked to Florence Nightingale for authority; and there was also the Neo-Spartan school who attempted to deal with epidemics by refusing to acknowledge their existence.

This approach is well-illustrated by the words of the Glasgow father who wrote to his new-boy son at Uppingham when the scarlatina epidemic was at its height:
"Stick into your work and don't mind such a trifle."
Thring comments admiringly: "That is education."

As for the boys who paid such a grievous price for the failures of their elders, there is only the tribute of Housman's sombre lines to the young who fell in the First World War:

"Life, to be sure, is nothing much to lose;
But young men think it is, and we were young."

= = = = = = = = = = = =

EPILOGUE

The Public School system is a living organism which has been developing for some six centuries. Its objectives have changed with the years. Today some of them may seem to us good, some bad, and the extent to which these different objectives have been achieved has also varied. From Wykeham's day to ours there has no doubt been the target of 'education' in a general sense, but there has always been, implicit or explicit, a goal at which that education was directed. Wykeham and Henry VI were very conscious of the need to educate men to serve church and state, the clergy who constituted the Civil Service, and men like Wykeham himself. The Reformation produced a revolution in the status of the clergy, and the Renaissance a revolution in the literary content of education.

As the national tongues developed their own genius, Latin ceased to be the lingua franca of all educated men, and became the object of, and the material for, scholarship - which it has been ever since. The 18th century, for reasons described in Chapter 3 *(Corruption)*, saw the Public Schools dwindling purposelessly. In the 19th century the aim (to which a large and growing majority of the upper middle class subscribed) was to produce Christian gentlemen - the kind of men, in fact, needed to administer the growing British Empire, and to supply the priesthood which an increasingly serious-minded Church of England required.
We are back, in fact, to the 'Church and State' of Wykeham.

By the opening of the 20th century a decline in religious activity has begun, a wider variety of careers has opened up, and social considerations have loomed larger and larger. Now the two Great Wars have produced their shattering effects; the British Empire is one with Nineveh and Tyre; and only a minute proportion of Public School boys become clergymen.

As for the Public Schools, they are left as - what? Surviving defenders of standards of excellence? Or the last bastions of the crumbling castle of social snobbery? A passage from a letter written by Thring in 1875 may serve as a text:

"There is no point on which my convictions are stronger than on the power of boarding schools in forming national character. There is a strong feeling growing up among the merchant class in England in favour of the public schools; and hundreds go to schools now who thirty years ago would not have thought of doing so. They want their children to learn to be manly and independent, and I think myself that it is this which has made the English such an adventurous race; and that with all their faults, and you know how decided my views are on this side, the public schools are the cause of this manliness.
As regards class feeling, the thing, if wisely managed, settles itself. As soon as it is possible to make a good boarding school work over a wide area, only those who have time to stay five, six, seven years or more at the school have a chance. This at once silently decides that none but the monied classes can form the bulk of the school.. This soon makes an educated class, and then endowments in England are used to help forward the poorer and less powerful but intelligent workers."

If this seems a rather secular statement of ideals, it should be added that Thring goes on to state firmly that "a school such as Uppingham cannot exist unless there is a very strong religious feeling in the ruler. To be responsible and independent, to bear pain, to play games, to drop wealth and home luxury – this is a priceless boon, which is all too often overlooked." In this trechant sentence he sets out to justify the prefects, corporal punishment, athletics and Spartan living conditions.

In these matters, as so often, there is a golden mean to be sought. On the one hand, the horrors of the Long Chamber at Eton under Keate, the reign of terror experienced by young Oman at Winchester, the firelighting at 3.30am by fags at Westminster. On the other hand, the permissiveness and 'pupil power' of today or - to put it in terms of Thring's period - the luxurious, indulged and pampered life of rich children brought up at home. As for fagging, one can argue (perhaps) that in most Victorian Public Schools the institution was neither despotically exploited by seniors nor resented by the fags themselves, especially in the days when all middle-class homes had servants.

In the matter of Games, too, there is a golden mean to aspire to. The 'mean' here is between the lounging, bullying and poaching which provided the boys with their fun in pre-Games days, and the compulsory, scientifically organised, often joyless Games of a later age, to say nothing of the professional materialism and the hysterical spectator-madness of today.
It is difficult to draw precise lines, and at any one time one school would have differed from another in the importance attached to Games; but one can safely say that before 1830 most schools could have done with more attention to Games, and after 1900 most schools could have done with less.

What are the extremes in the academic programme? Exaggerating a little for the sake of clarity, we find on the one hand the education derided by Sydney Smith consisting entirely of Latin and Greek grammar, the learning by heart of quantities of Latin poetry, and the writing of thousands of Latin verses. On the other hand we have the educational system of today, where every boy takes a wide range of subjects and has a large choice available to him if he reaches the Sixth Form. (Girls as well, of course, but this is a book about boys).

It is hard to argue against increased choice. But with this come exams, tailored to suit every age, and it is these exams that dog today's boys throughout their school careers; and when they leave, they are automatically stamped with their appropriate qualifications, like the little price-tickets that are stuck on every package and tin in a supermarket.

More seriously, this domination by exams leads both masters and boys to focus all their attention on exam syllabuses, and - worse - leads boys to choose the easiest subjects, which are also, of course, the subjects most readily picked up from out-of-school reading, and therefore the least necessary elements in the school curriculum. Hence the vast increase in the numbers studying English Literature, sociology, economics, geography, and the decrease in the numbers studying classics, modern languages, science and mathematics.

In many respects the Public Schools in the latter half of the 19th century appear, by and large, to have been fairly successful in striking a happy medium, while the criticism most commonly levelled at Public Schools today (whether justifiably or not) - that they are socially divisive centres of privilege - is totally inapplicable to the 19th century situation. Practically nobody then considered that the division into classes, which undoubtedly existed, was a result of the educational system.

There were plenty of humane thinkers who wanted to alleviate the hardships of the poor and to extend the benefits of higher education to those capable of profiting from it. Arnold would have said that these results would automatically follow if the Public Schools turned out well educated Christian gentlemen of sound moral and religious principles. This aim was, of course, far from being universally realised, but a case could be made out that the Public Schools were more successful in achieving it between 1850 and 1900 than before or after.

If we are right, then, in seeing these years as a kind of golden age for the Public Schools, there can be no doubt that much of the credit for it must be given to the remarkable series of Headmasters who ruled those schools - 'very superior men', as Thring called them when he was organizing the first Headmasters' Conference. Men like Arnold and Temple of Rugby, Thring himself of Uppingham, Kennedy and Moss of Shrewsbury, Vaughan and Montagu Butler of Harrow, Ridding of Winchester, Cotton and Bradley of Marlborough, Percival, who went from Rugby to start Clifton and duly returned to Rugby - the list could easily be extended.

How did these Headmasters do it, and why is the breed extinct? One quality they all had was enormous energy and industry. They usually taught the Sixth form; ran a boarding house (often without the aid of a house-tutor) as well as the school; kept, as best they could, the school accounts; preached and prepared boys for confirmation. They had, in general, no bursar or secretary to help them. They had no typewriters and wrote all their own letters, calling sometimes on their womenfolk, or on prefects to do their copying. Thring records sometimes writing forty letters in a day, and it is a remarkable fact that when Moss retired from Shrewsbury it was found that no less than nine men were required to replace him.

Evidence of devotion and sincerity is particularly striking when men are prepared to contribute money in the furtherance of their aims. Among a host of contributors, assistants and Headmasters alike, Ridding, Montagu Butler and Fry (of Berkhamsted) all dug deep into their own pockets to finance building schemes for their schools; Bradley left a far more lucrative post at Rugby to become Headmaster of Marlborough; and Thring's expenditure on his school left him continuously harassed by debt.

One way in which Victorian Public Schools differed from those that we know today is that they were almost invariably so much smaller. Various factors made for size after 1900. If your school is bigger, it is easier to cater for a wide choice of subjects in the Sixth form, your 1st XI will win more matches, you will get more scholarships to Oxford and Cambridge, your prestige will grow, and with it, in a questionable if not vicious spiral, your numbers. Your losses, however, though harder to estimate, are considerable.

Thring had very definite ideas on the subject. No house should have more than 30 boys and no school more than 300, and the Headmaster should know every boy in the school personally. Most of the great Headmasters worked in schools of about this size or less. Eton, of course, was far larger, and that may be why no Eton Headmaster features on our list. It was the housemasters and tutors at Eton who knew the boys personally.

There was a further difference between the Headmasters of the 19th century and those of today - the religious atmosphere in which they worked. A hundred years ago most middle class parents took their children to church. Fifty years ago they may have stayed at home, but they probably sent the children to church. Today church-going is a minority activity, and the school chapel service is generally shorn of much of its influence and associations. Now, whether one believes in Christianity or not, there can be no doubt that a more or less unquestioning acceptance of a certain moral code by boys, masters and parents is a powerful weapon.

All that is gone forever. Democracy, in Arnold's day almost a synonym for anarchy, is 'in'; and the word 'democratic' is used, as often as not without much regard to its real meaning, but as equivalent to 'good'.

Today Headmasters cannot sack an inefficient caretaker, much less a master, without risking a legal action; staff-meetings and sometimes pupil councils are apt to demand good and sufficient reasons for all decisions; and even where these are not demanded, Headmasters feel, perhaps rightly, obliged to give them.

It is just at this time, when Headmasters have lost much of their spiritual authority, that their energies are distracted by pressures of a totally new kind. Not only have most of their parents ceased to be churchgoers, but the old patterns of marriage and family life are being everywhere challenged. Divorce or separation, once rarities, are now a regular feature of middle-class life. Into the ensuing unhappiness and confusion the school is drawn as never before. The telephone and motor car have bridged the gap between home and school, and in all the family quarrels and scandals the school has to assume responsibilities and take a moral stand.

In a nutshell, this means that Headmasters, for good or ill, are exchanging the lonely responsibilities of the autocrat for the role of counsellor and co-ordinator. The Public Schools are setting out on a new voyage to a different goal from any they have sought before, and it would be rash indeed to forecast their history for the next twenty years. To do so, of course, is not our purpose.

We have tried simply to describe the past impartially, doing justice to its merits without condoning its faults. Even in the changed circumstances of today some lessons may be learnt from the mistakes of the past, and we venture to hope that some inspiration also may still be drawn from the heroic figures of the last century.

Robert Stanier and Leslie Wilson
January 1975

ACKNOWLEDGEMENTS

Grateful thanks from Tom Stanier to:

Tim Hands and Tom Wheare for their warm encouragement and wise suggestions; to Claire Trousdale for transforming the original battered typescript into a digital document; to Amy Ashton for her cover design; to Prontaprint of East Sheen for various kindly services; and in particular to Eleanor Stanier for kickstarting the whole project.

And finally, posthumous thanks to E.J.Sullivan (1869-1933) who did the original illustrations for Tom Brown's Schooldays.

BIBLIOGRAPHY

Adams, H. C.	Wykehamica, 1878
Ainger, A.C.	Eton Memories 1917
Arnold, R.	The Whiston Matter, 1961
Askwith, J.	The Lytteltons, 1973
Bamford, T.W.	Arnold, 1960
Bell, E.H.	Giggleswick School . 1912
Berkeley, G.F'.E.	Wellington College, The Founders of the Tradition , 1948
Blackie, J.	Bradfield College, 1976
Blunden E. (ed.)	Christ's Hospital
Brady, H.C.	Letters from Rugby,
Brown W.H.	Charter house, 1879
Bryans, E.	St Peter's College, Radley, 1897
Bryant, P.M.H.	Harrow, 1926
Butler, Samuel	Life of Samuel Butler, 1896
Byrne, L.S.R..	Changing Eton, 1937.
Carleton, J.D.	Westminster School, 1965
Christie, C.R.	A History of Clifton , 1935
Clarendon	Commission's Report, 1864
Coleridge, A.D.	Eton in the Forties, 1896
Connell, J.	Wavell 1980
Coulton, G.G.	Hart of Sedbergh, 1923
Cust, L.	Eton College, 1899

Douglas-Smith, A.E.	City of London School, 1937
Druitt, W.W.	Harrow through the ages, 1935
Edwards, D.L.	King's School, Canterbury, 1957
Farrar, F.W.	Eric, or Little by Little 1858
Findlay, J.J.	Arnold of Rugby, 1925
Firth, J.D.E.	Winchester College,
Fisher, G.	Annals of Shrewsbury School, 1899
Fitch, Sir J.	Thomas and Matthew Arnold, 1897
Frangopulo, N.J.	QEGS, Ashbourne 1925
Garnons-Williams, B.H.	A History of Berkhamsted School, 1980
Hughes, T.	Tom Brown's Schooldays, 1858
Hutton, T.W.	King Edward's Birmingham, 1952
Icely, H.E.	Bromsgrove School, 1953
Jameson, E.	Charterhouse, 1937
Kipling, Rudyard	Stalky & Co. 1899
Laborde, E.D.	Harrow School, 1948
Lamb, G.F.	The Happiest Days, 1959
Leach, A.F.	Winchester College, 1899
Loather-Clarke, H..	Sedbergh School, 1925
Lubbock, A.	An Old Etonian, 1899
Lyte, H.C. Maxwell	Eton College, 1904
Macdonald, A.	History of Repton, 1929
Mack, E.C.	The Public Schools & Brit Opinion, 1941
Mackenzie, R.J.	Almond of Loretto, 1905
Mansfield, R.B.	School Life at Winchester, 1870

Marcus, S.	The Other Victorians
Markham, F.	Westminster Town Boy, 1903
McDonnell, M.F.J.	St Paul's, 1905
Milford, L.S.	Haileybury College, 1909
Minchin, J.G.C.	Old Harrow Days, 1898
Moberly, C.A.E.	Dulce Domum, 1911
Monserrat, A.	An Uneasy Victorian, 1980
Moss, Mrs.	Moss of Shrewsbury, 1932
Newdome D.	History of Wellington 1959
Oldham, J.B.	Shrewsbury School 1952
Oman, Sir Charles	Memories of Victorian Oxford, 1941
Parkin, G.R.	Letters of Thring, 1898
Percival, A.	Very Superior Men, 1973
Price, A.C.	Leeds Grammar School, 1919
Raine, A.	St Peter's School, York, 1924
Rendall, E. and G.	John Smith of Harrow, 1913
Rivington, S.	A History of Tonbridge , 1925
Rose, K.	Superior Person, 1969
Rouse, W.H.D.	A History of Rugby School, 1898
Rowbotham, J.F.	Rossall School, 1890
Sanderson of Oundle	by Various Contributors, 1923
Sandford, E.G.	Archbishop Temple, 1906
Sargeaunt, J.	A History of Bedford School, 1925
Somervell, D.C.	Tonbridge School, 1947
Simon, B. and Bradley, I.	The Victorian School, 1975
Stanier, R.S.	Magdalen School, Oxford, 1958

Stanley, A.	Life of T. Arnold, 1845
Temple, W.	Life of Percival, 1921
Tennyson, Sir C.	The Tennysons, 1974
Trevor, N.	The Arnolds 1973
Tristram, H.B.	Loretto School, 1911
Winterbottom, D.	Doctor Fry, 1977

INDEX OF PROMINENT HEADMASTERS

Almond Dr H.H. (Loretto)   98, 165-166

Arnold Dr T. (Rugby)   50, 55, 77, 83-87, 93-96, 102-104
,   118, 141-144, 153-155, 198, 216

Balston, Rev. E. (Eton)   87-88

Benson, Dr E.W. (Wellington)   139-142, 200-201, 221-222

Bradley, G.G (Marlborough)   155, 176

Busby, Dr (Westminster)   40

Butler, A. G. (Haileybury)   167

Butler, Dr George (Harrow)   31-32

Butler, Dr H.M. (Harrow)   98-102, 134, 158, 169

Butler, DrSamuel. (Shrewsbury)   18-20, 39, 139, 146-147, 164

Carey, Rev.W.   28

Cotton, Rev.G. (Marlborough)   127, 176

Davies, Dr D. (Eton)	13-14
Dupre, John (Berkhamsted)	64
Elwyn (Charterhouse)	107, 128
Foster, Dr J. (Eton)	12-13
Fry, Dr T.C. (Berkhamsted)	217-218
Gabell, Dr H.D.(Winchester)	24
Gill, Dr (St Paul's)	37-38
Goddard, Dr W.(Winchester)	68
Goodenough, J. (Bristol)	63
Gray, Dr H.B. (Bradfield)	195
Hawtrey, Dr E.C.(Eton)	49, 68, 88, 185
Hessey Dr (Merchants Taylors)	207-208
Dr Ingles (Rugby)	16-17

Keate Dr J. (Eton)	14-15, 39-41, 145, 162, 186-187, 216
Kennedy, Dr B.H. (Shrewsbury)	30, 107, 116, 113, 149, 150, 162
Langley Rev. (Ashbourne GS)	64
Millard, Dr J.E. (MCS, Oxford)	108, 182
Moberly, Dr G. (Winchester)	87, 90-91, 153, 168, 217
Moss, Dr (Shrewsbury)	192, 230
Mulcaster, Robert (St Pauls)	37
Pears, S.A. (Repton)	102
Percival, Dr J. (Clifton)	91, 103, 159, 200, 203
Ridding, Rev. G. (Winchester)	43, 162, 168
Dr Russell (Charterhouse)	50-51
Sanderson, E.W. (Oundle)	77-92
Sewell, Rev. W. (Radley)	24, 157-158

Temple, DrF. (Rugby)	82, 103, 108, 130, 135, 155-156, 164
Thring, E. (Uppingham)	53-54, 96-97, 105-107, 114, 123, 130, 140-141, 153, 159 167, 183, 185, 218-221, 225
Vaughan, DrC.J. (Harrow)	107. 133-134, 155, 210-211
Vincent, Rev.W.	27-29,
Warre, Dr E. (Eton)	190, 200
Warton, Dr J.. (Winchester)	21-24, 60
Whiston, R, (Rochester)	56, 67, 74-76
Wilkinson (Rev M,) (Malborough)	33-34
Wilson, W. (St Bees)	66

= = = = = = = = = = = = =

OTHER NOTABLE FIGURES

Brown, Tom	207
Clarendon (Lord)	70-71, 97, 115
Coubertin, Baron de M	94
Disraeli, Benjamin	205
Gladstone (William)	39-40, 80-81, 147, 201
Hunt, Leigh	147
Johnson, Doctor	39-40
Kaiser Wilhelm II	190
Kingsley, Charles	203
Lamb, Charles	110
Nightingale, Florence	215-217
Smith, Sydney	78-79, 117, 199
Strachey, Lytton	80, 83
Thackeray, William	199
Wolsey, Thomas	36-37

THE END

Made in the USA
Charleston, SC
22 January 2017

NECK PAIN SUCKS

The 5-Step Method to Solving Your Neck Pain

Caelum Trott

NECK PAIN SUCKS
Copyright © 2021 Caelum Trott
All rights reserved.

ISBN: 9798524124326 (Paperback)
Imprint: Independently published

No parts of this publication may be reproduced, stored in a retrieval system, or transmitted in any form or by any means, electronic, mechanical, photocopying, recording or otherwise, without the prior written permission of the copyright owner.

Disclaimer

The advice provided in this publication is general advice only. It has been prepared without taking into account your individual health or circumstances. Before acting on this advice, you should consider the appropriateness of this advice, having regard to your own individual health and circumstances. To the maximum extent permitted by law, the author disclaims all responsibility and liability to any person arising directly or indirectly from any person taking or not taking action based on the information in this publication.

Declaration of interest

The NECKspert only forms partnerships with brands and products that he genuinely believes will improve the health of his readers and clients. It should be made clear, however, that he may at times receive financial incentives from some of the brands that he promotes. You can be certain that The NECKspert will never recommend a product that does not align with his mission of creating widespread health and NECKcellence, but he feels as though it is important to declare that financial partnerships do exist with some of these brands.

www.neckspert.com.au

To my mother, who raised me to live with courage and a purpose larger than myself.

To my wife, whose ongoing love, support and belief in me fuels me each day.

To my clients, past, present and future – you are my greatest teachers.

Table of contents

Introduction 1

Section 1 9

    Getting to know your neck 11

    Understanding pain 23

    Framework for success 43

Section 2 59

    Introducing the 5 Steps 61

    Step 1: Structure 65

    Step 2: Stress 133

    Step 3: Sleep 163

    Step 4: Supplements 199

    Step 5: Subconscious Mind 245

Section 3 283

    Staying NECKcellent 285

    In closing 303

Introduction

If you are reading this book, then it's likely you've been searching for answers for your neck pain. Answers that, up to this point, you've been unable to find or have not worked for you. I'm sure your journey has been a long and painful one and I truly feel for you – I've been there too.

Navigating health information can be tricky, especially when you're in pain. There is so much misinformation out there that it can feel like navigating through a minefield trying to decipher what to believe.

That is why I have created a simple 5-step method to creating a pain-free and excellent neck. It is designed to cut through all of the complicated jargon and unscientific claims you have been reading online and to give you a clear step-by-step plan to follow, based on both the latest science and tried-and-tested wisdom.

Despite all of your suffering, I genuinely believe that there is an important process at play in the experience you've had. I believe that all of life's challenges are an opportunity for growth and personal evolution. Pain is one of the biggest motivators for change and it is often a tool that our body uses to let us know we are off track and need a push back on course. So, the fact you are now holding this book in your hand is no coincidence (I don't believe in coincidences). Your journey with neck pain has brought you to this point and you are now ready for change.

INTRODUCTION

If followed correctly, this book will allow you to fix your neck pain – but it goes beyond that. It will also change other aspects of your life: your sleep, stress levels, nutrition, fitness, gut health, mood, energy, passion, happiness, relationships and your overall satisfaction with life.

If you had already fixed your neck pain with ease, then you wouldn't have given yourself the opportunity to create massive change in all aspects of your life – the opportunity to steer your ship back on course. This book is that opportunity. You have found your way to this book at exactly the right time and under the perfect circumstances – any earlier and you would not have been ready or committed to implement it.

Your struggle with neck pain has been real, but if you search deep down, you might be able to find a little flicker of truth that your journey up to this point has laid the perfect groundwork for this moment: the moment where you are now finally ready to create the changes to your health that you truly need and deserve. The changes that this book is offering.

***

This book is about you and your neck. But before we begin, I want to give you some context about how I came to dedicate a large part of my life to being 'The NECKspert' and helping people fix their neck pain.

Well before becoming a physiotherapist, I decided that neck pain sucks. From having a regularly kinked neck in primary school, to being a surfing-obsessed teenager, I was no stranger to neck pain.

My experience with truly crippling, life-impacting neck pain didn't arrive until I was studying physiotherapy at university, however. It seemed as though university was the perfect storm for my neck. I spent hours upon hours sitting in lectures and studying with bad posture, my stress levels were through the roof and I developed poor sleeping habits. On top of all that, I was lifting heavy weights in the gym to impress my new female classmates.

By my second year at university, I had developed chronic neck pain, postural headaches, migraines and neck-related dizziness, which for a physiotherapy student seemed like a cruel irony!

I began seeking answers and treatment from my university lecturers, who were some of the brightest minds in neck research, but despite seeing more than 10 different health professionals (physiotherapists, chiropractors, doctors, neurologists), not one of them was able to fix my neck.

After several months of failing to improve and thousands of dollars later (which for a self-funded university student felt like millions), I began to feel depressed. I started having anxiety attacks. My mental health was starting to reflect my physical health. Rock bottom came one day when one of my neck-related headaches progressed into a migraine, with

INTRODUCTION

flashing lights, dizziness and crippling pain, and I ended up in the office of a neurologist, having CT (computed tomography) scans on my neck and brain to see if I had a tumour.

After an hour of sitting in his waiting room, nervously awaiting results, he came out to collect his next patient. As he was walking away, I called out, 'Any results yet doc?' He looked back at me, searched his brain for who I was (despite seeing me just one hour earlier) and then replied nonchalantly, 'Oh, results were all fine, you can leave.' I couldn't believe that this was how a 'specialist' treated his patients. 'Is there anything you can do for me?' I asked. 'I could give you a script for pain and migraine tablets if you want, but I don't think you need them.' He turned and walked away.

I have come to find that more often than not, our lowest points in life can light a fire inside us that provides a catalyst for change. They inspire action and set us on a new path. This was one of those days for me. At that moment I became determined to fix myself and also to focus my physio career on helping others who had struggled with neck-related pain and dysfunction.

Over the following months I began to implement the steps that you will come to learn about in the *NECKcellent* method. These steps were a trial-and-error blend of things I had learnt at university, strategies and concepts that I had read about outside of the university walls, ideas and techniques I learnt through yoga, and a dash of intuition.

It didn't take long before the strategies I was implementing began to work. Within 2 weeks I felt better. Within 3 months my neck pain was gone. I still haven't had a migraine in over 10 years.

With a new lease on life, I forged ahead with my physiotherapy degree and upon graduating was awarded The University Medal (High Distinction average) and The Dean's Scholar Award (first place in the cohort). I went on to do an Honours thesis that included an academic paper on neck pain which was published in a medical journal. I tell you this not to boast, but to reinforce how passionate and driven I am when it comes to neck pain.

Over the past 10 years I have been refining my treatment methods for neck pain and helping people create thriving lives. My physiotherapy clinics help thousands of people with neck pain every year, my corporate health company has taught thousands of people how to have a healthy neck at work and I continue to work with schools to implement postural strength programmes for their students.

My main objective as The NECKspert is to take the existing neck-related research out there, cut through the crap, layer my own experience on top, and create simple, practical and easy-to-understand content that creates results for people like you.

Writing this book was the next logical step in achieving my mission as The NECKspert: *To help as many people as*

INTRODUCTION

possible achieve NECKcellence: a strong, pain-free and healthy neck.

I have structured the book very deliberately to ensure that you get better – and *stay* better:

Section 1 will give you a basic overview of the neck in terms of anatomy, all of its amazing functions and how all of the systems in the body are connected (especially to the neck). We will explore the concept of pain science and why there is much more to the complex experience of pain than meets the eye. I will also give you a framework for how to best approach the *5 Steps to NECKcellence* that will be explored in Section 2, through the science of behaviour change and habit formation.

Section 2 will unveil the five practical aspects of achieving a pain-free, strong and healthy neck forever. This is the section that you came for!

Section 3 explores life beyond pain, maintaining NECKcellence and ensuring your new, healthy neck remains that way forever. In Section 3, you will also learn the *one true secret* of how to heal your neck. The reality is that everything in the body is connected. All systems. This means that everything within the body influences the health of your neck: alignment of the hips or feet, health of the gut, eye function – even your heart and lungs. The same is true in reverse: the health of the neck can and does influence every other system in your body! I'll explain this in more detail in later chapters, but for now just take my word for it – the body is amazing!

With that in mind, it is worth noting that whilst this book is focused on the neck, the interconnectedness of everything in the body also means that many of the concepts and principles in this book can also be applied to other areas of pain in the body (e.g. lower back, knee, hip or shoulder, and chronic diseases such as cardiovascular disease, gut and digestion disorders, and even mental health conditions such as depression and anxiety).

Let's get started – I'm very excited about helping you achieve NECKcellence.

Yours in health,

Caelum Trott
The NECKspert

Section 1

The Fundamentals

Getting to know your neck

Your body is amazing and complex. You have between 50 and 75 *trillion* cells in your body, each with its own lifespan. Some cells live for a few days before they are replaced, others live for years, but it's true to say that in 12 months from now, you will quite literally not be the same person you are today.

That includes your neck, which should give you great hope. Every daily choice you make influences the health of your cells and the vitality of your body.

Whether or not you are currently aware of them, I assure you that there are numerous habits and behaviours that are contributing to your neck pain or preventing your injury from healing. By the end of this book, you will know them all and have a roadmap to change them.

Even before you get to that point, I want to take you through a little exercise that peers into the future, to give you some insight into where you are heading and the importance of making the changes that this book suggests.

Close your eyes and think about one harmful habit that you already know is not serving your neck or your health and imagine yourself repeating this behaviour every day for a whole year.

Look at yourself in the mirror and see the version of you 12 months from now, after continuing that negative habit. How do you look? How do you feel? What is your energy like? How are your pain levels? What activities are you missing out on due to your pain?

Now, imagine you have continued this habit every day for 5 years. What does your body look like? Pay attention to the bags under your eyes and your skin quality. How bad is your neck pain? What is it preventing you from doing? How do you feel? How are your energy levels?

Next, imagine that you have been repeating this negative habit every day for 10 years. A whole decade has gone past. Look at yourself in the mirror and analyse what it has done to you. Are your eyes bloodshot? Have you lost confidence in your voice? Is your posture slumped in defeat? Perhaps you've gained a lot of weight from an inability to exercise? How severe is your pain? Are you relying on pain medication to function? Are you missing out on life?

I now want you to revert back to the present moment. This time you are going to replace that negative habit with one that you already know is a better option for your neck. One that you know is supporting your health and vitality, even without yet knowing the 5 Ss of NECKcellence.

Imagine repeating this new habit daily for 1 year. Look at yourself in the mirror after a full 12 months of doing this. How do you look? How do you feel? What is your energy like? Can you notice how good your neck feels? What activities are you able to participate in due to your health?

Then imagine you have continued this habit every day for 5 years. What does your body look like? Pay attention to the clarity of your skin and eyes. Notice the strength and mobility in your neck. What activities have you now started doing? How do you feel? What are your energy levels like?

Lastly, imagine that you have been repeating this positive habit every day for 10 years. A whole decade has gone past. Look at yourself in the mirror and analyse what it has done to you. Notice your strong body and upright posture. Listen to the confidence in your voice. Now that you can exercise without pain, what has that done to your weight? Pay attention to the absence of pain in your neck. What are you now able to do because of your pain-free body and abundant health? How does it feel to be in this body? How does it feel to be this version of you?

The majority of this book is about giving you the knowledge and tools to make the right choices in order to create a pain-free neck, healthy body and a better life. But before we get into the practical aspects of the book, we first need to get a few key concepts and foundations out of the way.

Whilst you don't necessarily need to know a great amount of detail about the anatomy or function of the neck in order to have a healthy one, developing an understanding and

GETTING TO KNOW YOUR NECK

appreciation for just how amazing the neck is and how it works is an important place to start.

It may be very tempting to jump ahead to Section 2 and dive straight into the 5 Steps of NECKcellence, but I assure you that this book has been structured in a very deliberate fashion.

Section 1 is about setting you up for success. By gaining a basic insight into how the neck works, understanding pain and getting clear on how to effectively implement the 5 Steps, you will have the knowledge and tools to create positive changes in your neck that will last forever (rather than the short-lived results you've had in the past).

Anatomy 101

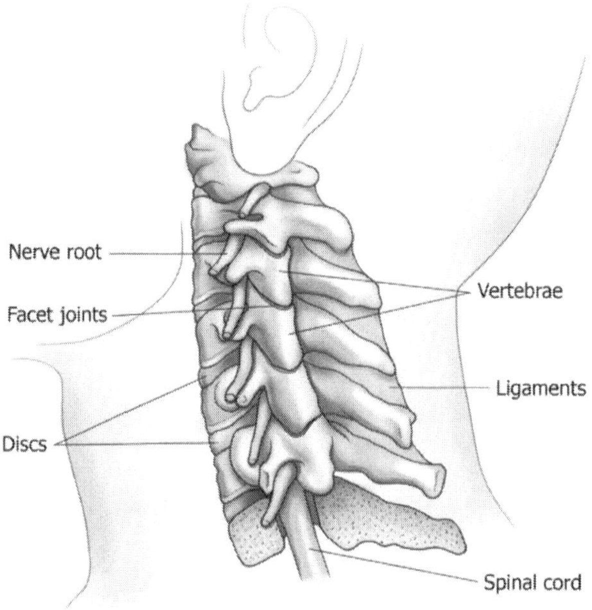
Nerve root
Facet joints
Discs
Vertebrae
Ligaments
Spinal cord

Let's start with the basic anatomy:

- The cervical spine (neck) is made up of seven bones called vertebrae.
- In between each of the bones is a little cushion (shock absorber) called an *intervertebral disc* (disc problems are often blamed for neck pain, but you'll see in later chapters that this is often incorrect).
- There are also two smaller joints between each vertebra called *facet* joints. These sit at the back of the vertebral column (one on each side) and assist with movement. The shape of the facet joints in the

neck allows movement in many directions (rotation, side bending, looking up and down).

- The *spinal cord* (bundle of nerves) runs through a hole in the centre of each vertebrae called the vertebral canal. Think of the spinal cord (and nerves) as the electricity supply to the whole body.

- Little nerves run off the spinal cord and exit through holes in between each vertebral level (on both the left and right). Each of these *spinal nerves* controls movement and sensation on different parts of the arms.

- Around each of the joints in the neck you have structures called *ligaments*. These are tight bands of tissue that are designed to stop too much movement from occurring.

- You also have large blood vessels that pass through your neck that carry blood between your heart and your brain.

- In front of your vertebrae, you have the *oesophagus* (carries food from your mouth to your stomach) and *trachea* (carries air to and from your lungs).

- Then you have the muscles. These control the position of your neck through active movement. The smaller and deeper muscles are designed for controlled and specific movements of each segment and are your postural muscles (they have longer endurance so can stay on for long periods of time without fatigue). The larger outer muscles are designed for bigger movements (usually of multiple segments at once). They are more powerful, but also fatigue more quickly.

So, as you can see, there is a lot of action going on in a very small area! Not just any action, but most of the critical functions of your body pass through the neck.

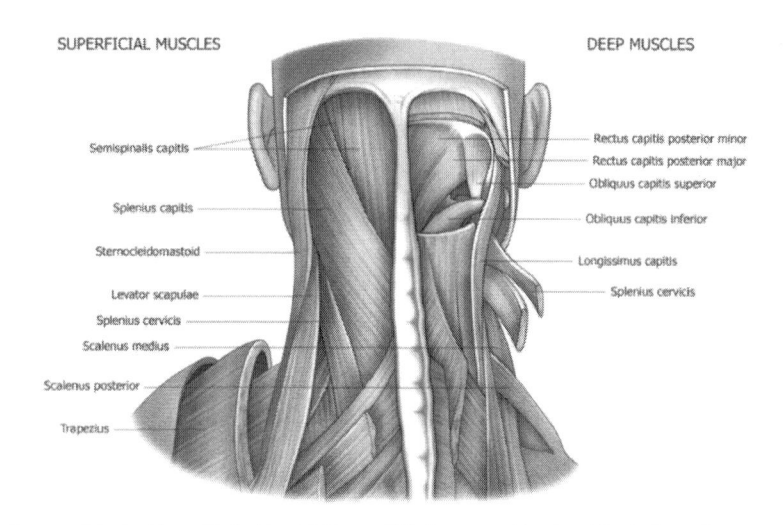

Source: Adapted from Stathakios J & Carron MA. Anatomy, Head and Neck, Posterior Cervical Region. [Updated 2020 Jul 31]. In: StatPearls [Internet]. Treasure Island (FL): StatPearls Publishing; 2021 Jan. Available at: https://www.ncbi.nlm.nih.gov/books/NBK551521.

Function 101

Now that you have a better understanding of what it looks like under your skin, let's explore some of the amazing functions of your neck:

- Almost every nerve in your body first travels through your neck (via the spinal cord). Second only to the brain, your neck holds the power supply to your entire body.

- The nerves that exit in between the vertebrae in your neck control both the movement and sensation in your arms and hands. That is why a pinched nerve in the neck can be felt all the way down in the forearm or hand (usually as pain, tingling or numbness).

- The nerves from your upper neck are responsible for sensation on your face and head. This is why it's possible to experience a headache that is in fact not coming from your head at all, but actually originating in your neck. Neck-related headaches are called *cervicogenic headaches*.[1]

- Your neck allows you to control the position of your head, thereby influencing your vision (via the eyes), balance (via the vestibular system inside the ear) and your hearing (by positioning your ears).

- Due to the important relationship between the positioning of your head and your vision, the muscles that control your eyes are closely linked to those controlling the neck. If there is dysfunction in your neck and the messages to the brain about head position do not match the messages from your eyes, this can result in dizziness, blurry vision and unsteadiness. This is referred to as *cervicogenic vertigo* (meaning dizziness coming from the neck).[2]

- Your neck houses the *vagus nerve*, which is one of your cranial nerves – known to have an incredibly important role in the health of your whole body. The vagus nerve is the main nerve in your body responsible for the 'rest and digest' response and for regulating stress (more to come on this). It helps to control your heart, liver, gut, breathing and inflammatory responses.

- The muscles and joints in your neck have 10 times more *proprioceptors* than any other part of the body. Proprioceptors are little receptors that send messages from your muscles and joints to your brain about the position of your body. The extra proprioceptors in the neck are due to the importance of head positioning (controlled via the neck) on your survival (through balance, vision and hearing accuracy). Whilst this is a good thing, it also means that any dysfunction in these proprioceptors can result in dizziness and increased pain sensitivity.

- Some joints in the body are designed for *stability* and do not allow movement in multiple directions (e.g. the knee), whilst others are designed for *mobility* and allow large amounts of multi-directional movement (e.g. the shoulder). The neck plays an important role in ensuring you can accurately position your head (mobility), whilst also creating optimal stability for the important functions of the face and head (such as vision and hearing). This results in the neck containing a large number of very mobile joints, overlayed with a network of both 'stability' and 'mobility' muscles. The complex relationship between these mobile joints and the two types of muscles that control them results in a beautiful system when working well, but one that has the potential to result in significant pain and dysfunction when things go wrong.

- Your neck has a very strong relationship to your jaw (TMJ or 'temporomandibular joint') and they share multiple connections through muscles and fascia. Dysfunction in the neck is therefore a common cause of jaw pain, and vice versa. We will explore the concepts of stress, jaw clenching and associated neck pain in later chapters.

As you can now appreciate, it is possible (and common) for the neck to be the cause of headaches, shoulder pain, jaw pain, blurry vision, dizziness, stress, anxiety, pain or tingling in the hands and even issues with gut function.

Hopefully this insight into the deep connection between your neck and the rest of your body can help you understand some of the strange symptoms you may have experienced.

Understanding pain

In order to overcome pain, it helps if you understand it. This has been proven through studies showing that people experience an improvement in their pain, and a reduction in disability, simply by learning about basic pain science principles.

Whilst the idea of reading about pain science may seem daunting or boring – don't worry, I've made it super simple and easy to grasp. In fact, don't be surprised if this next section is one of your favourite parts of the book! It's a fascinating topic and what you will learn about pain will feel liberating.

Pain is bloody horrible. But it is actually an incredibly important experience that keeps you safe, informs you about danger and helps you avoid harm. Without pain, you would be doing crazy and damaging things to your bodies without realising it – but your pain systems don't always work perfectly.

Pain and the brain

Once upon a time, scientists believed pain was a message sent from our body to our brain informing us that damage had occurred. What we have now discovered is that these early scientists had it the wrong way around. Pain occurs *in* the brain. It may be hard to believe, but pain doesn't actually tell you about how much you have *damaged* your body; it tells you about how much *danger* your brain *believes* you are in. This may be potential danger or real danger.

Let's look at an example: when you cut yourself, a message is sent to your brain to let you know something is wrong. The brain takes in this information, analyses the environment, draws on past experiences that were similar, decides how much danger it thinks you are in and then produces a pain response in proportion to this.

So, the pain you feel doesn't necessarily equal the amount of harm that occurs to your body. The hurt you feel actually equals the amount of *perceived threat* by the brain. Sometimes this perceived threat is accurate, but often it's not.

Pain doesn't equal damage
Think about the last time you stubbed your toe… it's excruciating! Even though the amount of tissue damage is small, the pain response is often big. Now, if you were a professional runner and you did this, the pain would be much greater because of the perceived threat to your livelihood, especially just before a big race. If last time you stubbed your toe, you fractured the bone and were on crutches, you would feel even more pain this time because of the memory of your past experience.

On the flip side, if you stubbed your toe with the exact same force whilst running away from an aggressive dog, you probably wouldn't feel any pain in your toe at all, because the brain has more important things to worry about. As you can see, there are many factors involved in pain, such as context (how could this injury affect my livelihood?), environment (am I being chased by something that could kill me?), past experience (what happened last time?) and your current emotional state.

Acute and chronic pain

When you sustain an injury, you experience pain to alert you to the fact you have done something to your body. This initial pain can be severe and it's a clever way of your brain telling you to protect the area so it can heal. During the first few days after an injury (called the *acute* stage), inflammation occurs, which is the body initiating its healing response. After these first few days, inflammation subsides and the pain plateaus and then gradually reduces over time.

UNDERSTANDING PAIN

There's an issue in the tissue!

How long this takes is based on the severity of the injury and which tissues are involved (bone, for example, takes longer than muscle tissue). This is a normal pain response and one that you would have definitely experienced in the past.

Unfortunately, the brain and body aren't perfect and sometimes things can go wrong. If pain persists beyond normal healing timeframes, it is called *chronic* pain.

Pain: what's actually going on?

Let's shrink ourselves and go on a virtual tour of the body to see what happens during a pain response.

The detectors

You have tiny little detectors throughout your body that tell you what's happening in your tissues. If these detectors notice a big enough change, such as excessive pressure (punch or pinch), temperature (too hot or cold) or changes in chemistry (chilli or acid on your skin), they will send a message to the spinal cord saying, 'Hey, something is going on over here, pay attention.'

If the messages from the detectors are small or brief, then the spinal cord may not be interested. If the detectors continue to be stimulated, they will become more sensitive and will bombard the spinal cord with alerts, until it says, 'OK, OK, I'll do something about it.'

The spinal cord and the brain

So, something is going on in your body tissues and the detectors want you to do something about it. They've sent enough messages to your spinal cord that it has now said, 'OK, I'll listen.' Your spinal cord is now excited. It's so excited, in fact, that it decides to let the brain know there could be some potential danger.

Until this point, no pain has been experienced. But now your brain has been alerted to the fact that something isn't right, so it assesses the situation.

Your brain looks at the surrounding environment and it draws on past events:
'Is this a familiar experience?'

It reviews your beliefs and expectations, and it decides:
'How much danger do I appear to be in right now? How threatening is this situation?'

Your brain will then give you a pain response in proportion to how it answers these questions. This whole process takes place in milliseconds, completely outside of your awareness. Pretty clever!

Protection mode
When your brain decides there *is* danger and gives you a pain experience, what is actually going on? A mix of chemicals are released in your brain and nervous system that cause you to feel an intense unpleasantness, fear and even loathing.

Your entire body kicks into protection mode and activates the *sympathetic nervous system*, better known as your 'fight-or-flight response'. Your body is preparing for action, so your muscles tighten up, your heart rate and breathing become rapid and you become hyper-vigilant. The detectors in your body tissues become more sensitive and your nerves, spinal cord and brain get better at sending and receiving danger messages.

The pain experience: Meet Borris

Let's look at two different examples to help you understand how the same injury can be experienced differently by two people.

In the first scenario, a man – let's call him Borris – is doing some labouring on a construction site. He picks up a 20kg rock and feels something 'go' in his neck. It was a bit too heavy and he has strained one of the joints in his neck.

The detectors in the joint sense a change and send a message to his spinal cord, which alerts his brain.

Borris had something similar happen 5 years ago, which kept him off work for 4 weeks. He has a mortgage, so missing work would be a real problem, especially as he's already a bit worried about his finances. Borris also has a belief that his neck is quite fragile and one of his close friends recently had neck surgery.

In a split second, his brain has analysed all of this information and concluded, *'Borris, we are in real trouble here, mate'* and it sends him a crippling pain experience.

UNDERSTANDING PAIN

MEET BORRIS & DORRIS

Meet Dorris

Borris has a twin sister, Dorris. In this scenario, Dorris is camping with her husband and kids. Dorris loves camping and she is unloading the car with a bit too much enthusiasm. She lifts the 20kg tent bag and feels something 'go' in her neck.

She has sustained the exact same injury as her brother Borris: same force, same area of the body and same severity. The brain has been made aware of an issue and assesses the situation.

Dorris had been really excited about the trip, so was in a particularly good mood. She experiences neck pain a few times each year – it usually lasts a few days then gets better. She grew up playing sport with her brothers, so she reckons she is pretty tough and resilient.

In a split second, without Dorris knowing, her brain has analysed this information and concluded: *'Dorris, I think we are alright here, love. I'm gonna send you a small pain experience just so that you take it a bit easier over the weekend, but I don't believe you're in too much danger.'*

So, from Borris and Dorris's scenarios, you can see how exactly the same extent of tissue damage can produce two very different, but equally as real, pain experiences. The fact that they have experienced pain, albeit at different intensities, is a good thing as it will give the injury a chance to heal through rest. But the difference in the pain experiences they each had is likely to influence how each of them respond to the injury and how effectively they manage it.

When things go wrong

Persistent pain
In a normal and healthy pain response, all of the elements that make up your pain experience will reverse and return to normal over time, in line with the healing of the injured tissue. But sometimes, things don't behave as they should and pain persists. There is no simple answer for why this occurs and there are often a number of different factors, each unique to the individual case.

Regardless of the reasons, the fact of the matter is that your danger alert system has malfunctioned. Whilst in a normal scenario the level of pain will diminish as the injury heals, with chronic pain the level of pain you experience remains the same or even worsens over time, **even if the injured area is healing normally.**

When pain becomes chronic, the pain you feel is no longer an accurate representation of danger or damage in your body. This may be hard to believe at first, but it will make more sense in the coming pages.

The detectors

You may remember that there are detectors in your body that monitor pressure, temperature and chemical changes. In order for these to send a danger message to the spinal cord, the stimulus has to be strong enough. For example, if you touch your skin lightly right now, you won't feel pain because the pressure isn't strong enough to activate the danger detectors. The same is true of pressing a warm object to your skin. But if you pinch yourself hard or place a boiling hot object on the skin, this activates the detectors, which will send a message to the spinal cord.

When pain persists, these sensors begin to change the way they work. They start sending danger messages to the spinal cord even if the stimulus isn't dangerous, such as light pressure or a tiny change in temperature. And instead of just sending one message, they send lots and much faster. Think of it like opening the floodgate – you now have detectors that are oversensitive and sending false danger messages.

The spinal cord
Now, our good friend the spinal cord, as you will recall, needs to become excited enough before it will alert the brain to danger. In states of persistent or chronic pain, the spinal cord becomes overexcited, a bit like an untrained puppy.

Danger messages that the spinal cord would normally ignore coming from the detectors seem like a big deal and it rushes off to inform the brain. In fact, it multiplies the danger messages and makes them even bigger.

When the danger messages reach the brain in chronic or persistent pain, the brain says to the spinal cord: 'Hey, good job getting really excited about this potential harm. I want you to get even more protective!' The spinal cord then releases more chemicals to enhance the danger messages.

You now have oversensitive detectors *and* an overexcited spinal cord that are both alerting your brain about danger that either doesn't exist or is overexaggerated.

The brain
When pain persists, your brain begins to change to get better at protecting you. The word *neuroplasticity* describes how your brain is 'plastic' in the way it can adapt and change. There are several ways in which your brain adapts to become more protective.

One of these is related to the body-map that you have in your brain for sensation. When your danger system is working normally, your brain can accurately identify the area of potential harm in the body. With chronic pain, your brain map for sensation begins to smudge and the outline of the painful body part begins to expand. To you, this may feel like the pain is spreading and covering a larger area. In reality, this is just the brain trying to be clever and protect more ground.

Another way that your brain changes with pain is by becoming really efficient at activating the areas and chemicals associated with the sensation of pain. The longer you feel pain, the more effective your brain becomes at producing the experience. It's like anything – the more you practice, the better you get.

Other body systems

Because your brain has interpreted that there is danger and has produced a pain response, it now calls on the other body systems to enter 'fight-or-flight' mode. Your sympathetic nervous system is very effective in helping you escape from danger and prepares your body for action, such as increasing your heart rate and breathing. It also gives less attention to things like digestion, sexual function and your immune system when you are in imminent danger.

Whilst a short blast of fight or flight can be good, in chronic or persistent pain you often remain in this heightened nervous state for long periods. The result of this can be anxiety and panic, restlessness, sexual dysfunction, problems with digestion, chronic fatigue, a weak immune system and higher levels of alertness to pain. Can you identify with any of these things?

All of this can have a huge impact on your life, and later in the book we will talk about techniques to try and switch from fight-or-flight mode (stressed) to 'rest and digest' mode (relaxed), which is controlled by the *parasympathetic* nervous system.

Chronic pain is reversible

Pain is real, but it's not always accurate
When pain becomes persistent or chronic, the outcome is a pain response that no longer represents an accurate picture of true harm. The brain and body have overcalculated the level of threat and are sending pain messages, even though the original injury may no longer be problematic.

This does not mean that the pain is not real! Chronic pain is very real – it is just no longer an accurate interpretation of the injury.

Take this analogy: when you stare into the sun and then look away, you can still see white spots in your eyes. This is because the stimulus was so intense for the detectors that even after it's gone, they are still firing. It's similar at a loud concert: your ears are exposed to such intense noise that after you leave, they often still ring for hours because the detectors were overstimulated.

It's no different with pain: even after the injury or danger has gone, the pain response can keep playing on.

Pain is reversible: detectors and spines
Whilst the changes in the body and brain associated with chronic pain can seem complex and extensive, the good news is that all of it is reversible!

You have approximately 37 trillion cells in your body. The life of a human cell is generally pretty short, and you are constantly replacing cells all the time. The detectors that sense danger in your tissues only last a few days before they are replaced, so with the right training you can replace these oversensitive sensors with ones that are more accurate.

Your overexcited spinal cord can also be tamed, just like a well-trained puppy. Just as the brain can tell the spinal cord to be more protective and vigilant, it can also release chemicals that make it less sensitised and ask it to only relay danger messages that are really important. This is how many drugs like paracetamol (called acetaminophen in some countries) work, but the body has its own chemicals that are even better.

Pain is reversible: neuroplasticity
Remember the word *neuroplasticity*? If you've forgotten, it means the brain can change and adapt, just like plastic. The various changes that occur in your brain that make you better at feeling pain can all be reversed. You have about 80 billion brain cells, called neurons, and each cell can

form thousands of links with other cells – the average brain has over 100 trillion connections.

A famous scientist once said: 'neurons that fire together, wire together', which means the more often you practice something, the stronger the connections in the brain become. The skills you will learn in the first step to *NECKcellence* will 'fire' the right parts of the brain, resulting in less pain and the ability to 'rewire' the brain back to a healthy state.

Scans and myths about discs

By now you may have thought: 'Hold on, if pain doesn't equal damage, then why does my X-ray and MRI show damage?' This is a very valid question.

What we now know about imaging (such as X-ray and MRI, or magnetic resonance imaging) is that it does *not* correlate very well with pain. The below table shows the percentage of **pain-free** individuals at different stages of life that display spinal changes on their scans.

Systematic Literature Review of Imaging Features of Spinal Degeneration in Asymptomatic Populations

W. Brinjikji, P.H. Luetmer, B. Comstock, B.W. Bresnahan, L.E. Chen, R.A. Deyo, S. Halabi, J.A. Turner, A.L. Avins, K. James, J.T. Wald, D.F. Kallmes, and J.G. Jarvik

Imaging Finding	\multicolumn{7}{c|}{Age (yr)}						
	20	30	40	50	60	70	80
Disk degeneration	37%	52%	68%	80%	88%	93%	96%
Disk signal loss	17%	33%	54%	73%	86%	94%	97%
Disk height loss	24%	34%	45%	56%	67%	76%	84%
Disk bulge	30%	40%	50%	60%	69%	77%	84%
Disk protrusion	29%	31%	33%	36%	38%	40%	43%
Annular fissure	19%	20%	22%	23%	25%	27%	29%
Facet degeneration	4%	9%	18%	32%	50%	69%	83%
Spondylolisthesis	3%	5%	8%	14%	23%	35%	50%

Source: Brinjikji W, Luetmer P, Comstock B, et al. (2015). Systematic literature review of imaging features of spinal degeneration in asymptomatic populations. *American Journal of Neuroradiology* 36(4): 811–816. https://doi.org/10.3174/ajnr.A4173

If we took 100 healthy people in their 30s who had no pain at all and scanned their spines, over half would have disc degeneration.

If we did the same with 50-year-olds (with no pain remember), 60% would have disc bulges. In 70-year-olds with no pain, 93% would have degeneration and 75% would have bulges or arthritis... but no pain.

This is similar in all joints: rotator cuff tears in the shoulder, cartilage tears in the knee and arthritis in the hips. These are all normal signs of ageing and will often cause no pain at all.

Think of them like you think of wrinkles in the skin… a normal part of life as a human. Just because you have some internal wrinkles in your joints, it does not mean that your body part can't function normally, and it definitely does not mean that it is causing your pain.

Dr Google and well-meaning friends

In the age of technology, the internet can be a scary place – especially when it comes to health. Have you ever typed mild flu symptoms into a search engine and been informed that you probably have cancer? There is an infinite amount of health information online, and whilst some of it is credible and written by qualified health professionals, much of it is not.

People love to write their own pain horror stories online and relay anecdotes of a family member that needed surgery for pain similar to yours. Even your close friends will offer well-meaning advice about your condition, based on a situation relating to their father or aunty.

Please, for the sake of your recovery, do not listen to the internet or well-meaning (but unqualified) friends for advice. This is a sure-fire way to make your pain worse, given what you now know about how thoughts and beliefs influence the pain experience.

The power of knowledge

You now have an understanding of what pain is, how it occurs, why pain is actually very important, but how it can sometimes malfunction. Scientific research has shown that one of the most important factors in overcoming persistent pain is understanding the biology of pain. Congratulations – you've already accomplished one of the key steps to getting your life back!

It can be extremely scary experiencing chronic pain and feeling like your neck is not improving or that it is even worsening. But you should now understand that persistent pain does not accurately reflect the damage in your body and is actually due to the brain and nervous system becoming a bit too good at protecting you and misinterpreting danger messages.

You should feel great about this. It doesn't mean that you should ignore your pain – it still needs to be respected – but just know that your body is incredibly good at healing your tissues, and with chronic pain, it's much less about what's going on in the tissue. In Section 2 we will explore practical ways that you can rewire your body and brain so that your protection system can begin to function normally again.

Summary:

- Pain is an important protective mechanism
- The level of pain you experience is determined by how much danger your brain *believes* you are in
- It does not tell you about how much damage there is to your tissues
- Chronic pain is rarely an accurate assessment of danger to your body
- All of the changes in your body associated with chronic pain are reversible

Now that your pain-science knowledge is up to scratch, let's keep moving.

References:

1. Page P. (2011). Cervicogenic headaches: an evidence-led approach to clinical management. *International Journal of Sports Physical Therapy* 6(3):254–266.
2. Reiley AS, Vickory FM, Funderburg SE, Cesario RA & Clendaniel RA (2017). How to diagnose cervicogenic dizziness. *Archives of Physiotherapy* 7:12.

Recommended readings:

- Butler DS & Moseley GL. (2013). *Explain Pain*. Adelaide: Noigroup Publications.
- Jull G, Falla D, Treleaven J & O'Leary S. (2018). *Management of Neck Pain Disorders: A Research-Informed Approach*. Amsterdam: Elsevier.

Framework for success

The 5-step approach to NECKcellence that I will unveil in Section 2 is a tried and tested formula for success, but only if it's implemented correctly. The best knowledge in the world is useless if not acted upon strategically, systematically and with a plan in place. Before we dive into the *5 Ss* of a healthy neck, we need to ensure you succeed in following them through by first putting an important framework in place.

Committing to success

In order to overcome your neck pain and create genuine and lasting health, you must commit to some real changes in your life. Some who read this book will take in the information and then not act upon it. Others will read it and temporarily change, only to revert back to old ways. Then there are those who will create long-term and sustainable behaviour changes that will transform their life forever.

Which category will you choose to be in?

If you believe you will be in one of the first two categories, then you might as well stop reading here. If you are committed to being in the third category (which you do have the ability to achieve), then read on.

Changing your health and your life does not occur through chance. It occurs through making small and incremental changes to different aspects of your life that eventually create results. The beautiful thing is that there's a science and an art to changing behaviours and making them stick long term. Let's explore how you're going to make this happen.

Behavioural change

Behaviours: *The ways in which a person behaves in response to particular situations or stimuli.*

The accumulation of your daily behaviours and actions ultimately shapes who you are and how you function in the world. Unfortunately, many of the behaviours you undertake each day are not optimal for your health.

Whether it's inadequate sleep, excessive sitting or an overfondness for chocolate and wine, your daily choices all add up and have a significant impact on your health.
In order to change a behaviour, you need three key ingredients:

1. **Knowledge**

Knowledge is the theoretical paradigm: the *what?* and the *why?* This book will give you the knowledge you require.

2. **Skill**

Skill is the *how?* This book will also teach you the skills.

3. **Desire**

Desire is the motivation: the *want*. This is something you will need to search inside yourself to define. In the coming pages we will undertake an activity to make this process easier.

To successfully integrate a new behaviour into your life, you must have all three ingredients. It's often a painful process to change a behaviour, because it usually involves ceasing an old one. The change needs to be motivated by a higher purpose, a willingness to subordinate what you think you want now for what you know you want later. But this process, if successful, defines happiness.

There is a gigantic difference between changing a behaviour once, or for a few weeks, and changing it forever. Whilst you do have control over your daily routines, behaviours and actions, in reality they are occurring on autopilot most of the time. That's where *habits* come in (enter stage left).

Habit formation
Habit: *A regular behaviour or practice that has become automated, especially one that is hard to give up.*

The secret to creating sustainable and long-term changes to certain behaviours in your life is through the power of *habit formation*. To achieve life-transforming results you must turn your new behaviours into long-term *habits*.

Over 90% of your waking life is spent largely unconscious. What do I mean by this? Whilst it might be nice to believe that you are constantly making calculated, conscious decisions all of the time, in reality the vast majority of your day is spent on autopilot, simply repeating commonly practiced behaviours (habits) without any great awareness that you are doing so.

Think about the last time you drove home from work. Did you pre-plan your trip and analyse the fastest way home, or did you simply jump in your car and get lost in a stream of thoughts, only to arrive at your destination and wonder how you got there? What about your last trip to the supermarket: when you entered through the doors, did you consciously decide which aisle to walk down first, or did you naturally follow the same path you always take?

The process of automating your behaviours is your brain's clever way of preserving precious brain energy. If you had to deeply analyse every single daily decision, you would be constantly exhausted. Your brain is a hungry little energy sucker, so it is constantly finding ways to take shortcuts and save energy.

In the early stages of behaviour change, using the three ingredients of *knowledge*, *skill* and *desire* is an essential place to start. But as time goes on, this conscious process will not be enough to sustain the new behaviour over the long term.

In order for the new behaviour to successfully become a part of your life forever, it has to become a habit. It must become your default decision without you even consciously thinking about it. As much as you may like to think that your willpower is strong enough to keep you exercising daily or avoiding sugar, I can assure you it is not. The behaviours that always win long term are the ones that become habits.

Thankfully, some very clever people have already done the hard yards in figuring out how to turn behaviours into habits. In the early 1900s, a marketing genius called Claude Hopkins was given the task of trying to convince Americans to use toothpaste. At the time, just 6% of Americans brushed their teeth. Through careful analysis of people's behaviour, he realised that there were three characteristics of a habit: a *cue*, the *behaviour* and a *reward*.

By hacking this process, he was able to sell his idea of brushing teeth with toothpaste to America by identifying the *cue* of 'fury teeth' and designing the sensory *reward* of bubbles and a minty taste in the mouth. His ability to habituate teeth-brushing by creating a clear cue → behaviour → reward circuit resulted in an increase of American teeth-brushers from 6% to 68% over 10 years and made Claude a very rich man.[1]

More scientific approaches to understanding habit formation were undertaken in the 1980s, through university-based studies on monkeys. The key finding of these studies was that if a habit circuit is performed for long enough, it eventually creates *craving*.[2]

The sensation of craving is the release of chemicals in the brain that creates a desire and expectation to undertake the key behaviour in order to experience the associated reward. Craving is the key piece of the puzzle that closes the habit loop and makes you retain a certain behaviour.

The habit loop:

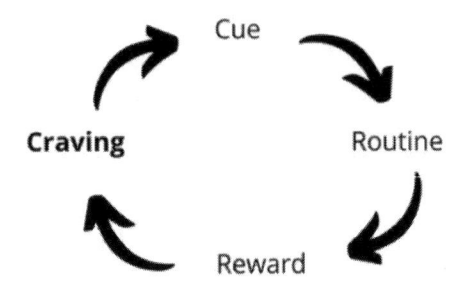

```
        Cue
   ↗         ↘
Craving      Routine
   ↖         ↙
       Reward
```

An example relating to your neck pain could be habitually using a standing work desk to improve posture. The *cue* is opening your laptop or turning on your computer. The new *behaviour* is elevating your standing work desk or putting your computer up on a stack of magazines. The *reward* is a pain-free neck. Do this for long enough and you will *crave* your new work posture, because it makes your neck feel so good.

The new behaviours you seek to turn into long-term habits will be determined and driven by your goals, so let's now turn our attention to *goal setting*.

Goal setting

Whether you're a regular goal setter or you think goal setting is cheesy and would rather go with the flow, the fact of the matter is, goal setting is essential. It is simply choosing the end destination and then mapping out how you are going to get there.

Imagine going to Central Station and getting on the first train you see. You might end up somewhere nice, you might end up in the ghetto, but chances are you'll end up a long way from where you really want to be. It's the same with goal setting: if you don't carefully choose the destination and clearly define the steps required to get there, then it's unlikely you'll ever make it.

You've probably heard of SMART goals (Specific, Measurable, Achievable, Realistic and Time-bound) and until recently, this was the style of goal setting I recommended. But research has now emerged that suggests there is a better way to set goals.

An example of a SMART goal would be:

In 6 weeks, I will swim 10 laps of the pool, at a comfortable pace, without an increase in my symptoms.

There are two key problems with SMART goals. Firstly, they encourage you to delay your happiness until you reach your goal. Secondly, if you fall even slightly short of the target you have set then you have essentially failed. There is a new style of goal setting that is proving to be much more effective: *open goals*.

Open goals are about setting an intention without defining a specific outcome. They are open-ended and do not rely on hitting any particular numbers or targets.

Examples of an open goal would be:

Let's see how little sitting I can do.

I want to see how often I can get 8-hours of sleep per night.

Whilst this may seem a little fluffy, various studies have shown that people actually perform better when they set open goals over SMART goals.[3–5] Undertaking a new task is less daunting with an open goal, and the journey is much more enjoyable because your happiness is not tied to a future event.

More importantly, if things aren't going to plan then you are more likely to quit a SMART goal, because you begin to think, 'What's the point? I'll never reach it.' With an open goal you tend to persevere and just do your best.

Think about it. If you set a goal of walking 10,000 steps per day, versus a goal of simply seeing how active you could be, can you see that you would be more likely to enjoy your walking in the second scenario? Do you agree that you would be more likely to continue being active if you only achieved 5000 steps each day than if you were emotionally tied to walking the 10,000 steps but weren't succeeding?

For each of the 5 steps to NECKcellence, you will be asked to set yourself an open goal and create a positive intention for achieving it. This will ensure you are both heading in the right direction *and* enjoying the journey.

Now is your opportunity to set your big overarching goal for your body and life. The reason you're reading this book: to heal your neck and change your life.

This goal will be your guiding light over the coming weeks and months. It will give you strength in times of darkness. It will drive you forward and give you energy to implement the 5 steps of NECKcellence. The goal must be open and should also include the true motivation for why you've set it.

Your overarching goal should not be: *'In 12 weeks I want to be pain-free.'* This does not describe what you want, but what you're trying to escape. It does not disclose why you want to achieve this.

Let's look at some examples of the kind of goal you are going to set:

- *Over the next 12 weeks I am going to see how many new healthy habits I can integrate into my life that support my neck health. This will help me achieve my true underlying motivation, which is to be a good mother, provide for my family, and be an energised and happy partner.*

- *Let's see how many times each day I can engage in an activity that contributes to my well-being. This will support my aim of getting back to surfing, which is my true passion.*

- *I want to see how frequently I can catch myself engaged in a habit that doesn't support my neck and then swap it for a positive alternative. My true underlying motivator for this is to create a healthy body that allows me to thrive in my professional and personal life.*

Now it's your turn. Set yourself the big goal. Why are you reading this book? What are you looking to achieve in your life that your health is currently preventing you from achieving? Write it down (research tells us that simply writing your goal down makes you 42% more likely to achieve it).

My Big Goal:

_____

_____

Now, I want you to share this goal with three people you trust. Choose three people that won't put you down, but will support and energise you towards achieving it.

Now you are committed.

Baby steps

Whilst embarking on this journey of healing your neck, it's important to try and let go of frustrations about your current level of function and to not compare how you are now with how you were before your condition started. This will really hold you back.

Instead, try and look at your inputs (what you're implementing to assist with your recovery) rather than your outputs (the immediate results you're feeling). The results will come, but it won't always feel like you're heading in the right direction.

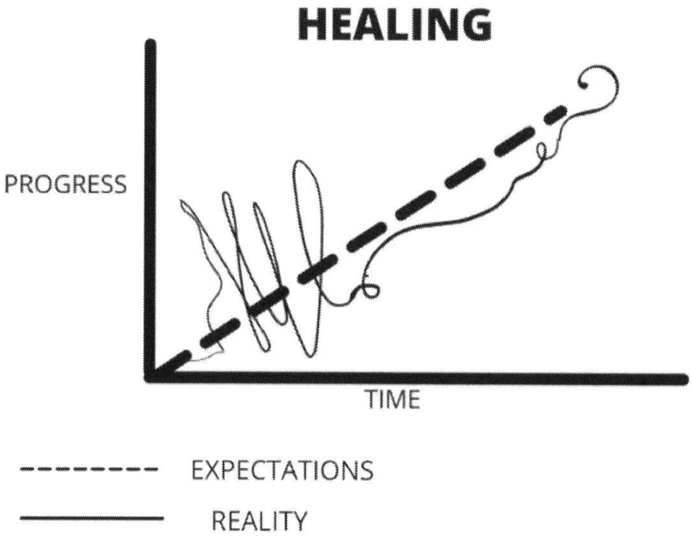
HEALING
PROGRESS
TIME
EXPECTATIONS
REALITY

The team approach

Just like anything in life, it's easier to achieve results when working as a team. The persistent pain journey is not one you have to take alone, which would certainly not produce the best outcome for you. Through this book, I will give you a step-by-step approach to overcoming your pain and creating NECKcellence, but I do genuinely believe that you will have the greatest success if you have a team of high-quality health professionals helping you implement the steps.

Build a team of health professionals that understand persistent pain, who you trust, who listen to you and who communicate with each other to strive towards achieving the best results for you as an individual.
I strongly recommend utilising a good physiotherapist, a naturopath or nutritionist, and a psychologist. If you are on any prescription pain medications then work with your doctor to slowly reduce these.

Be wary of practitioners that describe your condition in scary or threatening language or make you fearful of movement. You now understand that with chronic pain, the body tissues are not the main problem, so being 'cracked back into place' week after week is not the answer. Hands-on treatments can be effectively used in conjunction with the other approaches described in this book but are not adequate when used alone.

If consulting multiple health professionals is not financially viable for you (I empathise – when I was suffering with neck pain, I was a university student and every spare cent I had was spent on trying to fix my neck, which really broke the bank), then utilising one holistic and open-minded practitioner who can play a few different roles is an adequate solution.

The objective is to have someone in your corner, giving you good advice and keeping you motivated and on track when times get tough. Unfortunately, finding high-quality therapists that you like, trust and that have the best intentions for you is not always an easy task. Make a habit of interviewing health professionals before you hire them. You are putting your health into their hands, so they better be the right person for the job! Here is a list of questions you should ask any health professional before you let them be on your NECKcellent dream team:

1. **Can you give me a brief summary of pain physiology and how it works?** (If their answer sounds vastly different from what you've read in this chapter about pain... fire them)

2. **How useful are imaging and scans for my condition?** (If they don't discuss the poor correlation between imaging and pain... fire them)

3. **How important is movement and exercise for my neck?** (If they tell you to never move your neck, or to be overcautious and overprotective... fire them)

4. **What's the relationship between stress and my neck pain?** (If they can't give you three good relationships... fire them)

5. **What's the relationship between sleep and my neck pain?** (If they can't give you three good relationships... fire them)

6. **How important is nutrition and supplements for my condition?** (If they don't discuss the relationship between nutrition and inflammation, pain perception and tissue healing... fire them)

7. **How do emotions influence pain?** (If they can't provide a clear answer... fire them)

8. **Have you ever experienced significant pain or injury yourself?** If not, I wouldn't bother with them.

This list might seem harsh, but in order for you to create NECKcellence, your dream team of health professionals must be up to date with the latest research, be experienced in treating persistent neck pain, understand the diverse influences of the condition and recovery, and ideally be able to empathise with you through their own experience of overcoming significant injury (I believe the best health professionals have all overcome their own ailments).

Now, I have laid out clear guidelines for finding your dream team, but if you want to take a shortcut and go straight to the best, I have a team of NECKcellent therapists that can be your personal coach through this process, via online consultations from anywhere in the world, or face to face if you're in Sydney (Australia).

Head to https://www.neckspert.com.au/consulting/ to find a NECKcellent therapist.

***

You now have a framework for successfully implementing the 5 Ss of NECKcellence.

Recap and action steps:

1. Commit to success. Right now.
2. To change a behaviour, you need *knowledge*, *skills*, *motivation* and *belief*.
3. To make a new behaviour stick, it needs to become a habit.
4. To create a new habit: identify the cue/trigger, perform the new behaviour, understand the reward, repeat until you begin to crave it.
5. Set an *open* goal, understand your true motivation for setting it and make sure you believe that you can achieve it.
6. Take it one step at a time. It won't always feel like you're improving, but if you stick with the steps then you will always be heading in the right direction and you will get there.
7. Find a team of high-quality health professionals to help you put this book into practice.(https://www.neckspert.com.au/consulting/)

References:

1. Duhigg C. (2013). *The Power of Habit*. London, England: Random House Books.
2. Schultz W, Apicella P & Ljungbergb T. (1993). Responses of monkey dopamine neurons to reward and conditioned stimuli during successive steps of learning a delayed response task. *The Journal of Neuroscience* 13(3):900–913.
3. Swann C, Keegan R, Crust L & Piggott D. (2015). Psychological states underlying excellent performance in professional golfers: "Letting it Happen" vs. "Making it Happen". *Psychology of Sport and Exercise* 23:101–113. https://doi.org/10.1016/j.psychsport.2015.10.008.
4. Hawkins R, Crust L, Swann C & Jackman P. (2020). The effects of goal types on psychological outcomes in active and insufficiently active adults in a walking task: Further evidence for open goals. *Psychology of Sport and Exercise* 48:101661. https://doi.org/10.1016/j.psychsport.2020.101661
5. Swann S, Schweickle MJ, Peoples GE, et al. (2020). The potential benefits of nonspecific goals in physical activity promotion: Comparing open, do-your-best, and as-well-as-possible goals in a walking task. *Journal of Applied Sport Psychology* [published online 16 Sep 2020]. https://doi.org/10.1080/10413200.2020.1815100.

Recommended readings:

- Fogg BJ. (2019). *Tiny Habits: The Small Changes That Change Everything*. Boston, MA: Houghton Mifflin Harcourt USA.

Section 2

The 5 Steps to NECKcellence

Introducing the 5 Steps

The 5-step approach to a strong, healthy and pain-free neck is *simple*, but it is certainly not *easy*.

The approach is simple to understand and follow but implementing each of the steps and sticking to them long term requires commitment and dedication to your health. If you've read this far, then I am confident you will see the steps through and achieve NECKcellence.

The 5 Steps are designed to be executed in the correct order, from one through to five. Avoid the temptation to jump ahead or to try and do them all at once. Skipping ahead before you nail one step will make the next step harder to achieve. Starting them all at once will likely result in you becoming overwhelmed and not completing any of them.

You may wish to read through all 5 Steps before coming back to the first step and beginning the process of implementing them. Alternatively, you may prefer to get started straight away and tackle each step before exploring the next. Either strategy is fine, and I will leave it up to you to decide.

INTRODUCING THE 5 STEPS

Without further ado, here they are! The five Ss of NECKcellence:

1. **Structure**
2. **Stress**
3. **Sleep**
4. **Supplements**
5. **Subconscious Mind**

Think of the 5 Steps to NECKcellence as 'the pillars of a healthy neck'. I use the word *'pillar'* here for two reasons:

Firstly, *pillar* is a pretty darn good definition of a neck itself (a vertical structure that creates support).

Secondly, if you were to remove one of the pillars that support a building, then the building would become unstable and possibly even collapse. Similarly, if you remove one of the pillars of NECKcellence, then the whole method becomes less robust and unlikely to result in success.

I want to point out that whilst the 5 Steps are designed to create a healthy neck over the long term, this does not necessarily mean that you will never experience neck pain again. In fact, this would be very unhealthy, as you should now understand that pain in the right context is an important and very useful thing!

What it *does* mean, is that if you were to injure your neck in the future, for example through sport or lifting something too heavy, then your pain response would be healthy – the level of pain consistent with the level of tissue damage; the pain resolves quickly as the injured tissue heals; everything returns to normal rapidly.

Wrapping yourself in cotton wool and withdrawing from activities you love in order to avoid pain is no way to live. What I am encouraging instead, is that you create the perfect environment for your neck to withstand the demands that you and the world put on it. And should those demands ever exceed your neck's capacity and you do get injured, an environment in which the healing process is rapid and effective, leaving you pain-free and fully recovered in normal timeframes.

So, my friend, let us begin your 5-step journey towards creating a NECKcellent life. I'm excited to walk alongside you, one simple step at a time.

A journey of a thousand miles begins with a single step.
– Chinese proverb

Step 1: Structure

The first step to NECKcellence relates to the *structural* aspects of your neck: alignment, mobility, strength, endurance, control and posture. This is the classic focus of treatment when you see a physio or chiro.

There's a good chance you've already spent a considerable amount of time and money focusing on this step. There are two likely reasons this has not worked for you so far:

1. It was implemented poorly (bad advice, poor hands-on techniques, inadequate strength programmes, incorrect analysis).

2. This is only the first step of the five. Even if you had an amazing physiotherapist that nailed all of the structural elements of the neck, had magical hands and made you feel temporarily better every time you saw them, if you didn't get past Step 1 then you missed the forest for the trees.

Unfortunately, you may not know if you've had average (or poor) structural treatment, because many health professionals portray a great deal of self-confidence and believability even if they are completely lost. Some are well-meaning but poorly educated, others are just crooks, but either way you need to be very wary of health professionals (chiropractors, physiotherapists, osteopaths,

STEP 1: STRUCTURE

doctors etc.) that are over-servicing your neck without achieving long-term results.

If you ever hear a therapist say anything like the following, run for the hills:

Your spine is really crooked – I'm going to need to see you twice per week for a year to get it straight

You've got a slipped disc – I'm going to need to see you twice per week for a year to get it back in

Your neck has arthritis everywhere – if I don't see you twice per week for a year then you'll be crippled

You get the picture.

These sorts of comments and approaches show that the therapist is either outdated in their knowledge base or they are more interested in your money than in your recovery.

> ***You:*** *But my chiro showed me the X-ray and I could see that my neck was crooked and that my discs were degenerated.*
> ***Me (The NECKspert):*** *Put your scans in the top of the cupboard and forget you ever had them. Right now, please.*

The below table from Section 1 is such an important concept to understand that we are going to review it again here.

Research tells us that what we see on scans (such as X-ray, MRI, or CT) is largely unrelated to pain and dysfunction. Remember, this table shows the percentage of people that have degenerative changes in their spine on MRI scans, but *no* pain:

Systematic Literature Review of Imaging Features of Spinal Degeneration in Asymptomatic Populations

W. Brinjikji, P.H. Luetmer, B. Comstock, B.W. Bresnahan, L.E. Chen, R.A. Deyo, S. Halabi, J.A. Turner, A.L. Avins, K. James, J.T. Wald, D.F. Kallmes, and J.G. Jarvik

Imaging Finding	20	30	40	50	60	70	80
Disk degeneration	37%	52%	68%	80%	88%	93%	96%
Disk signal loss	17%	33%	54%	73%	86%	94%	97%
Disk height loss	24%	34%	45%	56%	67%	76%	84%
Disk bulge	30%	40%	50%	60%	69%	77%	84%
Disk protrusion	29%	31%	33%	36%	38%	40%	43%
Annular fissure	19%	20%	22%	23%	25%	27%	29%
Facet degeneration	4%	9%	18%	32%	50%	69%	83%
Spondylolisthesis	3%	5%	8%	14%	23%	35%	50%

Source: Brinjikji W, Luetmer P, Comstock B, et al. (2015). Systematic literature review of imaging features of spinal degeneration in asymptomatic populations. *American Journal of Neuroradiology* 36(4): 811–816. https://doi.org/10.3174/ajnr.A4173

If we took 100 *pain-free* 40-year-olds off the street and did an MRI of their spine, half would have disc bulges, 68% would have disc degeneration and one-third would have disc protrusions... but no pain. The likelihood of finding spinal degenerative changes on scans increases with age, even in pain-free bodies.

What this tells us is that many of the 'scary' findings we see on imaging (*arthritis, disc bulges, degeneration*) are

STEP 1: STRUCTURE

simply age-appropriate changes, like wrinkles in the skin. And they certainly do not mean you're destined for a life of pain.

Regardless of how crooked your neck looks on X-ray, or how degenerated your discs are on MRI, you can still be pain-free. I understand that having a picture you can point to that explains your pain may be comforting, but please for the sake of your recovery, forget about the scans you have of your neck and trust me when I say that they don't matter nearly as much as many health professionals would have you believe.

Is there a role for imaging at all? Absolutely – for suspected fractures and nerve-related symptoms like numbness or loss of power and reflexes it can be important. But it should never be used to scare people into excessive 'adjustments' and 'manipulations' over long periods of time in order to 'fix' a problem that isn't really *the* problem.

Apologies if that felt like a rant, but health professionals that use scare tactics to drum up business is one of my pet hates. Luckily for you, you're now armed with the knowledge (backed by scientific research) to no longer fall prey to health professionals that don't have your best interests at heart... raise a toast to that!

> *You: So, just to be clear, are you saying my C4 disc bulge isn't causing my pain?*
> *Me (The NECKspert): It might be a part of your pain experience (it also may not be), but ultimately it doesn't really matter. By improving the strength, mobility, endurance and movement control of your neck and body (in conjunction with the other four NECKcellent steps), you can heal your pain and improve your function, even if your scans are still showing an imperfect result.*

I would now like to run through some common diagnoses and break them down into language you can understand:

Disc bulge: Discs are shock-absorbers that sit in between each of your vertebrae. They are very strong. All of the tissues in your body (including your discs) adapt and change shape based on the things you do in life. If you play sport, lift heavy objects or sit in a similar position for long periods of time, your discs will change their shape to accommodate for this. A disc bulge is simply a part of your disc that has become thicker in one region in response to what you do in your life. Most of the time, disc bulges are not an issue. In fact, the area that has a bulge in it is often stronger than the rest of the disc.

Disc degeneration: As you age, you get wrinkles in your skin. But we don't call it 'skin degeneration'. When a radiologist describes your discs as 'degenerated', they are describing a very normal age-related change in the thickness of your discs. Whenever you read or hear 'disc

STEP 1: STRUCTURE

degeneration' from now on, I want you to think of it as 'age-appropriate wrinkles in the discs'.

Arthritis: Osteoarthritis refers to a reduction in the thickness of cartilage in a joint. Similar to wrinkles in the skin as we age, we naturally have a reduction in the thickness of cartilage in all of our joints. Studies show that cartilage thickness does not correlate closely with pain. Many people have 'bone on bone' (as many doctors unfortunately say) with no pain at all, whilst others have full cartilage thickness and lots of pain. If you have neck arthritis showing on your X-ray and are having a hard time believing me, you may choose to go and get an X-ray of another joint in your body that is completely pain-free (such as your knee or hip) and see how much 'arthritis' you have in there – I'd bet my bottom dollar there is a bit (but no pain)!

Foraminal stenosis: The little holes on either side of your spine that your nerves exit from are called foramen. These will often become narrower with age, known as *stenosis*. Occasionally they can become so narrow that they push on the nerve, which can cause nerve pain and symptoms. A small amount of foraminal stenosis is pretty normal and often not an issue, but if it begins to create ongoing nerve issues then it may need to be decompressed surgically.

Canal stenosis: This refers to narrowing of the spinal canal where the spinal cord travels. Again, some narrowing is common and often non-problematic, unless causing significant neurological symptoms (in which case surgery should be explored).

Whiplash: They couldn't have come up with a scarier word if they tried! *'Whip-Lash'*. Terrible name. There are different grades of whiplash, but they typically all include a strain to the tissues within the neck (muscles, joints, ligaments and nerves) after stopping rapidly, such as in a car accident or sporting tackle. Despite being very painful, whiplash rarely involves any significant damage to the structures in the neck and it should completely resolve when treated effectively.

Nerve root compression: I have had many patients tell me that something is 'crushing' their nerve (they have been told this). No wonder they have so much pain – if I was told that my nerve was crushed then my brain would produce a pretty severe pain message too. All nerves touch other structures and have some pressure on them – they literally run alongside blood vessels and muscles, constantly touching other body tissues. If they become aggravated from too much pulling, pressure or inflammation, then they become less OK with being touched. Most of the time this sensitivity can be reduced in the nerve by avoiding aggravating positions, creating less tension on the nerve through exercises or hands-on treatment, or even a cortisone injection to reduce inflammation around the nerve. The nerve will then tolerate being 'compressed' again, as it is no longer grumpy.

Hopefully the above explanations have demystified some scary medical jargon for you.

Movement as medicine

When you've had persistent pain, it's easy to become fearful of movement. Often you can't walk as far, can't sit or stand for as long, and your emotional state and relationships are also affected. Physical activity is often painful and it's easy to withdraw from movement. It's important to know that movement makes your tissues healthy and that the right movement in the right dose is one of the most powerful ways to rewire the brain and reduce pain.

When it comes to persistent neck pain, the discomfort you feel with everyday movements is less about excessive strain being placed on your tissues, and more about your overprotective system incorrectly alerting you to potential danger. It's trying to help but it's gone a bit too far.

You can reverse this process by gradually exposing your body to more and more movement over time. By doing this, you will teach your body and brain that it is safe to move and you will gradually remove the brain's perception of threat. This must be done slowly and with precision, and I will guide you through how to achieve this safely and successfully.

Beautiful movement
I believe beautiful movement has a simple equation:

**Beautiful, pain-free movement = strength + endurance + movement control + mobility
(proportional to the physical demands of your life)**

If you lack any one of these four ingredients, then you will begin to experience dysfunctional movement patterns, pain, tightness and a not-so-excellent neck.

Let's briefly explore these four ingredients before diving in a little bit deeper on each of them.

Strength: *The capacity of a structure to withstand load or force.*
Your body must be strong enough to withstand the demands that life puts on you. There are certain demands that are common across everyone, such as having the strength to withstand gravity, and then there are individualised demands related to the type of work or sport you do. The strength requirements around the neck are significantly greater for a rugby player than an accountant, for example.

At a basic level, you must have enough strength and endurance in your neck muscles to keep your head supported on your shoulders against gravity in various positions, such as standing, bending over and sitting. You must also have enough strength to move your neck and

STEP 1: STRUCTURE

head through various movements, such as lifting it up off a pillow.

Endurance: *The capacity to withstand load over an extended period of time.*

If you regularly perform tasks that require you to be in sustained neck positions for long periods of time, like a painter looking up at the roof for hours each day, then you must train your muscles to be able to withstand these physical requirements. Your endurance muscles allow you to remain in these sustained positions without fatigue.

Movement control: *The process of initiating, controlling and regulating purposeful voluntary movement via the nervous system.*

You must also have adequate control of your movement, in terms of muscular sequencing, timing and coordination. In other words, using the right muscles at the right time to perform a task. This is something that we should all ideally learn as babies as we move through our developmental milestones, but it is incredibly common for people to either:

1. Never have learned these movement control programmes adequately as a baby.

2. Have adopted new and poor-quality movement habits later in life, utilising sub-optimal control programmes in the brain and nervous system (think of a computer running dysfunctional software).

<u>Mobility</u>: *The ability to move freely through an appropriate range of motion, as dictated by joints, muscles, nerves and connective tissues.*

As well as adequate strength, endurance and control, you also need sufficient mobility in your joints, muscles, nerves and connective tissues (fascia and ligaments) in order to achieve healthy and beautiful movement.

Root cause

When I refer to the importance of strength, endurance, control and mobility, I'm not just talking about your neck in isolation. Your painful neck is often a victim rather than a culprit. Just because you are experiencing pain in your neck, it does not mean that the neck is the true source of the dysfunction. Good therapists know that the root cause of pain is often a long way away from where the pain is felt. If you lack strength, endurance, movement control or mobility *anywhere* in the body, this has the potential to create neck pain.

This is truer for the neck than anywhere else in the body. Your brain always wants your head to be level (eyes horizontal for vision, ears level for your balance system), so if you are leaning or tilting elsewhere in the body, your neck will usually adapt its position so that your head can remain level and centred. This is why it's important to have a good therapist that looks at the bigger picture of your body.

STEP 1: STRUCTURE

Take this example:

Helen broke her ankle when she was 21 (let's just say that she wasn't dancing on a table when it happened). She didn't do any rehabilitation when she came out of the plaster and whilst it is no longer painful, she never got her full strength or mobility back. Helen loves walking and running and because she has been doing so with a shortened stride on her left leg for 10 years (due to her ankle dysfunction), her body has compensated.

Specifically, she has developed a very minor right-sided tilt of her head to make up for the ankle discrepancy (this has allowed her eye level and balance detectors to remain level, even though her ankles are not). This mild head tilt over a long period of time has resulted in Helen developing neck pain and headaches. When she gets treatment on her neck, she feels temporarily better, but because nobody had treated the root cause, it always came back.

By treating Helen's ankle, I gave her whole body the opportunity to come back into alignment so that her neck did not have to compensate for her ankle dysfunction. The area of pain is often not the root cause!

Let's now dive a little deeper into strength, endurance, control and mobility, from both educational and practical perspectives.

Strength, Endurance and Control

There are muscles and there are muscles. Not all are created equal.

Some common complaints I hear are 'strength exercises make me worse', or 'I've done so much strengthening but I'm still in pain.'

This is because there are different types of muscles that need to be strengthened and controlled in different ways.

In your neck and throughout the rest of your body, you have both deep and superficial muscles. Think of the deep muscles as the *stabilisers* and the superficial muscles as the *movers*. Your deep muscles are considered 'postural' muscles and are designed for endurance. These smaller muscles contract at a low level for long periods of time and have many attachment points, meaning they can control each level of the neck with precision. They allow for control and stability whilst moving.

Your superficial (outer layer) muscles are designed for big movements and usually span larger areas. They are more powerful, but they are designed for shorter duration use (like sitting up from lying down) and they fatigue more easily.

STEP 1: STRUCTURE

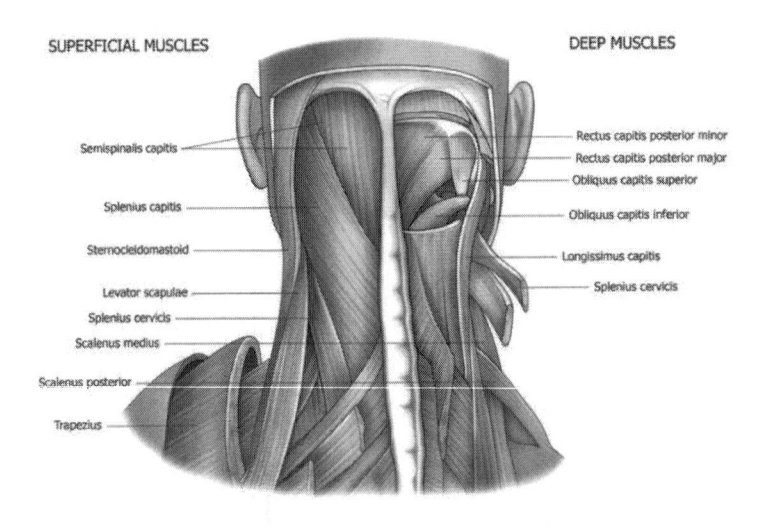

SUPERFICIAL MUSCLES — Semispinalis capitis, Splenius capitis, Sternocleidomastoid, Levator scapulae, Splenius cervicis, Scalenus medius, Scalenus posterior, Trapezius

DEEP MUSCLES — Rectus capitis posterior minor, Rectus capitis posterior major, Obliquus capitis superior, Obliquus capitis inferior, Longissimus capitis, Splenius cervicis

Source: Adapted from Stathakios J & Carron MA. Anatomy, Head and Neck, Posterior Cervical Region. [Updated 2020 Jul 31]. In: StatPearls [Internet]. Treasure Island (FL): StatPearls Publishing; 2021 Jan. Available at: https://www.ncbi.nlm.nih.gov/books/NBK551521.

A common cause of neck pain is an overreliance on the superficial muscles and poor control or endurance of the deeper postural muscles. When you rely on your superficial muscles for stability, they become tight, fatigued and painful from overuse.

Before you try complex movement patterns and exercise regimes, it's important to spend a few weeks learning how to retrain and strengthen your deep neck muscles.

The first step in this process is *movement control*. This refers to your ability to switch on the right muscle at the right time and requires you to improve the connection between each group of muscles and your brain. Once you relearn (or perhaps learn for the first time) how to find your deep stability muscles and improve your movement control through muscle sequencing and activating the right muscle for the right task, you will find that your neck can tolerate more without becoming sore and tight.

The key principle of movement control is *repetition*. Movement control refers to your ability to coordinate and sequence voluntary movements in your body via nerve pathways in your brain and nervous system. In order to create new movement patterns, you must repeat new movements over and over again until you form a new nerve pathway. Do this for long enough and it becomes *automatic* and overwrites the old one. For this to occur, you will need to practice hundreds of repetitions per day (e.g. three sets of 30 repetitions, three times per day).

The next step is to then improve the strength (the amount of load you can resist) and endurance (the amount of time you can resist that load for) of both your deep *and* superficial muscles. These exercises must then be slowly progressed by increasing the load (either via gravity or adding resistance via bands and weights) and the duration of the exercises (which will help with endurance). There is no point trying these exercises until you have mastered the control of your deep stability system, otherwise poor technique will create pain and tightness.

I have created a series of NECKsercise videos to guide you through each phase of muscle control and strengthening. These can be found at: www.neckspert.com.au/resources

STEP 1: STRUCTURE

Whole system strength and control

The illustration on page 78 shows the deep stability muscles of the neck, but in reality, you must also learn to control and strengthen the deep stabilisers of the rest of your body, such as your lower back, pelvis and hips.

Overactivity in the superficial muscular system anywhere in the body can create increased forces on the neck and contribute to pain and dysfunction. It may seem daunting that there are so many areas of the body that you need to learn to control in order to create a healthy neck structure, but don't worry – the NECKsercise videos on my website will focus on whole system strength and you will learn really simple exercises that tackle all of the important areas.

Diaphragmatic breathing

Try something right now: put one hand on your chest and the other on your belly. Take a deep breath in. Which hand rises first? Does your stomach expand and stick out like a pot belly when you breathe in? Or do you suck in your stomach and breathe into your chest?

If you're breathing correctly, your belly should expand first (hello, Buddha belly!) followed by chest expansion second. If your stomach draws in and your chest expands straight away, you have a dysfunctional breathing pattern that is likely creating issues for your neck.

One of the most important muscles related to improving neck pain is the *diaphragm*. The diaphragm is the muscle that you use to breathe. It is controlled by your *autonomic nervous system*, meaning it contracts automatically and outside of your awareness. The diaphragm sits just under your lungs, at the bottom of the rib cage, and when it contracts it draws air into your lungs by creating negative pressure.

When you use your diaphragm effectively to breathe, called *diaphragmatic breathing*, two very important things happen. The first is that you create more pressure in your abdomen, which acts as an important stabiliser of the spine. Second, you draw air right down into the base of your lungs, where you have more blood vessels, resulting in more oxygen from each breath than when you just breathe into your upper chest.

But here's the issue: most people in our society (especially people with neck pain) don't breathe diaphragmatically!

Why is this? I believe there are two main reasons:

Number one relates to ego. If you watch a young child breathe, they allow their belly to expand as they breathe in, meaning they are using their diaphragm effectively. This is a very natural process and does not require any thought for kids. But if you watch a teenager breathe, they will often puff out their chest and suck in their stomach, usually because they have just become aware of the opposite sex. This is then reinforced by society as we are bombarded by the media showing us people with flat stomachs and big chests, so we continue to adopt this poor breathing pattern. After a while it becomes an automated pattern in our brains and nervous system, requiring us to unlearn it through breath training.

The second reason is related to stress. Many of us lead stressful lives and when our nervous system becomes stressed, we adopt a rapid and shallow breathing pattern (this is part of the fight-or-flight response you will learn about in the next chapter). Stress makes you breathe into your upper chest, rather than using your diaphragm, and the changes in oxygen and carbon dioxide that this creates leads to more stress, creating a self-perpetuating cycle.

What are the implications of a dysfunctional breathing pattern on neck pain?

As mentioned earlier, when you breathe with good diaphragm activation ('Buddha belly breathing'), you create more pressure in the abdomen, which acts as a stabiliser for your pelvis and spine. If you have a stable base of support for your spine, then you will have better neck alignment and posture. Poor stability around your pelvis and lower back means your neck needs to work very hard to control its position, resulting in poor alignment, overactive neck muscles and pain.

The next key impact of upper chest breathing is related to oxygenation. As mentioned earlier, there are more blood vessels in the bottom of your lungs, so when you breathe 'low' you are able to absorb more oxygen from your lungs into your bloodstream. With an upper chest breathing pattern, there is reduced oxygen absorption, so the body compensates by using muscles around the neck and upper chest to try and expand the rib cage to get more air in.

The muscles that achieve this are called 'accessory respiratory muscles' because they assist with breathing when oxygen requirements increase. They are most often used during exercise to help the body get more air into the lungs, but if you have a dysfunctional breathing pattern then they can commonly be used at rest. This has *huge* implications for your neck, because your accessory muscles (which surround your neck) become overused, fatigued and will create compression and poor neck alignment.

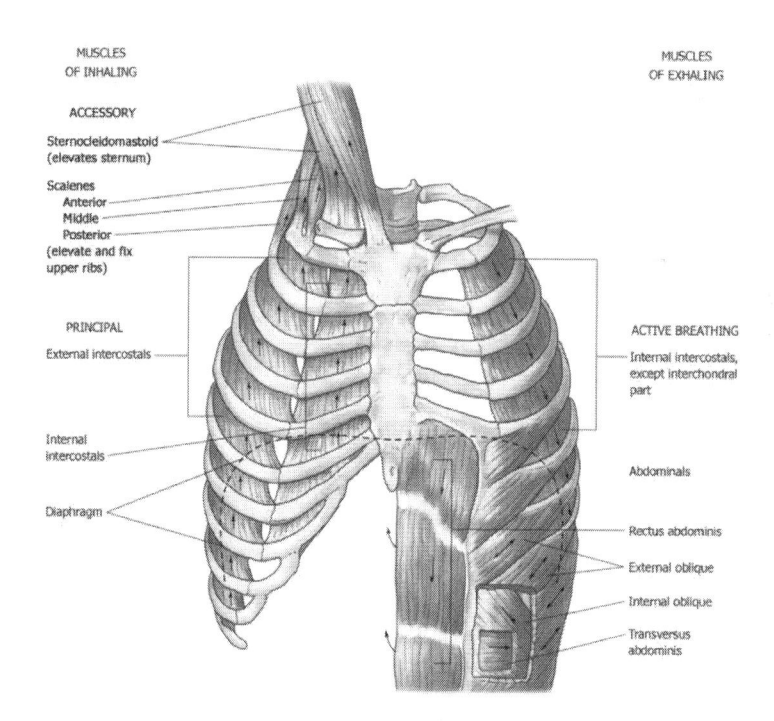

Source: Adapted from McConnell A. (2013). *Respiratory Muscle Training: Theory and Practice.* Oxford: Elsevier.

STEP 1: STRUCTURE

Another important element of good oxygenation is *slow* breathing, because slow airflow goes to the bottom of the lungs ('*slow flow goes low*'). This occurs naturally when you breathe through your nose, because the nasal passages are smaller than the mouth, which reduces the air flow rate. If you have blocked sinuses then it promotes mouth breathing, which results in upper chest breaths and accessory muscle use.

Seeking treatment for blocked sinuses can help you transition into becoming a nasal breather, which is very important for NECKcellence.

NB: Sinus sprays are more of a symptom reliever than a treatment for the root cause of the sinus congestion. Sinus congestion is typically due to mild allergies and intolerances (to food or environmental allergens), which can often be addressed via optimising gut health. The chapter on *Supplements* (Step 4) will offer tips on improving gut health.

You can find diaphragmatic breathing exercises in the NECKsercise videos: www.neckspert.com.au/resources

Mobility and Range of Movement (ROM)

Remember the equation for beautiful movement? We've now covered strength, endurance and movement control, so the next piece of the puzzle is *mobility*.

A common misconception is that everyone needs more flexibility. Whilst this is true for many people, there are also a large number of people who are *hypermobile* (very flexible), who actually need control and stability rather than more mobility. Hypermobility is genetic (you are born with it) and is determined by how stretchy your ligaments are, as well as the length of your muscles and fascia (connective tissue).

There is a very simple test to determine whether you are genetically hypermobile (flexible) or hypomobile (inflexible). It's called the Beighton Score and is a mark out of 9, with a higher score indicating more mobility.[1] Let's do it right now:

STEP 1: STRUCTURE

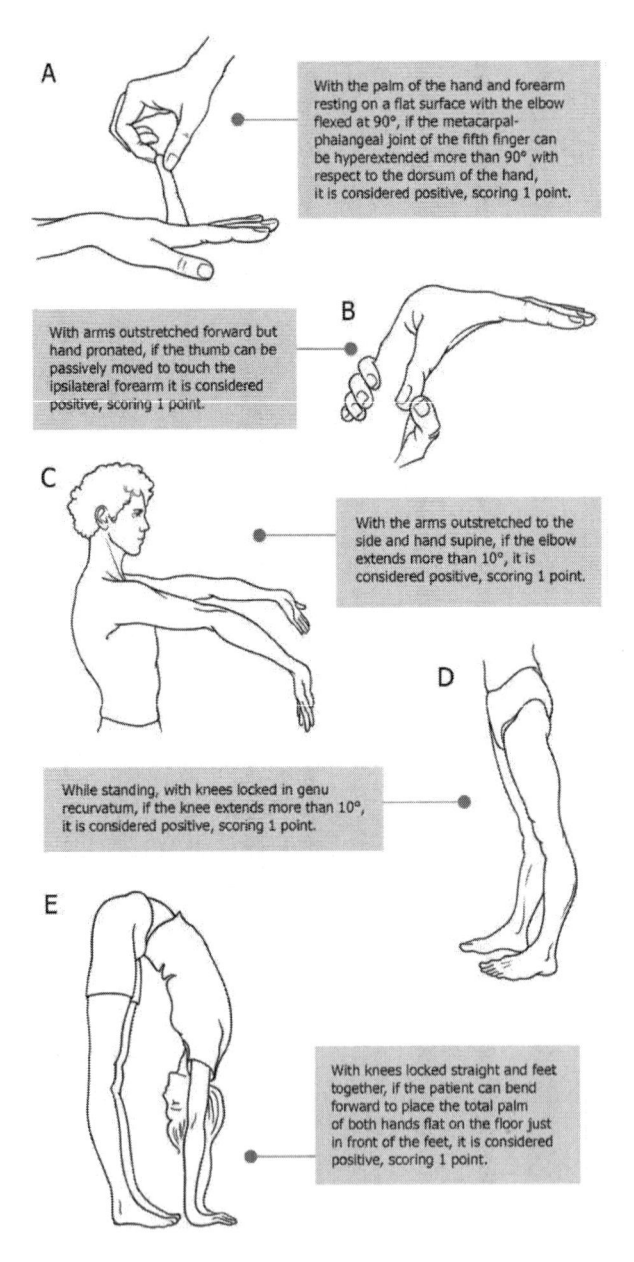

A — With the palm of the hand and forearm resting on a flat surface with the elbow flexed at 90°, if the metacarpal-phalangeal joint of the fifth finger can be hyperextended more than 90° with respect to the dorsum of the hand, it is considered positive, scoring 1 point.

B — With arms outstretched forward but hand pronated, if the thumb can be passively moved to touch the ipsilateral forearm it is considered positive, scoring 1 point.

C — With the arms outstretched to the side and hand supine, if the elbow extends more than 10°, it is considered positive, scoring 1 point.

D — While standing, with knees locked in genu recurvatum, if the knee extends more than 10°, it is considered positive, scoring 1 point.

E — With knees locked straight and feet together, if the patient can bend forward to place the total palm of both hands flat on the floor just in front of the feet, it is considered positive, scoring 1 point.

Source: Adapted from Ghali N, Sobey G & Burrows N. (2019). Ehlers-Danlos syndromes. *British Medical Journal* 366:l4966. https://doi.org/10.1136/bmj.l4966

You get one point for each side in items A–D and one point for E, with a maximum possible score of 9.

If you scored 4 or above, then you are considered to have joint hypermobility. This is not something to be concerned about, but it's important to be aware of because it will change the style of rehabilitation that is best for you. If you have joint hypermobility then you should not be spending much time (if any) on stretching, trigger pointing and massage or manipulation. Small amounts of these in the right places may be beneficial, but where you really need to be spending your time is on strength and postural control exercises. Your flexible body needs support, not more mobility, so too much muscle-release work (stretching, massage, manipulations and adjustments) will likely make you worse.

If you scored below 4, then whilst you still need to do the strength and control work, you will also need to work on your mobility and flexibility.

As a side note, if you've ever wondered why some people are naturally better at some sports than others, hypermobility and hypomobility play a big role. Hypermobile people are naturally better at swimming, surfing, dancing and gymnastics, whilst hypomobile bodies tend to be better at running, and agility and power sports.

STEP 1: STRUCTURE

Mobility over the lifespan

Neck movement	20–29 years	30–39 years	40–49 years	50–59 years	60–69 years
Flexion (looking down)	63–64°	58–59°	52–58°	50–52°	53°
Extension (looking up)	80–82°	63–69°	63–66°	56–60°	46°
Lateral flexion (side bend)	43–47°	34–38°	34–38°	30–32°	26°
Rotation (looking over shoulder)	72–76°	68–72°	57–63°	56–62°	54°

Source: Hole DE, Cook JM & Bolton JE (1995). Reliability and concurrent validity of two instruments for measuring cervical range of motion: effects of age and gender. *Manual Therapy* 1(1), 36–42. https://doi.org/10.1054/math.1995.0248.

This diagram shows that you inevitably lose a bit of your movement as you age. These are population averages and many people in each age bracket would have more or less mobility than is outlined here, but the general trend is a progressive reduction in flexibility as you get older.

Does this mean you are destined to have pain as you age? Absolutely not. I have a large number of elderly clients that have significantly reduced neck mobility and scans showing vast 'degeneration' and 'arthritis' who are pain-free and enjoy excellent function.

It's important to understand that you will never have the same level of neck mobility as you did when you were in your teens or early 20s, so this should not be the goal. What we are aiming for with your neck flexibility is age-appropriate mobility (where possible), more symmetry between your left and right sides, and a reduction in painful *trigger points* (more on these soon).

Causes of stiffness and inflexibility

Whilst it's true that a certain amount of your mobility is controlled by your genetics, there are many aspects that can be improved. There are four key structures in the body that influence flexibility:

1. Muscles
2. Fascia
3. Nerves
4. Joints

We will explore each of these as concepts first and then discuss how to improve them at the end.

Muscles

In the same way that your muscles adapt to force (they get stronger when exposed to more and weaker when exposed to less), they also adapt to *length*. When a muscle is held in a shortened position for a long period of time, the muscle adapts by literally shortening itself through removing muscle cells (why keep what you don't need?). The same is true of prolonged lengthening: by maintaining a lengthened

STEP 1: STRUCTURE

muscle position for a long period of time, cells are added to the end of the muscle to make it longer.

In reality, when you feel 'tight' in your muscles, it is unlikely that a true change in your muscle *length* has occurred, as it takes weeks of a sustained position to influence true muscle length changes. There are three other influences on your perception of muscle tightness that are much more common.

The first of these are *trigger points*. When a muscle is used repetitively over time (particularly to the point of fatigue) or sustained in a shortened position, it can develop painful knots in the muscle belly called trigger points. These are tight and tender muscle fibres that can be felt as lumps in the muscle. If you have trigger points in the muscles around your neck (if you sit for long periods throughout the day, have high stress levels or do repetitive upper body exercise then it's very likely that you do), it will often feel as though your muscles have become short, tight and painful.

Unlike the true change in muscle length via loss of cells that occurs from sustained shortening over several weeks, trigger points cause the muscle to shorten through contraction and can be treated very quickly with massage and trigger point therapy.

The problem that I often see in people with neck pain is they will get treatment for painful trigger points that makes them feel temporarily better, but does not address the cause of *why* the trigger points have emerged, so they always return.

Fascia

Fascia seemed to be an ignored structure in anatomy for a long time. It is a strong, white connective tissue that sits on top of your muscles. I remember being in the university laboratory learning anatomy on cadavers (dead bodies) and looking at these thin strips of white tissue throughout the bodies. These white bands of fascia included the iliotibial band (ITB), the plantar fascia (underneath the foot) and the thoracolumbar fascia (across the back). What I have since come to learn is that the rest of the fascia was simply dissected and thrown away by the laboratory assistants, so that the cadavers reflected what was drawn in our anatomy textbooks.

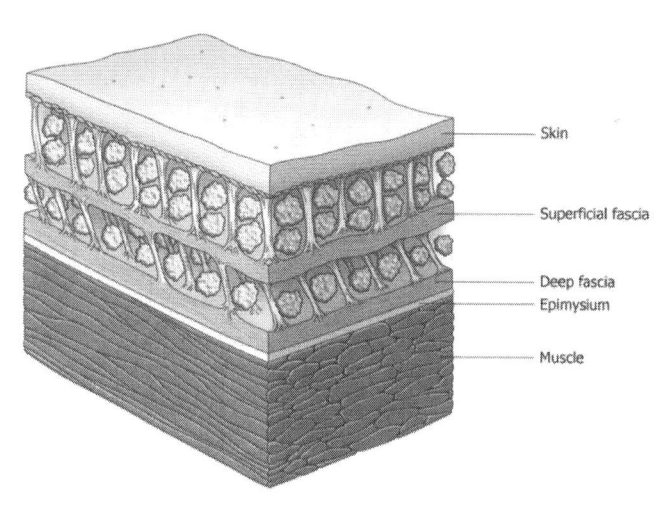

Source: Adapted from Stecco C, Macchi V, Porzionato A, Duparc F & Caro RD. (2011). The fascia: the forgotten structure. *Italian Journal of Anatomy and Embryology* 116(3):127–138.

STEP 1: STRUCTURE

In reality, fascia is a continuous network of tissue that runs throughout your whole body, without interruption. Rather than having a few distinct bands of fascia in the body (such as the ITB) like most anatomy textbooks would have you believe, it is more like a second skin that overlays the top of your muscular system. In fact, you have deep and superficial fascial systems, so it's like a second and a third skin!

The story gets even more interesting; it was previously believed that fascia was a *passive* system, meaning that it did not have the ability to contract like muscles do. Research has now shown that the fascial system *can* contract in a way similar to muscle (with a lot less force, but still in a way that significantly impacts how you move), meaning the length and tension of your fascia can be readily changed.

Now that you can visualise the fascial system as an internal body-bag, you should be able to appreciate just how *connected* everything is. If you become tight in one part of your fascia, it will change the position and length in every other part of the fascial network.

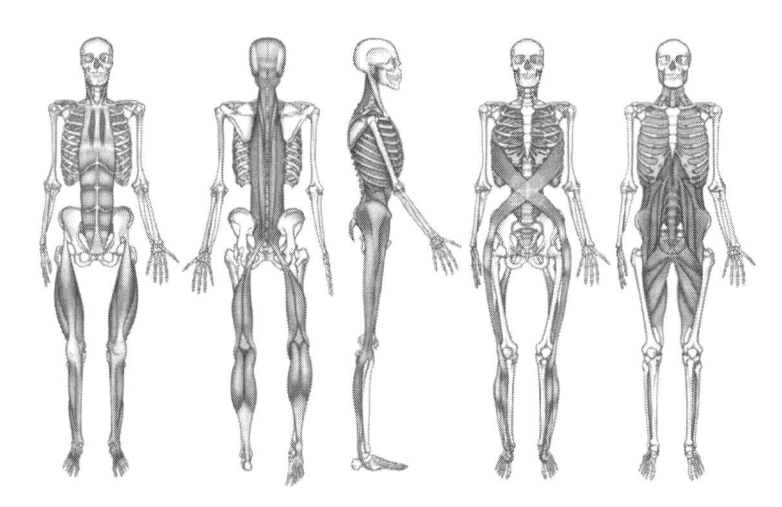

Source: Myers TW. (2001). *Anatomy Trains: Myofascial Meridians for Manual and Movement Therapists.* Edinburgh: Churchill Livingstone.

Imagine you and a friend are holding opposite ends of a large beach towel (one corner in each hand). If one of you pulls harder on one hand (mimicking a fascial contraction or tightness), you would feel that it changes the tension within the *whole* towel, with some parts getting tighter and others becoming looser. The same is true of your fascial system; tension in your leg can easily influence tension in your neck and vice versa.

Nerves

Nerves control both your ability to move and your ability to feel. Nerves are like long pieces of string (or rope in the case of your larger nerves) that conduct electrical messages between your body and spinal cord or brain.

There are small receptors in your muscles and joints that inform you about any movement that occurs. When you begin to stretch a muscle or joint, this information is

STEP 1: STRUCTURE

communicated along your nerves to the spinal cord and brain so that you become aware of it and decide if you should do something about it. You could have the tightest muscle in the world, but without a nerve to communicate this information, you wouldn't feel it.

The less you move your muscles and joints, the more intolerant your nerves become to movement. Your stretch receptors and nerves can become sensitised and your ability to move is reduced because the nerve sensitivity produces pain.

When you stretch your muscles, you become more 'flexible' not because the muscle is becoming longer, but because your *perception* of tightness is reducing. In other words, the nerves that are sending your brain messages about the stretch within the muscle are becoming less protective and allowing you to stretch further before they send a pain message.

It's not just a lack of movement that can create nerve sensitivity. If a nerve becomes impinged, overstretched or inflamed, it can become irritated and less tolerant to movement. It often feels like a tight muscle and if lengthened will produce an intense stretch feeling and pain. This is called *neural tension*.[2]

In the neck, this is commonly felt with flexion (looking down), rotation (looking over your shoulder), side-bending (ear to shoulder) and arm movements. Neural tension is treated very differently to muscle and joint stiffness so it's important to determine if this is the type of tightness you're feeling. There are specific tests to assess for neural tension, which you can view at www.neckspert.com.au/resources.

Joints

Joints are the connection points between bones, and there are four key aspects of joints that determine their mobility. The first is related to the muscles and fascia spanning the joint. The tighter the muscles or fascia around the joint, the greater the joint *compression*. Compressive forces around a joint create increased stiffness and decreased mobility. There are often local (deep) muscles and global (superficial) muscles contributing to joint compression.

The second is called *synovial fluid* and you can think of this as the lubricating oil in your joints. The role of the synovial fluid is to reduce friction between the cartilage surfaces of a joint, to allow for enhanced mobility. The more you move, the more synovial fluid is produced. The less you move, the less you produce. This is one of the reasons you may feel stiff when you first get out of bed in the morning, only to find that your neck mobility improves once you get moving.

The third structure in your joints that dictates mobility is the cartilage. The ends of your bones have a slippery surface called *hyaline cartilage*. This low-friction tissue ensures that the joint surfaces glide over each other beautifully. As you get older, you will likely have a reduction in the thickness of this cartilage, known in the medical world as *osteoarthritis*.

STEP 1: STRUCTURE

This word sounds scary and is often thrown around by doctors as an irreversible cause of pain, but I believe there needs to be a change in the medical community when discussing osteoarthritis. There is no doubt that a reduction in the thickness and quality of cartilage in a joint does impact its mobility and can contribute to pain, but let's compare the old-school description and treatment of osteoarthritis with a newer and more evidence-based version.

Old-school: *You have arthritis in your joints. This is wear and tear in the cartilage, which means you now have bone on bone, creating pain and stiffness. You should give up impact activities and take pain medication.*

New-school: *You have a reduction in the thickness of your joint cartilage. This is actually quite normal and just like you start to get some wrinkles in your skin as you age, you also get some wrinkles in your cartilage. Research shows that the thickness of your cartilage and your pain levels are quite unrelated, as many people with significant cartilage loss have no pain at all. The most important thing you can do for your joints is exercise, keep moving and stay strong.*

The fourth determinant of joint mobility is ligament tension. The main role of a ligament is to prevent a joint from moving excessively. As discussed in the earlier section on hypermobility, the tightness or laxity of your ligaments is largely dictated by genetics. Ligaments can be stretched or thickened based on your activities, but rather than trying to influence this it's more useful to know your

Beighton score and then tailor your exercises to this – a stretching and mobility focus if you're *hypomobile* and a stability focus if you're *hypermobile*.

So, you should now understand the key components of beautiful movement: strength, endurance, movement control and mobility. We've discussed how to improve the first three, so let's round it out by discussing how you can improve your mobility.

Improving your mobility

When it comes to improving your range of movement, there are self-management strategies and therapist-based strategies. The best results will come from a combination of both, but over time you should aim to significantly reduce the frequency of therapist-based treatment and move towards a self-management routine with occasional physio sessions to keep you on track.

There are various mobility techniques, but not all are created equal. It's important to use the right strategy, at the right time, in the right body part, to ensure the best results.

Let's start with therapist-based mobility techniques.

Things your physio can (and should) do to increase your mobility
Firstly, I want you to flick back to the top of this section and re-read the part about *root cause* and the story of Helen. Pain in the neck is not always due to dysfunction in

STEP 1: STRUCTURE

the neck (remember, victims and culprits), so the first and most important thing that any good therapist must determine is the true source of your pain. The dysfunction (such as weakness, tightness, poor alignment, altered messaging) may be anywhere in the body, such as the rib cage, pelvis, foot, or even in the visual or balance systems (or any combination of areas), and until this root cause is uncovered your neck pain will keep coming back.

Even if the root cause of your pain is not in the neck, there are some hands-on techniques (like massage) that may still be beneficial *in* the neck, as it has likely been compensating for dysfunction elsewhere in the body for long enough that it too has started to become dysfunctional. But this is not always the case and the important message here is that hands-on treatment does not necessarily need to be in the neck area in order to heal your neck pain. Get a thorough assessment from a good therapist who looks at your whole body.

Once the correct area to be treated has been found, if poor mobility is part of the dysfunction then there are various techniques that can be used to improve this.

Cracking, manipulations and adjustments
There seems to be a passive-aggressive (or sometimes overtly aggressive) tension between physiotherapists and chiropractors when it comes to treatment technique selection. The age-old debate about whether cracking joints or releasing muscles is superior has raged on for years, with

varying degrees of intensity from both sides of the fence (from mild disagreement through to all-out warfare).

The reality is that there are great physiotherapists and there are terrible physiotherapists, just like there are great chiropractors and terrible chiropractors, and the health outcomes are more likely representative of the overall quality of the practitioner than the use of one mobility technique over the other.

That said, here is my argument for why I believe a muscular–fascial-based approach is superior.

Cracking a joint is simply releasing the nitrogen gas that has built up naturally from within the joint. If a joint is poorly aligned then there will be an increase in pressure within the joint, hence you will feel as though it needs to be cracked to release this pressure.

In order to crack a joint, it must be taken to the end of its range of mobility, then quickly pushed beyond this. Once this has occurred, the release of gas will give you a sense of relief due to the decreased pressure and therefore increased mobility within the joint. There are two key issues I see with this strategy as a long-term solution to improving mobility.

The first issue is that despite the lack of scientific evidence confirming that joint cracking causes damage to joints, the mechanism in which the crack occurs requires taking joints beyond their normal range of motion. If this is done

STEP 1: STRUCTURE

repetitively, then it would be likely to create a small degree of tissue trauma to the ligaments and joint capsule over time.

Joint damage aside, there have been numerous instances in which people have incurred injuries to their vertebral artery following a neck adjustment, resulting in a stroke. Studies have found that improvements in neck pain are similar when comparing manipulation (i.e. cracking or adjustments) with joint mobilisation (gently oscillating the joint up and down but without taking it beyond its range and eliciting a crack). Given this, the benefit of cracking a neck does not seem to make sense to me when I weigh up the risk versus the reward, especially when gentle mobilisations produce the same improvements in pain.

The second issue is that cracking a joint does not address the reason it has become 'misaligned' in the first place. The positions of your bones and joints are controlled by your muscles and fascial system. If you feel like you need to crack a joint, it's because it is sitting in a non-optimal position, which is the result of tight muscles pulling it into that position or weak muscles not holding it in the correct position.

Let's use an analogy: imagine you have seven bricks stacked on top of each other and there are two ropes attached to every brick, each pulling in opposite directions. Borris and Dorris are standing on either side of the brick tower holding the ropes, preparing to play a game of tug-of-war.

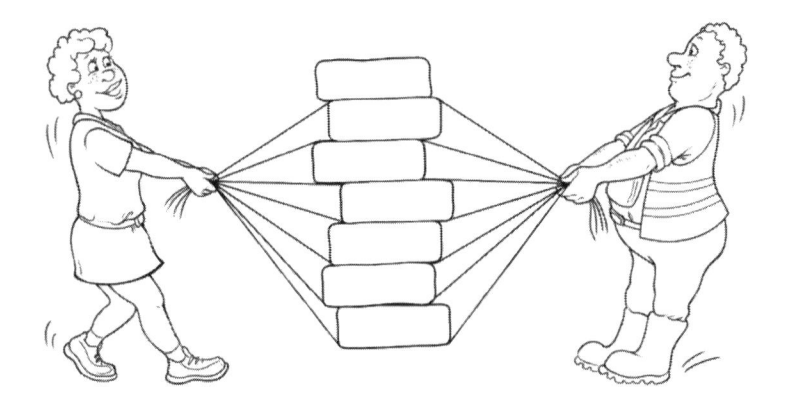

Now, if Borris and Dorris both pull with the same force, the brick tower will stay perfectly straight. But if one of them becomes weak or pulls a little harder, the tower will begin to look asymmetrical.

By now you may have worked out that the bricks in this example are your vertebrae and the ropes are your muscles. If the bricks were able to feel their position during this game of tug-of-war, they'd probably be telling you that they are stiff, sore or need to be manipulated back into better alignment.

Let's now imagine that a bricklayer (therapist) comes along and gives each brick a little 'adjustment' to create a well-aligned tower. If the tug-of-war is still playing out in an asymmetrical way, how long do you think it will be before the bricklayer needs to come back again and give the tower another adjustment? Not long.

STEP 1: STRUCTURE

If, however, we adjusted the length of all of the ropes to create symmetry and ensured that all of the opponents were pulling with the same force, can you see how the bricks will again become balanced and the bricklayer will no longer need to put them back into place?

Joints become compressed due to tightness or weakness within the muscles and fascia, so I believe you will always get more bang for your buck over the long term by addressing these issues as opposed to joint cracking.

Am I totally opposed to cracking joints? No.

Do I do it often? No, because once I release the forces compressing a joint, it rarely needs to be cracked as it has regained mobility and freedom to move.

Cracking joints can feel temporarily great, but I'm yet to see someone who gets more than a few days relief from it. If you're not releasing the muscles that are pulling the joints into a position where they feel like they need to be cracked, then the joint will quickly return to the same position and the desire to be cracked will be there all over again.

In the rare instance that I do crack a joint, it will be because I have released all of the surrounding muscles that are causing joint compression or tension but there still seems to be movement restriction *within* the joint. In this situation, I may crack it, but I know I have already addressed the reason it has become misaligned (i.e. released the ropes) and given the patient instructions about appropriate exercises to perform to prevent the ropes from tightening again.

Releasing the ropes

Now that I've given you my two cents' worth about the importance of muscle and fascial releases, let's explore the best ways to achieve it. No doubt you have come across some of these techniques during your neck pain journey and if you're thinking, 'I've tried all of these and none of them have worked,' remember that they're only effective if applied to the right muscles, in combination with an appropriate exercise programme and alongside the other steps to NECKcellence.

Massage
I'm not a big fan of full-body massages for people that have specific injuries. I believe a specific and targeted approach is more important. There will be tight and shortened muscles or fascia either within your neck or between your neck and the root cause area that are creating asymmetrical forces. Once identified, these can effectively be released through massage, which relaxes and lengthens contracted muscle fibres and tight fascia.

Trigger point therapy
Like massage, *trigger point* therapy is a soft tissue technique designed to relax and lengthen overactive muscle tissue. A trigger point is a focal area of muscle tissue that is contracted and tender. By applying sustained pressure to

the trigger point, the muscle is temporarily starved of the oxygen it needs to keep contracting, causing it to relax and therefore interrupting the neural feedback loop keeping it tight.

Dry needling

This is my favourite release technique. As described above, trigger points are tight bands of muscle fibres that are on a feedback loop of contraction (the nerve that supplies the muscle is telling it to contract). Applying an acupuncture needle into the trigger point can stimulate the nerve endings within the muscle and cause the whole muscle to contract (twitch response). This resets the electrical activity within the muscle and allows it to 'switch off' and relax.

Muscle energy technique (MET)

MET improves the position and mobility of joints through contracting and relaxing the muscles around them.[3] After a muscle has contracted, it relaxes and lengthens more than prior to the contraction. Similarly, by contracting an opposing muscle (one that creates the opposite movement), it creates a relaxation effect in the muscle you're wanting to release. MET uses these principles to achieve the desired response within and around a joint.

Stretching

Static stretching has copped a fair bit of flak in the physio community over the last decade, based on research that suggested it did not reduce injury risk. The research also concluded that it did not produce a true change in muscle length (unless sustained for several weeks, such as with splinting), but rather a change in the perception of pain during stretching (the onset of pain was later in the stretch).

Unfortunately, I feel as though the baby was thrown out with the bath water in this instance. Whilst stretching may not cause muscle fibres to increase in length, there are certainly benefits to using a greater range of motions in your joints as a result of increased flexibility before pain onset. Secondly, this particular study did not investigate the effects of stretching on the fascial system. A lot of the tightness we feel in the body is in fact due to fascia, not muscles, and stretching can certainly have a positive effect on the length and mobility of fascia in the body.

I therefore do recommend static stretching as a technique for improving mobility and 'releasing the ropes', but only after warming up.

Nerve glides

The *neural tension* (nerve tightness) described earlier can be treated through various nerve gliding techniques. The goal of nerve gliding is to reduce the sensitivity of the nerve through graded exposure to stretch, as well as to improve the mobility of the neural tissue that is being irritated.[2] This should be started with a *sliding* or *gliding* technique, where one end of the nerve is pulled and at the same time the other end is taken off stretch (similar to flossing teeth). This can then be progressed to a nerve *tensioner*, where both ends of the nerve are pulled in opposing directions. Nerve tensioners must be approached with caution as they have the ability to increase pain if not done correctly.

Self-release techniques – becoming your own physio

Whilst it's important to get a thorough assessment by a therapist to determine the specific areas that should be released, the real work should take place outside of the physio clinic. If you are spending 1 hour per week with a therapist who is using the above mobility techniques on you, that means there are 167 hours left in the week where you could be working on your own mobility exercises.

The goal is to become less reliant on a therapist doing passive techniques *to* you and to begin implementing a strategy in which you can treat yourself, by using self-release and strength exercises to reduce or remove pain when it occurs and prevent it from returning.

Until you really start to get your pain under control, I recommend a minimum of 20 minutes per day of self-guided release techniques. Down the track this can be reduced to 20 minutes every 2–3 days, but it should definitely become a part of your life.

Rather than trying to explain these exercises via text, I have created a series of self-release and mobility exercise videos that you can view and perform anywhere, anytime: www.neckspert.com.au/resources

Muscles become tight for a reason, so regardless of the techniques used to release them, the key thing is that they have to be coupled with exercises that are designed to prevent them from tightening again. This is typically a combination of strength, endurance and control exercises that are designed to improve posture and movement mechanics, as outlined earlier in this section.

Posture and ergonomics
There's a pretty good chance that right now, as you are reading this, you're sitting down.

We live in a society where most of us now sit for the majority of the day. We wake up, sit to eat breakfast, we sit on the way to work, sit at work, sit at lunch, back to sitting at work, sit on the commute home, hopefully get an hour of exercise in after work, sit to eat dinner, sit to read or watch TV and then off to bed again.

STEP 1: STRUCTURE

How many hours do you sit for in a day?

Activity	Hours
Breakfast	
Commute to work	
Morning work	
Lunch	
Afternoon work	
Commute home	
Dinner	
Relaxing	
Total Daily Sitting Time	

I will discuss the dramatically negative consequences of this on your neck and overall health shortly, but first let us take a short stroll back through time so that you can appreciate just how recent and problematic this phenomenon is.

Human beings have evolved to move. We have been evolving to move for about 4 million years. Our ancestors would walk, run and climb for hours on end in order to hunt for food, escape from danger and find shelter.

The below graph shows where *Homo sapiens* (us) sit on the timeline of human evolution. *Homo sapiens* (the modern human) have been around for about 200,000 years, as shown by the bottom bar on the graph, and if you divide just that little bar into 20,000 slices then the final slice represents the last 100 years of human life.

In that last little slither of time, smaller than your eyes can see on this graph, some big changes took place.

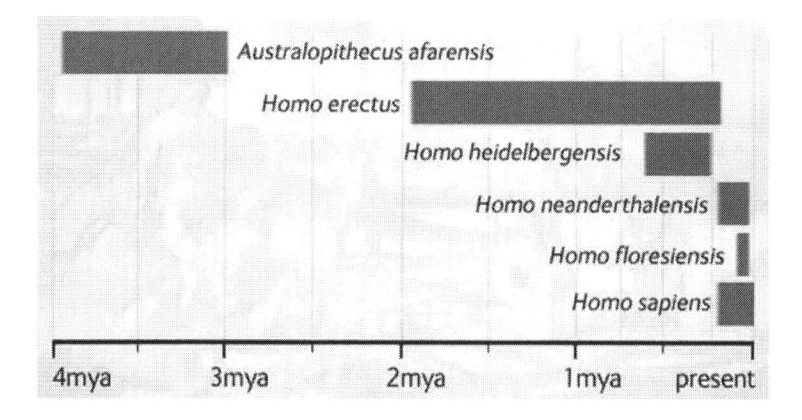

```
Australopithecus afarensis
Homo erectus
Homo heidelbergensis
Homo neanderthalensis
Homo floresiensis
Homo sapiens
4mya    3mya    2mya    1mya    present
```

mya = million years ago
Source: National History Museum, UK.

Transport

In 1913 the first ever commercially accessible motor car, the Ford Model T, was released. By 1927 there were over 15 million cars globally. Now there are 1.4 billion cars worldwide (with 20 million in Australia – almost one per person). The past 100 years is the first time in human history that we have had the option to choose sitting over walking as a common form of transport (horse and cart was an option for the wealthy, but not the majority of people).

Work

By the mid 1900s, there was a large transition from manual jobs to desk jobs. As computers became more prevalent in the 1980s, this marked the beginning of a largely sedentary workforce.

STEP 1: STRUCTURE

Technology

In 1927, the television was invented. Since that point, technology has evolved in a way that ensures we can enjoy entertainment for hours per day without lifting a finger (well, maybe one finger to change the show). From addictive video games to television shows that auto-play the next episode and YouTube rabbit holes, the pleasure centres in our brains are now being rewarded by this content for being lazy. Whilst there are obvious benefits to the way technology has evolved, there's no denying that it has created a society that sits more than ever before.

Another change in technology that has influenced human behaviour is the widespread use of food delivery apps. Our ancestors hunted and gathered in order to eat. Our grandparents farmed and gardened in order to eat. We can order home-delivery meals from an app on our phone whilst sitting on the couch.

Neck pain aside, the amount of energy our ancestors used to expend sourcing and preparing food was often more than the energy gained from eating it. You don't need to be a mathematician to figure out that the number of calories one would obtain from eating a home-delivery meal far outweighs the calories burned whilst tapping your phone to order it. Hello stored fat!

OK, so we sit... what's the issue?

Excessive sitting is one of the worst things you can ever do for your neck. Prolonged postures put incredible amounts of strain and stress on the muscles, joints and tissues of the body, causing overload and pain. Beyond neck pain, sitting is also a major risk factor for heart disease, stroke, diabetes, mental health disorders and many types of cancer.[4-6] The position you sit in dramatically changes the forces on your neck and how hard your muscles need to work to keep your head on your shoulders.

Your head weighs about 5kg if you have an average-sized noggin. When you are sitting with good posture and your head is centred over your body, your neck is working to hold your 5kg melon upright. Once you begin to slump and your head pokes forward in front of your body (like 99% of people working on computers), your neck is now working three times harder to keep your head on your shoulders. Put another way, your neck is now holding up three 5kg watermelons. Sounds like it could get pretty sore, right?

It gets worse. When you begin to look down at your phone to scroll Instagram or use a computer in your lap, your neck is now trying to support **30kg of load** (the word *laptop* is suddenly much less appealing)! That's six times more load than when your head is resting comfortably on your shoulders (which is what naturally happens in standing). The true weight of your head has obviously not changed, but the amount of effort required by your neck to support your head in this position is the equivalent of holding up a 30kg bowling ball... ouch.

STEP 1: STRUCTURE

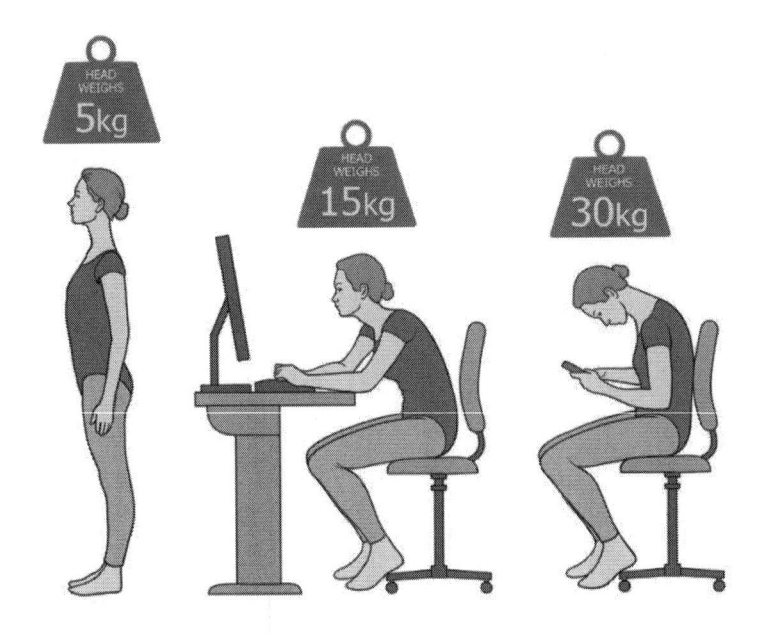

If you're struggling to wrap your head around this, hold a 5kg object up to your chest with one hand. Then stretch your arm straight out in front of you, holding the same object. Which one is harder for your shoulder muscles? Now, imagine holding that object at arm's length for 8 hours straight during a full workday. Are you starting to see the significance of sitting posture?

Sitting posture
One of the simplest yet most important things that you can do for your neck is to sit less. We are about to get into some strategies to reduce sitting time, but let's be real – there will always be times when sitting is a necessity. So, when you are sitting, *how* you sit will make all the difference.

There are three key tips I recommend when it comes to sitting posture:

1. Ricky Martin
2. Nipples up
3. Apples

Now that I've got your attention, let's break these down.

Ricky Martin – it's all in the hips
When you are sitting down, you are sitting on your pelvis. Given that the pelvis is the base of support for your whole spine, pelvic alignment is essential for good sitting posture and to ensure your neck ends up in the correct position.

Before you sit down, put your hands on your hips and tilt your pelvis as far forward as you can and then as far back as you can, just like a Ricky Martin dance. The mid-way point between full front-tilt and back-tilt is the neutral position and this is the position you should sit in.

Nipples up
It's easy to slump into a posture with a rounded upper back and shoulders whilst sitting, which as you now know can increase the load on your neck by up to six times. In order to prevent this, think about lifting your nipples 2cm higher by sitting up straight. Could I have said lift your chest higher? Sure, but you wouldn't have remembered it. Nipples up!

STEP 1: STRUCTURE

Adam's apple – 'An apple a day keeps your neck pain at bay'
Now that you're sitting on a neutral pelvis with a lifted chest, it's time to get the neck right. Imagine you have an apple under your chin, and you are gently holding it there by tucking your chin to stop it from falling to the ground. This creates space at the base of your skull, rather than the tightness that occurs when your chin pokes forward.

For a video demonstration of perfect sitting technique, head to www.neckspert.com.au/resources.

You've now mastered the three simple tips for good sitting posture. If that's too hard to remember or grasp, then just do this: sit 5% taller, like you have a rope around your head that's pulling you up to the sky.

Ergonomics

When it comes to ergonomics, a good chair is a great place to start. It takes a lot of effort to maintain good sitting posture throughout the day, so finding a chair that does most of the heavy lifting for you is a solid option. You want to find something that is supportive, puts your spine in a neutral position and reduces your tendency to slump into a 30kg head posture. If you want some inspiration, check out *Ergohuman*'s range. They're the best quality chairs I've come across, and whilst I don't recommend sitting for long periods, when you do need to be plonked on your backside it should be done in the right chair (www.neckspert.com.au/recommendations).

Next, you need to get your computer setup sorted:

1. The top of your computer screen should be at eye level. If you're using a laptop then you will need to get a separate keyboard, otherwise you will have to lift your arms too high in order to type.

2. Your keyboard should be close to your body so that you're not overreaching and causing your shoulders to pull forward.

3. Keep your mouse close to your body, again to avoid rounding your shoulders.

4. Buying a sit-to-stand work desk will be the best decision of your life.

Standing and moving

Regardless of your job, you have the ability to stand and move more. Whilst it is possible to have poor standing posture, terrible standing posture would still trump average sitting posture for your neck. The forces and loads on the neck are much lower when standing and there are a whole host of other health benefits gained from getting out of your chair regularly.

There are two excuses I commonly hear for why people think they can't stand to work on a computer. The first is they think they won't be able to concentrate well and the second is they don't have a sit-to-stand desk. Let's address both of these now.

1. Concentration

When you sit, this position signals your brain and nervous system that it's time to switch off. Your brains become less alert, there is less blood and oxygen flowing to your muscles and most of your body systems are less active. Your brain and body have evolved this way, because when your ancestors sat around campfires, it meant that it was time to wind down after a long day of hunting and gathering. It's a bit like power-saving mode. Despite thinking you have better concentration in sitting, you do not.

When you stand up and start moving, something pretty cool happens: the change in body position tells your brain that you need to be focused and ready for action, so your thinking becomes clear and more alert. You engage more muscles, pumping fresh blood and oxygen around your body, flooding it with nutrients and washing away toxins. Your bones and muscles get stronger, your digestive system functions better and all of the cells in your body become healthier.

2. Equipment

Purchasing a good sit-to-stand desk will save you money on medical bills over the long term, so it's a solid investment. Check out my personal favourite, *Omnidesk* (www.neckspert.com.au/recommendations).

Making it happen

Just like it takes a while to get fit for sport, if you're not used to standing much throughout the day, then don't expect it to happen overnight. Getting 'stand-fit' can take a few weeks and I've included a guide below to help you achieve this. It may seem basic but following this guide will give your muscles and joints a chance to adapt and strengthen so they can support your new dynamic posture!

Week 1: Stand whilst working for at least 10 minutes straight every hour
Week 2: Stand or walk whilst working for at least 20 minutes straight every hour
Week 3: Stand or walk for half of every hour (all at once or in smaller chunks)
Week 4: Try to limit sitting to a maximum of 15 minutes per hour

Other strategies to stand and move more

- Walk and stand in meetings to keep focused and energised
- Move around whilst you're on the phone
- Take the stairs
- Set a 30-minute reminder on your phone to do a lap of your office or get a glass of water
- Get off the bus or train before your station and walk (or if working from home then walk around the block regularly)
- Place the phone and rubbish bin out of arm's reach so you have to move to get to them.

STEP 1: STRUCTURE

> **You:** *I sit while I work, but I also do 1 hour of exercise every day so I'm fine, right?*
> **Me (The NECKspert):** *Wrong.*

Research now shows that even if you get the recommended dose of physical exercise (30 minutes of moderate to vigorous intensity exercise, 5 days per week), sitting for long periods throughout the day can still have seriously negative effects on waist circumference (obesity), blood pressure, blood glucose (diabetes), triglycerides (fats) and cholesterol.[7] A term has been coined for people who sit all day but still get their exercise requirements: *the active couch potato.*

A 2014 study estimated that for every 2 hours you sit, the benefits of 20 minutes of exercise are cancelled out…[8] What a waste!

Left of field

We've covered a lot under the topic of *structure* and how to create better strength, movement quality, alignment and posture, but there are a couple of other pieces of the puzzle we need to touch on.

Dizziness, headaches and funny vision

You will remember from Section 1 that your neck plays an important role in your vision, balance and also the sensation in your head and face. It is common with neck pain to also experience dizziness, blurry vision and headaches related to the neck.

It is important to note that these symptoms can also come from many other conditions unrelated to the neck, so it's vital to get them assessed by a health professional to confirm their origins.

The muscles and joints of the neck are closely linked to those controlling the eyes, both of which talk to the balance system in your inner ear (called the vestibular system). This is due to the important relationship between the positioning of your head with your vision and balance. If there is dysfunction in the neck and the messages to the brain about head position do not match the messages from the eyes or the vestibular system, this can result in dizziness, blurry vision and unsteadiness. The medical term for this is *cervicogenic dizziness*.

The structures that detect the position of your neck are called *proprioceptors* and it is possible to assess the function of these, as well as retrain them to become more accurate. Once your neck proprioceptors are functioning more accurately, the communication between your neck, eyes and balance system will become more streamlined, which should reduce any neck-related dizziness.

It is also possible to experience headaches as a result of dysfunction in the neck. These are known as *cervicogenic headaches* and may be the result of referred pain from the upper vertebrae and neck muscles (due to the shared nerves between the neck and head), or be a secondary symptom of cervicogenic dizziness.

STEP 1: STRUCTURE

The assessment and treatment of headaches and dizziness are often very individualised and should always be conducted by a qualified health professional.

Imagine that!

The brain is pretty cool. If you close your eyes right now and imagine yourself running, the same areas of the brain light up as if you were actually running in real life. Professional athletes have known this for a long time, which is why they practise their skills through visualisation. By doing this, their brain gets used to this movement and they can then perform it with more precision.

This trick can be used just as effectively to relieve pain. Close your eyes now and imagine yourself performing a movement that normally hurts. It is likely that you will feel pain, even though you haven't moved. You may also find it difficult to visualise the movement.

I'm going to give you an exercise: three times each day for a week, I want you to close your eyes and visualise yourself performing that painful task 30 times in a row. It might be looking over your shoulder, reaching into the cupboard or doing a push-up. You should notice that it gets easier to visualise each day and causes less pain. This may seem like a trivial or silly exercise, but I assure you that I would not have bothered putting it in this book if I hadn't experienced first hand the benefits it will bring you. If it's good enough for Usain Bolt, it's good enough for you!

Surgery

I have intentionally left the topic of surgery until last in this chapter, as I believe it should be the absolute last avenue explored in regard to improving the structure of your neck.

You may have had a surgical procedure. You may be considering having one. You may be trying to avoid one. Regardless of where you sit, it's worth understanding the basics of surgical options for neck pain, including if it's right for you, how successful it is and what it means long term.

Let me start by saying that for the right person, surgical procedures such as microdiscectomies, disc replacements and laminectomies can have very good results. That said, you should still do everything you can to avoid surgery. Why? Because through improving posture, alignment, strength and mobility, it is often possible to 'decompress' the spine without an operation, therefore eliminating the inherent risks of surgery.

Surgery is not a silver bullet for many types of neck pain, and even when it is effective the 5 Steps of NECKcellence are still critical to ensure it doesn't relapse. Failing to address any of these will very likely result in your neck pain returning at some point.

The role of surgery is to fix injured tissues that do not have the capacity to heal themselves. Unless your injury is the result of an acute event (such as severe whiplash or traumatic disc herniation from a tackle in football), then the injured tissue is usually the result of progressive dysfunction over time (like poor posture or weak muscular control).

It is important to remember that surgery does not fix the *root cause* of the injured tissue if the dysfunction has occurred progressively over time, and if the underlying problem is not addressed then pain is likely to come back.

Who should consider surgery?
There are a couple of conditions for which I believe surgical intervention may be an appropriate option (I have not included traumatic injuries such as unstable fractures here, for which surgery may be an obvious choice):

Severe nerve root compression resulting in neurological impairment

When a nerve root becomes compressed, either through a disc herniation or narrowing of the exit foramen (hole where the nerve root exits the spine), it can cause severe pain, numbness, pins and needles, loss of strength and loss of reflexes in the arm and hand. In many cases, this can be resolved through physiotherapy (hands-on techniques and corrective exercises), but if there has been no improvement after 6–12 weeks then surgery may be an option. Before undergoing surgery, it is worth considering a localised cortisone injection to the affected nerve root, which may improve symptoms and reduce the likelihood of surgery.

It is worth noting that many health professionals will tell you that delaying surgery on a compressed nerve will result in permanent nerve damage. In my experience, I have seen many people recover from nerve root compression without surgery, even after several months of neurological deficits such as weakness, numbness, tingling and pain. Personally, I would not suggest delaying a surgical opinion for longer than 6–12 weeks if no improvements have been made with physio treatment, but I do not agree that surgery is essential before the 6-week mark (or perhaps even 12 weeks) for nerve root impingement, and I have not seen any scientific evidence to support immediate surgery.

Severe spinal canal stenosis with neurological impairment

Spinal stenosis is a progressive narrowing of the spinal canal over time.[9] If this progresses to the point in which it causes severe pain, weakness or numbness in the arms and hands, then surgery may be an option (usually a laminectomy).

Just to be clear, I am not against surgery. I simply believe that surgery should be treated as the last option for non-traumatic neck injuries, and should only be considered after a good quality physiotherapy programme and the 5 Steps to NECKcellence have been attempted.

If you have already had surgery and did not get a good result, don't worry – you still have the potential to improve your pain by following the 5 Steps in this book.

STEP 1: STRUCTURE

Making Step 1 work

That just about brings us to the end of Step 1 – Structure. Before we jump into the next step, I want to remind you about the importance of implementing each of the elements in this chapter through a slow and systematic approach.

Successfully improving your structure and function requires three elements:

1. Measure
2. Goal setting
3. Pacing

Measure

What you measure, you improve, so it's really important to figure out where you're starting from. As an example, let's say that vacuuming is something that triggers your pain. You need to identify how many minutes of vacuuming you can do before your pain starts or increases. This may seem trivial, but it's an essential step in your gradual recovery and will also help you to avoid flare-ups.

See if you can identify your 'pain point' with a range of everyday activities, such as working on the computer, exercising, cleaning the house, cooking, watching TV or reading. Record these in the below table, so you can track your improvements day to day.

It's important to use tangible numbers such as length of time, distance, or the number of times you can perform a task before pain starts or becomes too much. Once you've established this, then you can start setting goals.

Activity	Time/distance/repetitions until onset of symptoms	Pain score/10	Time for pain to settle
Cooking	*20 mins*	*7/10*	*1 hour*

Goal setting

Jump back to Section 1 and review how to set *open* goals and use these principles to set yourself some structure-related goals around strength, mobility, function, sitting time and posture.

Pacing

Pacing is all about slowly increasing the demands you place on your neck and allowing it to adapt before moving to the next phase. The exercise videos I have created to improve structure have been presented with pacing in mind. You will notice there are levels, which become progressively harder as your function improves. You should only move on to a higher level once you can achieve your current level with ease and without any significant pain.

Focus on how much you are able to do each day, rather than your limitations. As your function progressively increases, celebrate the little wins. Even if it's not much in

STEP 1: STRUCTURE

the grand scheme of things, small improvements mean you're heading in the direction of recovery.

As you perform your daily exercises, be OK with a little bit of pain. You should try to avoid flare-ups by knowing your pain point and not overdoing it (especially when you feel good), but stick to your targets and do a little more each week, even if it hurts a bit. Remember, persistent pain is not an accurate representation of danger or damage to your neck, and by choosing to move you are telling your brain that it's safe to do so.

THE STORY OF MICHELLE

Michelle was a 45-year-old woman who worked in finance. She had two children (8 and 10 years old) and a husband who was a lawyer. Michelle loved doing exercise classes at the gym and was very fit, although she did work very long hours, which often involved sitting for the majority of the day. Beyond this she had a great diet, slept well and managed her stress effectively.

Michelle came to me for treatment after 2 years of worsening neck pain and headaches. She had been going to another therapist for regular treatment (massage and adjustments), but she found that she was only getting temporary relief. The pain had started to become so constant and intense that it was impacting her ability to exercise and work. She had also started to experience some mild dizziness when working on her laptop.

When I assessed Michelle, she had a lot of tenderness and increased muscle tone in her neck, as well as poor rotation. By assessing her whole body and function, I was able to see that despite her neck being the location of pain, she had some key areas of dysfunction away from her neck that were causing the issue. Whilst treating Michelle's neck had produced some temporary relief for her, it was not the root cause of her pain.

The first issue I uncovered in Michelle was that she had a dominance in her *global* muscle system. She was using her large muscle groups for exercise and to support her posture, but she had poor *deep* system control and endurance.

Secondly, she had an upper chest breathing pattern, meaning she was relying on her neck muscles to try and get more oxygen into her lungs.

Michelle's third major driver of her neck pain was her sitting habit at work. She had a decent ergonomic chair but would often sit for 8–10 hours per day at work.

Lastly, due to the way she held her children when they were younger, Michelle had a slight rotation in her upper rib cage that was pulling her neck into a poor position. In order to fix Michelle's neck pain, she needed a holistic and specific approach to improving her structure. Michelle worked her way through the different levels of NECKsercise, including learning how to activate her deep core muscles and relax her superficial muscles. She also learned how to breathe diaphragmatically which relaxed the overactive muscles around her neck.

Next, she began standing more at work and progressively managed to sit for just 50% of her workday, which significantly reduced the load on her neck. I also worked on correcting the twist in her upper rib cage through hands-on techniques and gave her corrective exercises to address the dizziness she had started experiencing.

Over 8 weeks, Michelle's neck pain was completely resolved, and I hardly touched her neck. We achieved this by finding the root causes in her body, changing her sitting habits, improving her strength and mobility, and correcting poor movement patterns and posture.

Step 1 Recap

- Imaging results are not closely related to pain
- There is a big difference between the deep and superficial muscular systems
- Beautiful and pain-free movement = strength + endurance + movement control + mobility (proportional to the physical demands of your life)
- The root cause of neck pain is often not in the neck
- Getting good quality hands-on treatment from a therapist is important, but it's only part of the picture

- How you breathe has a huge impact on your neck pain
- Mobility naturally declines as you age
- It's important to know if you're genetically hypermobile or hypomobile
- Improving posture and ergonomics is critical
- Sit less and move more
- Surgery is the best option in only a very small number of conditions
- Improve your strength, endurance, movement control and mobility by doing NECKsercise: www.neckspert.com.au/resources

My open goals for structure: *e.g. Over the next 6 weeks, let's see how much I can improve my neck strength and mobility by performing my NECKsercises as often as possible. Let's see how little I can sit throughout the day.*

_____

_____

Success checklist:

- ☐ I am doing my NECKsercises daily (strength, endurance, control, mobility)
- ☐ I have had a high-quality therapist explain the root causes of my pain

STEP 1: STRUCTURE

- ☐ I am working with a high-quality therapist every couple of weeks to help with muscle releases, joint mobility and to monitor my exercise technique
- ☐ I am able to breathe diaphragmatically both at rest and during exercise
- ☐ My body is hyper/hypo-mobile (select one) and I am therefore more focused on control/mobility (select one)
- ☐ When I am sitting, I am using a high-quality chair (find Ergohuman's range at www.neckspert.com.au/recommendations)
- ☐ I am sitting for less than 4 hours per day and I have purchased a standing work desk if I have a sedentary job (find Omnidesk's range at www.neckspert.com.au/recommendations)
- ☐ I am visualising myself performing activities that I want to return to each day
- ☐ I am measuring my progress with pain and function scores

References:

1. Malek S, Reinhold E & Pearce G. (2021). The Beighton Score as a measure of generalised joint hypermobility. *Rheumatology International* [published online 18 Mar 2021]. https://doi.org/10.1007/s00296-021-04832-4.

2. Fernández-Carnero J, Sierra-Silvestre E, Beltran-Alacreu H, Gil-Martínez A & La Touche R. (2019). Neural tension technique improves immediate conditioned pain modulation in patients with chronic neck pain: a randomized clinical trial. *Pain Medicine (Malden, Mass.)* 20(6):1227–1235. https://doi.org/10.1093/pm/pny115.

3. Thomas E, Cavallaro AR, Mani D, Bianco A & Palma A. (2019). The efficacy of muscle energy techniques in symptomatic and asymptomatic subjects: a systematic review. *Chiropractic & Manual Therapies* 27:35. https://doi.org/10.1186/s12998-019-0258-7.

4. Levine JA (2015). Sick of sitting. *Diabetologia* 58(8):1751–1758. https://doi.org/10.1007/s00125-015-3624-6.

5. Booth FW, Roberts CK & Laye MJ (2012). Lack of exercise is a major cause of chronic diseases. *Comprehensive Physiology* 2(2):1143–1211. https://doi.org/10.1002/cphy.c110025.

6. Patel AV, Maliniak ML, Rees-Punia E, Matthews CE & Gapstur SM. (2018). Prolonged leisure time spent sitting in relation to cause-specific mortality in a large US cohort. *American Journal of Epidemiology* 187(10): 2151–2158.

7. Bailey DP, Hewson DJ, Champion RB & Sayegh SM. (2019). Sitting time and risk of cardiovascular disease and diabetes: a systematic review and meta-analysis. *American Journal of Preventive Medicine* 57(3):408–416. https://doi.org/10.1016/j.amepre.2019.04.015

8. Kulinski JP, Khera A, Ayers CR, de Lemos JA, Blair SN & Berry JD. (2014). Association between cardiorespiratory fitness and accelerometer-derived physical activity and sedentary time in the general population. *Mayo Clinic Proceedings* 89(8):1063–1071. https://doi.org/10.1016/j.mayocp.2014.04.019

9. Mayo Clinic. Spinal stenosis. Available at: https://www.mayoclinic.org/diseases-conditions/spinal-stenosis/symptoms-causes/syc-20352961 (accessed June 2021)

Step 2: Stress

Life can be stressful. Especially when you're in pain. The link between pain and stress is actually a closed loop: pain causes stress, but stress can also cause pain.

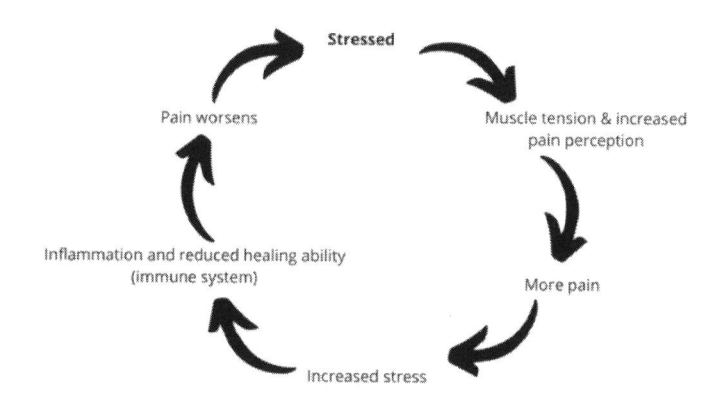

Stressed → Muscle tension & increased pain perception → More pain → Increased stress → Inflammation and reduced healing ability (immune system) → Pain worsens → Stressed

Stress is an imbalance between your perceived demands (stressors) and your perceived ability to cope (tools and resources). The stress response is an inbuilt strategy that prepares your body and brain for action.

When your brain believes you are in danger, it creates a response that prepares you to run away or stay and fight. You may have heard this called the *fight-or-flight response*. It causes an increase in your heart rate and blood pressure, blood rushes to your muscles, your pupils dilate and you become hyper-alert.

You are ready to protect your life.

STEP 2: STRESS

This is a healthy and natural response to a perceived threat, and it has helped humans survive throughout history. If you were not physically or mentally prepared to deal with danger, then it would be much harder to escape it.

When the danger passes, your blood pressure drops, your breathing and heart rate slow, and blood moves away from your muscles and prioritises your immune and digestive systems. You are then ready to rest and recover, often referred to as the *rest and digest response*.

Whilst short bursts of the stress response are normal and healthy, problems start to emerge when you experience *prolonged* and *chronic* stress.

Our modern society has a lot to say for itself when it comes to chronic stress. In the developed world, we are constantly being bombarded with marketing to *have more stuff*, *be more successful* and *look more beautiful* – all to make us spend money. Much of this marketing creates unrealistic expectations of what we should *be*, *want*, *do* and *have*, resulting in extreme levels of prolonged stress.

Currently in Australia, USA and much of the developed world, two thirds of the population experience unhealthy levels of stress on a daily basis.[1,2] This is not how the human body is designed to function, and the health ramifications are becoming increasingly clear.

Stress and your neck pain

All stress comes from either past or perceived future events. The danger may not be real, it may be made up in your mind, but the physical response in your brain and body is real regardless.

In order to appreciate just how dramatically stress impacts your neck pain, let us take a closer look at the nervous system and how it behaves when you are stressed.

Your nervous system can be broken down into two different parts: a *voluntary* system and an *involuntary* system. The voluntary system, also known as the somatic nervous system, controls your muscles and movement via your conscious control: you tell your neck to rotate and it performs the task.

The involuntary nervous system, called the autonomic nervous system (ANS), is a vast network of nerves reaching out from the spinal cord, directly affecting every organ in your body. It operates outside of your awareness, controlling things like your heartbeat, breathing and digestion. This is happening right now and in every moment of the day, without you even needing to give it a thought.

I just want you to ponder that for a moment, because it's easy to take your body for granted, but it is so incredibly complex and intelligent that I want you to give yourself a pat on the back and thank your body for being truly incredible.

Every single day your heart beats about 120,000 times, you breathe about 25,000 breaths and you magically convert food into the cells that make up your body. Pretty amazing.

The autonomic nervous system has two branches, the *sympathetic* and the *parasympathetic* branches, which have opposite effects. The *sympathetic* nervous system helps you deal with dangerous situations by initiating the 'fight-or-flight' response, preparing you to run away or protect yourself.

When our ancestors were hunting in the jungle and encountered a lion, this physical response was essential for getting them out of danger. Once the lion was gone, they would transition back into a *parasympathetic* state (rest and digest), where their bodies would begin to heal, recover and rejuvenate.

Let's contrast this to our current world, where instead of dangerous animals prowling the neighbourhood causing occasional stress, we have mortgages, work deadlines and car repayments that often sit in the back of our minds *constantly*. You can't escape your manager or the bank by hiding up a tree, like our ancestors could a lion.

If you do not quickly transition back into a parasympathetic (rest and recover) state as you are designed to do after danger passes, then you are left with a chronically over-stimulated mind and body, causing significant health problems.

Below is a list of some of the physical responses that occur during a stress response and the direct impact on neck pain.

Fight-or-flight response	Impact on your neck pain
Rapid and shallow breathing	Rapid and shallow breathing results in less oxygen delivery, which causes the muscles around the neck to start tensing up in order to help with lung expansion in an effort to get more oxygen. This results in tight and painful muscles due to overactivity.
Increased muscle tone	The sympathetic response causes muscle tension to assist with running or fighting, but prolonged muscle tone causes pain and impacts bone alignment.
Reduced immunity	Blood and energy are directed to the muscles instead of the immune system (to assist with escaping immediate danger) and this reduced immune energy impacts your healing ability and injury recovery.
Adrenal fatigue	Prolonged release of stress hormones (such as adrenaline and cortisol) causes exhaustion and adrenal fatigue. This reduces tissue healing, increases

STEP 2: STRESS

	inflammation and also increases pain perception by impacting mood and emotional regulation.
Poor digestion	Similar to the immune system, blood flow and energy is directed to the muscles instead of the digestive system (to assist with escaping immediate danger). This negatively impacts absorption of nutrients and vitamins that assist with injury recovery.
Inflammation	Prolonged stress causes inflammation in the body, creating pain and poor tissue health. Inflammation occurs through poor gut health (due to digestive issues), cortisol and insulin resistance (hormonal issues) and altered immune system responses.
Hypervigilance	The fight-or-flight response causes increased mental alertness (to detect danger), which makes us hyper-sensitive to pain.
Jaw clenching	Jaw clenching and overactive facial muscles are a common symptom of stress. The jaw and the neck have many connections and dysfunction of one can cause pain in the other. Clenching when stressed is a common cause of headaches, jaw pain and neck pain.

Beyond neck pain, there are a large number of other health implications associated with chronic stress that you should be aware of:

Physical impact of chronic stress	Mental impact of chronic stress
Heart disease	Anxiety disorders
Gut and digestive issues	Depression
Diabetes	Attention and focus deficits
Thyroid disorders	Phobias
Autoimmune diseases	Mental exhaustion and burnout
Cancer	Alzheimer's disease

The solution

Ironically, I'm sure it has been very stressful reading about all of the negative health effects of chronic stress!

I want to reiterate that small bursts of stress are healthy and important. It is *prolonged* exposure to stress, alongside poor coping strategies, that results in serious health problems.

Regardless of your age, sex, socioeconomic status, profession or any other factor, you will have to deal with external pressures in your life. It is part of the human experience. Therefore, I do not suggest that you try to adopt stress *reduction* strategies, as this is a sure-fire way to fail.

Instead, let us focus on stress *management* strategies, so that regardless of the stressors you are facing, you have the tools and skills required to effectively deal with them in a productive way.

There are healthy ways to deal with stress and there are unhealthy ways. Unhealthy strategies often feel good for a short period of time, but then compound the effects of stress soon after, thereby creating a vicious cycle that actually increases stress.

Some examples of commonly used stress-relievers that actually intensify problems include alcohol, medications such as sleeping pills and muscle relaxants, recreational drugs, social withdrawal, overindulging on unhealthy food, and watching excessive amounts of overstimulating television.

While these solutions may make you feel temporarily better, they never have a restorative or healing effect on the body and nervous system, and they always result in increased physical and mental stress once the short-lived pleasure chemicals wear off.

Conversely, there are a large number of well-researched, evidence-based and highly effective strategies to manage stress. Some of these include:

- Exercise: as discussed in detail in Step 1 (*Structure*)
- Diaphragmatic breathing: as discussed in detail in Step 1 (*Structure*)
- Sleep: as discussed in detail in Step 3 (*Sleep*)

- Herbal supplements: as discussed in detail in Step 4 (*Supplements*)
- Emotional release work: as discussed in detail in Step 5 (*Self-Care*)
- Mindfulness and meditation

As you can see, there is a pattern in each of the steps in this book: they all improve and enhance each other. Each have strong healing and therapeutic effects on the nervous system, which bring you from a prolonged fight-or-flight response into a healing parasympathetic state.

Five of the six above stress management tools are discussed in detail in other chapters of this book, so the focus of this section will be mindfulness and meditation.

Mindfulness and meditation

For me personally, starting a daily meditation practice was one of the most impactful of the 5 Steps of NECKcellence when fixing my own neck pain. I have experienced the results in my own body and advocate for it as one of the most important health practices you will ever undertake.

By this point in the book, you now understand that pain is strongly influenced by your thoughts, beliefs, expectations and feelings. These factors can impact your nervous systems, hormones, the release of chemicals in the brain, and ultimately increase or decrease your pain experience. If your mind is free to run wild with fear, anxiety and frustration, this can really turn up the pain dial. Scientific studies have proven that practising mindfulness and meditation techniques can reduce pain, stress and anxiety, and physically change the structure of your brain in a positive way.

It's important to note that meditation is an evidence-based practice and not just some hippy habit. Meditation is now widely researched by the best academic institutions and utilised by the world's best athletes, business executives and health professionals.

I should also point out that mindfulness and meditation is accessible and achievable for everyone. Something that I commonly hear when discussing meditation with clients is that they don't feel as though it would be possible for them to achieve, because they have a busy mind and cannot sit still. Let me assure you that I have taught incredibly highly strung, restless and stressed people effective strategies for practising mindfulness and meditation, which most of them have successfully implemented.

NOW

The reality of your life is always *now*. Seeing this can set you free. Understanding this is the key to happiness. We spend most of our lives successfully ignoring the present moment. We avoid *being* happy while we attempt to *become* happy.

I'll be happy when: I get out of pain... I get the promotion... I meet someone... I leave someone... I make more money... I get to Fiji... I lose 10kg...

We try to fulfil desire after desire and as a result we spend our lives being far less content than we could be. We fail to notice the little things and rarely appreciate what we have until we've lost it. This ongoing dissatisfaction with the present and striving for the next 'thing' results in stress, discontentment, depression and pain.

This is not your fault – we're in a world where we've been conditioned to think like this, through advertising and marketing. We see the billboard of the model with the perfect body: 'I'll be happy when I look more like that'... We see the happy couple on Instagram posting photos from a beach in Italy: 'I'll be happy when I'm doing that'... We see the advertisement of a person driving a luxury car, smiling and looking happy: 'I'll be happy when I have that'... All day, every day we are exposed to these messages.

There is a way off the merry-go-round. A way to break the constant state of dissatisfaction and 'I'll be happy when...' mentality. This is achieved through meditation and mindfulness.

Mindfulness versus meditation
These two terms are often used interchangeably, but there is a key difference between them.

Meditation is the *practice*, the time you set aside each day to sit in stillness. There are various techniques and forms of meditation, but they all have the common thread of focusing your mind on a single point, to bring awareness and calmness into the mind and body. It is not about stopping thoughts – it's about becoming aware of the space between thoughts, which get longer the more you practise. It's about observing thoughts as if you are removed from them, like they are not yours.

Mindfulness is the *result*. Mindfulness is the experience of increased focus, awareness and presence that occurs as a result of meditating.

We are now at a point in history where meditation is widely accepted as a scientifically validated health practice that can manage stress, reduce pain and enhance both mental and physical health through improving the immune, cardiovascular, hormonal and nervous systems.[3-5]

But meditation existed long before scientists did. In fact, the oldest records of people practicing meditation date back to 1500 BC.

Ancient Indian Hindus – 1500 BC
Taoist China and Buddhist India – 500–600 BC
Japanese Buddhism – 8th century
Sufi/Islam – 11–12th centuries
Christian/Judaism meditation – 12th century
Western Buddhism – 1900s
Yoga and transcendental meditation – 1960s
Modern mindfulness (mindfulness-based stress reduction, cognitive behavioural therapy) – 1970s

Benefits

For meditation to have stood the test of time for that long, you can probably bet your bottom dollar that there are some benefits in there for you. Below are some of the proven health effects that will balance the stress response in your body and directly reduce your neck pain:[4-7]

- Improves immunity
- Reduces stress
- Regulates emotions
- Reduces pain
- Improves cortisol sensitivity
- Changes brain physiology (shape and size)
- Improves mood and happiness
- Reduces inflammation
- Lowers risk of multiple chronic diseases

How does it work?

When you begin to meditate, you initiate a response in your nervous system that quickly transitions you from a sympathetic (stressed) state to a parasympathetic (relaxed) state. Your breathing deepens, your heart rate slows, your muscles relax and your mind becomes still. Your brain and body are responding to a sense of perceived safety and therefore allow your digestive and immune systems to heal, and generally repair your body.

Meditation even changes the size and shape of your brain.[8] MRI studies have shown reductions in the size and activity of the amygdala,[9] which is one of the key brain regions associated with fear, stress and pain. It also increases the size of the brain regions associated with memory, decision-making, learning, cognition, emotional regulation, perspective, empathy and compassion.

And the best part: these visible changes in the brain are seen after just 8 weeks.

Brain waves
Another key impact of meditation is its influence on your brain waves. There are four types of brain waves (electrical activity) to understand:

Beta waves: associated with day-to-day wakefulness.
Alpha waves: active during periods of relaxation, whilst you're still awake.
Theta waves: slower in frequency and greater in amplitude than alpha waves.
Delta waves: the slowest and highest amplitude brain waves. Delta waves are characteristic of sleep.

During meditation, two types of waves are most prominent:

- **Theta waves** are most abundant in the frontal and middle parts of the brain. These types of wave originate from a relaxed attention that monitors our inner experiences. Theta waves indicate deep relaxation. These are more prominent in meditation than sleep.

- **Alpha waves** are more abundant in the back parts of the brain and are characteristic of wakeful rest. The amount of alpha wave activity increases when the brain relaxes from intentional, goal-oriented tasks. This is a sign of deep relaxation – but it does not mean that the mind is void. Research shows that activities that promote alpha wave activity have positive health benefits.

There is very little delta activity during meditation, confirming that meditation is different from sleep.

Awareness of beliefs

What you *do* is one way to change your pain and improve your health, but how you *think* is equally important. We will explore the importance of *beliefs* in detail in Step 5, but let us now briefly touch on the link between beliefs and pain and the role that meditation can play.

Research has shown that genetics only play a small role in the development of disease. The exact amount varies depending on which study you read and the type of condition, but genetics seems to account for just 15% of your health on average.[10] The other 85% comes down to your lifestyle, beliefs and behaviours.

This means that even if neck pain runs in your family, 85% of your neck pain is related to your exercise habits, sleep, stress levels, the food you eat, how you process emotional challenges and your beliefs about your neck.

This is the science of *epigenetics*. If your genes are the gun, then epigenetics are the trigger. Your belief systems about your health (which are usually subconscious, meaning you're not aware of them) are one of the triggers of your genetic gun, determining the health of your cells. This might sound a bit like science fiction, but I assure you it's fact.

So where does meditation fit into all of this? Meditation lets you become aware of your subconscious thoughts and beliefs. You become mindful of *what* and *how* you are thinking and can begin to uncover some of the harmful and negative scripts that sit in your subconscious brain. You begin to question where these beliefs came from and become conscious of the negative impact they are having.

Remember, your beliefs and the way you think about your neck (and therefore your behaviours that follow) account for around 85% of the reason you have ongoing pain, so using meditation to become aware of your beliefs and rewrite them is a very valuable investment of your time.

Practical strategies to get you started

Meditation is not typically learned via written words, but let's give it a go anyway. I'm going to introduce you to a really simple and effective technique:

Sit in a comfortable chair, close your eyes and just scan your body from head to toe, relaxing any areas of tension. Do this over a couple of minutes. Once you feel like your whole body is relaxed, move your attention to your breath and simply follow the inhale all the way in, and then the exhale all the way out. Count up to 10 breaths, and then back down to zero. Repeat this for a few minutes, and when you catch your thoughts wandering just reset and return to the breath.

When starting out, I have found that using audio-guided meditations can be very helpful. You can download some of my free meditations at www.neckspert.com.au/resources.

Knowing the benefits of meditation is all well and good but implementing an ongoing meditation habit is another kettle of fish. You'll remember that in Section 1, we discussed the science of habit formation and behaviour change. Using these principles, below is a 6-step guide to making sure it sticks:

Forming the habit:

1. Find your motivation for starting: this one is easy – you've learned about the benefits of meditation for stress, the nervous system and neck pain, so you should have a clear motivator for getting started.

2. Start with just 5 minutes per day, at the same time and in the same place.

3. Do a course and choose a simple technique that resonates (www.neckspert.com.au/resources)

STEP 2: STRESS

4. Create a comfortable space and minimise distractions (such as in the lounge, before the rest of the house wakes up in the morning).

5. Set a challenge (e.g. meditating for 30 days in a row).

6. Detach from the outcome of each session. Some will feel awesome, some terrible, and you need to be OK with that. It's all a part of the process.

In case you're still not totally convinced that meditation is something you need in your life, I'm going to leave you with this list of influential meditators:

- Albert Einstein
- Sir Paul McCartney
- Jeff Weiner (CEO LinkedIn)
- Oprah Winfrey
- Tim Ferris
- Clint Eastwood
- Russell Simons
- Ariana Huffington
- Padmasree Warrior (CTO of Cisco)
- Rupert Murdoch
- Ray Dalio (billionaire founder of Bridgewater Associates): '*Meditation has been the single most important reason for my success.*'

Other strategies for stress management

Understanding the science
I stated earlier that stress is actually a healthy and important phenomenon in the body. It's *chronic* stress that is the issue. But the story is about to get even more interesting!

In 1998, a study was conducted on 28,000 adults. Participants were asked two questions:

1. How much stress have you experienced in the last year?
2. Do you believe that stress is harmful for your health?

The adults were then monitored for 8 years to see what happened to their health. The results showed that high levels of stress increased their risk of dying by 43%... **but only for those people who also believed that stress was harming their health.**[11]

In other words, people who experienced high stress but believed that stress was healthy and not harming them did not have the same detrimental effects as those who believed that stress was a problem.

If you believe stress is harmful for your health, it perpetuates the response and becomes much worse long term. When you change your mind about stress, you can change your body's response to it and stop it from becoming chronic and harmful.

STEP 2: STRESS

> ***You***: *Didn't you just tell me that science has confirmed all of the negative effects of stress? It sounds like you're now telling me to ignore the science and try to believe that stress is not harmful.*
> ***Me** (The NECKspert)*: *I'm telling you to stop believing that short bursts of stress are harmful. When you feel stressed, use it to your advantage and take action using the additional energy it will give you. Then you must rest and recover. This healthy relationship with stress will mean you will stop it from becoming chronic, which is where the issues arise.*

Next time you are triggered and feel a stress response occurring in your body, know that it's your body rising to the challenge and feel appreciation for that, rather than getting worried about feeling stressed. Remember that stress is essential and healthy for growth and development, and notice how this outlook changes your stress response.

Perspective

You will recall that the stress response in your mind and body is the same regardless of whether the stress is real or imagined. With this in mind, it is worth asking yourself when you begin to feel stressed, *'Is this stress in response to real danger? If so, is it in proportion to the level of danger? And if so, how likely to occur is this dangerous situation?'*

As major stressful events do not typically occur frequently in life, there is a tendency to 'catastrophise' the more common minor stressful events. As humans, we often find ourselves losing perspective and overreacting. Have you ever blown something out of proportion and then eventually realised that it wasn't so important after all?

Here's a simple process for recalibrating your stress response whenever you feel it coming on:

1. Create reference points: On a scale of 1 to 10 (1 being insignificant and 10 being life-threatening), where does this stressful situation really sit?
2. Take a breath
3. Recalibrate your stress response based on the true level of threat
4. Acknowledge that the stress is there to help you deal with the situation at hand
5. Welcome the stress (the new appropriately proportioned amount of stress)
6. Utilise the stress response in your body to deal with any aspects of the threat that are within your control
7. Recover back to a restful state

Gratitude

Science has confirmed that gratitude is one of the most positive thought systems for both your mental and physical health.[12,13] It creates pleasure chemicals in the brain and a neurological response of safety and protection.

It may seem a bit cheesy telling you to think of something you're grateful for, but I promise that if you develop a regular 'gratitude practice', you'll change your life in 2 weeks.

STEP 2: STRESS

Gratitude for experiences in your life, big or small, helps to kickstart your parasympathetic nervous system, releases brain chemicals related to safety and switches off your fight-or-flight response. Sometimes this may be the 'big' things, such as having a loving partner, a close friend or your children. On other days it might be something smaller, like a nice meal, a good workout or when your team wins the footy. You may struggle to think of anything at first, but you will find that as the habit develops, this exercise becomes easier.

Write down three things that you're grateful for right now and make them the first thing you think of when you wake up in the morning and last thing you think of before closing your eyes at night.

1. _____
2. _____
3. _____

Service and giving back
By giving, you can strengthen feelings of self-worth, belonging, purpose and happiness. Studies have shown that giving produces a parasympathetic response and can reverse stress and anxiety, as well as strengthen your mind and body. Research also indicates that people who have a greater interest in helping others are more likely to rate themselves as happy. One such study demonstrated that by

committing to an act of kindness once per week over a 6-week period, individuals experienced an increase in well-being compared with the control group who did not.[14–16]

When you have pain, it's easy to feel sorry for yourself and fall into the depths of self-pity. By performing acts of service, you are able to support others less fortunate than you, which recalibrates your stress response and reduces your own pain perception. When was the last time you gave something away? When was the last time you were given something? Which one made you feel better?

Make a commitment that once every day you will give up a small amount of your time or possessions to help someone in need. It will change your life.

Social connection
Meaningful social relationships and human connection are two of the major building blocks of happy, thriving people. They are even used as a measure of well-being in research. In our modern society, we are more connected online, but less connected than ever as humans. In Australia, like many other western countries, people are finding themselves feeling isolated, having fewer close friends and spending more time using technology – especially since COVID-19.

When you were younger, did you know your neighbours? Did you eat dinner with the family at the table? Did you spend a lot more time outdoors with friends? Today, what percentage of your Facebook friends could you call for a chat? When was the last time you spoke to your best friend? Is there a regular time each week you meet socially with others?

It's very likely that you spend much less time engaged in meaningful human relationships and connecting with others than you used to, and certainly than our human ancestors did, and this can have a very negative impact on your health.

One of the most effective ways to manage stress is by connecting with others – and your body knows this! When you are stressed, a hormone called oxytocin is released in the body. Oxytocin, sometimes referred to as the cuddle hormone, motivates you to be social, hug someone and find support by rewarding this behaviour with pleasure chemicals. Oxytocin is also a natural anti-inflammatory and strengthens the body through cell regeneration, both of which are very positive for your neck pain.

Next time you're stressed and in pain, give someone a big old cuddle and let oxytocin work its magic!

THE STORY OF JACK

Jack is a 49-year-old chartered accountant who came to me with neck pain. He had been experiencing severe neck pain and headaches for over a year when we first met, as well as some tingling in his right arm that would come and go. He had seen multiple therapists to try and resolve his pain and was contemplating seeing a neurologist and surgeon.

Jack had a history of playing rugby when he was younger and had disc bulges at C3/4 and C6/7, but despite this he had not experienced pain or headaches until recently. He was a partner at his accounting firm and was under large amounts of stress on a daily basis, both at work and at home with three 'moody' teenagers.

Despite having already transitioned to a standing work desk, getting regular treatment on his neck and being diligent with his rehab exercises, he had only experienced a very slight improvement in his symptoms.

During Jack's assessment, it became evident just how significant his stress levels were and the effect they were having on his pain and overall health. He had been living in fight-or-flight mode for the past couple of years, since becoming a partner, and was now having issues with his digestion and immune system, as well as showing signs of chronic fatigue. We realised that his neck pain was always worse during stressful weeks, even when he adhered to his neck rehab and treatment sessions.

STEP 2: STRESS

Jack's stress levels were largely responsible for his neck pain and headaches, in three ways:

- His nervous system was in overdrive, which had increased his pain perception and nerve sensitivity
- Living in fight-or-flight mode had caused him to adopt an upper chest breathing pattern, meaning he was relying on his neck muscles for breathing, which caused overactivity, pain and fatigue in the neck
- Due to his stress levels, his body's healing response (immune system) was not functioning effectively, and he was not absorbing nutrients due to poor digestive function (creating poor tissue healing).

In treating Jack, I did not change the exercise programme or treatment techniques from his previous therapist, as I thought they were well implemented (though not tackling the underlying cause of his pain). I guided Jack through a comprehensive stress management programme, which included meditation and mindfulness, breathing technique training, a gentle cardio exercise programme, advice to spend more time connecting with his family, and enforcing a better work-life balance and daily gratitude practice.

Over several weeks, Jack's stress levels reduced significantly, his new breathing pattern resolved the tension in his neck, and he began to have a reduction in the intensity and frequency of his pain and headaches. His neural sensitivity decreased, and his arm pain ceased. His digestion improved and he began feeling much more energised throughout the day. He was also sleeping better at night.

It took 4 months for Jack's symptoms to completely resolve. Every now and again he still gets a slight headache if work gets out of control, but he now has the tools and strategies to manage his stress levels, which were the key underlying cause of his neck pain.

Step 2 Recap

- Stress is an imbalance between your perceived demands (stressors) and your perceived ability to cope (tools and resources)
- The stress response is an inbuilt strategy that prepares your body and brain for action, which is important for your survival
- Chronic and excessive stress is where the problem lies
- Stress can cause pain, and pain can cause stress: Stressed → muscle tension and increased pain perception = more pain → increased stress → inflammation and reduced healing ability (immune system) → pain worsens → more stress...
- Top ways to manage stress:
    - Exercise
    - Sleep
    - Breathing techniques

STEP 2: STRESS

- Meditation
- Nutrition and herbal supplements
- Emotional release
- Understanding the science of stress
- Gratitude practices
- Perspective and stress recalibration
- Acts of service and giving back
- Social connection

You now have the tools and skills to successfully manage stress in a healthy and effective way, bringing you one step closer to a pain-free neck.

My open goals for stress: e.g. *Over the next 6 weeks, let's see how quickly I can relax my mind and body when I begin feeling stressed. I can achieve this by aiming to meditate, do my gratitude practice and improve my social connections as often as possible.*

Success checklist:

- ☐ I am completing a meditation practice daily
- ☐ I am breathing diaphragmatically
- ☐ I have a daily gratitude practice
- ☐ Whenever I feel stressed, I find perspective by rating the issue on the recalibration scale
- ☐ I am exercising daily

- ☐ I am giving back through community service, charity or random acts of kindness
- ☐ I am nurturing my social connections and relationships

References:

1. Australian Psychological Society (2015). *Stress & Wellbeing: How Australians are Coping With Life*. Available at: https://www.psychology.org.au/getmedia/ae32e645-a4f0-4f7c-b3ce-dfd83237c281/stress-wellbeing-survey.pdf (accessed June 2021)
2. American Psychological Association (2017). *Stress in America: The State of Our Nation*. Available at: https://www.apa.org/news/press/releases/stress/2017/state-nation.pdf (accessed June 2021)
3. Black DS, O'Reilly GA, Olmstead R, Breen EC & Irwin MR. (2015). Mindfulness meditation and improvement in sleep quality and daytime impairment among older adults with sleep disturbances: a randomized clinical trial. *JAMA Internal Medicine* 175(4):494–501. https://doi.org/10.1001/jamainternmed.2014.8081
4. Black DS & Slavich GM. (2016). Mindfulness meditation and the immune system: a systematic review of randomized controlled trials. *Annals of the New York Academy of Sciences* 1373(1):13–24. https://doi.org/10.1111/nyas.12998
5. Zeidan F & Vago DR. (2016). Mindfulness meditation-based pain relief: a mechanistic account. *Annals of the New York Academy of Sciences* 1373(1):114–127. https://doi.org/10.1111/nyas.13153
6. Davidson RJ, Kabat-Zinn J, Schumacher J, et al. (2003). Alterations in brain and immune function produced by mindfulness meditation. *Psychosomatic Medicine* 65(4):564–570. https://doi.org/10.1097/01.psy.0000077505.67574.e3
7. Merkes M. (2010). Mindfulness-based stress reduction for people with chronic diseases. *Australian Journal of Primary Health* 16(3):200–210. https://doi.org/10.1071/PY09063

STEP 2: STRESS

8. Hölzel BK, Carmody J, Vangel M, et al. (2011). Mindfulness practice leads to increases in regional brain gray matter density. *Psychiatry Research* 191(1):36–43. https://doi.org/10.1016/j.pscychresns.2010.08.006
9. Gotink RA, Vernooij MW, Ikram MA, et al. (2018). Meditation and yoga practice are associated with smaller right amygdala volume: the Rotterdam study. *Brain Imaging and Behavior* 12(6):1631–1639. https://doi.org/10.1007/s11682-018-9826-z
10. Rappaport SM. (2016). Genetic factors are not the major causes of chronic diseases. *PLOS ONE* 11(4):e0154387. https://doi.org/10.1371/journal.pone.0154387
11. Keller A, Litzelman K, Wisk LE, et al. (2012). Does the perception that stress affects health matter? The association with health and mortality. *Health Psychology* 31(5):677–684. https://doi.org/10.1037/a0026743
12. Emmons RA & McCullough ME. (2003). Counting blessings versus burdens: an experimental investigation of gratitude and subjective well-being in daily life. *Journal of Personality and Social Psychology* 84(2):377–389. https://doi.org/10.1037//0022-3514.84.2.377
13. Seligman ME, Steen TA, Park N & Peterson C. (2005). Positive psychology progress: empirical validation of interventions. *The American Psychologist* 60(5):410–421. https://doi.org/10.1037/0003-066X.60.5.410
14. Rowland L & Curry OS (2019). A range of kindness activities boost happiness. *The Journal of Social Psychology* 159(3):340–343. https://doi.org/10.1080/00224545.2018.1469461
15. Whillans A, Dunn E, Sandstrom G, Dickerson S & Madden K. (2016). Is spending money on others good for your heart? Health Psychology 35(6):574–583. https://doi.org/10.1037/hea0000332
16. Buchanan KE & Bardi A. (2010). Acts of kindness and acts of novelty affect life satisfaction. *The Journal of Social Psychology* 150(3):235–237. https://doi.org/10.1080/00224540903365554

Step 3: Sleep

Sleep is an incredibly fascinating phenomenon that happens to you every single night. Given that you spend approximately one third of your life sleeping, it's worth knowing a bit about sleep and the importance of it.

Sleep is certainly not just the absence of wakefulness. It is a beautifully complex and critical process that rejuvenates your brain and body at the end of each day, and is one of the most essential aspects of your health.

Over the past couple of decades, we have seen an explosion of sleep science emerge that has helped us to understand exactly what happens to us when we hit the hay each night. This includes the benefits of obtaining good quality sleep, but also the disastrous impact of inadequate sleep, especially on pain.

In this chapter we will explore the relationship between sleep and pain by learning a little bit about sleep science (just enough to understand how cool and critical it is), what happens to your brain and body when you don't get enough good quality sleep, the upside of when you do, and most importantly, how to actually make high quality sleep happen.

STEP 3: SLEEP

> *You: I know that getting enough sleep is important, but my pain keeps me awake at night.*
> *Me (NECKspert): I hear you. Pain can make sleep very challenging and often creates a negative feedback loop (Pain → Poor sleep → Worse pain → Worse sleep → Around we go), but there are ways to break this cycle, and with the practical strategies you will learn in this chapter you will be able to start improving your sleep quality (Pain → Improved Sleep hygiene → Better quality sleep → Less pain → Better Sleep → Less pain etc.).*

What happens in the land of nod?

Let's start by briefly exploring the science of sleep. It may seem unnecessary for you to understand the mechanism of sleep and instead be tempted to jump straight into the practical aspect of fixing it, but I promise you that gaining a basic understanding of how it all works will assist you in realising the impact of your daily habits on your sleep quality at night and making the implementation of any necessary changes much more successful. Plus, sleep science facts go down great at dinner parties.

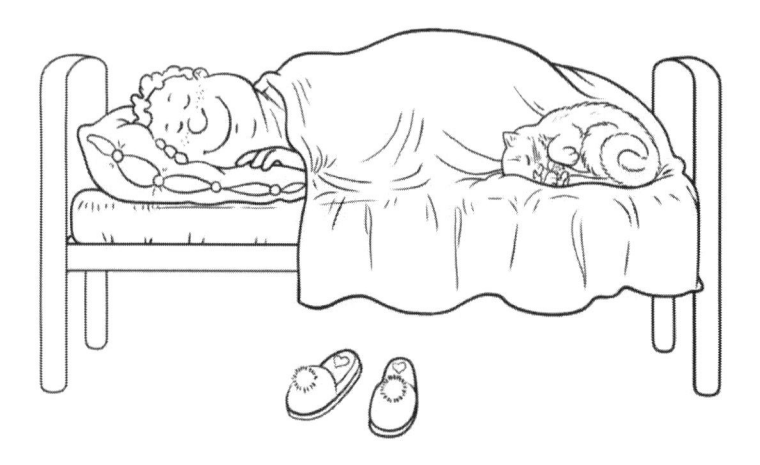

What causes sleep?

There are two key things that determine when you are awake and when you are asleep. The first is your *circadian rhythm*, which is your internal clock that tells you whether you should be up and about or getting some shut-eye.

The second factor is a chemical that progressively builds up in your brain throughout the day called *adenosine*. As soon as you wake up in the morning, adenosine starts to build up and it increases the longer you're awake. The more adenosine accumulates, the more tired you become, creating what is known as *sleep pressure*.

Thing 1: Circadian rhythm

Your circadian rhythm is the timekeeper in your brain that lets you know when you should be awake or asleep. It also determines when you feel like eating and drinking, your mood, metabolism, core body temperature and even how much you pee. Your circadian rhythm is not perfectly accurate, so it uses something constant to keep it on track –

sunlight. Daylight is the most constant thing in this world, so your brain relies on the trusty old sun (even through clouds) to keep your internal sleep clock ticking accurately.

When the sun sets in the evening, your brain registers this and a couple of hours later it starts releasing a hormone called *melatonin* that prepares you for sleep. When the sun comes up in the morning, the light through your eyelids tells your brain to stop producing melatonin and begins the process of wakefulness.

There are a few key issues we are now facing in society that are negatively impacting our circadian rhythms and therefore our sleep.

Artificial lights

In the not-so-distant past, when the sun went down in the evening, the only remaining light was from the moon, stars and fire. In our modern world of phones, televisions and computers, we are exposed to artificial light late into the night. This light tricks our brains into thinking it's still daytime and therefore negatively impacts our circadian rhythm.

Studies have shown that exposure to artificial light delays the release of melatonin by between 1 to 3 hours,[1] so when you're lying in bed at 10pm trying to sleep, your body may think it's only 7pm. It also shortens melatonin release, meaning you are more likely to wake up before getting a full 8 hours of sleep.[2] Even dim lights can suppress melatonin release by 50%, but LED lights have double the impact.

Whilst the use of smartphones, laptops and televisions are now very normal in the evening, we can be quick to forget how recently this technology was invented. The iPhone was only released in 2007, LED lights were created in 1999, laptops and computers were rare in homes 30 years ago and televisions only became a common household item in the 1950s. We really are the first guinea pigs in this unprecedented experiment of an artificially lit world – and the results are starting to show.

Regulated temperature

Just as the fading sunlight lets your brain know that it's time to initiate the sleep process, so does a drop in temperature. As the sun sets in the evening, the temperature begins to decline, and this signals your brain to start releasing melatonin. In order to fall asleep, your core temperature needs to decrease by about one degree Celsius. I'm sure you can recall those hot and sticky summer nights when falling asleep is a challenge!

Unlike our ancestors who were much more exposed to the elements, today most of us live within controlled environments with little variation in temperature ranges. Changes in temperature throughout the day and night play an important role in healthy sleep, but our modern world creates a very constant temperature through air-conditioned or heated homes, workplaces, shops and cars. This can affect the core body temperature cooling required for high-quality sleep.

International travel

Once upon a time, travelling across to the other side of the world would take months and months on a ship. This incredibly slow mode of transport meant that a traveller's body clock gradually adjusted to new time zones in real time. Fast forward to the present day and it's not uncommon (well, at least before COVID-19) for a businessperson to fly from Sydney to London for a meeting on Monday, see clients in Hong Kong on Wednesday and then return home for family dinner by Thursday night. Did somebody say jet lag? Whether it's a regular occurrence for work or an infrequent holiday by-product, most of us have experienced this unpleasant phenomenon.

Jet lag is a mismatch between your internal body clock (circadian rhythm) and the sun in the new location. Your body tells you that it's midnight and you should be asleep, but the glaring morning sunshine is insisting that you should be up and about. As you now know, sunlight helps to keep your body clock ticking accurately, so over the following days it gradually resets the circadian rhythm at a rate of 1 hour per day (e.g. 8 days to reset to an 8-hour difference).

It's worth noting that you no longer even need to leave your living room to experience the effects of international travel. In our globalised world, many companies expect employees to attend online meetings in international time zones, many people watch international sporting matches in the middle of the night, and overseas friends and family will schedule video calls at all hours. We can now all experience jet lag in the comfort of our own home – yay!

Chronotypes

Not all circadian rhythms are created equal. Do you spring out of bed in the morning, ready to tackle the day, only to become tired and ready to sleep by 9pm? Or could you sleep until midday, take ages to get going in the morning, but feel wide awake at 11pm? Perhaps you're somewhere in between?

Your biological preference for wakefulness and sleep is known as your *chronotype*. It is believed that approximately 40% of the population are 'morning larks' (early risers and early sleepers), 30% are 'night owls' (late risers and late sleepers) and 30% are 'in-betweeners', although this is variable with age and sex.[3]

There seems to be an evolutionary explanation for why humans tend to have an in-built variability in their preference for when they are awake or asleep. Human tribes throughout history have slept in groups and if everyone was to fall asleep and wake up at the same time, it would make a clan vulnerable to predators. With a mix of morning larks and night owls, the group would only collectively be asleep at the same time for 50% of the night (i.e. 4 hours instead of 8), increasing the tribe's chances of survival.

With this long evolutionary history, your chronotype is an in-built feature in your genetic make-up and shouldn't be fought. This can obviously be challenging in a world with fixed school and work start times (especially for night owls), but knowing your chronotype and trying to structure your life around this will do wonders for your sleep quality and health. A number of chronotype tests are available online if you're not sure which you are.

Stress
There's a good chance you've had the unpleasant experience of lying in bed awake for hours trying to tame a stressed and busy mind. The impact of stress on your sleep can be disastrous. The hormones and chemicals your body releases when you're stressed are designed to make you alert and ready to escape danger – not ideal for sleep. Studies into the impact of stress on sleep consistently show decreased periods of both deep sleep and rapid eye movement (REM) sleep (more on this soon), poorer 'sleep efficiency' (the amount of time spent asleep versus trying to sleep) and an increase in the frequency of waking up at night.[4,5]

We've spoken a lot about stress in the last chapter so I'll keep it brief here, but in a nutshell, excessive or poorly managed stress will wreak havoc on your sleep quality.

Thing 2: Adenosine and sleep pressure
Alongside your circadian rhythm, the second dictator of when you sleep is a chemical called *adenosine*. From the

minute you wake up, this chemical begins to accumulate in your brain and increases in quantity throughout the day.

The more adenosine builds up in the brain, the more tired you become. This is known as sleep pressure. When sleep pressure hits a critical threshold, you can no longer keep your eyes open and you are carried away on a magical cloud to the land of nod.

During the night, your brain cells shrink in size to allow cleansing fluid (*cerebrospinal fluid*) to come in and wash away all of the adenosine and other plaques and toxins that have built up throughout the day. This is comparable to vacuuming your house daily and all of your furniture temporarily shrinking to make cleaning easier... this is the magic of your brain! As a side note, this process is thought to also remove amyloid plaques, which are the underlying cause of Alzheimer's disease, drawing strong connections between poor sleep and dementia.[6,7]

If you have poor quality or insufficient sleep then not all of the adenosine will be cleared overnight, so the next day instead of starting with a clean slate, you start accumulating new adenosine on top of yesterday's build-up – you didn't finish the vacuuming. You wake up feeling tired, groggy and grumpy.

This is where things can get interesting: remember the little adenosine receptors that tell you how much adenosine has built up in your brain and signals for you to feel tired? Well, it turns out these receptors also have a fondness for another chemical: *caffeine*. Caffeine binds to adenosine receptors in the brain and blocks them, thereby masking fatigue.

We will also discuss caffeine in the next chapter on supplements and nutrition, but due to its impact on sleep, it also deserves a place here in the sleep chapter.

Ingesting caffeine is the equivalent of putting a sticker over the fuel light in your car so you can't see when you're running on empty. It tricks you into feeling alert and awake. Adenosine continues to build up, but you don't know because the sleepiness signal is being blocked by the caffeine. Once the caffeine wears off, there is a big crash. Not only does caffeine impact sleep quality, but it also enhances your pain perception by activating the fight-or-flight response that we discussed in detail in the last chapter.

Caffeine is present in tea, coffee, cola, dark chocolate and workout powders. Its effects peak about 30 minutes after you ingest it and it stays in your system for about 12 hours. This is worth noting because even a lunchtime coffee can impact your sleep quality at night. Some people are more caffeine sensitive than others (due to the quantity of an enzyme in the liver that breaks down caffeine), but it does have an effect on everyone to some degree.

Many people drink coffee because it makes them feel more alert and 'on the ball', but interestingly it does not result in high-quality work. NASA did a study in the 1990s where they gave spiders various drugs and then analysed the webs they made.[8] The results below speak for themselves.

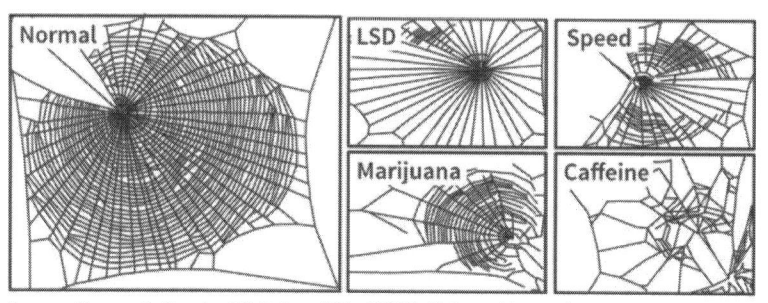

Source: Noever R, Cronise J & Relwani RA. (1995). Using spider-web patterns to determine toxicity. *NASA Tech Briefs* 19(4):82.

Even compared to LSD, speed and weed, the spider's caffeine-inspired webs were unbelievably bad. Next time you reach for a coffee before an important task, remember this picture and ask yourself: can I afford to spin a caffeine web on this task?

There are some health benefits of coffee, but for someone looking to resolve chronic pain, the importance of high-quality sleep and calming the nervous system mean that these health benefits are outweighed by the negative impact of caffeine on your pain cycle.

Sleep phases

Hopefully you've held on through the science of circadian rhythms and adenosine. Before we discuss some practical solutions to improve your sleep, there are a few more aspects of sleep science that are important to understand.

There are five stages of a sleep cycle. The first four are all stages of non-REM sleep. The fifth stage is REM sleep, which gets its name from the fact that the eyes dart back and forth during this sleep phase.

It takes approximately 90 minutes to complete a full sleep cycle, and the quantity of REM versus NREM sleep in each cycle varies throughout the night. The first half of the night is dominated by NREM sleep, whilst the second half is REM dominant. If you go to bed later than usual, you'll miss out on the majority of your NREM sleep. If you get up earlier than usual, you'll miss out on most of your REM sleep. Both phases are critical for different functions and the next day you'll have impairments corresponding to the phase you've missed.

NREM sleep
The main function of NREM sleep is best thought of as storing important information from the day (facts, skills, experiences) and deleting unnecessary content. During this phase, the brain takes raw information and memories and decides what it should keep and what it should delete. It then converts the important content from short-term to long-term storage, like transferring files from a universal serial bus (USB) stick to a hard drive. This creates space in the short-term memory bank for new content the following day and ensures that important facts are safely stored for future recollection.

REM sleep

The REM phase of sleep is where you dream. During this phase you problem solve, reflect and create insights about raw information. Your brain waves during REM sleep are very similar to when you're awake (busy and chaotic), but paradoxically your physical body is paralysed (a clever trick by your brain to stop you wildly acting out your dreams).

During REM sleep, there is an activation of the visual, emotional and autobiographical memory parts of the brain. There is also a deactivation of regions that control rational thought. This allows you to look past the raw facts you have stored during NREM sleep and begin to draw insightful conclusions, overcome complex problems, fine-tune your emotional responses and develop creativity.

In a nutshell, NREM makes you *remember* information, whilst REM makes you *understand* that information in a meaningful and insightful way.

Sleep and your pain

You now know more about sleep science than 99% of the world's population – congratulations! Next, let's explore the relationship between sleep quality and your pain.

As you learned in Section 1 of this book, pain is a complex phenomenon that is influenced by your emotional state, past experiences, environment and context. I'm sure you've had the unpleasant experience of straining your neck at the

STEP 3: SLEEP

end of a long day at work when you were exhausted and your whole world came crashing down: you were fed up with your injury, you didn't have the energy for it any more, enough was enough, you burst into tears. Sound familiar?

Perhaps you can recall another instance where you had slept well and were feeling upbeat and energised, but then your neck 'went' on you? Whilst it hurt like hell and probably put you in a shitty mood, you were able to get through a day at work, make a joke about your dodgy neck with a colleague and still go out to dinner with your friends that night.

Same neck strain, but very different experience. Here's why:

Natural painkiller
Scientific studies have shown that poor quality or reduced duration of sleep results in a huge increase in pain sensitivity.[9] The parts of your brain that are responsible for processing pain are 40% more sensitive after sleep deprivation. To put this into context, your 5/10 pain after a good night's sleep just became a 7/10 pain after sleeping poorly.

When sleep quality improves, these brain regions become less sensitised. Painkillers like oxycodone act on the same part of the brain, so you can think of sleep as a natural painkiller (and pain increaser when you don't get enough).

Sleep and the immune system

There is also a lot of scientific evidence showing that sleep improves the immune system,[10] which is the main system in your body that heals injured body tissues (such as muscle, bone and nerves). A large factor in pain is *inflammation*, which can become excessive and persistent in chronic conditions.

Getting sufficient sleep has been proven to reduce inflammation and promote a healthier immune system response, therefore creating faster tissue recovery times and stimulating the repair of cells in the body. Studies have even shown that long-term sleep loss is a *predictor* of increased injury rates.[11,12]

Sleep and movement quality

When pain has been around for a while, it is usually accompanied by poor movement patterns in the body. Sometimes these play a role in creating the injury, other times they are developed as a result of the pain, but in both cases, they are involved in maintaining the pain.

With this in mind, it should come as no surprise that improving the quality of how you move is critical to overcoming your pain (refer back to Step 1 on *structure* for a refresher). It turns out that learning new movement patterns and exercises is heavily impacted by the quality of your sleep. Studies have shown that skill learning (e.g. improving the quality of how you rotate your neck) is improved by 25% after high-quality sleep.[13]

When sleeping after practising a new movement pattern, your brain begins to rewire your brain pathways and turns the various components of the new skill into an effortless and automated task. If you fail to obtain good sleep after all your hard work practising your *NECKsercises,* then they're unlikely to stick.

More specifically, the last 2 hours of NREM sleep is where the majority of skill automation happens in the brain, so cutting your sleep short to wake up early will negatively impact your ability to learn high-quality movement patterns around your neck.

Sleep and physical performance

Due to the amount of money involved in professional sport, a lot of health and fitness research comes from this area. Studies into how sleep impacts your physical performance have uncovered a decreased ability for your body to function at a high level when you sleep less than 8 hours per night.[14–16] Even if you're not an athlete, each of these effects will also impact your everyday life and your pain:

- Time to physical exhaustion during exercise drops by 30%
- A 30% drop in muscle power
- Decreases in both maximal strength and endurance
- Increased lactic acid build up
- Reduced oxygen uptake

Whether the above effects are experienced during exercise or just during activities of daily living, they all result in bad movement patterns and pain. To put a positive spin on it, if you can achieve 8 hours of quality sleep per night then you will experience increased muscle strength, power and endurance, less physical exhaustion and improvements in how your body uses energy. Each of these will have dramatic benefits on your neck pain.

Sleep and emotions
You should recall from Section 1 that pain is heavily dependent on your emotional state. One of the biggest determinants of your emotional stability is the amount of REM sleep you get each night. During REM sleep, emotions are processed through dreams and your brain is able to detach from emotionally challenging experiences. If you do not get sufficient REM sleep, you will experience emotional volatility, which will increase your pain levels.

Sleeping position

You spend one third of your life in your bed, so the position you sleep in has an enormous impact on your posture and the position of your neck and spine.

It's very challenging to get someone to sleep in a new position, because as soon as they fall asleep, they will unconsciously get back into their favourite position – even if it's terrible for their neck.

That said, the first rule of sleeping positions when overcoming neck pain is don't sleep on your tummy with

STEP 3: SLEEP

your head in full rotation. You need to become a back or side sleeper.

Secondly, you need good quality pillows. The thickness of your pillow should ensure that your head is neutral when sleeping on your side. If you draw a line down your forehead and through your nose, the line should then continue perfectly straight along your sternum. If your pillow is too thick or too thin then your neck will be flexed or side-bent all night, which is not OK. My favourite pillow is the *Ecosa* pillow. It's comfortable, supportive and ticks all the boxes.

Next, you need a good mattress. More specifically, you need the right density for your body. If your mattress is too soft, your spine will be in excessive flexion (forward bent). Too firm and it won't allow for the natural curvature of your spine. Similar to your pillow test, if you draw a line along your spine when lying down on your side, the line should be dead-straight.

Again, for mattresses I recommend *Ecosa*. The mattress is firm and supportive but very comfortable. They offer the best mattress on the market at an affordable price (under A$1,000), and you can even test it for 100 nights to make sure it's right for you. I've personally been using an *Ecosa* pillow and mattress for a while now and they were a total game-changer, so I'm a big fan. You can find them at www.neckspert.com.au/recommendations.

Your whole system

Whilst this book is about your pain, it's important to remember that everything in the body and brain is connected, all of the body systems are interrelated, and that dysfunction in one part of the body will impact the health of your whole system.

With this in mind, the below table is a holistic overview of some of the negative health implications associated with sleep deprivation. I haven't included this to scare you, but simply as a reminder of the importance of prioritising high-quality sleep, not just for your injury but for your overall well-being.

Mental/nervous system	Physical
Alzheimer's	Cancer
Anxiety	Diabetes
Depression	Weight gain and obesity
Suicide	Heart attack
Chronic pain	Infertility
Bipolar disorder	Immune deficiency
Stroke	Early mortality

If reading this does scare you, then hopefully it's enough of a nudge to start treating sleep with the respect it deserves. Currently, about 40% of Australians and one third of Americans don't get enough sleep, so I want to ensure that you get on the right side of that statistic.[17,18]

The upside

Let's not dwell on the negatives. The benefits of sufficient sleep for your whole system should be just as much of a motivator to implement change as fear of the downside.

Anti-ageing (physical and mental)	Reduced risk of heart attacks, stroke and diabetes
Enhanced memory and learning	Enhanced mood and happiness
Boosted creativity	Appetite regulation and gut health
Help with metabolism and body weight	Accurate pain perception
Reduced cancer and dementia	Boosted immune system
Regulated insulin and blood glucose levels	Reduced anxiety and depression

If you could package up these benefits into a pill with no side effects, it would sell for millions. But luckily for you, it's completely free. Getting 8 solid hours of shut-eye each night is all it takes to experience the above results.

> ***You***: *Thanks NECKspert, but getting 8 hours of quality sleep is easier said than done. I can't fall asleep quickly and I can't help waking up multiple times per night. The only way I sleep through is if I take sleeping pills.*
> ***Me (NECKspert)***: *You're not wrong – it can be a real challenge for many people to sleep well. But I promise that if you follow my plan below, you will dramatically improve the quality and duration of your sleep. Before I lay out the plan, let me first address your point about sleeping pills.*

Sleeping pills

Whilst taking sleeping pills might feel like a simple solution, they are toxic and do not lead to the health benefits of real sleep. Rather than inducing natural sleep, sleeping pills sedate the brain and prevent REM sleep.

Ironically, sleep studies have shown that sleeping pills hardly improve the time it takes to fall asleep, even though people thought they had fallen asleep quicker (the placebo effect).[19] Once asleep, sleeping pills do not allow you to get into the deep, restorative phases that occur during natural sleep, resulting in fatigue and grogginess the next day. This often sets up a vicious cycle where you need caffeine during the day to offset the side-effects of sleeping pills, and pills at night to offset the caffeine... around we go.

STEP 3: SLEEP

Where natural sleep enhances learning and memory, pill-induced sleep actually unwires brain pathways, erases memories and weakens learning. A big study into sleeping pill use showed that over a 2.5-year period, heavy users were five times more likely to die than natural sleepers, and even light users (only 18 pills per year) were still three times more likely to die (take note if you are a frequent flyer and use pills to sleep on planes). Some of the causes of death included infection (due to suppressed immune system), car accidents, heart disease, stroke and cancer.[20]

It shouldn't surprise you that getting off sleeping pills can be a painful task. Be aware that you will likely go through a period of what is known as *rebound insomnia,* where sleeping is incredibly hard, especially if you've been taking pills for a long time. I urge you to stay strong through this period, avoid reaching for the pills and know that it will pass. It may take days to weeks, but deep and natural sleep will eventually return, and true benefits of sleep can then begin to take place.

The solution!

By now, I'm sure you will agree that getting 8 hours of high-quality sleep is one of the single most important things you can do for healing your pain, enhancing your health and transforming your life. But how do you actually make it happen?

Below I have mapped out your 11-point plan for optimal sleep. My advice is to make a copy of this plan and use it as a nightly checklist. Put it somewhere visible so that you can read through it as the sun starts to set in the evening and review it daily until it becomes second nature.

1. **Lighting**: You now understand the impact of artificial lighting on your circadian rhythm, so as the sun sets you should dim any bright lights, turn on soft lamps and light candles. Replace any bright white light bulbs with warm, low-intensity bulbs. This will tell your brain that night is here so that it can begin melatonin release at the right time, meaning you'll get off to sleep easier. You should also remove any artificial lights from your bedroom, such as alarm clocks, and block outside lights with black-out curtains (if you don't have any external streetlights then it can be nice to leave curtains open, so sunlight enters in the morning).

2. **Reduce screen time**: If you're really serious about optimising your sleep then you should ideally cut out all computer, smartphone, tablet and television use at night in order to minimise blue light exposure. If that is unrealistic, apply 'night-shift' filters to your devices to minimise blue light exposure. There are also great options for glasses that filter out blue light.

3. **Read a book before bed:** Reading is a very relaxing and therapeutic pre-sleep activity as it can distract your mind from focusing on the stresses in your own life. *How* you read is very important though. One study looked at the impact of 2 hours of reading on a tablet/device before bed versus 2 hours of reading a

paper book.[21] The results were dramatically different: reading with a tablet instead of a paper book resulted in a 50% reduction in melatonin release, as well as a 3-hour delay in melatonin release. It took tablet users longer to fall asleep, they had reduced REM sleep, were more tired the next day, and they had an ongoing lag in rising melatonin levels for several days after tablet use ceased (digital hangover).

4. **Temperature**: The optimal room temperature for sleeping is 18 degrees Celsius, so if you sleep with air-conditioning then set it to this. You need your core body temperature to cool by one degree to initiate sleep, and a helpful trick is to have a *warm* shower or bath just before bed. The body will create an internal cooling response due to the hot water, drawing blood to the surface of your skin, which cools your core body temperature. Having a warm shower or bath before bed makes you fall asleep faster and can give you 10–15% more NREM sleep.[22,23]

5. **Go to bed and wake up at the same time daily**: Research has shown that this is one of the most important aspects of high-quality sleep, so try to resist the urge to have long lie-ins at the weekend.[24,25] If life permits (e.g. work, kids, commitments), also try and match your sleep times to your chronotype. For example, if you are a night owl, perhaps you can negotiate with your employer about starting and finishing work later or have a discussion with your

spouse about your preference for doing school pick-up rather than drop-off.

6. **Stress management**: Your own mind can be one of your biggest barriers to sleep. Before bed, write down a to-do list for the following day so that you can clear your head for the night. You should then spend 5–10 minutes doing a mindfulness activity like following your breath or a relaxing body scan. You can use the audio-guided mindfulness recordings from my website: www.neckspert.com.au/resources

7. **Exercise**: There are many benefits to your sleep from regular exercise, such as an increase in deep NREM sleep, improved sleep quality and duration, and reduced time to fall asleep. Sleep also has a big influence on exercise capacity, with poor strength and fitness results seen after inadequate sleep. Sleep and exercise feed each other, with regular exercise leading to better sleep, but good-quality sleep also increasing your likelihood of regular exercise due to having more energy. Important tip: don't exercise right before bed as your core temperature will be too high. You should finish training 2–3 hours before bed.

8. **Caffeine**: The half-life of caffeine is 6 hours, meaning half of the drug quantity is still in your system 6 hours after you ingest it (and that it can take up to 12 hours to be completely removed). Given this, you should avoid caffeine after midday, or remove it from your diet

STEP 3: SLEEP

altogether. Try switching to herbal teas or soda water with fresh lemon as an alternative.

9. **Alcohol**: Alcohol prevents you from entering REM sleep. You should always aim to go to sleep with a blood alcohol concentration of zero. It takes approximately 1 hour for your liver to process one standard drink, so if you are having a drink at night, ensure you give your body enough time to clear it from your system before hitting the hay. An even better solution is to swap your wine or beer for a non-alcoholic alternative, at least on the majority of nights.

10. **Diet**: Avoid going to bed too full or too hungry as this can impact sleep quality. A lower carbohydrate diet has been shown to result in better sleep, so reduce your carbohydrates and increase fibre intake at dinner. Getting up to urinate multiple times per night is a common cause of sleep disturbance, so reduce your liquid intake before bed. There are a number of natural herbal supplements that can assist in sleep quality, without the negative side-effects of sleeping pills. I will discuss these in the next section on *supplements*.

11. **Equipment**: Make sure you have a good quality pillow and mattress, such as the Ecosa products.

You now have all the skills you need to drift away to the land of nod each night... *bonne nuit*!

THE STORY OF ANNA

Anna had been suffering from neck pain for 8 years when I first met her. She was in her early 60s and despite needing to continue working for a few more years for financial reasons, she was contemplating retiring from her administration job due to her pain. Anna lived alone as her two kids were now grown up and she had separated from her ex-husband 10 years earlier.

The only thing that seemed to work for relieving Anna's neck pain was strong pain medication. She got temporary relief from massages and joint mobilisations, but the pain always came back. She had also been suffering from poor sleep since her divorce a decade ago and had recently started taking sleeping pills.

Through my assessment of Anna, I determined that despite having a number of factors contributing to her pain, sleep was the biggest driver. This was due to the influence of poor sleep on her pain perception, stress, postural alignment and immune system dysfunction. She told me that she was just naturally a bad sleeper and didn't think she could do anything to change it, but I was able to identify a number of habits impacting her sleep quality: she stayed up late watching television, drank coffee after midday, consumed alcohol every night and was very stressed about the prospect of having to retire due to her pain.

STEP 3: SLEEP

The main focus of my treatment plan for Anna was sleep optimisation. First, I guided her on getting the right pillow and mattress for her body. We then implemented an evening routine that involved turning off all the main lights in the house and just using lamps, she started reading a book instead of watching television and she had a hot shower just before bed each night. She swapped her afternoon coffee for a herbal tea and committed to drinking just one glass of wine every second night, well before bedtime. She also commenced a pre-sleep mindfulness and breathing exercise to help reduce stress and mental stimulation.

As she introduced all of these changes, she also began to taper down her sleeping medication until the point she was no longer taking them.

Despite noticing an improvement in her sleep within the first 2 weeks, it took Anna 3 months until she achieved her first full 8-hour sleep without waking up once. This was a huge achievement as she previously averaged about 4 hours of broken sleep per night.

As Anna began to consistently sleep well at night, she noticed that her pain levels progressively improved and she even had mornings where she would wake up pain-free. She was also noticing benefits in other aspects of her life, such as improved energy levels throughout the day, she was more productive at work and enjoyed being there, and her stress levels improved dramatically.

After 4 months of working on Anna's sleep and the other smaller influences on her pain, she was rarely feeling neck pain and felt as though she had regained control of her life. She was confident she would be able to keep working for another 5 years but thought she would aim for another 10 years of work as she loved the company.

By taking control of her sleep, Anna was able to heal her neck pain.

Step 3 Recap

- You need 8 hours of good-quality sleep every night in order to thrive
- Sleep is controlled by your circadian rhythm and the build-up of adenosine
- Your circadian rhythm is influenced by lights, temperature, stress, international travel, age and your chronotype
- Adenosine can be masked by caffeine, tricking your brain into thinking it doesn't need sleep
- There are five phases of sleep, four of which are NREM and the fifth being REM
- The main function of NREM sleep is storing important information from the day and deleting unnecessary content
- The REM phase of sleep is where you dream. During this phase you problem solve, reflect and create insights about raw information.

STEP 3: SLEEP

- Sleep is a natural painkiller and sleep deprivation can increase pain sensitivity by 40%
- Getting sufficient sleep has been proven to reduce inflammation and promote a healthier immune system response, resulting in faster tissue recovery times
- Poor sleep reduces movement quality, which increases injury risk
- Sleep impacts emotional volatility, which influences your pain response
- The right sleeping equipment is important. Get a good quality pillow and mattress that is right for your size and shape.
- Sleeping pills do not allow you to obtain good quality, restorative sleep and come with a long list of dangerous side-effects
- The below success checklist outlines your recipe for good-quality sleep!

My open goals for sleep: e.g. *Over the next 6 weeks I am going to see how often I can get 8 hours per night of good-quality sleep, by implementing a pre-bed routine and following the steps in the success checklist.*

_____

_____

Success checklist:

- ☐ I have improved my lighting (warm bulbs, no LEDs, mood lighting)
- ☐ I have reduced or ceased screen time at night (and use blue light filters on screens)
- ☐ I now read a physical book before bed, as opposed to using e.g. a tablet or Kindle.
- ☐ I have a hot shower before bed
- ☐ My bedroom temperature is around 18 degrees Celsius
- ☐ I know my chronotype and have made adjustments for this
- ☐ I'm going to bed and waking up at the same time daily
- ☐ I'm doing a mindfulness breathing exercise before bed to reduce stress and calm my mind
- ☐ I'm getting adequate exercise during the day, but not within 2 hours of bedtime
- ☐ I'm avoiding caffeine after midday
- ☐ I'm not going to bed with any alcohol in my system
- ☐ I'm reducing carbohydrates and increasing fibre in my diet, especially at dinner
- ☐ I'm replacing sleeping pills with natural herbal supplements
- ☐ I now minimise liquid intake within 1 hour of going to bed
- ☐ I've purchased an Ecosa pillow and mattress (www.neckspert.com.au/recommendations)

STEP 3: SLEEP

References:

1. Tähkämö L, Partonen T & Pesonen AK (2019). Systematic review of light exposure impact on human circadian rhythm. *Chronobiology International* 36(2):151–170. https://doi.org/10.1080/07420528.2018.1527773
2. Gooley JJ, Chamberlain K, Smith KA, et al. (2011). Exposure to room light before bedtime suppresses melatonin onset and shortens melatonin duration in humans. *The Journal of Clinical Endocrinology and Metabolism* 96(3):E463–E472. https://doi.org/10.1210/jc.2010-2098
3. Fischer D, Lombardi DA, Marucci-Wellman H & Roenneberg T. (2017). Chronotypes in the US—Influence of age and sex. *PLOS ONE* 12(6):e0178782. https://doi.org/10.1371/journal.pone.0178782
4. Kim EJ & Dimsdale JE. (2007). The effect of psychosocial stress on sleep: a review of polysomnographic evidence. *Behavioral Sleep Medicine* 5(4):256–278. https://doi.org/10.1080/15402000701557383
5. Kalmbach DA, Anderson JR & Drake CL. (2018). The impact of stress on sleep: pathogenic sleep reactivity as a vulnerability to insomnia and circadian disorders. *Journal of Sleep Research* 27(6):e12710. https://doi.org/10.1111/jsr.12710
6. Sprecher KE, Bendlin BB, Racine AM *et al.* (2015). Amyloid burden is associated with self-reported sleep in nondemented late middle-aged adults. *Neurobiol Aging* 36(9):2568–2576. http://doi.org/10.1016/j.neurobiolaging.2015.05.004
7. Ju YS, Ooms SJ, Sutphen C, et al. (2017). Slow wave sleep disruption increases cerebrospinal fluid amyloid-β levels. *Brain: a Journal of Neurology* 140(8):2104–2111. https://doi.org/10.1093/brain/awx148
8. Noever R, Cronise J & Relwani RA. (1995). Using spider-web patterns to determine toxicity. *NASA Tech Briefs* 19(4):82.
9. Staffe AT, Bech MW, Clemmensen S, Nielsen HT, Larsen DB & Petersen KK. (2019). Total sleep deprivation increases pain sensitivity, impairs conditioned pain modulation and facilitates temporal summation of pain in healthy

10.   participants. *PLOS ONE* 14(12):e0225849. https://doi.org/10.1371/journal.pone.0225849
11.   Besedovsky L, Lange T & Born J. (2012). Sleep and immune function. *Pflugers Archiv: European Journal of Physiology* 463(1):121–137. https://doi.org/10.1007/s00424-011-1044-0
12.   Gao B, Dwivedi S, Milewski MD & Cruz AI, Jr. (2019). Chronic lack of sleep is associated with increased sports injury in adolescents: a systematic review and meta-analysis. *Orthopaedic Journal of Sports Medicine* 7(3 Suppl):2325967119S00132. https://doi.org/10.1177/2325967119S00132
13.   Milewski MD, Skaggs DL, Bishop GA, et al. (2014). Chronic lack of sleep is associated with increased sports injuries in adolescent athletes. *Journal of Pediatric Orthopedics* 34(2):129–133. https://doi.org/10.1097/BPO.0000000000000151
14.   Kuriyama K, Stickgold R & Walker MP. (2004). Sleep-dependent learning and motor-skill complexity. *Learning & Memory (Cold Spring Harbor, N.Y.)* 11(6):705–713. https://doi.org/10.1101/lm.76304
15.   Azboy O & Kaygisiz Z. (2009). Effects of sleep deprivation on cardiorespiratory functions of the runners and volleyball players during rest and exercise. *Acta Physiologica Hungarica* 96(1):29–36. https://doi.org/10.1556/APhysiol.96.2009.1.3
16.   Skein M, Duffield R, Edge J, Short MJ & Mündel T. (2011). Intermittent-sprint performance and muscle glycogen after 30 h of sleep deprivation. *Medicine and Science in Sports and Exercise* 43(7):1301–1311. https://doi.org/10.1249/MSS.0b013e31820abc5a
17.   Mah CD, Mah KE, Kezirian EJ & Dement WC. (2011). The effects of sleep extension on the athletic performance of collegiate basketball players. *Sleep* 34(7), 943–950. https://doi.org/10.5665/SLEEP.1132
18.   Liu Y, Wheaton AG, Chapman DP, Cunningham TJ, Lu H & Croft JB. (2016). Prevalence of healthy sleep duration among adults — United States, 2014. *Morbidity and Mortality*

Weekly Report 65(6):137–141.
http://dx.doi.org/10.15585/mmwr.mm6506a1

18. Adams RJ, Appleton SL, Taylor AW, et al. (2017). Sleep health of Australian adults in 2016: results of the 2016 Sleep Health Foundation national survey. *Sleep Health* 3(1):35–42. https://doi.org/10.1016/j.sleh.2016.11.005

19. Sateia MJ, Buysse DJ, Krystal AD, Neubauer DN & Heald JL. (2017). Clinical Practice Guideline for the Pharmacologic Treatment of Chronic Insomnia in Adults: An American Academy of Sleep Medicine clinical practice guideline. *Journal of Clinical Sleep Medicine* 13(2):307–349. https://doi.org/10.5664/jcsm.6470

20. Kripke DF, Langer RD & Kline LE. (2012). Hypnotics' association with mortality or cancer: a matched cohort study. *British Medical Journal Open* 2:e000850. https://doi.org/10.1136/bmjopen-2012-000850

21. Chang A-M, Aeschbach D, Duffy JF & Czeisler CA. (2015). Impact of light-emitting eBooks before bed. *Proceedings of the National Academy of Sciences* 112(4):1232–1237. https://doi.org/10.1073/pnas.1418490112

22. Tai Y, Obayashi K, Yamagami Y, et al. (2021). Hot-water bathing before bedtime and shorter sleep onset latency are accompanied by a higher distal-proximal skin temperature gradient in older adults. *Journal of Clinical Sleep Medicine* 17(6):1257–1266. https://doi.org/10.5664/jcsm.9180

23. Tai Y, Saeki K, Yamagami Y, et al. (2019). Association between timing of hot water bathing before bedtime and night-/sleep-time blood pressure and dipping in the elderly: a longitudinal analysis for repeated measurements in home settings. *Chronobiology International* 36(12):1714–1722. https://doi.org/10.1080/07420528.2019.1675685

24. Phillips AJK, Clerx WM, O'Brien CS, et al. (2017). Irregular sleep/wake patterns are associated with poorer academic performance and delayed circadian and sleep/wake timing. *Scientific Reports* 7:3216. https://doi.org/10.1038/s41598-017-03171-4

25. Phillips DJ, Savenkova MI & Karatsoreos IN. (2015). Environmental disruption of the circadian clock leads

to altered sleep and immune responses in mouse. *Brain, Behavior, and Immunity* 47:14–23. https://doi.org/10.1016/j.bbi.2014.12.008

Step 4: Supplements

Whilst nutritional and herbal supplements are a major focus for this step, the larger concepts are food, diet and gut health. In reality, a more appropriate name for this step would have been *Nutrition*, but then instead of the 5 Ss of NECKcellence we would've had the 4 Ss and 1 N, which obviously doesn't cut it. I'm sure you can forgive the slightly misleading title.

We'll begin by exploring the impact of certain foods on your neck pain and overall health, before moving onto some very important supplements that will assist you in the healing process.

You are what you eat

There is more truth to the old saying 'You are what you eat' than you may realise. When you eat food, the cellular structure of that food is absorbed into your body and quite literally *becomes* your body. The food you eat becomes the building blocks for your body's cells, which are constantly being replaced.

If you were building a house, the quality of the house would largely be dependent on the quality of the materials you used to build it. Use cheap and flimsy bricks and timber, you will get a poor-quality house. Consume unhealthy and low nutritional food and drink, you will have a flimsy and poor-quality body that is prone to disease.

STEP 4: SUPPLEMENTS

It's all in the gut

In order to understand the impact of nutrition on your pain and overall health, you first need to understand the role and importance of your gut.

The gastrointestinal tract, AKA the *gut*, is the passage from the mouth to the anus that includes all of your digestive organs. It includes the oesophagus, stomach, small intestine and large intestine, as well as the accessory organs of digestion such as the tongue, pancreas, liver and gallbladder.

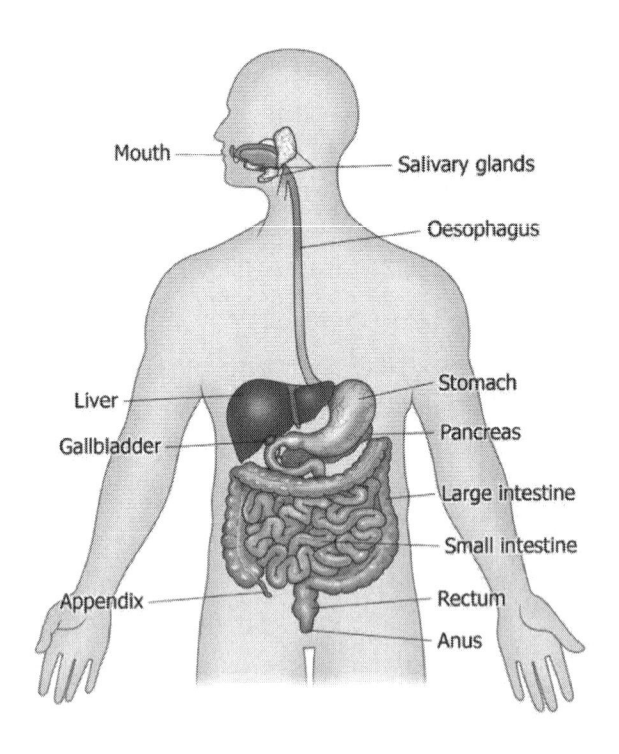

Source: Adapted from *Encyclopædia Britannica, Inc.*

When you eat a meal, the digestive process first begins in your mouth via chewing and the enzymes in your saliva. The food then passes from your mouth into the oesophagus, where it runs down into your stomach. The stomach is the second place in which the food is digested, with digestive enzymes and gastric acid that break it down into smaller molecules.

Next, the food begins its journey through the small intestine. This is where the majority of nutrient and mineral absorption occurs. Carbohydrates, proteins, lipids (fats), vitamins and minerals are absorbed from the small intestine into the bloodstream and then transported to the liver, where the nutrients are screened for toxins and harmful substances. Once cleaned in the liver, the nutrient-rich blood travels to the heart where it can then be pumped around the body for your cells to use as fuel for energy production and other vital processes.

Lastly, any food that has not been absorbed is transported to the large intestine. In this part of the digestive process, water is absorbed by the body along with any last nutrients and minerals that can be captured. Unlike the speedy small intestine, the large intestine can process undigested food for up to 16 hours, meaning it has time to find and absorb all of the goodies that were missed in the last chamber (such as calcium and B vitamins). The remaining indigestible waste is then stored as faeces before being removed by your morning bathroom ritual.

STEP 4: SUPPLEMENTS

Macronutrients

There are three main macronutrients that make up the food you eat: carbohydrates, fats and proteins. These are absorbed into your blood in the small intestine before being transported around the body. Despite what many fad diets would have you believe, all three macronutrients are essential for your body to function and thrive, but the type, quality and quantity of each macronutrient will determine your health.

Carbohydrates
Carbohydrates are the main source of fuel you use to make energy. They include sugar, fibre and starch, but they all eventually break down into sugar molecules (AKA glucose). When you consume simple carbohydrates like sugar, white bread and pasta, there is a big spike in your blood glucose levels (sugar in the blood), which often feels temporarily good. Unfortunately, this tends to be closely followed by an energy crash as the body pumps out a hormone called insulin to get your blood sugar levels back under control.

More complex carbohydrates such as wholegrain bread, brown rice, fruits and vegetables take much longer to be broken down and absorbed by the body, preventing the rapid spike and drop in blood glucose levels.

The spikes and dips in your blood sugar levels are called your glycaemic variability and research has shown that high glycaemic variability is associated with inflammation (affecting your neck pain), diabetes, obesity, heart disease and cancer. The more simple carbohydrates you consume, the more glycaemic variability you will have. Eating complex carbohydrates levels out this fluctuation and is incredibly important for your health.

It's worth noting that one of the main reasons that sugar is so addictive is because it produces fast energy. Sugar used to be scarce to humans, so our primitive brains reward us with pleasure chemicals when we eat it. This would incentivise our ancestors to gorge on honey or fruit when they came across it, because when they would next be lucky enough to find such a rare stash of instant energy was unknown.

But these days sugar is everywhere. With 75% of the foods in our supermarkets containing added sugar, it's actually pretty hard to avoid.[1] The food industry knows our primitive brains still love sugar, so they get us addicted to their products by pumping sugar into them. Overconsumption of sugar and simple carbohydrates is a major cause of inflammation, diabetes and obesity, as any sugar not burned for energy is converted to fat and stored in the body. It's also incredibly damaging to your gut health, but more about that later.

Fats
Fat often gets a bad rap, but it is an essential macronutrient. It coats your nerves, surrounds your cells and regulates your hormones. It also produces double the energy per

STEP 4: SUPPLEMENTS

gram as carbs and proteins, but your body will use all of the sugars it has available before it starts asking fat to chip in.

Whilst carbohydrates, proteins, vitamins and minerals are absorbed into blood vessels, fat is absorbed into your lymphatic vessels. Lymphatic vessels transport immune cells throughout the body and remove fluid from cells. Whilst blood vessels take the long route from the small intestine to the heart by going via the liver for a detox, lymphatic vessels bypass the liver and go straight to your heart.

This means that the type and quality of fat you eat is critical, as it ends up in your heart and is not purified by the liver first. We will explore good versus bad fats shortly when discussing oils, meat and dairy.

Proteins

Proteins are chains of amino acids that create your DNA, make new cells, are integral to healthy liver detoxification and contribute to energy production. They increase the size and strength of your muscles and bones, repair damaged tissues after injury and strengthen your immune system.

There are 20 different amino acids, 11 of which can be created by your body and 9 that cannot, meaning they must be obtained through your diet. Eating a wide variety of both animal- and plant-based proteins will ensure that you obtain the essential amino acids your body requires.

The type, quality and quantity of meat you eat will play a major role in your health as we will discuss soon. Whilst there tends to be a general overconsumption of meat (especially poor-quality meat) in the western diet, there can also be major issues with a vegan or vegetarian diet. Plants rarely contain the full spectrum of amino acids the body needs, so a meat-free diet that does not lead to nutritional deficiencies is very difficult (but not impossible).

Carefully combining various plant proteins (such as soy, quinoa, chia seeds and buckwheat) in each meal can allow you to get the full array of amino acids, but the decision to eat a vegan or vegetarian diet should not be taken lightly and must be guided by an experienced health professional.

It's worth noting that I have seen patients with long-term pain who have had dramatic improvements in their symptoms after reintroducing meat back into their diet. On the flip side, my mother has been vegetarian for over 20 years and enjoys excellent health, so it really comes down to the individual and how dedicated they are to obtaining high-quality and diverse sources of protein.

Micronutrients

Along with the big macronutrients in food, there are also vitamins and minerals that are essential for your health. These are called micronutrients and are necessary for energy production, immune function, blood clotting, muscle growth, bone health and the vast majority of other processes in your body. They play an integral role in the

STEP 4: SUPPLEMENTS

millions of chemical reactions that occur inside your body every second to keep you functioning and alive.

One common example of the importance of micronutrients is iron deficiency. Low iron is known as 'anaemia' and is highly damaging to the human body. It can result in extreme fatigue, immune suppression, shortness of breath, anxiety, sleep disturbances, infertility and poor memory. And this is just one single nutrient deficiency – think about what could happen if you have three or four.

Whilst eating a healthy, balanced and varied diet should give you all of the vitamins and minerals you require to be healthy, this is not always the case. The quality of the soil in which fruit and vegetables are grown dictates much of the micronutrient content of the food. Unfortunately, modern agricultural practices have implemented the use of very poor-quality soil which produces food that has significantly lower quantities of vitamins and minerals. Organic and biodynamic farming practices tend to use more micronutrient-rich soil, so paying a little extra for organic fruit and vegetables will significantly improve your chances of getting adequate micronutrient content and avoiding vitamin and mineral deficiencies. You will also avoid the poisonous pesticides used on commercial farming crops.

Even if you're eating a healthy diet with adequate micronutrient intake, there can be other influences *within* the body that result in poor absorption of micronutrients. One common situation in which this can occur is through 'gut dysbiosis' – an imbalance of good and bad gut bacteria.

NB: Whilst blood tests may help you to identify if you have any significant vitamin or mineral deficiencies, it is also important to know whether the deficiency is due to your diet or another issue such as absorption difficulties from gut inflammation or a microbiome imbalance (or both). I highly recommend consulting a naturopath, nutritionist or dietician in order to investigate the underlying cause of any deficiencies in order to resolve them long term.

Microbiome (gut bacteria)

Let's head back into your large intestine.

Your gut microbiome is made up of microorganisms such as bacteria and fungi. The large intestine is home to 99% of all the bacteria in (and on) your body, equating to approximately 100 *trillion* microbes in your gut, made up of 700 different species of bacteria. It's worth noting that the importance of gut bacteria is a relatively recent discovery, and whilst we are now beginning to understand the complex role the microbiome plays in our health, scientists have only just scratched the surface.

There are very few bacteria in your small intestine, where most of the nutrient absorption takes place. This is important in ensuring they don't steal your food before you can absorb it. The vast majority live in the large intestine, feeding on the remaining undigested food that was not

STEP 4: SUPPLEMENTS

absorbed in your small intestine, where they produce useful by-products of the feast (such as vitamins) and support your immune system.

In a perfect world, you would only have bacteria that improved your nutrient absorption, healed your gut wall and improved your immune system. Unfortunately, your gut is in a constant battle between good bacteria that support your health and bad bacteria that create systemic problems. This eternal battle is a war on space.

Good bacteria enhance your gut's ability to absorb vitamins and minerals, as well as defend against damaging substances. They also provide information to the immune system and ensure it is operating appropriately. These goodies occupy space that prevents bad bacteria from making your gut home and produce natural antibiotics and acids that kill off the baddies. They also steal food from the bad bacteria, starving them and driving them away.

Bad bacteria, on the other hand, can provoke an immune response that causes widespread inflammation in your gut and beyond. This can impair the ability of your gut to digest and absorb nutrition to its full potential, as well as create numerous other issues including chronic pain, IBS (irritable bowel syndrome), autoimmune diseases and even mental health disorders like depression and anxiety.

The immune system in the gut

Your gut accounts for 80% of your whole immune system. The walls of the large intestine have a high density of immune cells and your gut bacteria play a vital role in the immune system's first line of defence.

Along your gut lining you have what are called 'antigen-presenting cells', which you can think of as bouncers at a night club or perhaps the captains of your immune army. These guys take samples of your microbiome and tell the rest of your immune cells what to attack and destroy in order to protect you.

The role of good bacteria in immune function is to help create immune cells, as well as accurately inform the immune system about what should be attacked and what should be allowed to pass through.

Another VIP in this area is your appendix, which sits just above the large intestine. Your appendix is made up purely of immune tissue and good bacteria, playing a critical role in repopulating the gut with a healthy microbiome after a bout of diarrhoea or food poisoning. If you have had your appendix removed, then assisting this repopulation with probiotics may be important.

What could possibly go wrong?
Your immune cells monitor everything in your gut in order to protect you from harmful substances, but this can sometimes become challenging. In the presence of

STEP 4: SUPPLEMENTS

excessive bad bacteria and fungi (or large, undigested food particles), your immune system can become overwhelmed.

Instead of a small and targeted attack, it may create an 'inflammatory flushing reaction', which is your immune system's attempt to protect your body from a perceived invasion, as it can't distinguish between what is safe and what is dangerous. Some signs and symptoms of an inflammatory flushing reaction include diarrhoea, itching, sneezing, mucous and pain (including neck pain).

Chronic inflammatory flushing reactions can lead to what's known as intestinal permeability (AKA 'leaky gut') and this is where a lot of chronic immune disorders can arise.

Leaky gut is when the cells in the mucosal membrane of your gut (which separates your digestive system from your other organs) become inflamed and damaged, allowing for large food molecules and bacteria to leak through. The result: your immune gut cells will mistake these food molecules for foreign invaders and attack them in an attempt to protect you, resulting in whole-body inflammation.

Inflammation through gut dysbiosis (excessive bad bacteria) and leaky gut has been linked to the onset of chronic pain, osteoarthritis, rheumatoid arthritis and various other health conditions,[2,3] such as:

- Type 1 diabetes
- Hashimoto's thyroiditis (autoimmune hypothyroidism)
- IBS
- Inflammatory bowel disease (IBD; Crohn's disease, ulcerative colitis)
- Liver disease
- Metabolic syndrome, insulin resistance and type 2 diabetes
- Cardiovascular disease
- Pelvic inflammatory disease
- Hormonal disorders such as endometriosis and polycystic ovarian syndrome
- Behavioural disorders (ADHD, or attention-deficit hyperactivity disorder, autism)
- Premature ageing

Inflammation

Inflammation in the right dose at the right time is a good thing. It is an important part of your immune system's attempt to keep you safe and heal your body. But when inflammation becomes prolonged and chronic, such as in gut dysbiosis, inflammatory flushing reactions or leaky gut, things can begin to go very wrong.

One of the key chemicals involved in inflammation is histamine. Chronic inflammation can result in 'histamine intolerance', which is when your body starts creating histamine in an uncontrolled manner. The cells that create histamine are in every single organ in your body, resulting in inflammation throughout your whole system.

STEP 4: SUPPLEMENTS

When it comes to neck pain, headaches or any musculoskeletal condition, excessive histamine will exaggerate your pain and prolong recovery by adding to the inflammatory process in an unhelpful way. Remember, inflammation in small amounts is important for your body to protect and repair itself, but when this becomes disordered it causes all sorts of turmoil.

The key take-away here is that the underlying nature of any chronic disease, including chronic pain, is disordered inflammation – and this will always come back to your gut health.

As Hippocrates, the great Greek physician of the Age of Pericles, said so many years ago: 'All disease starts in the gut.' Despite this, we're only recently starting to understand this in mainstream health practices.

Gut health and your neck pain

Hopefully you're beginning to see the relationship between nutrition, your gut and your neck pain. In case you got a little lost in the detail of the last section, let's quickly summarise the relationship so far:

- High-quality macronutrients (carbohydrates, proteins and fats) are the building blocks for healthy body tissues, such as the nerves, muscles, bones, joints and tendons in your neck.

- Micronutrients are essential for all of the chemical processes in your body, including tissue healing, cell repair and pain processing.
- You have trillions of bacteria in your gut and these play a major role in your immune system.
- An excess of bad gut bacteria can cause whole-body inflammation, reduce nutrient absorption, increase your pain perception, cause headaches, reduce tissue healing and contribute to depression and anxiety.

Now that you have an understanding of the impact of your gut health on your neck pain, let's explore some of the common ways you can create gut problems.

What actually causes gut dysbiosis?
There are four common ways to mess up your gut microbiome:

1. Diet
2. Medication
3. Stress
4. Illness

1. Diet

The food you eat largely dictates the type of bacteria you have in your gut. Good bacteria feed on healthy, unprocessed, unpackaged foods and produce vitamins, minerals and healthy fatty acids as they feast. Bad bacteria thrive on refined sugar, processed foods, alcohol and excessive amounts of meat. When there is an abundance of these types of food in your gut, bad bacteria and other microbes thrive, multiply and take over, producing inflammation and chronic illnesses.

You develop different types of gut bacteria from eating different types of food, so eating a wide range of healthy foods is essential for microbiome diversity. Our ancestors ate about 500 different plant crops, whereas today most of us eat only 17. We therefore miss out on many of the good gut bacteria that we would have by eating a broad spectrum of foods.

Even if you eat a relatively healthy diet, a large number of people have undiagnosed allergies and sensitivities to certain foods. When eaten, these foods set off an inflammatory response in the body and can create intestinal damage and pain.

Common food intolerances that may be causing dysbiosis and impacting your neck pain

There are a number of foods that people are commonly intolerant of or sensitive to, which create a negative immune and gut response when consumed. It's worth noting that even in the absence of a true allergy or sensitivity to the following foods, excess consumption will cause issues in everyone.

Dairy

Lactose is a sugar molecule found in dairy products, and whilst almost all humans have the enzyme required to break it down, most of us (over 75%) have a big reduction in the enzyme quantity as we age and are no longer reliant on our mother's milk.[4] The reduction in this enzyme can cause lactose intolerance, resulting in a grumpy tummy, but contrary to popular belief it does not seem to have any significant consequences on our health.

The real issue with dairy is due to a protein called *casein* (A1), which is found predominantly in cow's milk dairy products. People with casein sensitivity have a mild allergic response when they consume it, triggering inflammation. As you are now aware, chronic inflammation in the gut and body is a common cause of chronic pain (including in the neck), headaches, autoimmune disease and a whole host of other chronic illnesses.

If you're a dairy-lover and this makes you sad, don't worry – sheep and goat dairy have considerably less casein and have some seriously delicious cheese options (Chevre and Manchego being two of my personal favourites).

Gluten

Gluten is a protein found in most grains. In some people it is perceived by the immune system as a foreign invader and an immune response is triggered. Approximately 1% of humans have gluten intolerance, called coeliac disease, but as many as 13% have 'gluten sensitivity'.

STEP 4: SUPPLEMENTS

Whilst people with coeliac disease can become seriously ill when exposed to gluten, people with gluten sensitivity may be unaware of the low-grade immune response occurring in their bodies. Common symptoms of gluten sensitivity include joint pain, headaches, fatigue and stomach pain. I have seen a number of patients have a significant reduction in their neck pain simply by removing gluten from their diet.

Fructose (sugar)

Fructose is the sugar found in fruit, but the majority of items on supermarket shelves are also sweetened with fructose. A large number of people lack the enzyme that breaks down fructose, resulting in the undigested sugar passing through the small intestine and into the large, where it is happily gobbled up by bad gut bacteria. Even without a fructose intolerance, eating too much of it can have a similar result (and it's easy to eat too much when it's in most packaged food).

Fructose intolerance or overindulgence can also cause depression and increased pain perception. You may have heard of the 'happy hormone' called serotonin. This hormone is responsible for feelings of pleasure and also reduces your pain response. Fructose is used in the creation of serotonin, so malabsorption of fructose can lead to serotonin deficiency, which causes a reduced ability to experience happiness and an increased pain experience.

How do I know if I'm allergic or sensitive to fructose, dairy or gluten?
There are certain tests that your doctor or naturopath can order that detect allergies for these foods. It's important to be aware that often a 'sensitivity' will not be detected on an 'allergy' test, so even if you test negative, the ingredient may still be having a negative effect on your gut.

In the next section I will outline a gut health plan that will assist you in detecting any intolerances without necessarily needing to have specific allergy testing done.

What about other common foods?

Specific allergies aside, let's explore some of the common foods seen in the western diet that can cause gut dysbiosis and inflammation, and thus contribute to your neck pain.

Sugar
Sugar (the sugar you put in your coffee is sucrose) is the simplest form of a carbohydrate and therefore the most readily available and quickly digested form of energy for the human body. Whilst it can be great for a quick energy boost and that 'sugar high' we all know so well, excessive consumption is a major problem for your health. The tricky thing is, it's incredibly hard to avoid sugar in today's society and it's extremely addictive. This is an unfortunate result from a survival adaptation we continue to inherit from our ancestors in a time when sugar was much scarcer. It once served humans very well, but this is certainly not the case anymore.

STEP 4: SUPPLEMENTS

It is found in the majority of packaged foods in the supermarket, such as cakes, desserts, lollies, chocolate and soft drinks, but also in savoury foods like sauces, milk and cereal. Simple carbohydrates like white bread, white rice, pasta and crackers all quickly break down into sugars in the body, so can be regarded as simple sugars also.

Sugar is incredibly inflammatory for your body. When you eat an excessive amount of sugar, you are feeding the bad microbes in your gut that thrive on it.

Eating simple sugar also causes a fast spike in your blood glucose levels (sugar high), which is quickly followed by a drop (sugar crash). This dysregulation of your blood sugar levels causes a stress response in the body, releasing cortisol and adrenaline, and causing inflammation.

Sugar molecules release large amounts of energy, and any unused energy is stored as fat in the body. Simple sugars can also suppress the hormone that makes you feel full, leading to overeating and further weight gain. Excessive body weight compresses your joints, weakens your immune system and creates an ongoing inflammatory response in your body.

Remember, inflammation plays a key role in your neck pain. When you're fuelling your body with inflammatory foods such as sugar, you will have reduced tissue healing capacity and increased pain perception.

Alcohol

Alcohol damages your gut lining and can lead to dysbiosis and microbiome imbalance. Like sugar, this leads to inflammation and increased pain perception (90% of serotonin is made in your gut, and low serotonin results in increased pain perception). Alcohol can multiply your bad gut bacteria a thousand-fold, as well as cause gut wall permeability ('leaky gut'), triggering an immune response and inflammation in the body.

Lastly, alcohol prevents you from entering into REM sleep, which is essential for recovery and healing your body and nervous system. Preventing high-quality sleep through regular and excessive alcohol consumption can play a major role in prolonged pain. You will also be less likely to alter your sleeping position during the night when intoxicated, leaving you vulnerable to a poor sleeping posture for hours (you are more likely to adjust your neck position during the night if uncomfortable when sleeping without alcohol in your system).

Caffeine

Let me start by saying that I am a coffee lover. Despite this, I've got to stick with the facts.

As a stimulant, caffeine puts your body into a fight-or-flight response, stimulating the secretion of cortisol and adrenaline (your stress hormones). You will recall that a prolonged stress response results in whole-body inflammation and reduced healing capacity, contributing to a prolonged pain experience. It also increases your pain perception as the body is preparing for danger.

Caffeine dehydrates the body, affecting your electrolyte and fluid balances (important for blood flow and your immune system). It also disrupts your stomach acidity levels and can be inflammatory to your gut lining. Like alcohol, caffeine prevents you from entering REM sleep, limiting your ability to obtain restorative sleep for tissue healing and regulated pain perception.

Some people are much more tolerant of caffeine than others as they have more of the enzyme that processes it, so it's not a one-size-fits-all approach to coffee. If you've been drinking it for a while, it's likely you've become accustomed to the feeling and can't accurately detect its true impact on you any more. The best way to really assess its influence on your body is to cut it out for a month, then slowly reintroduce it and closely monitor your response.

If you've been a long-time coffee drinker, be prepared for debilitating withdrawal symptoms like headaches and fatigue when you go 'cold turkey'. Once you're clean, you'll be able to feel the true impact of caffeine again, and don't be surprised if that first coffee makes you anxious and jittery as the fight-or-flight response takes hold.

Oil

Oil is basically liquid fat. Whilst other nutrients are absorbed into your blood vessels, fat is absorbed into your lymphatic system, which is responsible for transporting immune cells throughout your body. Unlike blood vessels, which travel via the liver to remove toxins, fat absorbed into your lymphatic vessels goes straight to the heart without the detoxification process.

Given this, the type and quality of fat you eat is critical. Good-quality, cold-pressed extra virgin olive oil (unheated) is fantastic for your health – it promotes good gut bacteria, protects against inflammatory diseases and creates healthy nerves. High-quality olive oil can even be good for weight loss as it blocks an enzyme that converts carbohydrates to fats. Oils such as rapeseed, linseed or hemp seed contain *alpha-linolenic acid,* which is an anti-inflammatory like ibuprofen, without the side-effects of medications.

It's worth noting that heating oil can damage it, releasing 'free radicals' that cause inflammation of nerve and skin cells. Olive oil has a relatively low smoking point (the temperature at which damage occurs), so for cooking it is better to use butter, rapeseed or coconut oil (these have more saturated fat but are more stable when heated).

Cheap vegetable oils like canola oil should be avoided like the plague. They are high in omega-6 fats, which are highly inflammatory. Takeaway food and even high-quality restaurant meals are typically cooked in vegetable oil, meaning your heart, nerves and blood vessels are being exposed to toxin-filled, inflammatory and artery-clogging fat. This has negative effects both on your neck pain and your overall health.

STEP 4: SUPPLEMENTS

Meat and dairy
Without eating animal products, it is incredibly difficult to obtain the full spectrum of essential amino acids, B12 and iron required to thrive. Some people can maintain their health on a vegan diet, but they must be incredibly diligent about eating a wide diversity of vitamin-rich food and plant proteins, as well as have optimal gut health for mineral absorption. Whilst most people do require some meat and dairy to thrive, the majority of people in developed countries eat far too much of it. And poor-quality produce at that.

Fats found in meat and dairy products contain more *arachidonic acid* than vegetable fats. Arachidonic acid is converted into inflammatory chemical compounds called prostaglandins, which greatly intensify pain.

Excessive meat feeds the bad bacteria in your gut, causing inflammation and other chronic health conditions (even cancer). Eating smaller amounts of meat will ensure it is absorbed in the small intestine, rather than passing into the large to feed bad gut bacteria.

A major issue with mass-produced meat and dairy products is that you are exposed to antibiotics every time you eat them. The meat and dairy industry pump large quantities of antibiotics into their animals, which we then ingest when we eat them. Antibiotics kill both good and bad bacteria in the gut, making your gut very vulnerable to bad bacteria taking over as they repopulate.

The solution is to buy organic, grass-fed and biodynamic meat and dairy products. They are a little more expensive, but consuming smaller quantities can balance out the cost. Besides, the long-term cost of eating poor-quality and antibiotic-dense meat and dairy will be far greater than the few extra bucks per week you'll fork out for high-quality products.

It's worth noting that most of the oldest living and healthiest populations on Earth (called Blue Zones) do include meat in their diet, but it is all self-farmed and organic.[5] In these regions, red meat is only consumed once every few weeks, whilst fish is typically consumed daily.

Minimising meat consumption can play a big role in reducing your neck pain.

> ***You***: *You've just listed all of my favourite things. Does this mean I can no longer have any of these?*
> ***Me (NECKspert)***: *I know, it's a cruel world we live in. But luckily for you, the answer is no – you are not banned from ever having any of these things again. It's the same analogy as the cut on your finger: when it is sore and inflamed, you cannot irritate it by rubbing chilli on it. Once it has healed, it will tolerate having chilli rubbed on it without causing pain (unless you do it over and over again on a daily basis). Once your gut is healed (which we will explore soon), re-introducing small quantities of sugar, dairy, alcohol, bread and caffeine shouldn't be an issue. But during the healing process, they must be avoided.*

2. Medication

Before we dive into a discussion about medications, it's important to note that I am not a medical doctor. I am simply outlining some of the research around the below medications and the resulting impact on your body and pain. The below information is general in nature and you should always consult your doctor or pharmacist before changing any medication.

Antibiotics

Antibiotics kill both good and bad bacteria in the gut. This can lead to a dominance of bad gut bacteria and other microbes, sometimes for several months after the course of antibiotics has been finished.

When it comes to antibiotic medication, you should always ask your doctor if it is absolutely necessary to take, to ensure you can maintain healthy gut bacteria and avoid becoming resistant.

As mentioned earlier, you are exposed to antibiotics not only when you are prescribed them by a doctor, but also through eating meat and dairy products.

Painkillers

If you've had pain for a long time, there's a good chance you have taken a wide range of painkillers.

Whilst pain-relieving medication can be extremely effective in controlling pain after an acute injury, such as breaking a bone or post surgery, they should never be used as a long-term solution. When used after an acute injury, a few days of painkillers can allow you to commence a rehabilitation programme sooner and take the edge off, but even then, it could be argued that feeling pain is helpful in that situation as it's giving you information about what your tissues are ready to handle. Longer-term use of analgesics is where the true problem lies. They are disastrous for your health, their ability to control pain rapidly declines over time, and they can even make your pain levels worse. Let's explore how and why.

Firstly, pain medication has a negative impact on your gut bacteria. Your liver secretes bile, which improves your microbiome diversity, but the negative impact of painkillers on your liver results in altered bile secretions and impaired gut health. This results in disordered immune system function, leading to chronic inflammation throughout your body and causing long-term health problems.

> *You: I only take paracetamol daily, not those heavy-duty opioid medications.*
> *Me (NECKspert): Unfortunately, it doesn't matter. Even paracetamol use impacts your liver and gut health if used long term.*

When it comes to the stronger analgesics (opioids), there is a growing body of evidence that these can even make your pain more severe, especially when taken long term or at high doses. This is called 'opioid-induced hyperalgesia',

STEP 4: SUPPLEMENTS

which translates to 'increased pain sensitivity due to the use of opioid drugs'.

The longer these drugs are taken for, the less effective they are at relieving pain when you take them, and the more severe your pain will be when you do not take them.

Another negative impact of opioid painkillers is a reduction in your testosterone levels. This can result in muscle weakness, which is counterproductive when you are trying to improve your neck muscle strength.

They also affect the quality of your sleep, preventing you from entering into the healing stage of REM sleep, so whilst you may feel like you can sleep better after taking painkillers, the benefits of the sleep are significantly reduced.

Lastly, the reduction in energy and motivation experienced by taking strong pain medication is likely to prevent you from taking the challenging but important steps needed to resolve the root causes of your pain, instead opting for a symptom-relief approach that never fixes the true underlying causes.

> *You*: *That's all well and good in your fairy tale, but in the real world I cannot function without painkillers because I'm in so much pain.*
>
> *Me (NECKspert): Firstly, I'm sorry to hear you have got to that place. It is a colossal failure of our medical system. If we correctly viewed pain as an alarm system that informed us when our body was out of balance, we would begin to question whether it was productive to turn off that alarm system with drugs – especially when those drugs make it harder to detect the true source of the imbalance, let alone resolve it. Now that you have become dependent on these drugs, I am not suggesting that you simply stop taking them today. But what I am suggesting is the following:*
>
> - *Rather than seeing pain as the enemy, see it as a warning system that something is out of balance and needs to be shifted*
> - *Start to slowly taper down the medication you take, under the guidance of your doctor, whilst also implementing the 5 steps to NECKcellence*
> - *As you begin to treat the root causes of your pain rather than just the symptoms, your need for painkillers should steadily reduce over time.*

Important note: weaning off long-term pain medication can be dangerous and should always be done under the guidance of a doctor to ensure it is done safely and with minimal side-effects.

It's worth noting that your own brain actually produces much better versions of these painkillers in the form of neuro-chemicals. These pleasure chemicals are called *endogenous opioids* ('endogenous' means they are created by your own body) and by following each of the 5 steps carefully, you will promote the release of these endogenous painkillers.

At the end of this chapter, I will also recommend a range of natural herbal pain relievers that don't have the side-effects of pharmaceutical analgesics.

Anti-inflammatory medications

Non-steroidal anti-inflammatory drugs (NSAIDs) such as diclofenac or ibuprofen are commonly used in pain and injuries. They interrupt one of the body's inflammatory pathways and can therefore reduce inflammation.

It's worth noting that inflammation is an important immune response after damage. Following an acute injury, swelling and inflammation is your body's way of cleaning up the damaged tissue and beginning to heal the injured site.

Given this, how smart do you think it would be to take pills that stop this process? If you're asking my opinion, my answer would be this: not very bloody smart at all.

In the case of prolonged inflammation, my answer is a little different. If swelling or inflammation is hanging around beyond the standard timeframes of an inflammatory response, then a very short course of NSAIDs (up to 5 days) *may* be helpful in kickstarting your rehabilitation, if your doctor believes they are safe for you.

The long-term use of anti-inflammatories, however, is something that I believe should be avoided at all costs – you are essentially playing with your body's immune response, and that is not something to be sniffed at.

It is also worth understanding that there are typically underlying reasons for prolonged inflammation, many of which we have explored throughout this book (e.g. gut health, stress, poor sleep, diet). Simply taking drugs that prevent chronic inflammation does not address its root cause.

When it comes to your gut health, NSAIDs turn off the inflammatory pathway that produces protective mucosal secretions in your gut. This is why stomach ulcers are a common concern after the use of NSAIDs. This lack of protective mucosal lining in the gut often leads to leaky gut syndrome and its associated implications.

Sleeping pills

Look, I get it. Struggling to sleep sucks. But sleeping pills aren't the answer, for a couple of key reasons. Firstly, they do not allow you to enter into REM sleep, meaning you are missing out on many of the healing and therapeutic aspects of sleep. Secondly, they cause significant issues with your immune system. So significant in fact, that one study has shown that people who took sleeping pills regularly were five times more likely to die over the 2.5-year study period. Even more alarming was the finding that light users (only 18 pills per year) were still three times more likely to die. This impact on your immune system is not doing your neck pain any favours whatsoever.

We've explored in-depth strategies to help with sleep in Chapter 3, so speak with your doctor about weaning yourself off sleeping pills and addressing the true causes of your sleep impairment instead.

3. Stress

Whilst diet is obviously an important aspect of gut health, it's important that you understand the impact of stress on digestion and nutrient absorption. In a nutshell, you can have the most immaculate diet in the world, but if you're chronically stressed you won't be obtaining all the nutrients from your food.

In Section 2 we spoke about the two branches of your autonomic nervous system: sympathetic (fight or flight) and parasympathetic (rest and digest). When you are chronically stressed (sympathetic nervous system dominance), your body gives its energy to the body systems that are designed to deal with immediate danger, such as sending blood to your muscles, increasing your breathing and heart rate, and increasing your blood pressure.

The lack of priority given to your digestive and immune systems, which your parasympathetic nervous system takes care of, means that the digestive process is sub-optimal. Important vitamins and minerals are not absorbed, the immune system functions poorly, which impacts your gut microbiome, and regardless of how healthy your diet is, your nutritional intake can be impaired.

If you need a refresher on stress management tools, jump back to Step 2.

4. Illness

Whether it's a parasite that you picked up on an overseas holiday, or harmful bacteria ingested from undercooked chicken, our environment contains parasites, fungi and bacteria that can cause you to become ill.

When this occurs, your body will eliminate this from either the top (vomiting), bottom (diarrhoea), or both. Diarrhoea and vomiting can eliminate both good and bad bacteria from your gut, and once this occurs the gut is a vulnerable place. Remember, the battle between good and bad bacteria is a war on space, so after a bout of diarrhoea there is plenty of room for bad bacteria to call home.

To avoid ongoing gut dysbiosis after illness and ensure that good gut bacteria win the war, you should take probiotics once the diarrhoea ceases to help repopulate your gut with good bacteria. Supporting your liver and gut lining with healing, anti-inflammatory herbs such as turmeric and the supplement glutamine is also a good idea in these scenarios. We'll talk more about these and some other supportive options at the end of this chapter.

STEP 4: SUPPLEMENTS

How to heal your gut

Firstly, the following is a general guide only. Everyone is nutritionally unique, and I recommend getting specific and individualised advice from your qualified health professional about dietary changes, especially in regard to commencing herbs and supplements and weaning off medication.

Individuality aside, the following recommendations tend to be extremely beneficial for most people and are unlikely to cause any adverse responses.

Detox and gut cleanse
In order to heal your gut, you must undertake a strict 4-week gut cleanse. Over this time, the goal is to starve the bad bacteria by restricting the foods they eat, reduce the toxin load on your body and significantly reduce inflammation.

A gut cleanse contains three key components: cutting out inflammatory and unhealthy food, adding in a plethora of nutrient rich foods and taking appropriate supplements to help support gut healing, microbiome balance and liver detoxification.
The first two components can be summarised in the table below. Remember, you must be totally strict with this for the first 4 weeks!

Dietary guidelines

Cut out	Replace with
Gluten and white carbohydrates (bread, pasta, cakes, pizza bases)	Legumes, quinoa, brown rice, pulse pasta, gluten-free wraps
Processed sugar (soft drinks, lollies, chocolate, cake, biscuits)	Dark chocolate (85%+ cacao is best), apple or banana slices with natural nut butter, 'nice-cream' made from coconut milk and frozen banana, coconut yogurt with almond butter and frozen berries
Dairy	Dips such as hummus, 'cheese' made from cashews and macadamia nuts, coconut yogurt, almond milk, avocado instead of butter
Excessive red meat	Focus on oily fish (wild caught) such as mackerel, herring, salmon and sardines; organic chicken and lean cuts of organic meats; replace beef mince with turkey mince (e.g. for ragu); make sure your red meat is always *grass-fed* as this changes the inflammatory outcome of the protein and fat content
Meat and animal products with antibiotics and hormones	Organic (hormone- and antibiotic-free) and grass-fed as much as possible; you are better

STEP 4: SUPPLEMENTS

	off having good quality and less of it
Vegetable oil (such as soy, canola, sunflower)	Extra virgin olive oil, coconut oil, hemp seed oil, rapeseed oil, avocado oil, flaxseed oil
Alcohol	Soda water with fresh lime, bitters, lime and soda, mineral waters sweetened with stevia, kombucha, herbal teas
Caffeine	Herbal tea, turmeric or dandelion latte with almond milk and stevia
All packaged and processed foods – these contains lots of added sugar and vegetable oil (e.g. chips, dips, processed meats, sauces, fruit juice)	Fresh vegetables, fruit (ideally organic) and nuts. Aim to make your meals 60–70% vegetables, especially dark leafy greens. Lower-sugar fruits are ideal, such as papaya, kiwi fruits and dark-pigmented berries (blueberries and blackberries).
Deep-fried food	Grilled, oven-baked, pan-fried on low heat (with coconut oil)
Pre-packaged breakfast cereals	Organic rolled oats with chia seeds, pepitas, walnuts and almonds, mixed with fresh fruit and almond milk or coconut yogurt

During the cleanse you should also make a conscious effort to eat *prebiotic*-rich food. Prebiotic food contains fibre that can only be eaten by good bacteria, therefore promoting good gut bugs. These include foods like oats, leeks, asparagus, onions, garlic, artichokes and potatoes that are boiled and then left to cool.

A word of warning: you are going to be grumpy, irritable and unpleasant to be around for the first 1–2 weeks of this detox, especially if you typically have lots of sugar, alcohol or caffeine in your diet. Warn your partner and friends that they are about to experience you at your worst for up to 2 weeks. The cravings and headaches are real! This is just your liver detoxifying and your bad gut bacteria putting up a fight and dying off as you starve them of their food. Don't worry – it will pass, and you'll feel like a million bucks on the other side.

After 4 weeks of strictly following the above guidelines, you may choose to start slowly reintroducing *small* amounts of gluten, caffeine, alcohol or sugar back into your diet. The key word here is small! If you go back to regularly overindulging on these inflammatory foods, it won't take long for your gut health and immune system to become impaired again.

The other important rule for reintroducing these foods is to only add one thing per week. As you reintroduce it, carefully assess how it makes you feel. If you feel bloated, gassy, lethargic or your pain increases, I'd recommend ditching it forever. If you feel OK, see it as an occasional treat and allow yourself to have it from time to time.

Supplements

Whilst diet is important, supporting the healing of your gut and body through supplementation is also critical. This helps to rebuild the integrity of your gut wall and provide you with vitamins, minerals and nutrients that are high potency or difficult to come by through diet.

The first three are supplements that most people suffering from neck pain would benefit from taking long term, but should only be taken under the guidance of your healthcare professional (especially if you are pregnant or on any cardiovascular medication).

Probiotics

Probiotics are good bacteria that promote a healthy gut microbiome. The eternal battle between good and bad bacteria in the gut is a war on space. When you have a sufficient number of good bacteria, they occupy space and prevent bad bacteria from populating your gut.

Probiotics can be found naturally in many foods or taken as a supplement. They also have a very anti-inflammatory effect on your body as they work as 'immune-modulators', balancing out your immune response.

The benefits of probiotics are that they typically have no side effects, whilst supporting your immune system and reducing inflammation in your gut and body. Take them for the full 4 weeks of your gut cleanse protocol and then do another 4-week course every 3–4 months.

NB: If you notice that you get an upset stomach after taking probiotics, it is likely that you have a severe microbiome overgrowth. In this case, I highly recommend consulting a clinical naturopath to address this before continuing.

It is also a good idea to include probiotic-rich foods in your diet. Fermentation is a food preservation process that produces a probiotic effect in food – some of the common fermented foods you may have come across include:

- Kimchi
- Sauerkraut
- Yogurt (avoid during cleanse – dairy)
- Sourdough bread (avoid during cleanse – gluten)
- Kombucha
- Miso soup

Be aware that many supermarket-bought fermented foods have also been heated to kill off the microbes, hence losing the probiotic benefit. Your local health food store is the safest bet to find high-quality probiotic-rich foods.

Fish oil (omega 3)
Fish oil is rich in omega 3s (EPA and DHA), which change the inflammatory pathways in the body and the experience of pain. Omega 3s help to create anti-inflammatory chemicals and are extremely effective for improving chronic inflammation, pain and joint health.[6]

When it comes to fish oil, you definitely get what you pay for. Quality can vary significantly between products, so make sure it has been filtered and processed for heavy metal contamination. Oil from wild-caught fish is generally a better option. Some good brands include Nordic Naturals, Fusion and Bioceuticals.

Curcumin

Curcumin is one of the active constituents of turmeric, which works as a potent anti-inflammatory and antioxidant on the human body.[7] Curcumin tends to be poorly absorbed by the body, so a *liposomal curcumin* formula has been created to increase the uptake of the constituent, which can be prescribed by a naturopath. A high-quality over-the-counter curcumin is C3, which you can find in various brands globally, including Jarrows and Fusion.

Supplements and herbs for pain and sleep

There are other supplements that are more individualised and should only be taken under the strict recommendation of your healthcare professional.

The reason I am listing these is to highlight the fact that there are incredibly powerful natural supplements that can greatly assist with pain and sleep, but without the negative side-effects of pharmaceuticals. Again, you should discuss these supplements with a qualified health professional before taking them to ensure they are right for you and will not interfere with any other medications you are taking.

PEA: Palmitoylethanolamide (PEA) is a natural fatty molecule that helps to reduce the inflammatory process. It also helps to reduce pain signals by acting on the body's internal 'cannabinoid' system. This is fantastic for chronic pain, migraines, fibromyalgia and neuropathic pain.

Quercetin: An anti-inflammatory, anti-allergenic and antiviral. It acts as a potent antioxidant protecting your capillaries, veins and blood flow, which is important for healing and cardiovascular health. Quercetin is also a fantastic antihistamine for allergies.

Rehmannia: This is a herb known as an 'adrenal-tonic', which helps to restore your cortisol balance – important for your immune system and inflammatory control. It is particularly supportive for auto-immune conditions such as rheumatoid arthritis.

Medicinal mushrooms: Medicinal mushrooms, such as reishi (*Ganoderma*), are immune modulating and can reduce chronic inflammation.

Salix alba: This is the tree that aspirin was first derived from. It has potent anti-inflammatory properties, without the risk of stomach ulcers that NSAIDs carry.

Valerian: Valerian is the herb that the drug diazepam is derived from. It was discovered for its pain-relieving, sleep-inducing and nervous system-calming properties.

California poppy (*Eschscholzia californica*), Jamaican dogwood (*Piscidia piscipula*) and magnesium glycinate are some other great considerations.

STEP 4: SUPPLEMENTS

Again, talk to your health practitioner about which one is best suited for you.

THE STORY OF KATE

Kate had been experiencing severe neck pain for 8 months when she came to see me. Her pain had started a few weeks after she had been in hospital for a skin infection. She believed that her neck pain was related to being stuck in a hospital bed for 2 weeks with an unsuitable pillow.

As I explored each of the 5 Steps of NECKcellence in Kate's story, it was clear that she certainly had some issues with her structure (strength and mobility), her stress levels (she had a high-pressure job and two demanding children) and her sleep quality (she had struggled to get a full 8 hours ever since she left the hospital 8 months earlier.)

Despite a bit of bread, a couple of coffees each day and the odd glass of wine, Kate's nutrition was pretty flawless and therefore did not become a big focus of our treatment sessions.

After 3–4 weeks of treating Kate, we weren't making any significant progress with her pain, so I wanted to dive back into her history to see if there was something we had missed. After further questioning about her time in hospital, she informed me that she had been on three different types of intravenous antibiotics to treat the infection during her stay. I realised that this was the missing piece of the puzzle – her gut microbiome was decimated.

With the involvement of my clinical naturopath, we put Kate on a strict gut cleanse protocol that involved cutting out all sugar, caffeine, alcohol, gluten and dairy, and any packaged or fried foods. She then began to take high-dose probiotics and a number of supportive herbal supplements to help heal her gut lining.

Kate was very diligent and compliant with her treatment plan, despite getting severe headaches for the first week after cutting out coffee. After 2 weeks, she began to notice a significant improvement in her pain levels. By the end of her 4-week gut cleanse, her neck pain was completely gone.

Kate continues to do a quarterly gut cleanse and to the best of my knowledge, her neck pain has never returned.

Step 4 Recap

- High-quality macronutrients are the building blocks for healthy body tissues, such as the nerves, muscles, bones, joints and tendons in your neck
- Micronutrients are essential for all of the chemical processes in your body, including tissue healing, cell repair and pain processing
- You have trillions of bacteria in your gut and these play a major role (80%) in your immune system

STEP 4: SUPPLEMENTS

- An excess of bad gut bacteria can cause whole-body inflammation, reduce nutrient absorption, increase your pain perception, cause headaches, reduce tissue healing and contribute to depression and anxiety
- There are four primary ways to mess up your gut microbiome: diet (unhealthy food or intolerances), medication (antibiotics, painkillers and anti-inflammatory drugs), stress and illness (food poisoning)
- In order to heal your gut, a strict cleanse and detox protocol should be undertaken
- There are a variety of natural supplements that can assist with gut healing, pain, sleep, stress and tissue healing. Unlike pharmaceutical medication, these rarely have negative side-effects.

My open goals for supplements and nutrition: e.g. *Over the next 4 weeks I am going to cut out as many harmful foods as possible, as well as increase my intake of highly nutritional alternatives, and take a range of natural supplements to heal my gut, reduce inflammation and improve my pain and sleep.*

Success checklist:

- ☐ I have completed the 4-week gut cleanse, including dietary and supplement recommendations
- ☐ I have consulted my doctor about gradually weaning off all pain medication, anti-inflammatories and sleeping pills
- ☐ I am continuing my stress management techniques from Step 3
- ☐ I have consulted a well-regarded naturopath about a range of individualised herbal supplements to support my gut healing, pain, sleep, tissue healing and stress (my wife, Michaela Jean, is my go-to recommended clinical naturopath and nutritionist. You can book an online consultation with her at https://www.michaelajean.com.au)
- ☐ Upon completion of the initial cleanse, I have reintroduced small amounts of items on the restricted list, but have kept my diet almost identical to the cleanse protocol
- ☐ I am continuing to take my individualised supplements as directed by my naturopath

STEP 4: SUPPLEMENTS

References:

1. Popkin B & Hawkes C. (2016). Sweetening of the global diet, particularly beverages: patterns, trends, and policy responses. *The Lancet* 4(2):174–186. https://doi.org/10.1016/S2213-8587(15)00419-2
2. Schott EM, Farnsworth CW, Grier A, et al. (2018). Targeting the gut microbiome to treat the osteoarthritis of obesity. *JCI Insight* 3(8):e95997. https://doi.org/10.1172/jci.insight.95997
3. Zhang YJ, Li S, Gan RY, Zhou T, Xu DP & Li HB. (2015). Impacts of gut bacteria on human health and diseases. *International Journal of Molecular Sciences* 16(4):7493–7519. https://doi.org/10.3390/ijms16047493
4. Storhaug CL, Fosse SK & Fadnes LT. (2017). Country, regional, and global estimates for lactose malabsorption in adults: a systematic review and meta-analysis. *The Lancet Gastroenterology & Hepatology* 2(10):738–746. https://doi.org/10.1016/S2468-1253(17)30154-1
5. Buettner D. (2009). *The Blue Zones: Lessons for Living Longer From the People Who've Lived the Longest.* Washington, DC: National Geographic.
6. Goldberg RJ & Katz J. (2007). A meta-analysis of the analgesic effects of omega-3 polyunsaturated fatty acid supplementation for inflammatory joint pain. *Pain* 129(1–2):210–223. https://doi.org/10.1016/j.pain.2007.01.020
7. Hewlings SJ & Kalman DS. (2017). Curcumin: A Review of Its Effects on Human Health. *Foods (Basel, Switzerland)* 6(10):92. https://doi.org/10.3390/foods6100092

Step 5: Subconscious Mind

This chapter is about the powerful influences that sit under the surface – the aspects of your mind and body that your conscious mind is not necessarily aware of. We are focusing now on your *subconscious mind*: suppressed emotions, subconscious beliefs, and subconscious creativity through thoughts, language and behaviour.

This final step in achieving NECKcellence is the one that people most often struggle with, but it is also the one that will transform not only your neck, but also your whole life if you are able to implement it successfully.

The concepts and techniques in this chapter are not yet considered 'mainstream' medical science. They intersect science, meta-physics and eastern healing systems, and whilst they are becoming progressively better understood through scientific studies, the medical world still has a long way to go in successfully implementing these concepts on a large scale.

Whilst I have a great deal of respect for science and it is currently the best tool we have for assessing the world around us, it is imperfect. The imperfections in science exist for a number of reasons:

First, research is expensive, and it is therefore difficult to attract funding for research projects that do not result in financial gain to those funding it (pharmaceutical companies spend billions of dollars on clinical trials for certain medications because they will get a large return on their investment). The resources allocated to researching topics such as the impact of beliefs, emotions and the subconscious mind on pain and health outcomes is minimal because it is difficult to commercialise the results.

Next, there is a dramatic lag time between practise and research. Most scientific studies occur to test a hypothesis, or to validate what a clinician has already seen working. It often takes years of research to prove concepts that have already been successfully used by therapists, meaning that science is generally well behind what progressive clinicians are already doing.

Third, it is incredibly difficult to control and standardise many types of therapy. In drug experiments, half of the participants are given a pill, half are not, and the researchers can easily control the dose of the drug in each pill. Unlike medications, therapy techniques that are hands-on or verbal cannot easily be standardised, and each person will require a different technique or approach that is unique to their condition. Think about massage as an example: a therapist is not going to massage exactly the same area, at exactly the same pressure, for exactly the same amount of time in each of the participants in order to standardise the experiment, and if they did it is unlikely it would be equally helpful to each individual due to varying symptoms and causes.

Fourth, for a result to be statistically significant, the result must be achieved a minimum number of times. For example, if you gave a certain medication to 100 people and only one person obtained a particular result, this would not be considered statistically significant. Whilst this makes sense in some cases, there are many circumstances in which achieving a certain result is incredibly significant, regardless of the number of times it is achieved. If using a new therapy cured neck pain in only one out of 100 people, but it was free and had no negative side-effects, would you use it?

Lastly, data are highly malleable. Numbers and the wording of questions are commonly 'massaged' to support whatever the researchers are trying to prove. This is not to say that results are fabricated, but rather organised in a way that is most convenient to the desired outcome.

Remember this: *The absence of evidence is not the evidence of absence.* Just because there have not been any studies done on a subject, it does not mean it is implausible.

All of that said, I am still a scientist and believe that it is the best model we have when it comes to guiding treatment practices and medical intervention – I am just illustrating the limitations of it and want you to understand that just because something isn't mainstream yet, does not mean it won't be or should not be.

Many of the concepts in this chapter are supported by scientific studies, but some are a little ahead of the curve.

STEP 5: SUBCONSCIOUS MIND

Read and implement Step 5 with an open mind and I am certain it will change your life forever.

Suppressed emotions and trauma

Once upon a time (and still to this day in many circles), if somebody claimed that their emotions had caused their physical pain then they would likely be called a hippy or weird. But now, through the study of quantum physics, we are beginning to understand just how emotions impact our physical bodies and how important they are in both creating and resolving pain.

Everything in the universe, including your body, is simply matter vibrating at different frequencies. Everything is constantly in motion – even objects that appear to be stationary are in fact vibrating, oscillating and resonating at various frequencies. This includes both the things you can see and the things you cannot.

Emotions are simply energy. You can't see radio waves, but you know they exist because you can hear them. You can't see microwaves, but you know they exist because they heat your food. You can't see emotions, but you know they exist because you can feel them.

Just like radio waves, microwaves and light waves, emotions are another form of energy vibrating at different speeds that impact the cells of our body. If you listen to sound waves that are too loud, you can damage the cells in your ear. If you look at light waves that are too intense, you can damage the cells in your eyes. If you are exposed to excessive UV waves, you will burn your skin. Similarly, if you are exposed to an excessive amount of negative emotional energy (low vibrational frequency) then it should not be too much of a stretch of the imagination to understand that these can be harmful to your body.

The speed (frequency) at which your cells vibrate determines the health of your body. Healthy cells have high vibrational energy, whilst unhealthy cells vibrate at lower frequencies. You are more perceptive to this than you realise. When you meet someone that is vibrant, happy and positive, you *feel* their 'good vibes'. Conversely, when you walk into a room after two people have just had an argument, you *feel* like the energy in the room is 'so thick you could cut it with a knife' (low vibrational energy).

What you are experiencing in these scenarios is the vibrational frequency of the people you have just encountered, and whilst it cannot be seen by the human eye, it can certainly be felt.

The vibrational frequency of your cells is constantly being affected and influenced by everything around you, both externally and internally. External influences include the food you eat, the people you engage with, the television you watch, the music you listen to and the books you read. Internal influences include your thoughts, beliefs, language and emotions.

The more positive and uplifting the people, media, food, thoughts and emotions you engage with, the higher the frequency your cells will vibrate at and the healthier you become. Conversely, when you surround yourself with pessimistic people, watch violent media and entertain negative thoughts, you vibrate at a lower frequency and become unhealthy.

When different things come into contact, they will start to vibrate together at the same frequency. They 'sync up', which is known as *spontaneous self-organisation*. This is the reason that who and what you surround yourself with is so important!

If any of this sounds a bit wishy-washy, there are countless articles and books that take a much deeper dive into *quantum physics* and *resonance* than I will go into in this book, and I suggest you do some further reading into this incredible field of science.

Emotional trauma
There are a number of factors that determine the impact of emotions on the health of your body. First is the *intensity* of the emotion. A mild emotional response (such as frustration or amusement) will have a minimal impact compared with intense emotions (such as devastation or ecstasy).

The second factor is the *regularity* at which the emotion is experienced. The more frequently an emotional event takes place, the larger the impact on your cells. One-off traumatic emotional events can obviously have a massive influence on your health, but the effects are compounded if there are multiple such events or if the one event is replayed on a regular basis in your mind.

The third and perhaps most important aspect of how emotions impact your health is how they are *expressed*. As stated before, emotions are forms of energy that pass *through* your body. As the name *emotion* implies, they are *energy in motion*. They are supposed to be felt, expressed and released.

When emotions are suppressed, they become stagnant negative energy that is stored in the body and lowers the vibrational frequency of your cells. The flow of energy that should naturally occur through your body becomes blocked and you begin to experience pain. The flow, movement and high-vibrational frequency of the energy in your body (which is your natural state) becomes restricted and the cells of your body become sick. The pain is a signal to you that you are out of balance and something needs to be shifted, but without the knowledge of how to effectively unblock or release this stagnant energy, you can become trapped in the pain.

The suppression of emotions is particularly problematic in males who have been taught to be stoic and tough. The 'stiff upper lip' mentality of masculinity over time has meant that expressing emotions is seen as weak and therefore ridiculed. A world in which it is not acceptable to cry is a world with a lot of sick people. In women, the issue is more common that emotions are expressed ineffectively rather than simply suppressed (although stoicism is not exclusive to men, and many women also find it difficult to express emotions).

> *You: I am a highly emotional person and I still have pain.*
> *Me (NECKspert): There are effective emotional release techniques and there are ineffective, self-perpetuating ways of expressing emotions. We will explore some key aspects of emotional release techniques that are important to their success. There are certainly people that are constantly expressing their emotions who are still in pain, but they are likely missing one or more steps in the process. We will take a deep dive into this emotional release technique soon.*

It is also worth noting that emotional trauma can result not only from past experiences, but also fear of future events. This is often the by-product of a mind that is running out of control, producing chaotic and fearful thoughts. I have seen people begin to believe they are a bad person or become lost in self-loathing and guilt because they are ashamed of the thoughts they are having. It is important to know that you are not your thoughts. You can *have* thoughts, but they are not *who you are*.

The following process can be used to detach from your thoughts and help you to understand that you shape and change the way you think.

Suppressed emotion processing technique (SEPT)
I am about to teach you what I believe is one of the most important techniques you can ever learn. If done effectively

and regularly, it results in freedom from emotional pain and suffering and allows your mind and body to live in a state of flow, ease and balance.

The release and transfer of energy throughout your body is your most natural state. When your cells are vibrating with high-frequency energy, you are healthy and vital. When this does not occur, you experience pain (either physical or emotional).

SEPT is a technique that allows you to shift and express emotional energy, rather than suppressing and storing it in your body, which results in pain and illness. It allows you to raise your vibrational frequency and restore vitality to the cells of your body.

I actually came across a concept similar to SEPT before experiencing my own injury. I read about the process in a book and remember thinking at the time that there could be a lot of value in the technique, but I did not feel the need to apply it at that point.

Years later, when I was in the depths of pain and despair, something reminded me of the technique, and I revisited the process. I still remember vividly the first time I tried it. I burst into tears of joy and it felt like a massive weight had lifted from me. It's difficult to describe the feeling, but I knew I had just uncovered one of the root causes of my pain and the missing piece of the puzzle in my recovery.

Over the years I have adjusted and improved the process, based on my experiences with it. Whilst it has its foundations in the process I originally read about, it has been adapted to the point where I consider it a new technique altogether, which I have called S*EPT*.

Please note: I am not a psychologist and do not have any formal qualifications in trauma work. I found and adapted this technique for my own healing and had such incredible success with it that I began using it with clients, with equal success. If you are suicidal, have manic depression, bipolar disorder, post-traumatic stress disorder or any other severe mental health conditions, whilst I'm confident that this technique will be very helpful, I recommend you use it in conjunction with mental health services such as psychology and psychiatry, and not as a replacement or stand-alone technique. If you have a mental health disorder, then it may be best to first trial the technique in the presence of a therapist.

The process

SEPT can be an intense process, so it's important that you find a safe and comfortable place to practise it in. It is also a good idea to not schedule anything that requires too much energy or effort within the hour after finishing the technique, as it can be jarring going straight from an emotional release session back into work or socialising. Once you've found a private space, you can either sit or lie down, whichever is more comfortable. The process has five steps that you will move through in sequential order: *alignment, responsibility, expression, release and forgiveness*. The technique can take anywhere from 10 to 30 minutes to move through. It is important not to jump ahead – you want to feel as though you have completed each stage.

Before you begin, you must identify the suppressed emotion or past experience you are going to work through. The easiest way to find suppressed emotions is to ask yourself, 'What is the most painful emotional experience I have ever faced?' The first thing that pops into your head is usually the most important one to start with.

You will intuitively know the right place to start. Each time you sit down to practise SEPT, ask yourself this question and whatever experience comes up should be the focus of your session.

1. **Alignment**: The first step in the process is aligning with the emotion. You must release all judgement of yourself for whatever emotions come up. Feeling guilty for having particular emotions will prevent you from shifting them, so give yourself full permission to feel and fully express any emotion that arises.

2. **Responsibility**: When you encounter a painful life experience, it is common to feel as though it has been done *to* you. It is tempting to blame others for the experience, which creates even more negative emotion. Accepting responsibility for your emotional response does not mean you have to blame yourself for the experience – it simply means that you take full

STEP 5: SUBCONSCIOUS MIND

responsibility for your *emotional response* to the experience. Releasing the feeling of being a victim and taking responsibility for your emotional responses is one of the most liberating things you can ever do.

3. **Expression**: You will then allow yourself to feel and fully express all of the emotions that arise as you reflect on the experience you have chosen. If it's grief, then allow yourself to cry hysterically; if it's anger then feel and express that anger (punching bags can be very useful); if it's guilt then allow that guilty feeling in your stomach to arise. Feel each emotion completely, without limitation and let it flow from your body. Take as long as you need on this step. When you have no more emotion to give, then it's time to move to the next step.

4. **Release**: As the intensity of the emotion begins to reduce, you will then start the process of releasing it from your body by raising its vibrational frequency. As you feel the emotion, focus your attention on your stomach and imagine the emotion sitting there. You may want to visualise it as a dark ball of energy. You will then begin to take slow, deep breaths, and with each inhale, feel the emotional ball of energy in your stomach begin to rise up towards the chest. As you feel it gradually move from the stomach up to the heart, you will visualise the colour changing into a bright light. You will also feel the ball of energy begin to vibrate faster. Continue this process of gradually lifting and drawing this ball of energy from the heart up towards

the top of your head with each breath, feeling it glowing brighter and vibrating faster the higher it goes. By the time it reaches the top of your head, use 10 exhale breaths to release the emotional energy from your body. You have now raised the vibrational frequency of the stagnant emotional energy and removed it from your body. Sit in the stillness you have just created for as long as it feels right.

5. **Forgiveness**: Lastly, you must forgive all involved in the experience. This can be the most challenging step for many people. Resentment and blame of yourself or anyone else involved will prevent you from fully releasing the trauma. Forgive everyone involved in the traumatic experience, including yourself. Forgiveness is vital.[1]

You should perform SEPT every 2–3 days until you reach the point that thinking about the memories of the painful experiences no longer evokes a strong emotional response. This may take a single session for a mildly emotional experience, or regular sessions over several months to shift big emotional traumas.

Once you have begun to work through your bigger emotional traumas, you can start reflecting back through time, one year at a time, to identify some of the smaller emotional experiences you have suppressed. It is like peeling back the layers of an onion until you are no longer holding onto any past pain.

STEP 5: SUBCONSCIOUS MIND

Let's explore a real-life story of how an emotional trauma can cause chronic pain, and how SEPT can shift the suppressed emotions to assist in the healing process.

THE STORY OF SALLY

Sally was always quite healthy and happy. She was married with two kids, worked part-time, exercised daily and ate a healthy diet. She had experienced a few episodes of neck pain over the years, but nothing that didn't calm down after a few days.

One day, Sally received a phone call informing her that her father had been diagnosed with cancer. She had always been very close to her dad, so the news rattled her to the core. After an incredibly challenging 6 months of constant stress and worry, her father passed away.

Sally was grief stricken. Over the coming weeks and months, she felt sick to her stomach and would burst into tears constantly. She felt immense guilt that she hadn't spent as much time with her father in recent years, and as the weeks passed, instead of crying she became angry that she had lost her father before his time.

Three months after her father passed away, Sally developed severe neck pain and headaches. She was in agony from the moment she woke up in the morning until she went to bed at night.

When Sally came to see me, it was clear that she had been through an emotional trauma. She was carrying a certain heaviness about her and her anger, guilt and pain were palpable. As I assessed and explored the 5 Steps of NECKcellence with Sally, she scored very well on the first 4 stages: she had relatively good neck mobility, alignment and strength; her day-to-day stress levels were well managed through exercise; she was sleeping surprisingly well; and her diet was immaculate.

We then moved on to Step 5, where she began to tell me about her father. Despite Sally crying a lot in the early days of her father's passing, it was clear that she was not effectively shifting her grief. On the contrary, thoughts of her father filled her with guilt and anger, and every time she cried, she would cast blame for her loss (onto doctors, the hospital, the unfair universe). Self-pity had become her place of comfort.

As I worked with Sally, I introduced the concept of using SEPT for emotional trauma. I explained how suppressed emotions that are stored in the body create pain and illness, and the importance of shifting that stagnant energy in order to restore health. I taught her the 5-part SEPT technique of *alignment, responsibility, expression, release* and *forgiveness*.

Like many people, Sally felt slightly uncomfortable and sceptical about the concept of healing her neck pain through an emotional-release technique, but she was open to trying it.

STEP 5: SUBCONSCIOUS MIND

Starting with alignment, she released all judgement of herself for having feelings of grief, guilt and anger. She gave herself full permission to feel and fully express these emotions.

She then accepted responsibility for her role in the experience she was having. Not for the death of her father, but for the anger, guilt and pain she was experiencing because of it. She accepted that this was not something that was done *to* her but rather was a life situation that had occurred in which she could take responsibility for her response.

Next, she let go of blame. She forgave herself for spending less time with her dad in recent years. She forgave the doctors and the hospital for not keeping him alive. She forgave herself for having feelings of anger and blame.

She then allowed herself to feel and express each of the emotions that came up. She allowed herself to cry hysterically. She allowed herself to feel intense anger and guilt. And as she fully expressed each emotion that arose, she used the breathing and visualisation technique to shift and release the emotions from her body by raising their vibrational frequency.

Sally would leave our sessions feeling exhausted but lighter. Every time she came back, I could feel that her energy had lifted a little more. Over several weeks, her neck pain and headaches disappeared.

Now, when Sally thinks of her father, she still feels sad and misses him, but her anger and guilt have been replaced with gratitude for all of the wonderful times they spent together and the memories she has of him. Last time I spoke with Sally, she was still pain-free.

Subconscious beliefs

Your health is closely linked to your *beliefs*. Studies have shown that people who are optimistic and positive about their health have lower rates of disease and injury than those who believe they are destined for disaster.[2,3]

Have you ever had any of these thoughts?

My mum had arthritis in her neck so I'm sure to get it.

My dad had neck surgery and it runs in the family so I will need it one day.

I am prone to injury.

I am a slow healer.

I will always have pain.

Each of these are *beliefs*, not *facts*.

STEP 5: SUBCONSCIOUS MIND

Once upon a time, it was thought that genetics were one of the leading factors in determining a person's health. Whilst they certainly do play a role, we now understand that genes are only the tip of the iceberg and a much bigger factor in our health is *epigenetics*. Epigenetics refers to the factors that determine whether certain genes are expressed (turned on or off), including your lifestyle, behaviours and perhaps most importantly, your *beliefs*.

The size of the influence that genetics have on your health varies depending on which study you read and the type of condition, but they generally account for less than 15% of any condition. This means even if neck pain runs in the family, at least 85% of your neck pain is related to your subconscious beliefs about your pain and the ensuing behaviours you adopt because of them.

Take this example: Let's say your dad had chronic neck pain. When you were little he always complained about his neck and told you that one day you'd have to deal with the same because it runs in the family. He also told you that you were injury-prone and a slow healer. Your impressionable young mind then developed a subconscious belief that you will likely develop neck pain one day. At that point, your chances of developing neck issues just increased from 15% (pure genetics) to significantly higher because beliefs are *triggers* for genes to start expressing themselves.

Then one day, later in life, you develop some neck pain (which everyone does at one time or another), and your *beliefs* about your neck then take centre stage. You start *behaving* in a way that reflects your beliefs about having a fragile neck that is destined for injury and pain, such as becoming guarded and protective of movement. This creates more pain, unrelated to your genetics and due to your behaviour, but it fits with your belief that you are destined to have an arthritic neck and therefore strengthens the belief further. A loop has formed.

Even if you are someone who has developed neck pain as a result of physical trauma (like a car crash or a bad tackle in football), your subconscious beliefs around your health play a huge role in your recovery.

It does not necessarily have to be a belief about being destined to have neck pain. Perhaps instead it's a belief you developed as a child that *'nothing good ever happens to me'*, so now your ability to heal is impacted by a belief that recovery is unlikely because *'nothing good ever happens to me'*. Or maybe it was a doctor or health professional that made you believe your neck was permanently damaged, fragile and destined for life-long pain.

Regardless of the belief origin, it has the potential to significantly influence your well-being and life.

STEP 5: SUBCONSCIOUS MIND

> ***You****: My pain is from the whiplash I sustained in my car accident, which ruined my neck. It has nothing to do with my beliefs.*
>
> ***Me (NECKspert)****: I agree that your accident may have caused some damage to your neck and possibly created changes to its structure on scans, but it's important to remember three things:*
> - *Your body tissues can heal*
> - *There is poor correlation between scans and pain (terrible looking scans can be seen in completely pain-free patients)*
> - *Your pain response and ability to heal is heavily influenced by your beliefs, due to both epigenetics and the relationship between pain and your brain's interpretation of danger.*

I know this may be hard to believe, but this is now well understood by pain scientists and doctors that are up to date with current research (jump back up to Section 1 for a quick refresher on pain).

But here's the kicker: you are likely not even aware that you have these beliefs about your neck or your health, because they are subconscious. You developed many of them at a very young age (the younger you were, the more deeply ingrained they are) and they sit deep in your brain, governing most of the decisions you make in life – without you even realising it.

If most of our beliefs are subconscious and were formed when we were young, what can we do about them? Remember in Step 2, when discussing meditation and mindfulness, I touched on how they can help you become aware of and alter your subconscious beliefs? Through regular meditation and mindfulness, you become conscious of and perceptive to *what* and *how* you are thinking. You become perceptive to some of the harmful and negative scripts that sit in your subconscious brain, whereas in the past you would not have noticed them. You begin to question where these beliefs came from and become conscious of the negative impact they are having.

Most importantly, meditation then gives you the power to form *conscious* beliefs and rewrite your internal scripts about your health, your neck and your life.

As you become more mindful through meditating, you will begin to catch yourself thinking things like *'I will never be able to do that with my neck'*, *'My neck is fragile'* or *'I will always have pain.'*

I want you to begin to pay very close attention to your thoughts and language around your health and neck pain. Whenever you catch yourself having a negative thought or saying something that doesn't align with well-being, ask yourself three simple questions:

1. Is that thought, a fact or a belief?
2. Where did that belief come from?

STEP 5: SUBCONSCIOUS MIND

3. What would my life be like if I believed or thought something different?

And what is the best possible replacement thought you can have? *Gratitude.*

Here's an example:
You wake up in the morning, ahead of a big work meeting that day. As you are putting on your shirt, you feel a severe jolt of pain and your neck locks up. You immediately start running the negative scripts you have regarding your neck: 'Trust this to happen with *my* neck', 'Bad things always happen to me on important days,' 'My neck must be so fragile if simply putting on a shirt can damage me.'

Rather than letting these thoughts and beliefs take over your mind, run through your three questions:

1. *Are these thoughts factual or is it my belief system that has caused me to see things this way?*

If you explore them deeply, you will find that you have probably had many more important days that have *not* been ruined by neck pain than days that have. And that your neck has tolerated much more strenuous things than putting on a shirt, which haven't resulted in pain, but today was simply unlucky rather than a result of your neck being fragile. You will then find that these initial reactions were all beliefs and not facts.

2. *Where did that belief come from?*

Did your parents say things like that when you were growing up? Have people told you these things? How credible are they?

3. *How can I reframe this experience into something centred around gratitude?*

This is not an easy thing to do, but imagine what the rest of your day (and the rest of your life) would be like if you exchanged your initial thoughts for these ones:

Bummer, I'm going to have a bit of pain today... Oh well, at least I still have a healthy heart, lungs, brain and legs. Today will be OK and I'll get better quickly.

This pain is not fun, but I'm grateful for the reminder from my body that one of my 5 Ss is out of balance (structure, stress, sleep, supplements, subconscious)... I'll reap much greater rewards on my overall health than just resolving my pain by fixing my strength and/or stress and/or sleep and/or nutrition and/or emotions, so I'll use this pain as a message to get back on track.

Remember, your beliefs and the way you think about your neck (and therefore your behaviours that follow) account for around 85% of the reason you have ongoing pain, so using meditation to become aware of your beliefs and rewrite them is an incredibly powerful tool.

STEP 5: SUBCONSCIOUS MIND

As you begin to replace your negative thoughts and belief patterns with consciously positive alternatives, you will start to rewrite your reality. You will regain personal power rather than being the victim of subconscious negativity and over time your default thoughts and beliefs will become more positive because your brain will begin to rewire itself. Your positivity will become *automated* – and that's where life becomes oh so sweet.

Original thoughts are much less common than you would think, with many being repeats from yesterday. If you consciously change negative thoughts and beliefs to positive ones through the above process, you will begin to repeat these automatically the following day, then the next, then the next, until eventually your new positive belief system will become automated, subconscious and create incredible results for your mind, body and health.

Subconscious creation: thoughts, language and behaviour

Life is not a process of discovery – it is a process of creation. Most people create their reality subconsciously, living as a passive bystander and thinking that life happens *to* them. You will now learn how you can make it a conscious process.

Before we dive in, I want to preface this section by saying that whilst some of these concepts may seem a little fanciful, what I am talking about here is quantum physics. The science of energy and matter. Whilst these concepts may once have been considered 'woo-woo', scientists are now beginning to understand the process of how you *create* your life (rather than being a passive participant in it) and how you can master your own reality through making it a conscious process.

The way in which you create your reality is through a three-part process: thoughts, words and actions.

The first level of creation is thought. Nothing exists that was not first conceived as an idea, concept or visualisation. Every thing, every experience, every aspect of your life, began with a thought. The power of thought has been proven through various studies.[4,5]

The second level of creation is words. Words are simply thoughts expressed, with more dynamic and creative energy. Words vibrate at a different frequency to thoughts, so expressing a thought through words results in a greater impact on the creation of a situation or experience.

The third level of creation is action. This is the most potent form of creative energy. Action vibrates at an even higher frequency to thoughts and words. It is thought and word in motion.

If you think of something, but never speak or act on it, you are creating at a very basic level. Combining both thoughts and words together begins to create reality at a more complex level. When you think, speak *and* act on

STEP 5: SUBCONSCIOUS MIND

something, that is when you will make it manifest in your life.

How do thoughts, words and actions create our reality?

We have the genius Albert Einstein to thank for our current understanding of how this all works.

Thoughts, feelings, emotions, words and actions are all energy. As discussed before, these forms of creative energy all vibrate at different frequencies. Through what is known as the *law of attraction*, different forms of energy that vibrate at a similar frequency are drawn to each other and bind together.

When enough of the same type of energy binds together, it creates matter. To put this another way: when you have enough of the same frequency thoughts, words and actions, they combine together to create reality.

When you constantly think about your pain, speak about your pain and act in a way that reflects being in pain, guess what reality you are reinforcing?

> ***You**: But I am in pain! I can't simply pretend that I am not!*
> ***Me (NECKspert)**: Whilst it is challenging at first to break this cycle, it is possible (and completely necessary) if you are going to fully recover. By consciously choosing thoughts, words and actions that reflect health, rather than pain, you will create healthier cells and a new body.*

You cannot fool yourself by thinking, speaking and acting in a certain way if you do not believe it as truth. The reality you create will always come from the thought behind the thought. If you attempt to think about health, but the true underlying thought is one of illness, then you will not create health. It must be a genuine process, rooted in firm belief rather than weak hopefulness.

Take these two scenarios as examples:

The first person has long-term neck pain. They attempt to consciously change their reality through the process of creation that we are discussing here. They close their eyes and think about what it would be like to be healthy and pain-free, but they are fixated on what they are currently lacking and fearful they will never get to where they want to be. Even though they are trying to consciously think about health, their underlying thought is one of desire (the absence of what they want). This person is simply creating more of what they are thinking about: the absence of health.

The second person also has long-term neck pain. They too have decided to consciously create their own reality through thoughts, words and actions. This person understands that the process of creation must be authentic, and that the underlying thought cannot be one of lack or fear if they are going to create health. In order to create an underlying thought that reflects health and wellness, they focus all of their attention on every part of their body that is already healthy. They foster feelings of gratitude for their healthy legs, heart, brain and lungs, and they sit in a place of appreciation for this. They then visualise themselves living a life with a healthy neck, but instead of an underlying feeling of lack for what they're missing, they create a feeling of excitement for all of the things they will be able to do once they recover. They consider all of the things they can already do now (rather than dwelling on what they cannot), again sitting in gratitude for this, which gives them genuine belief and confidence that they will soon be able to achieve what they are visualising.

Do you see the difference here? The first person is trying to think about health but is actually focused on the absence of it. The second person is creating a new reality for themselves by using gratitude for what they currently have to propel excitement about what is possible and a belief that they will achieve it.

Becoming a conscious creator

All of this sounds good in theory, but how can you change the way you think, speak and act in order to change your health? There is a three-step process to this, which initially requires a fair bit of mental effort, but in time will become second nature.

1. First, you have to begin constantly watching, monitoring and editing your thoughts. When you have a thought that does not reflect perfect health and well-being, think again. Recognise that this type of thought pattern is no longer helpful and consciously decide to change it to something else. Like learning anything

new, becoming a *conscious* thinker will require a lot of attention and energy at first, but eventually you will rewire your brain to default to a health-affirming thought automatically.

Every time you catch yourself thinking 'I'll never get better,' 'I can't do that with my neck' or 'I'm destined for long-term pain,' think again. Swap it out for 'I'm healing every day,' 'There's so much I can do with my neck' and 'I'm destined for perfect health.' To ensure the thought behind the thought is rooted in belief rather than fear, write down or make a mental note of things you're currently grateful for in relation to your health, and attach that feeling of gratitude to your new thought about your healing and recovery.

2. As your thoughts about your inevitable recovery and health become stronger and more consistent, speak them out loud. Use words to reflect your new, consciously created, thought patterns. Speak them loudly, confidently, regularly and with steadfast belief in their truth. 'I am healthy,' 'I am strong,' 'I am healing quickly.' When you hear yourself say something that is not in alignment with health, decide not to say it again. Choose something else. Stop giving energy to your pain by constantly talking about it to others. Resist the temptation of discussing your neck pain and replace it with conversations about your current and steadily improving health, well-being and vitality.

STEP 5: SUBCONSCIOUS MIND

3. Begin to consciously act in a way that reflects your carefully chosen thoughts and words. When you notice yourself behaving in a way that does not reflect health and vitality, act again. Pay close attention to everything you do during each day to see if it reflects health or pain. Change the way you stand, change the way you move, choose health-affirming actions at every opportunity. Act in a way as if you are already where you want to be in achieving your goal (in a sensible way – I'm not suggesting you go and swim 10km without building up slowly, but begin taking steps towards it).

Become very clear about exactly where you want your health to be, then think, speak and act as if you are already there. Entertain no other possibility. Stop allowing unconscious thoughts, words and actions to create your reality. Choose how the rest of your life will look through this process of closely monitoring and refining the way you think, speak and act. Train yourself to do this until it happens automatically without any effort.

This is a calling to end a life of unconscious living. Choose what you want to experience. Be meticulous in what you think, say and do in relation to this. Release all doubt, fear and disbelief surrounding it. Be appreciative of your new reality even before it has arrived.

This is how to master your subconscious mind.

THE STORY OF MICHAEL

Michael had been suffering with chronic neck pain for over 5 years when he came to me. He'd had a car accident and sustained severe whiplash, which had left him with chronic neck pain that radiated into his upper back.

Michael was a builder who ran his own business, and since his accident he had largely come off the tools due to the pain. He loved working as a builder, so watching his team do the heavy work was a constant reminder to him of his injury. He had also given up his life-long passion of rock climbing and believed that he would never climb again.

Despite years of extensive physio, chiro, osteo, cortisone injections and Pilates, nothing had helped him. He was also heavily dependent on pain medication.

From the first time I met Michael, I could see how his belief structures, negativity bias and language were all significantly impacting his recovery. Whilst telling me his story, he kept referring to his family history of health problems, he blamed the other driver for his injury, he spoke about his pain as if it was never going to heal and would stop him from doing the things he loved forever.

I implemented some small strategies for Michael around his structure, stress, sleep and nutrition, but the big focus for my treatment plan with him was influencing his

STEP 5: SUBCONSCIOUS MIND

subconscious mind, which was the driving force behind why he was not recovering.

At first, Michael was very sceptical about my approach and he admitted to me later that he initially thought I was a quack when discussing these things with him. But he'd explored all other options, so he played along anyway.

First, I educated Michael about the insignificance of genetics in comparison to his behaviours and thought patterns. We explored his belief systems and uncovered some underlying beliefs he had about not being good enough, nothing good ever happening to him and life being hard. He worked on identifying that these were beliefs rather than facts, then came up with replacement beliefs ('life can be easy and something great is about to happen'), which he would affirm to himself whenever he noticed a negative belief sneaking in.

It also became apparent that whenever Michael had conversations with his friends or family, he would always end up steering the conversation to talking about his pain. It consumed his mind, and it was all he spoke and thought about. I coached him on the impact of thoughts, words and actions on creating his reality and the effect of his negativity on the vibrational health of his cells.

He began to monitor his thoughts very closely, became aware of his negativity bias and whenever he had a thought that did not align with health and recovery, he chose to think differently.

He stopped talking about his pain, and when people asked him about it, he would say 'It's getting better every day'. Even on bad days when his pain was intense, Michael would find something positive to focus on – he became obsessed with his recovery instead of his pain.

He spent 30 minutes every day simply visualising himself building and rock climbing, and even though his pain had not fully resolved, he slowly and carefully began resuming both activities. He started with a few minutes per day of each and gradually built this up over several months.

I worked with Michael for 6 months, and by the end of our sessions he was unrecognisable. He began to claim control over his subconscious thoughts, beliefs and behaviours, and over time his body began to respond. He had a spring in his step and a new energy about him. He spoke with so much positivity and optimism that his friends and family loved being around him. Most importantly for Michael, he got back to working on the tools full-time and was rock climbing 3 days per week. Every now and again his pain would flare up a little bit, but he didn't give it any energy – he would simply tell himself that his body was strong, healthy and would heal quickly, which it now did.

Michael still monitors his thoughts, words and behaviours closely. He became a master of *creating* his life rather than *enduring* it and he transformed both his mind and body by diligently implementing Step 5 of NECKcellence.

Step 5 Recap

- Emotions are energy that needs to be expressed
- When emotional trauma is suppressed, this energy is stored in your body and its vibrational frequency impacts your cells, creating disease and dysfunction
- Suppressed emotions are best released through the process of SEPT, which involves the five-stage process of alignment, responsibility, expression, release and forgiveness
- Your life is a reflection of your subconscious beliefs
- Many of these belief systems were developed when you were young and are often inherited from your parents
- Meditation and mindfulness are a very potent way of becoming aware of your underlying belief systems
- You can begin to consciously question and rewrite your beliefs through asking three questions: Is that thought a fact or a belief? Where did that belief come from? What would my life be like if I believed or thought something different?
- You create your reality through your thoughts, words and actions
- Most people create their lives unconsciously, unaware of their creative power, and simply feel as though they are a victim or passive participant in their world
- You can consciously and very deliberately create your own reality through constant monitoring, review and refinement of your thoughts, words and actions

- When you think something, say something or do something that does not reflect optimal health, change it.

My open goals for the subconscious mind: *e.g. Over the next 6 weeks, I am going to identify as many of the suppressed emotional traumas that have accumulated throughout my life as possible. I will see how frequently I can run the process of SEPT to begin shifting these stored emotions. In doing so, I will feel emotionally and energetically lighter and become aware of my self-limiting beliefs. I will see how many times I can catch myself thinking and saying something that does not align with my optimal health, and then change my thoughts, words and actions to something that will assist my recovery.*

_____

_____

Success checklist:

- ☐ I am practicing SEPT every second day, then weekly as things improve
- ☐ I am mindful of my underlying belief patterns and when I notice a thought arise that does not support my health, I rewrite it to ensure it is aligned with my imminent recovery and overall well-being

STEP 5: SUBCONSCIOUS MIND

- ☐ I am regularly focusing on evidence that supports the ability of my body to quickly and effectively heal itself
- ☐ I am constantly monitoring and carefully selecting my thoughts, words and behaviours, ensuring that I consciously create a healthy and pain-free body
- ☐ I am meditating daily, which gives me a greater ability to monitor all of the above, through presence and mental awareness.

References:

1. Harris AH, Luskin FM, Benisovich SV, et al. (2006). Effects of a group forgiveness intervention on forgiveness, perceived stress and trait anger: A randomized trial. *Journal of Clinical Psychology* 62(6):715–733.
2. Kim ES, Hagan KA, Grodstein F, DeMeo DL, De Vivo I & Kubzansky LD. (2017). Optimism and cause-specific mortality: a prospective cohort study. *American Journal of Epidemiology* 185(1):21–29. https://doi.org/10.1093/aje/kww182
3. Kim ES, James P, Zevon ES, Trudel-Fitzgerald C, Kubzansky LD & Grodstein F. (2019). Optimism and healthy aging in women and men. *American Journal of Epidemiology* 188(6):1084–1091. https://doi.org/10.1093/aje/kwz056
4. Scheier MF & Carver CS. (1993). On the power of positive thinking: the benefits of being optimistic. *Current Directions in Psychological Science* 2(1):26–30. https://doi.org/10.1111/1467-8721.ep10770572
5. Park N, Peterson C, Szvarca D, Vander Molen RJ, Kim ES & Collon K. (2014). Positive psychology and physical health: research and applications. *American Journal of Lifestyle Medicine* 10(3):200–206. https://doi.org/10.1177/1559827614550277

Recommended readings:

- Lipton B. (2011). *The Biology of Belief: Unleashing The Power Of Consciousness, Matter & Miracles*. London, UK: Hay House.
- Church D. (2018). *Mind to Matter: The Astonishing Science of How Your Brain Creates Material Reality*. Carlsblad: Hay House.
- van der Kolk B. (2014). The Body Keeps the Score: Mind, Brain and Body in the Transformation of Trauma. London, UK: Penguin Books Ltd.

Section 3

Life After Pain: Thriving and Avoiding Recurrence

Staying NECKcellent

If you've been implementing my suggestions as you're reading, by this point you will be very close to achieving NECKcellence (if you haven't already).

You have strengthened your neck, improved your movement control, increased your mobility, taken control of your posture and ergonomics, learned to breathe correctly and realised that pain does not equal damage.

You now understand the impact of chronic stress on your body, brain, nervous system and neck pain, and you have successfully implemented stress management strategies such as mindfulness, meditation, breathing exercises, gratitude practices and giving back.

Obtaining good-quality sleep every night is now a priority and you understand the importance of sleep for having a strong, healthy and pain-free neck and body. You have purchased the right pillow and mattress for your body and implemented a daily pre-bed routine that sets your body up for a good night's sleep.

You have become very careful of what you put into your body, cutting back on inflammatory foods and increasing your intake of healing and nourishing foods that fuel your health. You have prioritised your gut health as you understand its connection to the rest of your body, and you have safely weaned yourself off pharmaceutical pain medications and replaced them with high-quality herbal supplements.

The impact of suppressed emotions and subconscious beliefs on your neck pain and overall health is something you are now very aware of. You are regularly practicing SEPT and being conscious of your thoughts, words and behaviours, carefully reviewing and refining these to reflect your inevitable healing and recovery.

You have succeeded in the BIG GOAL you set for yourself back in Section 1 and the smaller goals you have set for each of the 5 Steps.

All of these changes have resulted in the progressive reduction in your pain, an increase in your function, the ability to participate in the things you love, abundant energy, improved relationships with your friends and family, more happiness, and, ultimately, a better life.

You should be proud of yourself. I am proud of you. I have said from the start that whilst the 5 Steps to NECKcellence are simple, they are not easy. It has taken courage, resilience, self-belief, determination and a complete shift in the way you have been living your life.

I'm sure there have been many struggles and dark days as you worked through these 5 Steps, but you have risen to the challenge, persevered and are now reaping the rewards of your efforts.

Take a moment to think back to where you were before reading this book – the pain, suffering, despair, hopelessness, fear and anger. I want you to spend 2 minutes remembering who that person was, the old you, and then say goodbye to that person for the last time.

Compare them with the person you have now become. Breathe in the magic of the new life you have created for yourself – the life you deserve.

But do not become complacent. The massive improvements to your neck and overall health that you have created can all be undone if you do not continue with the new habits and behaviours you have implemented.

The 5 Steps to NECKcellence are not a quick fix that you can use short term to improve your health, only to revert back to your old ways. To keep a strong, pain-free and healthy body, you must continue with the habits and lifestyle changes that you have worked so hard to introduce.

You should regularly review the BIG GOAL you set for yourself in Section 1. Look back at the smaller goals you set yourself along the way for each of the 5 Steps. It's important you keep coming back to these over time to ensure you are staying on track.

Section 3 is all about maintaining the results you have achieved, long term. I will keep this section short and sweet. It will give you a roadmap and some structure so that you stay NECKcellent forever.

Falling in love

It's time to fall back in love with your body. When you're in the depths of your pain, it's common to hate your body and want a new one. You've now seen that your body is amazing and has the ability to heal and thrive when it gets what it needs.

One of the key elements in maintaining NECKcellence is to fall back in love (and stay in love) with your neck and body.

Your body is an amazing and complex thing. You will remember from earlier in the book that every single day you breathe about 25,000 breaths, your heart beats about 120,000 times, and your body converts the oxygen in your bloodstream into energy that powers your whole system. All of this happens outside of your awareness. Pretty amazing.

You have between 50 and 75 *trillion* cells in your body, and each has its own lifespan. Some cells live for a few days before they are replaced, some live for a year, but it's true to say that you are quite literally not the same person today as you were before implementing the 5 Steps… you have changed the structure and health of all of your cells. It is amazing that your body has the ability to do this and you should love it for being able to heal and adapt like this.

It is critical that each day, you take 30 seconds to feel gratitude for the health and vitality of your body. Think of all of the incredible things it does for you and allows you to do and sit in that feeling of gratefulness. This may sound cheesy, but you must do this every day – gratitude keeps your mind and body healthy.

Keeping the 5 Steps rolling

The intensity with which you monitor your new habits and behaviours will naturally decrease over time. As time passes and your neck improves, a *slight* relaxation in your diligence is OK, as long as you maintain the bulk of your lifestyle changes.

Take this analogy: if you have a cut on your skin and you pour methylated spirits on it, it will really bloody hurt. You have to be incredibly diligent to keep the cut clean so that it can heal effectively. Once it has healed, you could pour a little bit on the skin from time to time and the pain wouldn't come back (not that I would recommend doing so). But soak your skin in methylated spirits too regularly and there's a good chance you'll do some damage to the skin again.

It's the same with your neck pain: in the early stages of recovery, you need to be incredibly diligent and follow all of the 5 Steps to the letter. Once your pain has healed and your health is back on track, if you slip up every now and again then you will be fine, but don't expose your body to too many negative habits or you'll be back where you began.

With this in mind, I have created a list of strategies to help you continue with the Steps long term, without feeling overwhelmed by them.

Structure

1. *Don't be a hero*: Now that your pain is under control and you are back doing the things you love, that is not a licence to be silly. You must respect your body tissues and how much you are asking them to do, and whilst I encourage you to fully participate in life and the things you love, don't be a hero. You don't have to be the biggest and toughest person in the gym, lifting heavy weights. You don't need to attempt that double-black ski run when you're only comfortable with blue runs. You don't need to play 18 holes of golf if your body is only used to 9 holes. You don't need to garden for 6 hours when you normally only do 2 hours. Manage your ego and exercise with balance.

2. *Service your car*: You wouldn't wait until your car breaks down to get it serviced, so why do it with your body? You should schedule regular services or check-ups with your health professionals to ensure you keep your body running in peak condition. When I say regular, I don't mean every week, but it is wise to catch up with your team of health professionals every 3 months.

3. *Sustainable NECKsercise*: Once your pain is under control, it may be tempting to stop doing your NECKsercises. Whilst you may not need to keep doing *all* of them every single day, you need to keep some ticking away in the background. I would suggest doing your favourite couple of NECKsercises for just 5 minutes each day, but do a more comprehensive neck strengthening and mobility session three times per week.

Stress

1. *Make meditation stick long term*: Daily meditation is something that you are going to want to keep around long after your neck pain is gone. The benefits are simply too good to miss out on, so just because you've fixed your neck pain, don't ditch the mindfulness!

    I've been meditating for a long time now, and if I can give you one piece of advice for making sure it's here to stay, this is it: do it first thing in the morning and last thing at night. If you don't do it as soon as you wake up, life will get in the way and you'll find every excuse under the sun to skip it. Get it done as soon as you get out of bed and go to the toilet. Getting in a second daily meditation just before you go to sleep is where the magic happens. It strips away all of the stress from the day and lets you hit the pillow with a clear head.

2. *Keep giving back*: Whether it's once per week, once per month or once per quarter, finding a few hours to donate to a good cause is a great way to benefit those

less fortunate, as well as yourself. It will keep things in perspective, reduce the perception of stress in your own life and boost your overall happiness. Even if you're the CEO of a multinational organisation, finding a few hours every couple of months to give back is something I strongly recommend.

3. *Journalling*: Once per month, I suggest taking 30 minutes to write down the following:

    a. What are the top three things that are currently stressing me out?
    b. On a scale of 1 to 10, how significant are each of these stressors? (How significant are the ramifications of not dealing with these?)
    c. How likely are they to occur?
    d. Who can give me some wise advice or assistance in overcoming these stressors?
    e. What are five things I'm grateful for now?
    f. What are some simple steps I can take that will create more of what I am grateful for?

This journalling process is a great way to clear your head and create some distance between the things stressing you out and your emotional reactions to them. You will find that simply writing them out will reduce the impact they are having on you and once you brainstorm some solutions, you will feel a greater sense of control in your ability to deal with them.

Sleep

Once you've been doing your pre-bed routine for a while, it will become habitual. You already had a pre-bed routine before reading this book (turn off the house lights, brush your teeth, set your alarm etc.) – you just may not have realised that it was a habit imprinted in your brain.

To ensure your new routine sticks long term, keep it simple. Set a reminder that pops up 2–3 hours before your bedtime each night (which should always be the same time) that simply says:

1. Lights
2. Temperature
3. Breathe
4. Diet

This will trigger you to:

1. Turn off main lights, turn on warm lamps, swap screen-time for a real book
2. Lower the room temperature (fan or air conditioning) and have a hot shower
3. Do your mindful breathing exercise before bed
4. Ensure you do not have caffeine or alcohol in your system, have a smaller dinner with low carbohydrate content, minimise liquid intake and take your sleeping supplements.

Many smartphones and watches have bed-time routine technology built into them, so see if yours has these capabilities before trying to recreate the wheel.

Don't treat sleep as something that will occur without laying the right foundations. Ultimately, you need 8 hours of sleep every night to thrive, so simplify your routine, practice it nightly and it will quickly become second nature.

Supplements and nutrition

1. Reduce or remove refined sugar, dairy, gluten, alcohol and caffeine from your diet. This may feel incredibly challenging initially whilst you starve the bad bacteria in your gut, but in time these foods will become foreign and unappealing.

2. Eat organic, grass-fed meat and minimise red meat intake altogether. This will reduce your exposure to antibiotics, which creates gut bacterial issues.

3. Eat a wide range of fresh vegetables and fruit daily (ideally organic). This is important for your micronutrient intake.

4. Eat only high-quality oils (such as cold-pressed olive oil) and avoid cheap vegetable oils, which are inflammatory and can increase your pain response.

5. Take your supplements daily, including probiotics, curcumin, fish oil and any other appropriate individualised supplements.

Subconscious mind

1. *Emotional flushing*: After regularly practising SEPT, you will notice that the bigger emotional traumas in your life no longer trigger intense emotional responses. This is a sign that you have effectively processed them. As you move past the bigger events, smaller events in which you have suppressed emotions will come to the surface for you to process. It's like peeling back layers of an onion, one suppressed emotion at a time.

   Practicing SEPT regularly in the beginning is recommended, but once you've worked through most of your bigger emotions you can reduce the frequency. I recommend scheduling half an hour every month to do a SEPT session, which will shift any smaller emotions you have suppressed over the month. You should also do a session soon after any new emotional experience, to ensure you quickly process and express the emotion before it is stored.

2. *Belief review*: After several months of closely monitoring and rewriting your beliefs, it will become an automated process. You will notice that your thoughts, words and behaviours automatically reflect your new health-affirming beliefs without any effort.

Despite this, it's still a good idea to check in with your beliefs once per month to ensure they are still supporting your health and that no old negative beliefs have crept back in. To do this, ask yourself the following questions and listen for an honest response from your subconscious mind:

- Am I a fast healer?
- Is my neck strong?
- Is my neck resilient?
- Am I in control of my health?

If your mind answers no to any of these, it's time to rewrite your beliefs. The best way to do this is to write a list of instances in which you have experienced the above to be true (e.g. times when your body did heal fast, experiences when your neck was strong and resilient, occasions when you were in control of your health) and then keep replaying those memories until they override the old belief.

3. *Forgiveness:* Whether you feel as though a health professional made you worse or the driver of the car that caused your whiplash accident is responsible, there can be a lot of residual blame surrounding long-term pain. You may also have events in your life that seem unrelated to your neck pain in which you are holding onto blame or resentment of those involved. Parents and ex-partners are common culprits, but it is also very likely that you are fostering blame and resentment towards yourself.

You will have worked through much of this with your SEPT practice, but there is a nice little exercise that I recommend doing once every 3 months (or monthly if it feels right for you):

- Write down or simply think about three people that you feel have done you wrong (one of those people may indeed be yourself)
- Forgive them for what they did to you (this may require professional counselling and assistance if the experience was particularly horrific or traumatic)
- Shower them with thoughts of kindness, love and compassion.

This is easier said than done but practicing this regularly will set you free.

Life beyond pain monthly checklist

This checklist is a summary of the above points. Set a reminder on your phone to review this list once per month to ensure you're sustaining NECKcellence:

- ☐ Don't be a hero
- ☐ Service your car
- ☐ Sustainable NECKsercise
- ☐ Meditate
- ☐ Keep giving back
- ☐ Stress journalling
- ☐ Sleep routine

- ☐ 'Happy gut' diet (clean and organic)
- ☐ Remove inflammatory foods
- ☐ Daily supplements
- ☐ Emotional flushing (SEPT)
- ☐ Belief review
- ☐ Forgiveness

5-finger check

Another nice check-in tool is the *5-finger check*. Each finger on your hand represents one of the 5 Steps of NECKcellence, so if you ever feel a niggle in your neck, look down at your hand and check that you haven't lost any fingers. Better yet, do it *before* you get a niggle by checking in every couple of weeks – prevention beats cure every time.

Have a coach

Whether it's one of your dream-team health professionals or someone external like a business or life coach, I strongly recommend having a long-term coach. Athletes, business executives and top performers in any field all understand and utilise the value of coaches and you should do the same.

Whilst it's nice to think that you can monitor your own habits and behaviours, you will have days and even weeks where you fall off the wagon. A good coach will keep you accountable, motivate you when you are off track and call you out on your excuses.

Coaching can seem expensive, but it's an investment in your own health, well-being and happiness, and is often the difference between success and failure.

I take on a very small number of clients in a coaching capacity each year, and I also have a team of health professionals I have trained as NECKspert coaches. If you are interested in personal NECKspert coaching, contact me at https://www.neckspert.com.au/contact.

Keep flashing forward

There will be days and moments in the future where you will be tempted to stray off track from the 5 Ss. It may be through being busy or boredom with the exercises, social pressure to eat and drink poorly, or a new emotional trauma that derails you. When you have become aware that you have commenced a bad habit or ceased a good one, I recommend repeating the flash-forward exercise we did at the start of this book.

Think about the harmful habit that you know is not serving your neck and imagine yourself repeating this behaviour every day for a whole year. Imagine looking at yourself in the mirror 1 year from now. How do you look? How do you feel? What is your energy like? How are your pain levels? What activities are you missing out on due to your pain?

Then imagine you have continued this habit every day for 5 years. What does your body look like? Pay attention to the bags under your eyes and your skin. How bad is your neck pain? What is it stopping you from doing? How do you feel? How are your energy levels?

Next, imagine that you have been repeating this negative habit every day for 10 years. A whole decade has gone past. Look at yourself in the mirror and analyse what it has done to you. Are your eyes bloodshot? Have you lost confidence in your voice? Is your posture slumped in defeat? Perhaps you've gained a lot of weight from an inability to exercise? How severe is your pain? Are you relying on pain medication to function? Are you missing out on life?

I now want you to revert back to the present moment. This time you are going to replace that negative habit with one that you know is NECKcellent. One that you know is supporting your health and vitality. One that is aligned with the 5 Ss.

Imagine repeating this habit daily for 1 year. Look at yourself in the mirror after a full 12 months of doing this. How do you look? How do you feel? What is your energy like? Notice how good your neck feels! What activities are you able to participate in due to your health?

Then imagine you have continued this habit every day for 5 years. What does your body look like? Pay attention to the clarity of your skin and eyes. Notice the strength and mobility in your neck. What activities have you now started doing? How do you feel? How is your energy?

Lastly, imagine that you have been repeating this positive habit every day for 10 years. A whole decade has gone past. Look at yourself in the mirror and analyse what it has done to you. Notice your strong body and upright posture. Listen to the confidence in your voice. What has regular exercise done to your weight? Pay attention to the absence of pain in your neck. What are you now able to do because of your pain-free body and abundant health? How does it feel to be in this body? How does it feel to be this version of you?

This activity is a sure-fire way to bring you back on track every time.

The secret to staying NECKcellent forever

Whilst other people (physiotherapists, doctors and surgeons) can assist you along your road to recovery and staying pain-free (and it is wise to have a team behind you), you and only you have the power to fix yourself.

This is a powerful and completely liberating truth. It means you are not relying on a mystical health professional to click you back into place and magically fix you. You are in the driver's seat.

As you've now experienced, you have the ability and power to heal your own body. The principles you've learned about in this book apply not only to neck pain, but to all aspects of health. Whether it's knee pain, shoulder pain, arthritis, digestive issues or mental pain, your ability to apply the 5 Steps from this book will play a huge role in your ability to recover.

Once you understand this and truly believe it, then and only then will you begin to transform your health and your life forever.

In closing

You are not the same person you were before reading this book. Whether you have completely transformed your lifestyle, or simply refined a few key habits, you have changed the shape and structure of your body on a cellular level. You have changed your thought patterns, beliefs and mindset. You have altered the energy in your nervous system. You have created a better life.

You *will* feel pain in your neck again, like all healthy humans should if they overload their tissues or their system is out of balance, but you now have the knowledge and skills to quickly fix it.

Being healthy does not mean never feeling pain again, but understanding that pain is a message from your body that you are out of balance and having the ability to quickly heal and resolve both the pain and the root cause.

You now have the steps that will guide you back to health whenever pain arises. Review the 5 Steps regularly, even when you are pain-free, as they will grant you not only freedom from long-term neck pain, but also ensure you enjoy a thriving mind, body and life.

IN CLOSING

There are various definitions of 'well-being', but a commonly cited one is:

A delicate balancing act between an individual's social, emotional, psychological and physical assets (resources) and the particular social, emotional, psychological and physical liabilities (challenges) they are facing in life and work at any one time.

Dodge, et al. 2012

I personally feel as though this definition is lacking, as it paints a picture of surviving rather than thriving. I have therefore created my own definition of well-being, which I personally feel is more comprehensive and aspirational:

Well-being is the resourcefulness to sustain abundant energy, razor-sharp focus and presence, a clear and creative mind, healthy relationships, a pain-free body, and a happy and purpose-filled life, even when facing external challenges.

The NECKspert

The first definition suggests you need to have *resources* (social, physical, emotional) to be well, but when your tank is on empty and you've got nothing left, it's your ability to be *resourceful* with what you've got (physically, mentally, emotionally and spiritually) to pick yourself up and create the life you want that defines true well-being.

That is what you have done. You came to this book when your resources were low. Your tank was empty. You had nothing left to give. You dug deep and you were resourceful enough with the physical and emotional energy you had left to start the long journey back to health and wellness.

For that, I applaud you.

It's true, neck pain sucks. But now you have fixed it and you've got the tools to fix it again if it ever comes back to remind you that you're out of balance. You are one of very few people who understand the power you hold when it comes to healing yourself.

There is a lot of pain in the world: physical, mental, emotional, spiritual and social. I urge you to talk about these five principles with others who are in pain. Lead by example. Share with kindness. Give this book to your friends and family who have pain (not just neck pain).

Together, let's create a world with a little less pain.

It has been an honour guiding you back to NECKcellence.

In health,

Caelum Trott
The NECKspert

Printed in Great Britain
by Amazon